PHILOSOPHICAL TURNS

PHILOSOPHICAL TURNS

Epistemological, Linguistic, and
Metaphysical

Robert Wess

Parlor Press
Anderson, South Carolina
www.parlorpress.com

Parlor Press LLC, Anderson, South Carolina, USA
© 2023 by Parlor Press.
All rights reserved.
Printed in the United States of America on acid-free paper.

S A N: 2 5 4 - 8 8 7 9

Library of Congress Cataloging-in-Publication Data on File

1 2 3 4 5

978-1-64317-370-2 (paperback)
978-1-64317-371-9 (hardcover)
978-1-64317-372-6 (PDF)
978-1-64317-373-3 (EPUB)

Index by Samantha McAlister. Cover design by David Blakesley. Cover photo by Samuele Errico Piccarini on Unsplash. Used by permission.

Parlor Press, LLC is an independent publisher of scholarly and trade titles in print and multimedia formats. This book is available in print and ebook formats from Parlor Press on the World Wide Web at www.parlorpress.com or through online and brick-and-mortar bookstores. For submission information or to find out about Parlor Press publications, write to Parlor Press, 3015 Brackenberry Drive, Anderson, South Carolina, 29621, or email editor@parlorpress.com.

Contents

Preface *ix*
Acknowledgments *xi*

1 Philosophical Turns *1*
2 McKeon's Pluralism *19*
3 The Linguistic Turn: A Narrative *51*
4 Meillassoux: Metaphysical Turn as Chaotic Pragmatism *129*
5 Harman: Metaphysical Turn as Perspectivalism *176*
6 Turn against Turn *233*

Works Cited *250*
About the Author *265*
Index *267*

For my Mother and Father.

Preface

This book originates in my experiences in Richard McKeon's classroom at the University of Chicago in the 1960s, even though much of what it examines did not exist at the time. I went to his classes as an auditor to learn more about pluralism, pluralism and Neo-Aristotelian literary criticism being the two main components of what I was learning at the time in the English Department, principally from my dissertation adviser, Sheldon Sacks, the founding editor of *Critical Inquiry*. While I did learn more about pluralism, I learned much more about philosophy, not a particular philosophy but philosophy in general as a distinctive mode of argumentation. Developments in philosophy since the 1960s that I have studied have tended to confirm in important ways things I learned about philosophy at that time.

Reading philosophy, one encounters arguments on every page, but McKeon teaches one to see these as trees in order to see the forest that orders them, the structure with a beginning, middle, and end, beginnings being particularly important. Beginnings are key to philosophical turns such as the widely known example of Kant's turn discussed in chapter one. Beginnings may literally appear at the beginning, as in the *Critique of Pure Reason*, but they may also drive a narrative, not appearing clearly until the end as in chapter three's narrative of the history of the linguistic turn.

Philosophical turns are charted in what McKeon calls "historical semantics," which is one side of his pluralism. Chapter two gives special attention to this side in its introductory overview of his pluralism. Historical semantics anticipates contemporary developments in philosophy, having enabled McKeon in the 1960s, when a turn to metaphysics appeared unimaginable, to predict that such a turn would be the next phase in philosophy, which appears to be happening in today's emergent metaphysical turn. This prediction was not a guesstimate but was based on a cycle of turns that has repeated itself in the history of philosophy.

The turns in this cycle change the subject matter of philosophy. They turn from the priority of one subject matter to the priority of another. Recognition of these changes may change one's view of philosophy. Consideration of these subject matters relative to one another in the final chapter leads to the book's main conclusion about philosophy, one that favors metaphysical turns.

Acknowledgments

In recent decades, a number of academics who found value in McKeon's classes have found one another on the internet and formed an informal chat room. These have been joined by others who have come to McKeon in other ways. These online discussions have been invaluable to me in deepening my understanding of McKeon. Participants include Richard Buchanan, Gregory Clark, David Depew, Eugene Garver, Andy Kaplan, Irwin Levenstein, Steven Mailloux, Will Selinger, and Jim Vice. We all miss the late Douglas Mitchell.

The Center for the Humanities at Oregon State University supported my work repeatedly for many years, first under Peter Copek, the founding director, then under David Robinson, his successor. Even in retirement, the Center gave me an opportunity to lecture on this project at an early stage of my research.

In addition, discussions with Oregon State colleagues about Harman and Meillassoux helped me begin to understand their work. I thank Evan Gottlieb in particular for alerting me to the importance of Meillassoux as well as for the reading group he ran at the time where most of these discussions occurred. Participants in these discussions, as best I can recall, included Bradley Boovy, Rich Daniels, Gilad Elbom, Anita Guerrini, Anita Helle, Jillian St. Jacques, Tim and Joy Jensen, Stephanie Jenkins, Brian Lindsley, Raymond Malewitz, Kersi Peltomaki, Ehren Helmut Pflugfelder, David Robinson, and Lily Sheehan.

Writing a book, at least for me, is a test of patience and endurance, so that Greig Henderson's and Gregory Desilet's encouraging comments on a partial draft at an early stage in my writing were much appreciated. And David Blakesley's interest and encouragement have been immensely helpful in bringing this book to conclusion.

My deepest thanks go to my wife, Sandra, my partner for life.

1 Philosophical Turns

> The history of the fashions of philosophizing may be sketched briefly by tracing the subject matters in which philosophers have found their basic distinctions.
>
> —Richard McKeon, *Freedom and History*, 164

The familiar phrase "the linguistic turn" is routinely used as shorthand for modes of language-centered philosophizing that flourished in the twentieth century. While these modes are still with us, they are being displaced in some quarters by what may be called "the metaphysical turn," an event generally deemed unimaginable during the heyday of the linguistic turn, though as we shall see later in this chapter there is in Richard McKeon an exception to this generalization that merits attention. One sign of this new turn is a book series announcement by the Open Humanities Press:

> The world is due for a resurgence of original speculative metaphysics. The New Metaphysics series aims to provide a safe house for such thinking amidst the demoralizing caution and prudence of academic philosophy. We do not aim to bridge the analytic-continental divide, since we are equally impatient with nail-filing analytic critique and the continental reverence for dusty textual monuments. We favor instead the spirit of the intellectual gambler, and wish to discover and promote authors who meet this description. Like an emergent recording company, what we seek are traces of a new metaphysical "sound" from any nation of the world. The editors are open to translations of neglected metaphysical classics, and will consider secondary works of especial force and daring. But our main interest is to stimulate the birth of disturbing masterpieces of twenty-first century philosophy. (www.openhumanitiespress.com)

The editors of this series are Graham Harman and Bruno Latour.[1]

---

1. Latour's appearance here is no doubt surprising to many because his 1979 book, coauthored with Steve Woolgar, *Laboratory Life: The Construction of*

What do such philosophical turns reveal about philosophy? What conclusions about philosophy in general might one draw from careful consideration of these two turns in particular, one longstanding, the other emergent? Can one find in philosophical turns themselves a reason to favor one turn over others? Answering these questions is the main aim of this book. Overall, then, this book is more a critical examination of philosophies than an assertion of a philosophy, though the final section of the last chapter will propose a next step for today's emergent metaphysical turn.

The Terminology of the Metaphysical Turn

The familiar "the linguistic turn" serves here as a template for "the metaphysical turn," a term I am using in preference to varying terms with varying fates that have been used to designate this new turn, principally "object-oriented philosophy," "speculative realism," and "object-oriented ontology." Harman, in addition to joining Latour in calling for a new metaphysics, is linked in notable ways to all three of these terms.

In the case of "object-oriented philosophy" (OOP), Harman coined the term in 1999 (*Towards Speculative Realism* 93) and features it on the opening pages of his first book, *Tool-Being*. This term never gained wide currency and has receded in importance even for Harman, although it continues to serve as the main title of his blog. But *Tool-Being* does spell out object-oriented-philosophy's rejection of human-centered philosophy, a fundamental tenet for Harman from which he has never wavered. Against Kant, Harman insists that "the true chasm in ontology lies not

---

Scientific Facts, was seminal in the study of the socially constructive view of science. By contrast, Harman is among the most prominent of the new metaphysicians. The "spirit of the intellectual gambler" even appears in the title of his second book, published in 2005, *Guerilla Metaphysics: Phenomenology and the Carpentry of Things*. At first blush, then, Latour and Harman appear to be an odd couple, although as we shall see they are actually very close. One sign of this is that Latour dedicates to Harman his 2004 essay, "Why Has Critique Run out of Steam? From Matters of Fact to Matters of Concern" (225). Readers can decide for themselves whether this essay corrects Latour's constructivism of science or, as Latour claims, clarifies that his true aim all along was more realist than was customarily thought. Harman, on his blog, seconds Latour's claim, explaining Latour's dedication to him by recounting email conversations in which he encouraged Latour to correct the misapprehension that he is a "stereotypical social constructionist" ("Answering").

between humans and the world, but between *objects and relations*" (2; unless otherwise noted italics are Harman's, as in this case).

Far more important to the metaphysical turn is the term "speculative realism," used to entitle an event at which Harman, Ray Brassier, Iain Hamilton Grant, and Quentin Meillassoux each gave a paper and responded to questions. Held 27 April 2007 at Goldsmiths, University of London, it was advertised as a "One-Day Workshop." Evidence that it was immediately recognized as important is that it was transcribed and published in *Collapse*, November 2007. Harman recounts that the four initially had no title for the Workshop. Meillassoux favored "Speculative Materialism," which appeared to be the best candidate, despite Harman's dislike of materialism, until Brassier came up with "Speculative Realism," which "had such appeal that it was adopted immediately by all members of the group" (*Quentin* 79–80). The announcement of the Workshop defined "speculative realism" as "not a doctrine but the umbrella term for a variety of research programmes committed to upholding the autonomy of reality, whether in the name of transcendental physicalism, object-oriented philosophy, or abstract materialism, against the depredations of anthropocentrism" (*Speculative Realism* 306). Subsequently, Harman goes on, Brassier and Meillassoux both distanced themselves from the term while Grant took "a turn in the direction of British Idealism," which left himself "as the only original Speculative Realist who still endorses the term wholeheartedly" (*Quentin* 80).[2] Harman offers in *Speculative Realism: An Introduction* another account of events leading to the 2007 colloquium, and he adds sections discussing each of the four presentations at the colloquium.

In a 2013 essay, "The Current State of Speculative Realism," Harman dismisses as "pointless debate over whether Speculative Realism 'really exists'" (22). As evidence, he parades publications about it, discussions

---

2. Additional relations among the four: (1) Brassier translated Meillassoux's seminal *After Finitude: An Essay on the Necessity of Contingency*; (2) Harman wrote *Quentin Meillassoux: Philosophy in the Making*, which has appeared in first and second editions; (3) Meillassoux's desire to have Harman's work appear in French led to *The Quadruple Object*, which actually appeared initially in French, as Harman explains in this book's Preface (1); (4) Harman and Grant have exchanged comments on one another: Harman, "On the Undermining of Objects: Grant, Bruno, and Radical Philosophy"; Grant, "Mining Conditions: A Response to Harman"; (5) Brassier now distances himself sharply from Harman, as evidenced by his "Postscript: Speculative Autopsy," appended to Peter Wolfendale's *Object-Oriented Philosophy: The Noumenon's New Clothes*.

of it in the blogosphere, its appearance in editorial policies of journals, graduate theses, postdoctoral topics, and classes at universities, as well as its crossing of national boundaries and becoming "a *term d'art* in architecture, archaeology, geography, the visual arts, and even history" (22). Not least, there is also a Speculative Realism series published by the Edinburgh University Press, edited by Harman. Recognizing that "it is always a badge of honour for intellectuals to refuse being stamped with any sort of label," Harman still insists entrepreneurially that such labels have value as a "brand" and that if it were up to him "not only would the name 'speculative realism' be retained, but a logo would be designed for projection on PowerPoint screens, accompanied by a few signature bars of smoky dubstep music" ("On the Undermining" 21).

"Object-oriented ontology" appears in relation to OOP in Levi R. Bryant's formulation: "'object-oriented ontology' (OOO) refers to any metaphysics which argues that being is composed of objects or substances. The relation between object-oriented ontology and object-oriented philosophy is thus a relation between genus and species" (Foreword xiii). Harman initially accepted OOO as "a good term for describing a range of object-oriented positions that differ in various ways from [his] own" ("Current State" 26.). Recounting his role in "kick[ing] off the OOO movement in April 2010 at Georgia Tech in Atlanta," Harman suggests metaphorically that "OOO can be seen as one of the 'states' within a larger Speculative Realist union" (*Bells* 7).

Regarding the adjective "object-oriented," Harman first introduced it a 1999 lecture to broaden philosophy beyond relations of the human subject to objects, that is, beyond the epistemological problem of human access to reality (*Towards Speculative Realism* 93). The broader alternative Harman advocates is defined by two contrasts. First, instead of limiting philosophy to questions about human interactions with objects, he broadens it to include also questions about what happens when, for example, "rocks collide with wood, when fire melts glass, when cosmic rays cause protons to disintegrate" (94). Second, he contrasts (1) epistemology's tendency to gravitate toward the abstract, "lump[ing] together monkeys, tornadoes, diamonds, and oil under the single heading of that-which-lies-outside," to (2) "an object-oriented philosophy, a sort of alchemy for describing the transformations of one entity into another, for outlining the ways in which they seduce or destroy humans and non-humans alike" (95). He finds a step toward this object orientation in Heidegger's famous tool analysis, which he regards in the 1990s, seven decades after its appearance in *Being and Time*, as still "the high water mark of recent philosophy" (96). This foreshadows his first book, *Tool-Being: Heidegger and the Metaphysics of Objects*, published in 2002.

An additional meaning of "object-oriented" emerged years after Harman introduced the term. This meaning appears in Alexander R. Galloway's Marxist critique of speculative realists, particularly Harman and Quentin Meillassoux, where Galloway links "object-oriented" to object-oriented computer programming.³ He elaborates on this linkage in a later text, characterizing Harman's object-orientation as "an ontology

---

3. In his critique, Galloway uses Marx's concept of mode of production but truncates it, attending only to the "means" of production, defined as "the most highly evolved technologies of post-Fordism capitalism" (347). By linking Harman to post-Fordist object-oriented programming and Meillassoux to the mathematics in post-Fordist technologies in general, Galloway concludes that speculative realism is "ventriloquizing the current capitalist arrangement" and is thus "politically retrograde" (363). But this "capitalist arrangement" includes "relations" of production too, the part of the mode of production that Galloway ignores. For Marx, the problem with capitalism is not the "means" (e.g., factories in Marx's time, post-Fordist technologies in our time) but the "relations," wherein capitalists own the "means" and workers own nothing more than what it takes to produce labor power day after day. Marx envisioned revolution occurring in advanced capitalist countries not by destroying the "means" but by changing the "relations." Commenting on the error of the Luddites, he said, "It took both time and experience before the workers learnt to distinguish between machinery and its employment by capital, and therefore to transfer their attacks from the material instruments of production to the form of society which utilizes those instruments" (554–55). One needs to consider both "means" and "relations" to get full analytic value out of the concept of mode of production. In Galloway's case, one has to look hard to find any nod in the direction of "relations." Tucked in a footnote, one can find the suggestion that whenever one uses Google one is performing unpaid labor from which Google extracts surplus value (358n15). This severely limited attention to "relations" calls attention to the extent to which Galloway generally ignores "relations" to focus on the "means." When one attends to both, one readily recognizes that post-Fordist technologies are one thing in capitalist "relations" of production, but could be something else in "socialist" relations. Some of these technologies might even help to move from capitalist to socialist relations. But such considerations are unthinkable for Galloway, because he essentializes post-Fordist technologies, demonizing them as a "totalizing nihilism" (365). Claiming to historicize in Marxist terms, he contradictorily gives post-Fordist technologies a capitalist taint ingrained forever. One irony is that to rid himself of this taint, Galloway should trash his post-Fordist word processor.

of encapsulated, withdrawn objects existing at different scales and connected in networks" (Bryant, "BREAKING"; Galloway's comment appears 10 December 2012). Harman responded in 2014 by contending that Galloway's linkage is based on nothing more than "an *intellectual pun* on the term *object-oriented*" ("Materialism" 51). But later, in 2018, in *Object-Oriented Ontology: A New Theory of Everything*, Harman finds more than a pun. Without mentioning Galloway, Harman remarks that he "borrows the phrase 'object-oriented' from the world of computers," explaining, "Whereas programs written in older computer languages were systematic and holistic entities, with all their parts integrated into a unified whole, object-oriented programs make use of independent programming 'objects' that interact with other objects while the internal information of each remains hidden (or 'encapsulated') from the others" (11). In short, parts without a whole in object-oriented programming are analogous to Harman's view "that objects—whether real, fictional, natural, artificial, human or non-human—are mutually autonomous and enter into relation only in special cases that need to be explained rather than assumed" (12). What Harman "borrows," then, appears to be a meaning that he adds to the meaning in his 1999 lecture "Object-Oriented Philosophy."

In *Object-Oriented Ontology*, Harman updates his views in two other notable ways. First, he remarks, "Object-Oriented Ontology (also known as 'Object-Oriented Philosophy') dates to the late 1990s" (8), but then concedes in an endnote that strictly speaking only "Object-Oriented Philosophy" originated in the late 1990s (279). The endnote appears to be there for the purposes of accuracy, while the main text suggests that for Harman the differences between OOP and OOO have disappeared, and that he now actually prefers OOO, which he says is properly pronounced "Triple O" (6). Second, in this recounting of the history of the development of his philosophy, Harman makes no reference to Speculative Realism, either the term or the 2007 event. This is surprising insofar as Harman describes this book as "the first comprehensive book on OOO aimed at a wide general readership" (255), which would appear to include many unfamiliar with the speculative realist context of Triple O. Having worked closely with both "object-oriented philosophy" and "speculative realism," Harman now appears to demote them in favor of "object-oriented ontology."

Harman's centrality in the cluster of terms associated with the metaphysical turn is part of his importance in this turn, but only part. His considerable importance derives mainly from his prolific output. Always engaging as a writer, even at his most difficult, his new metaphysics is now arguably the most fully fleshed out of any of the new metaphysical philosophies. Followers of his blog know he regularly lectures in many countries. His work has already been translated into many languages, not only European languages, but also Chinese, Korean, Japanese, Russian, and perhaps others. Harman will thus be the subject of my penultimate chapter, chapter five, concluding consideration of the metaphysical turn, before the final chapter's answers to the questions about what philosophical turning teaches, both about philosophy and about the relative values of different philosophical turns.

The one term that needs to be added to this cluster is "correlationism," which Meillassoux introduced to identify the metaphysical turn's antagonist. Evidence of the importance of the 2007 event at Goldsmiths appears in the frequency of references to it in discussions of this turn. But what appears to have triggered the turn more than anything appears in Meillassoux's work, the subject of chapter four. Evidence of his importance appears in Harman's *Quintin Meillassoux: Philosophy in the Making*, which quickly appeared in two editions, 2011 and 2015. Meillassoux is as important to the beginning of the metaphysical turn as Harman's prolific output is to its growing worldwide renown.

Meillassoux defines "correlationism" in *After Finitude: The Necessity of Contingency*: "the central notion of modern philosophy since Kant seems to be that of *correlation*. By 'correlation' we mean the idea according to which we only ever have access to the correlation between thinking and being, and never to either term considered apart from the other" (5). Writing in 2018, Harman calls *After Finitude* "the most famous individual work to have emerged from Speculative Realism," as evidenced in part by "its translation into a dozen or more languages in the first decade of its existence" (*Speculative Realism* 134). Meillassoux proved to be pivotal historically by providing disparate philosophers a common antagonist. Harman recounts that the four participants in the 2007 event differed among themselves but found that they shared an antipathy toward correlationism. "[T]he reason this mere term was able to catalyze an entire movement," Harman explains, "is because it nailed so perfectly the basic problem with all continental philosophy (and much analytic philosophy) since Kant" (*Quentin* 81).

Harman applauds Meillassoux even more strongly on his blog, predicting that "correlationism" is "headed for permanent enshrinement in the philosophical lexicon," that "people will still be referring to certain positions as 'correlationist' in 300 years, 500 years, maybe longer" ("New Post"). Whether this is hyperbole none of us will be around to tell. What is clear is that Harman registers the importance of the critique of correlationism at the birth of the metaphysical turn. Perhaps the best evidence of the quick success Meillassoux's stigmatizing of correlationism enjoyed appears the example of Peter Gratton, who accepts the premise that correlationism is something to be avoided so much that he insists that figures he wants to defend are not guilty of correlationism as charged: "My view is that those critiqued by the speculative realists, such as Martin Heidegger, Jacques Derrida, and several others, were not 'correlationists,' but were after a realism of time" (*Speculative Realism* 10). Correlationism quickly became a scarlet letter no one wanted to see pinned to anyone they wanted to defend.

Philosophical Turns

It is perhaps safe to say that the most widely known philosophical turn in the modern era appears in Kant's call to give up conforming thought to thing in favor of conforming thing to thought (*Critique of Pure Reason* 22, Bxvi). Thing is not prior to thought; rather, thought is prior to thing. Kant's turn, at least before Meillassoux's critique of correlationism, has typically been described approvingly, except sometimes his analogizing of his turn to the Copernican Revolution is questioned insofar as one is a decentering (Copernicus) and the other is a recentering (Kant). But that is a minor point. Modern philosophy's widespread agreement with Kant has been enshrined in supposed truisms such as the inaccessibility of the thing-in-itself, thinkable but not knowable.

As the Kant example suggests, philosophers typically treat turns dogmatically by aligning with one side, either agreeing with what is turned to or with what is turned from, with the appeal of being au courant typically giving the edge to the former. Turning to something new, one should add, can sometimes rehabilitate something old. "It is safe to say that Aristotle is not one of the most fashionable classic philosophers in present-day continental thought," Harman observes, then adds, "But once we start to look at individual things as the central topic of philosophy, Aristotle's dominant position is hard to overlook ("Aristotle" 246). Meillassoux goes farther, borrowing from Aristotle his "anhypothetical principle" (*After Finitude* 60–61), a principle that will receive extensive attention in chapter four.

But if one wants to see what philosophical turns teach about philosophy, one needs to refrain from taking sides and instead begin pluralistically by seeing what one can learn from the turns themselves. Instead of taking sides for or against Kant's turn, for example, consider that his turn suggests (1) that philosophy always has an ultimate priority, not priority in the Kantian sense of prior to experience, but priority in the deeper sense of that which is first in a philosophical explanatory structure, and (2) thing and thought are among the existents where this ultimate priority may be located.

A philosophical turn is a turn from a reigning ultimate priority to a new ultimate priority. The change in priorities is what is at stake, and it may take decades for completion of the change to occur. The importance of turns is a function of the importance of ultimate priorities. An ultimate priority does not follow anything in the structure of the philosophy in which it appears, for if it did it would be posterior to what it follows, no longer an ultimate priority. This feature makes an ultimate priority a beginning, something from which things follow but which itself follows from nothing within the philosophical structure in which it appears. Kant identifies this feature in his philosophy when he remarks, "This peculiarity of our understanding, that it can produce *a priori* unity of apperception solely by means of the categories, and only by such and so many, is as little capable of further explanation as why we have just these and no other functions of judgment, or why space and time are the only forms of our possible intuition" (*Critique of Pure Reason* B145–46). Perhaps, then, philosophies are exceptional among the disciplines in being ungrounded groundings, grounded in an ultimate priority from which everything follows in the philosophy it informs, but which itself is ungrounded, intuited rather than inferred. Ungrounded grounding may flesh out the meaning of "somewhere" in Harman's response to an interviewer pressing him to spell out why he starts with objects. Harman answers with the truism that "you have to start somewhere" ("Propositions" 33).

Importantly, does the evidence one finds in the turns themselves support the conclusion that turns are equal or that one is preferable to another? On this issue, the present book is limited insofar as it focuses on only a few examples of turns, but that may be enough to propose an answer to this question, at least a tentative one. A recurrent consideration relevant to this answer will be marked by the term "exemptionalism." Exemptionalism is something that some turns do to exempt themselves from something from which they do not exempt other philosophies. Whereas "exceptionalism," in the sense proposed above, is not a basis for a preferential order among the turns, exemptionalism could be a factor in deciding if there is one.

Turns, as Richard McKeon suggests in this chapter's epigraph, involve changes in "the subject matters in which philosophers have found their basic distinctions" (*Freedom* 164). Rather than privilege in advance one subject matter over another, pluralism examines turning to see what happens when an ultimate priority based on subject matter X is displaced in favor of one based on subject matter Y. Philosophical turning thus foregrounds the diversity of existents that can serve as ultimate priorities. In each case there is the dual problem of establishing the sense in which the ultimate priority is an existent, as well as the sense in which it can function philosophically as prior to all other existents. Kant, philosophizing the subject matter of thought, finds his basic distinctions in the subject matter of human faculties, exemplified preeminently in his three critiques. His ultimate priority is in the subject matter of thought, and from this priority he moves to the basic distinctions in mental faculties that organize his philosophy.

The subject matter of the linguistic turn differs from both Kant's subject matter and the subject matter of thing from which he turns. Chapter three takes up the history of the linguistic turn. The chapter takes the form of a narrative of discovery because this turn took decades to complete the turn to its ultimate priority. Late in its history, in 2013, Eileen Joy identifies Jacques Derrida as "one of the architects of the 'linguistic turn'" (28).[4] She is not alone because younger colleagues told me the same thing when I asked when they thought this turn began. But as we will see in chapter three, it began before 1930, the year Derrida was born. But Joy is right to the extent that Derrida plays an important part in the narrative's culmination. Those present at the turn's origin did not recognize all that it entailed. For recognition to occur would take de-

---

4. Interestingly, while the linguistic turn is mainly an Anglo-American phenomenon, Joy's application of the term to Derrida extends the term to continental philosophy. Insofar as Derrida's influence in the anglophone world appeared more in departments of literary and cultural studies than in philosophy departments, the linguistic turn did not bridge the analytic-continental divide, but it did establish a beachhead of sorts, one place where the divide lessened if it did not disappear altogether.

cades. A full history of this turn would require coverage of a multitude of figures. My chapter is necessarily very selective, best viewed as the skeletal form of such a possible history, designed to show that philosophical turning provides a standpoint for a corrective reading of the linguistic turn that illuminates its stages.

I see no reason to think that all turns unfold the same way. All that a philosophical turn entails to complete itself could very well appear at a turn's beginning. But as we shall see in the chapters on Meillassoux and Harman, chapters four and five respectively, what happened in the linguistic turn could happen again this century in a metaphysical turn. Chapters three, four, and five all offer examples of philosophical turns that draw on ingredients of what they are turning from that limit the extent to which they reach what they are turning to, thereby inadvertently leaving to others the job of completing the turn. In the case of the linguistic turn, its beginning, precisely because of the extent to which it relied on what it was turning from, even became the antagonist of later stages in the turn, so much so, as the example of Joy illustrates, that it ceased being recognized as the beginning. Whether that will happen in the case of the metaphysical turn remains to be seen. Perhaps the metaphysical turn will eventually profit from the lesson of the linguistic turn.

To be clear, in McKeon's view the subject matter of philosophy always involves thing, thought, language, and action. What changes in philosophical turns is that "basic distinctions," as McKeon puts it, are located sometimes in thing, sometimes in thought, and sometimes in language and action; language and action are joined because here "basic distinctions" center in whether "to treat sequential statements as forms of action or . . . purposive courses of action as instances of verbal rules" ("Principles" 395). A change in the subject matter of philosophy is thus a change in the order of priority. In the case of Kant's turn, there is no change insofar as philosophy continues to be about thing and thought. What changes is the order of priority between the two. Kant prioritizes thought in examining how thing conforms to thought. For the sake of avoiding circumlocution, I will usually refer to the subject matter of philosophy not by elaborating on the prioritizing that is involved but by simply identifying the dominant component, as in the Kantian example of a philosophical turn to the subject matter of thought.

Kant's subject matter of thought is epistemology, but for McKeon, as we shall see, the subject matter of philosophy is a reality, whereas there is a tendency to dissociate epistemology from reality. That this tendency is being corrected today is possibly a sign of the influence of the emergent metaphysical turn. In any case, one example is Adrian Johnston's insight that while Kant's philosophy is generally understood as distinguishing epistemology from ontology, and limiting philosophy to the former, Kant "arguably cannot avoid tacitly reintroducing an implicit ontology into his system" ("Hume's Revenge" 107). Amplification of Johnston's point appears in Markus Gabriel: "*Transcendental ontology investigates the ontological conditions of our conditions of access to what there is*. It sets out with the simple insight that the subject (in whichever way conceived) *exists*, that the analysis of the concept of existence is, hence, methodologically prior to the subject's access to existence. The subject with its conceptual capacities actually exists; it is part of the world" (ix; Gabriel's italics). Such existence, moreover, is fundamental, because the inferences in a philosophy whose ultimate priority is in this "subject with its conceptual capacities" will take their distinctive form from the distinctive characteristics of the reality of this "subject." We will return to this point at the end of chapter four in proposing an alternative to Meillassoux's critique of Kant.

Philosophical turns, then, call attention to the way the subject matter of philosophy is always a reality, albeit not the same reality.

Pluralism: James and McKeon

William James is credited with popularizing the term "pluralism": "The word, infrequently used prior to James's *fin de siècle* writing, has since taken on a life of its own" (Ferguson 15). But in a survey of pluralisms, "Types of Pluralism," Walter Watson excludes James, because he "argues for a pluralistic view of the universe as against a monistic view" (351). In other words, James's *A Pluralistic Universe* is a polemic rather than a pluralism encompassing opposing views. In it, James calls upon philosophy to descend from its conceptual ladder "to obey Bergson's call upon you to look toward the sensational life for the fuller knowledge of reality" (253). The "pulses of experience" escape the limits of "our conceptual substitutes for them" (256), James insists, concluding that "pluralism" presupposes "that every smallest bit of experience is a *multum in parvo* plurally related, that each relation is one . . . way of its being taken, or way of its taking something else" (274).

Whereas Watson excludes James because of his polemical advocacy of starting with experience rather than concepts, he includes McKeon precisely because in his pluralism different philosophies are "seen to be the result of the selection of different starting points or principles" (356). This focus on "starting points" distinguishes McKeon's pluralism among the pluralisms Watson surveys. What Watson means by "starting points or principle" is what I mean by "ultimate priorities." You have to start somewhere, and where you start has to be in some sense prior to all other possibilities. McKeon's focus, then, contributes to an inquiry into what philosophical turns teach about philosophy.

McKeon

One way to see McKeon's pluralism in action is to samples reactions to his teaching by his students. Dennis O'Brien, who went on to serve as president at Bucknell and the University of Rochester, recollects, "If one wished to derive the truths of McKeon's work, they would not be truths of doctrine, but truths about what it means to have, hold, or discover a doctrine" (89). Wayne C. Booth, known for *The Rhetoric of Fiction* and many other books, particularizes his experience with an array of examples. He recounts that the first course he took from McKeon was one on Plato's *Republic* that convinced him that McKeon was a dogmatic Platonist. But in later courses he came to realize that McKeon's dogmatism changed, like a chameleon's colors, from course to course. McKeon became in another course "an absolutely dogmatic Humean, not just eager to defend Hume from every conceivable attack but brilliant at exposing the stupidities of any of us who raised what seemed to us obvious objections to Hume"; Booth continues, "As any reader of McKeon might predict, I later met in him an equally persuasive dogmatic defender of Democritus, of Cicero, of Kant, of Dewey, and—somewhat peripherally from McKeon's point of view but highly important in my own thinking—of Anselm" (215). Thomas Farrell, author of *Norms of Rhetorical Culture*, remembers the closest thing to a doctrine in McKeon being the not "terribly satisfying one" of "the infinitely rich possible relationships among things, thoughts, and terms" (192).

Elder Olson, a colleague, wrote a short memoir of McKeon that concluded that he "produced no philosophy, as such, of his own, no system of doctrines," but instead, he formulated "a *metaphilosophy* which, in its systematic display of the oppositions and correlations of diverse philosophies, adumbrated a matrix from which all valid philosophies were generated, as well as a general dialectic explaining how the diverse dialectics operated" (306).

McKeon, then, is a charitable reader par excellence. George Kimball Plochmann, a McKeon student who later wrote a book on him to be considered in chapter two, captures this charitableness in recollecting McKeon once remarking that when reading Kant, "Do not worry at first whether space and time are really subjective forms in the mind, but worry instead about what Kant means when he says they are" (205n4). Rather than jump to the conclusion that an author is right or wrong, read charitably enough to take time to work out an author's meanings, even if that entails entertaining assumptions that seem far-fetched. One difficulty in some of McKeon's essays is that they include extended consideration of an astounding number of philosophical positions, not lumped polemically into easily understood categories of "right" and "wrong," but preserved in their distinctiveness, with McKeon providing a broad pluralistic framework within which each distinct position is shown to make sense.[5]

McKeon is sometimes described as a pragmatist, which might be construed as evidence that he is neutral in the sense of readiness to adapt views to particular circumstances rather than adhere dogmatically to a single realist view. A direct link to pragmatism came during his time in graduate studies in the 1920s at Columbia University, where he studied under John Dewey. At the same time, however, he also studied under Frederick J. E. Woodbridge, who supervised his dissertation on Spinoza (McKeon, *Freedom* 8), published in 1928 under the title *The Philosophy of Spinoza: The Unity of His Thought*. McKeon recollects that Woodbridge taught that ideas are "not inventions constructed by the mind, but discoveries forced upon us by compelling realities whose natures are basically intelligible" ("Philosopher" 46). David J. Depew's insightful study of this dual influence of Dewey and Woodbridge is aptly entitled "Between Pragmatism and Realism."[6] In one of his autobiographical es-

---

5. Among the rumors I heard while in graduate school at the University of Chicago was that R. S. Crane, a legendary professor, was known to remark that most of the books he read should have been condensed to articles. The reverse is the case for McKeon insofar as he sometimes wrote articles that should have been books.

6. Whereas Depew focuses on this "crossing," Peter Simonson only alludes to it insofar as he notes the influence of both Dewey and Woodbridge (23, 32), but Woodbridge appears only briefly in passing and what McKeon says about Woodbridge's influence is construed as "McKeon remind[ing] us of pragmatism's heterogeneity bred through many intellectual cross-fertilizations" (32),

says, McKeon recounts that this "crossing" of Dewey's pragmatism and Woodbridge's realism was more influential "than the teaching of either alone could have been" ("Philosopher" 45).[7]

This "crossing" of pragmatism and realism challenges one to find a sense in which combining pragmatism and realism is not a contradiction in terms. This combination appears most importantly in McKeon's view of philosophical turns. On the one hand, because these turns change the subject matter of philosophy, they are pragmatic in the sense that they presuppose that there is no one true subject matter. Stressing this pragmatic side of McKeon, even aligning McKeon with James and thereby lessening the distance that Watson finds between them, Robert Danisch concludes that for McKeon "truth is simply codification of a set of pre-

---

a construal that remains too general. Simonson's interest is in McKeon's pragmatic side and, particularly, in McKeon's making "communication" and "rhetoric" key terms in pragmatic thought. Pursuing this interest, Simonson offers admirable overviews of McKeon's biography and intellectual development.

7. This autobiographical essay, "A Philosopher Meditates on Discovery," before its reprinting in *Selected Writings of Richard McKeon*, volume one, was delivered as a lecture at "The Institute for Religious and Social Studies of The Jewish Theological Seminary of America." This lecture was part of a series of lectures during winter 1951–1952 in which each lecturer was asked to reach "back to some point, to some moment of experience, that brought him a clearer sense of direction and some vision of a goal toward which henceforth he must move" (MacIver ix). McKeon published two additional autobiographical essays. One was also a lecture at "The Institute for Religious and Social Studies of The Jewish Theological Seminary of America," this one in a series of lectures during the winter of 1949–1950. It was originally published in a volume entitled *Thirteen Americans: Their Spiritual Autobiographies*, where each chapter is entitled by the name of its author. The editor of the volume introduces it as an effort "to bring before the public types of personality, which seem to be contributing to the preservation and advancement of civilization" (Finkelstein xi). When McKeon's chapter was reprinted in *Freedom and History and Other Essays*, it was retitled "Spiritual Autobiography." The other essay, "The Circumstances and Functions of Philosophy," appears in *Philosophers on Their Own Work*, volume one of a multivolume series sponsored by the International Federation of Philosophical Societies. The "Foreword" to this inaugural volume indicates that the "first volumes" include members of the project's "Steering Committee" (xiii). This "Foreword" also explains that the series offers "self-critical article[s]" by philosophers, each "given its own title by its author," so that "the reader will get to know the respective philosopher under the impact of the elucidations given by himself of his own philosophy" (xii).

existing behaviors that we happen to call rational within the logic of a particular historical moment" (*Building* 141).

On the other hand, while a pragmatic consensus may form around one or another subject matter, the subject matter itself is a real existent independent of this consensus. The turns from subject matter to subject matter are limited in number and occur in a cyclical order, seemingly independent of human volition, like the seasons of the year. The reality of a subject matter evidences itself, moreover, in arbitrating in debates centered on this subject matter. Debates about epistemology, for example, are arbitrated by the reality of epistemology, a component of reality that Johnston and Gabriel identify. The most extensive example of such arbitration that this book offers appears in chapter three, where the reality of language is the arbiter.

In a philosophical turn, the pragmatic side appears in the specific problems philosophers solve in effecting a turn, problem-solving being, as Depew indicates, the characteristic mark of classical pragmatism (30). Turns occur not because all philosophers one day suddenly confront the same problem. Rather they occur when different philosophers address different problems whose solutions all involve turning in some way to the next stage in the cycle. The twentieth-century's turn to language and action entailed turns against the Kantian prioritizing of thought. As we will see, such turns against thought appear in logical positivism (chapter three) and in Heidegger (chapter five), but logical positivism and Heidegger take up different problems that they solve by toppling thought from its position of priority. An exhaustive study of one turn should find a range of distinct problems, all solved by turning in some way to the next stage in the cycle. McKeon's identification of turns thus invites scholars to examine the full historical record of turns.

While McKeon typically references one or more of these turns to contextualize analysis of specific philosophic treatments of problems, he occasionally departs from this practice to present the turns in general terms as a cycle that begins with thing, turns next to thought, then to language and action, then back to thing ("Philosopher" 51). Presented thus, the cycle implicitly claims a capacity for prediction at the level of ultimate priorities that is much more than a one-shot guesstimate. Questions about the future press forward when the focus is the present. In the case of the twentieth century, McKeon saw it as a period in the third of his three stages, so that his cycle predicts that the twentieth-century's linguistic turn will be followed by the twenty-first-century's metaphysical turn.

In classes, McKeon would often take time to review the most recent cycle of turns, beginning with the turn to thing in the seventeenth century, to contextualize the twentieth-century subject matter of language and action. But these reviews left open the question "what next?" The cyclicality of turns predicted a "next," but McKeon let that pass, just as he does in his publications. In one case, though, in 1967, in the heyday of the linguistic turn when nothing seemed more far-fetched that a turn to metaphysics, he did in a classroom lecture depart from his usual silence about the future to predict,

> We shall have another revolution in philosophy. And on the basis of that revolution, we shall proceed again to a choice between parts and wholes and to the establishment of principles in a new metaphysics. I want to confess that I am subversive in intention. But this course is not a revolutionary one. It is a simple introduction to philosophy as it is practiced today, rendered a little novel and difficult by exposure to its basis in rhetoric and communication. ("Experience").

While his use of "subversive" here seems to imply a metaphysical intention, that is speculative, and it is even more speculative to formulate his strategy for realizing his intention if it is metaphysical. In any case, the final chapter will suggest ways to construe McKeon's use of "subversive."

Additionally, the basis of McKeon's linkage in this passage of rhetoric to modern philosophy will be explained in chapter two, devoted to McKeon. Then, this linkage will be part of chapter three's skeletal narrative of the history of the linguistic turn, a part that has been noticed but still deserves more attention than it has received to date.

That the emergent metaphysical turn may confirm McKeon's 1967 predication lends credence to this book's view that his cycle of philosophical turns merits greater attention than it has received heretofore. More importantly, going beyond the value of prediction, one should view McKeon's cycle as a philosophical view of the history of philosophy in which philosophical turns are not historical contingencies, but revelatory of the role in this history of changes in the subject matter of philosophy.

This cycle, however, is only part of McKeon's philosophical pluralism. Placing this part in the context of his pluralism as a whole is the aim of chapter two. To accomplish this aim, chapter two will offer an introductory overview of the main stages in McKeon's development of his philosophical pluralism.

2 McKeon's Pluralism

> Words may be thought to designate things, signify thoughts, and induce actions, if things, thoughts, and actions are thought to exist apart from and prior to words. Or words may be thought to be the sources and causes of what things, thoughts, and actions are thought to be, and therefore, are.
>
> —McKeon, "Pluralism of Interpretations and Pluralism of Objects, Actions, and Statements Interpreted," p. 54

Reading McKeon, one encounters an extraordinary command of the history of philosophy, so much so that it is easy to conclude that he is more a historian of philosophy than a philosopher. That is a mistake. He is a philosopher who inquires into the nature of philosophy by examining closely the history of philosophy, principally in the West.[8] In another of his autobiographical essays, he traces this project to the influence of Etienne Gilson during his postdoctoral studies in Paris in the early 1920s, an influence he acknowledges in dedicating *Thought, Action, and Passion* to Gilson. "I learned from Gilson," he recalls, "to trace the basic patterns and unity of philosophical thought through the diversity of philosophic systems and expressions" (*Freedom* 12).

This Gilson influence adds to the combined influence of Dewey and Woodbridge a deep interest in "[p]erennis philosophia," Gilson's term in *The Unity of Philosophical Experience* "for philosophy itself" (318). For Gilson, this unity centers in metaphysics, which philosophy recurrently returns to after departing from for reasons attributable to metaphysicians themselves. Metaphysics is about being, which is paradoxically in all things yet in different things in different ways (312). It is all there in the beginning in Thales, who makes a claim about all things, being, but names it water, reducing being to a particular sensible thing, this naming making Thales vulnerable to critique (311). This slippage is the typical

---

8. His inquiries occasionally extend beyond the West. An example would be his "Foreword" to *The Edicts of Asoka*, edited and translated by N. A. Nikam and Richard McKeon, U of Chicago P, 1959. Asoka was an emperor of India, ca. 274–232 BCE.

error metaphysicians make: "a particular determination of being, or a being, will be invested with the universality of being" (315). Contrastingly, Plato, Aristotle, and St. Thomas Aquinas, Gilson's three greatest metaphysicians, aimed "not to achieve philosophy once and for all, but to maintain it and to serve it in their own times, as we have to maintain it and serve it in ours" (317). But this relativism perhaps strikes a disappointing note of discord with his earlier strong rejection of all forms of historicist accounts of philosophy (303–04).

Leaving that aside, Gilson's "unity" thus centers in a problem that seems insoluble, solved insofar as being is conceived and not solved insofar as the conception reduces being in a way that makes metaphysics a target of criticism that brings it into disrepute. McKeon's unity, his *"perennis philosophia"* if you will, centers in the combination of philosophical and historical semantics in his pluralism, which this chapter introduces. This book draws particularly on historical semantics to inquire, as noted in chapter one, into (1) what such turns reveal about the nature of philosophy and (2) whether what these turns reveal provides a basis for preferring one to the others. The former, what turns reveal, appears in varying ways in every chapter. The latter is addressed mainly in the final chapter.

Historical semantics centers on changes in the subject matter of philosophy. It will frame chapters three, four, and five. Philosophical semantics explains why philosophers analyzing the subject matter in place during a historical period disagree with one another.

PHILOSOPHICAL SEMANTICS

The best record of the early emergence of what would become philosophical semantics appears in Plochmann's *Richard McKeon: A Study*, mentioned in chapter one. Plochmann first encountered McKeon in a classroom at Columbia University in 1934, when McKeon was 34; then, after McKeon moved to the University of Chicago, he followed him there in 1936 (2,5). He also returned to Chicago after WWII for additional work with McKeon in the late 1940s (11). Plochmann's recounting of McKeon's teaching is invaluable insofar as it is the best record we have of the earliest stages in McKeon's pluralistic philosophizing. Plochmann himself went on to become a professor of philosophy at Southern Illinois University.

Plochmann recounts that McKeon's earliest pluralism "was reminiscent of Coleridge's famous remark that everyone is born a Platonist or an Aristotelian" (46). In a course at Columbia, McKeon would put "Plato" and "Aristotle" on the blackboard, then list contrasts under these names to identify pluralistic options. One essay evidencing this practice, simplistic compared to McKeon's mature pluralism, is "Literary Criticism and the Concept of Imitation in Antiquity," published in *Modern Philology* 1936, then reprinted in *Critics and Criticism: Ancient and Modern*, the principal volume of what came to be known as the "Chicago School" of literary criticism that combined critical pluralism with the use of Aristotle's *Poetics* as a model for literary criticism. Here, analogous to his classroom practice, McKeon presents extensive analyses of the different meanings of "imitation" in Plato and Aristotle in which Aristotle is to literal meanings as Plato is to analogical meanings (*Critics* 149–59, 160–68).[9] These two sections take up most of the essay, but after the Aristotle section there is a brief section that begins,

> The word [imitation] was used in still other senses by other writers in antiquity, but considerations of method are not so important in the fashions of their usage, and the systematic implications are not so subtle. None of the writers on literature employed the dialectical method of Plato in any but a highly attenuated and faltering manner. Their definitions are literal like

---

9. The "literal" prioritizes the proximate cause of each distinctive thing. In the age of New Critical formalism, the Chicago School drew on Aristotle for a model of art as an autotelic object in which the proximate cause of the object is the form in the object. While the literal thus descends to proximate causes, the "analogical" goes in the opposite direction. Encountering two things, the analogical ascends dialectically to something common between both and may ascend higher and higher to more and more inclusive levels, offering in place of the specific, direct causes of distinct things on the literal level, a general cause of many things with great differences, ultimately a cause beyond existents such as Platonic ideas. McKeon uses this literal/analogical distinction in "The Philosophic Bases of Art and Criticism" that originally appeared in the early 1940s before its reprinting in *Critics and Criticism*.

Writing in 1982, McKeon misremembers this 1936 essay, not only by saying it was published in *Classical Philology* rather than *Modern Philology*, but also and more importantly by saying it includes a section on Democritus, which is not the case ("Criticism" 39–40). He appears to be referencing the analysis of imitation in Greek antiquity that he produces in "Imitation and Poetry," which appears in 1954 in *Thought, Action, and Passion*.

> those of Aristotle, but in their writings the term "imitation" does not appear in a context of subject matters distributed in various scientific disciplines. Rather, the meanings in which they use the term are derived for the most part from the meanings which it assumed in Plato's dialogues, usually degraded and rendered static or, what amounts to the same thing, in a meaning which "imitation" might have had if Aristotle had used it in some other work than the *Poetics*, as, for example, the *Rhetoric*. (168)

Having depicted these "footnotes" to Plato and Aristotle as degradations of Plato and Aristotle, McKeon then groups them together to conclude: "A third variant to the meanings of Plato and Aristotle may therefore be said to derive from the tradition of writers on rhetoric" (168). Rhetoric is thus marginal in McKeon's earliest pluralism, offering an alternative pluralistic option, albeit one dependent on Plato and Aristotle. This marginality is reversed in the later historical semantics.

What would become philosophical semantics began to develop when McKeon substituted concepts for names: in place of Plato, "holoscopic," view from the whole; in place of Aristotle, "meroscopic," view from the part (Plochmann 47). Later, Democritus became the exemplar of meroscopic and Aristotle was moved to a position between meroscopic and holoscopic (49). "Holoscopic" and "meroscopic" remained in McKeon's pluralism throughout its development, eventually serving to distinguish kinds of principles in his "Schema of Philosophic Semantics" ("Philosophic Semantics" 218). As philosophic semantics developed, other pluralistic options were added as parts of this "Schema," whose evolution is Plochmann's principal concern. The key essay in Plochmann's account is "Philosophic Semantics and Philosophic Inquiry," which McKeon delivered as a lecture in 1966 at Southern Illinois University, presumably at Plochmann's invitation (Plochmann 68). McKeon never published this lecture in his lifetime, but it became legendary among his students as he used mimeographed copies of it in classes I took in the 1960s; it was published posthumously in both *Freedom and History and Other Essays* (242–56) and *Selected Writings of Richard McKeon*, volume 1 (209–21).

In this "Schema," there are four fourfolds: four "principles," four "methods," four "interpretations," and four "selections." A combination of principle, method, interpretation, and selection is a semantic profile. Different profiles explain differences among philosophers analyzing the same subject matter during a historical period. McKeon recorded profiles on note cards that have been published, where they are arranged in varying ways for comparative purposes (*On Knowing—Social Sciences* 360–84). In essays, partial rather than complete profiles are typically enough to position philosophers in relation to one another for a particular purpose. One of the best places to see extensive use of philosophic semantics in conjunction with historical semantics is "Imitation and Poetry," among the McKeon essays that should have been a book (*Thought* 102–221, 239–85 [endnotes]).

References to philosophic semantics in the chapters that follow will be incidental. The main overlap with philosophic semantics appears in the term "ultimate priority." This term is not McKeon's, but it does overlap with his term "principle." The terms overlap insofar as both mean "beginning" or "starting point." Harman glimpses offhandedly the philosophical significance of a "beginning" when he remarks, "I suppose any philosophy probably has some ungrounded first principle" ("Propositions" 30), that is, an ungrounded grounding, which marks philosophy's exceptionalism among the disciplines, as suggested in chapter one. "Ultimate priority" also takes a step beyond this overlap in directing attention to a distinctive feature of philosophical turning.

The other three components in McKeon's "Schema," taken together, lead to the ultimate priority of principle. McKeon distinguishes these three in terms of the number of terms required in each. "Selection" is a single term, a simple, at most a kind of pointing, though there are distinguishable modes of pointing. To say anything about this simple, one needs two terms, an "Interpretation," with modes of interpretation distinguished on the basis of whether they stay on phenomenal level in two possible ways or go above or below the phenomenal. To support an "Interpretation" with argument, "Method," one needs three terms, as seen most simply in the syllogism. Modes of method are distinguished broadly between universal modes applicable to all subjects and particular modes relative to distinguishable subject matters, with two kinds on each of these two levels. Solutions to the three problems thus comprise together an inferential structure in need of grounding.

It finds this grounding in a principle. Principles are either "meroscopic" or "holoscopic," as noted earlier, with two variants of each. Principles are always ultimately prior within the philosophies in which they appear. But in a philosophical turn, ultimate priority is also on a level beyond individual philosophies, which is among the more important things philosophical turns teach. At this level, the existent that is the ultimate priority philosophers are turning to becomes the arbiter in debates among these philosophers. As arbiter, it overlaps with the individual philosophy or philosophies in which it appears, but goes beyond this overlap in changing the subject matter of philosophy. As noted in chapter one, philosophy is always about the quartet of thing, thought, language, and action, but changes in the order of priority among them change the subject matter of philosophy; in the pages ahead, references simply to changes in the subject matter of philosophy will be shorthand for changes in this order of priority. By establishing a new order of priority, an ultimate priority changes the subject matter. To do this, an ultimate priority must establish a sense in which it is prior not only to the ultimate priority in the subject matter it is turning from but also to the ultimate priority in the other, the third possible subject matter, as well. Focusing on the ultimate priority's reprioritizing in this change in subject matter, as chapter three will illustrate more extensively than any other chapter, adds a level of interpretation that can correct interpretations that ignore this level. On this level, ultimate priority goes beyond its overlap with "principle" to the issue of priority among the subject matters in McKeon's cycle.

Ultimate priorities illustrate the interrelation between philosophical and historical semantics. They appear in all philosophies (philosophical semantics), but they take different forms in different philosophical subject matters (historical semantics). The philosophical turns in the history of philosophy indicate that ultimate priorities appear in thing, thought, and language and action. That means that philosophers have found in each of the three subject matters in McKeon's cycle of turns an existent that in a certain sense is prior to ultimate priorities in the other two subject matters. Paradoxically, that makes possible a turn to and from each, a turn to each as a priority and a turn from each as posterior to one of the others.

It is speculative but possible that philosophy's exceptionalism is paradoxically omnipresent in all disciplines, at least potentially, if you accept McKeon's view that any problem pushed far enough becomes a philosophical problem (*On Knowing—Natural Sciences* 2). More often than not, philosophy is below the surface, but it may always be there. Philosophy's exceptionalism, then, would not separate philosophy from the other disciplines, but might instead provide a foundation for anyone who wanted to undertake the daunting task of offering an account of the relations among the disciplines.

An example of an ultimate priority appears in "Metaphysical Arguments," where Bernard Williams offers a brief argument for a specific metaphysics to illustrate metaphysical argument in general. Williams begins with a review of inductive and deductive arguments. Ingredients of such arguments may appear in metaphysical argument (55–56), but metaphysical argument is distinct from both, for the metaphysician "will try to show that some concept on which we rely is secondary to, or presupposed by, some other concept which he has introduced or extended from elsewhere." In other words, the metaphysician will establish an order of priority. Williams adds that the more widely the metaphysician uses this concept, "the more systematic will his philosophy be" (58).

Williams advances his specific metaphysics with the example of the hypothetical experience of mistaking a boot for a cat in the dusk. In this perceptual experience, what exactly is seen? It is not a cat, because there was no cat there, only a boot. It is not a boot either, because it is perceived to be a cat. In other words, something is seen that is neither a cat nor a boot. "So the experience you have in both cases must be something neutral between really seeing a cat and really seeing a boot," Williams goes on, "something common to both and less than either." This "something" evidences the priority in the order of perception; as Williams explains, "the having of visual experience must be more basic than the seeing of real objects; for one can have visual experiences without in fact seeing the appropriate, or indeed any, sort of object, but we cannot see an object without having visual experiences" (53). "Visual experience," in short, is prior to seeing an object. This is a priority in the subject matter of thought, the location of "principles of knowledge in thought or perception" (McKeon, "Future," 299).

By identifying an ultimate priority, Williams thus uncovers a subject matter. The ultimate priority Williams identifies "can lay the foundations," as he puts it, for an empiricist metaphysic using the notion of an 'idea' or a 'sensation'" (54), presumably an idea in a Humean sense. The posterior moment construes the visual as an object. This construal may be mistaken, while the prior "sensation" is certain, happening automatically, even if it is not seen as such insofar as one thinks one sees an object (e.g., cat). Its certainty makes it foundational for a metaphysics in which purely "visual experience" is the fundamental reality, the ultimate priority in the consequential order of perception in which interpretive construal, which may err, is dependent on a purely empirical experience that is certain. Interpretive construal may be so ingrained that the prior "visual experience" may not register in consciousness, a seeing that is paradoxically not seen.

This empiricist ultimate priority is discovered, not invented, in an intellectual process. The mistaken cat and boot perceptions are data in this process. "Ultimate priority" explains why Williams can put "empirical" and "metaphysical" together, two terms more commonly put at loggerheads. What legitimates the combination is the sense in which the empirical "visual experience" is an ultimate priority, an existent that functions as foundational to what is posterior. In the strictest sense, "metaphysics" may be said to refer to an order in reality based on an ultimate priority that is absolutely independent of and indifferent to humans, located in Meillassoux's "*great outdoors*," to be taken up in chapter four. But, as Williams shows, "metaphysic" can be used more broadly to refer to orders in reality that involve humans, such as the order in "visual experience." For "visual experience" is still independent of and indifferent to humans in the sense that its occurrence is something that cannot be altered in a normal human being.

While "visual experience" is only a part of reality, indeed, a small part when compared to what is usually meant by references to reality, it is nonetheless as a reality that it can function as an ultimate priority and arbitrate in debates among philosophers. Because there are ultimate priorities in each of the subject matters in McKeon's cycle, one can speak of a metaphysics of each one. "Empiricist metaphysic" illustrates this point. McKeon himself will illustrate it later in this chapter in characterizing the sense in which philosophizing in each of the subject matters in his historical semantics is a distinctive metaphysics. Importantly, because philosophical turns are from the reality of one ultimate priority to the reality of another, the commonplace opposition between antirealism and realism will be of no use later, in the final chapter, when considering whether the evidence of the turns themselves provides a basis for a determination of a preferential order among them.

One may view Williams's discovery as a kind of reverse engineering that begins with the hypothetical mistaking a boot for a cat in the dusk and that ends with the structure of prior and posterior moments in an "empiricist metaphysic" to explain this hypothetical. Sensory intuition is involved but it is secondary to the intellectual figuring out on the supersensible level of the explanatory structure of prior and posterior moments. Ironically, even though the ultimate priority is the immediacy of "visual experience," it takes intellectual work, which is far from immediate, to arrive at the order of prior and posterior that explains the combination of this experience with the mistaking of a boot for a cat. Williams seems to be talking exclusively about sensible experience, yet he obviously goes beyond it to figure out the order of priority that explains what he finds in it.

Williams's discovery is an intuition, not an inference from a premise, for that would make this premise ultimate not the priority that Williams intuits. Ultimate priorities are intuited, accessed directly. Ultimate priorities are premises that ground inferential structures, but are themselves ungrounded, intuited rather than inferred.

But Williams, while identifying establishing an order of priority as the distinctive characteristic of metaphysical argument, does not describe the grasping of the ultimate priority in this order as intellectual intuition, or anything else for that matter. He simply does it. In this respect he is like most of the others to be examined in this book. Meillassoux is the main exception. He explicitly recognizes the dependency of metaphysics on intellectual intuition and develops a form of intellectual intuition based on a borrowing from Aristotle. Silence like Williams's will reappear particularly in examples of "exemptionalism" that deny the possibility of direct access, yet base their denial on an ultimate priority accessed directly.

This silence would appear to be attributable at least in part to Kant's influential argument that one cannot access directly the thing-in-itself, the noumenon. Kant himself does not always abide by this rule, as we shall see at the end of chapter four, but that has done little to weaken his influence. Dogmatic dismissals of intellectual intuition have become commonplace. An example appears in Brassier's "Concepts and Objects," an important essay to be considered in the final chapter. Brassier, moreover, dismisses accessing intuitively the metaphysical reality of thought as well as thing. Yet Brassier does seek to access objects independently of concepts. He does find a way, albeit one that is embarrassingly minimalistic, little more than ostensive pointing, but his discovery ironically depends on direct access to language. He eschews direct access in general, yet relies on a mode of direct access in the end, albeit without acknowledgement.

"Modern skepticism," McKeon observes, "partly precedes the Critical philosophy, partly springs out of it; it consists solely in denying the truth and certitude of the supersensible, and in pointing to the facts of sense and of immediate sensations as ultimate" ("Dialogue" 147).

McKeon wrote this in 1956, when logical positivism was still in recent memory, before "immediate sensations" lost their authority as a source of intuitive knowledge during developments in the linguistic turn in later decades of the twentieth century. But those developments do not undermine McKeon's broader historical point, which also appears in Hilary Putnam's "How Old Is Mind?," where Putnam observes that "during the last two or three hundred years, especially in English-speaking countries, the mind has been virtually identified with sensation." Putnam finds in Descartes the beginnings of the hegemonic position sensory intuition came to enjoy. While Descartes had reservations about secondary qualities, he had none about primary qualities, which are both visual and measurable. For primary qualities, Putnam explains, "the 'extension' of the material object, its size and figure," did "retain the classical view that these are present in the mind *and* in the object, that (in this respect) I have the very form of the object within my own mind (though not, of course, its matter)" (32, 37).

Putnam illustrates this broader classical view with Aristotle, who gets the first word in Putnam's "Aristotle after Wittgenstein," first published in 1993 and later reprinted in a collection of his essays: "In Book 3 of *De Anima*, Aristotle writes that 'the thinking part of the soul, while impassible, must be capable of receiving the form of an object; that is, must be potentially the same as its object without being the object.'" Later in the same essay, Putnam elaborates on Aristotle's intellectual intuition of "form": "to give the form of, say, a living thing is to give the way it is organized to function, its capacities and functionings and the interrelationships among those capacities and functionings: in short, what it is capable of, and how it accomplishes what it is capable of" (62, 71). Descartes, in effect, retains this classical view but reduces form as "organized to function" to form as visual "size and figure," elevating the sensory to an authoritative level.

In later chapters, Putnam's "organized to function" will serve to mark places where something like intellectual intuition appears to be occurring without acknowledgement, as in Williams, where he explains the experience of mistaking a cat for a boot by giving an account of how the prior and posterior moments in his "empiricist metaphysic" are "organized to function." Rather than purport to offer a theory of intellectual intuition, which would be a huge undertaking unto itself, this book will suggest that a reevaluation of it is in order because of evidence of dependency on it without acknowledgement, as in Williams, or even in the face of explicit denunciations of it, as in Brassier. It may have become modern skepticism's blind spot, that which is needed but cannot be acknowledged without reevaluation of this skepticism, seemingly cherished dogmatically. More importantly for the purposes of this book, evidence of reliance on "organized to function" in all the turns will be a factor in the final chapter's consideration of whether there is a preferential order among the turns. Specifically, it will be a factor in considering how to view the turns if one gives up skepticism's claims to superiority.

Putnam qualifies his formulation of form as "organized to function" by adding that he will not try to explain "how Aristotle thought a form could be 'in' the soul *minus* its matter" ("Aristotle" 62). Explaining that would no doubt be a thorny issue in theorizing intellectual intuition. One possible way to approach this issue might be by analogy with an architectural plan for a house. The plan is the form. The plan does not contain the matter of the house, but it does identify what matter is to be used and where it is to be put. Matter is part of the form of the actual house, but not part of the form of the architectural plan. Michail Peramatzis finds a similar distinction in Aristotle: "For a form does not depend, for its being what it is, on particular perceptible bits of matter [e.g., wood]. It does depend, though, on appropriate types of material feature, the matter from which the form is made up [e.g., the particular kind of wood that is to go in a particular place in an architectural plan]" (53–54).

One thing missing from these Putnam essays is consideration of Aristotle's distinction, presented in *Posterior Analytics*, book one, chapter two, between what is better known to us and what is better known in nature:

> there is a difference between what is prior and better known in the order of being and what is prior and better known to man. I mean that objects nearer to sense are prior and better known to man; objects without qualification prior and better known are those further from sense. Now the most universal causes are *furthest* from sense and particular causes are nearest to sense, and they are exactly opposed to one another. (71b34–72a5, *Basic Works* 112; see also *Physics* 184a17–21, *Basic Works*)

Mistaking a boot for a cat in the dusk is better known to us; the explanatory functional interrelation of prior and posterior in Williams's "empiricist metaphysic" is better known in being. The level of sense is crucial;

that is the level where inquiry begins and which is always involved. But one must always use the intellect to go beyond this level.

This distinction recurs in *Posterior Analytics*, most often in varying ways Aristotle considers an eclipse of the moon. We can conclude this initial commentary on intellectual intuition with two passages in which Aristotle imagines watching an eclipse of the moon while standing on the moon. The two passages appear inconsistent; if one wants to read charitably, one can remove the inconsistency by reading the later one as presupposing the earlier one. These passages can serve to dissociate Aristotle's intellectual grasping of what is better known in being from "presence," critiques of which became commonplace in the linguistic turn. Translated into Aristotle's terminology, one can say that the mistaken identification of presence with being arises from the mistaken conflation of what is better known to us and what is better known in being in the logocentric assumption that both can be grasped simultaneously and immediately.

This assumption appears in the later passage if one reads it without assuming that it presupposes the earlier passage:

> if we were on the moon . . . both fact and reason would be obvious simultaneously. For the act of perception would have enabled us to know the universal too; since the present fact of an eclipse being evident, perception would then at the same time give us the present fact of the earth's screening the sun's light, and from this would arise the universal. (90a27–31; *Basic Works* 160).

The earlier passage corrects this later one:

> for perception must be of a particular, whereas scientific knowledge involves the recognition of the commensurate universal. So if we were on the moon, and saw the earth shutting out the sun's light, we should not know the cause of the eclipse: we should perceive the present fact of the eclipse, but not the reasoned fact at all, since the act of perception is not of the commensurate universal. I do not, of course, deny that by watching the frequent recurrence of the event we might, after tracking the commensurate universal, possess a demonstration, for the commensurate universal is elicited from the several groups of singulars. (87ba38–88a3; *Basic Works* 154)

Sensory experience of an eclipse is "present" but the universal, grasped through intellectual intuition, is not. Such movement from the sensory to the intellectual is consistent with Charles H. Kahn's view, in his penetrating "Aristotle on Thinking," that "intellectual activity is for Aristotle a joint action of sentience and intellect" (363). But this joint action consists of two distinct stages. The intellect comprehends the way a thing, as Putnam puts it, "is organized to function." Such organization is not "present" to the senses.

Historical Semantics

Historical semantics charts philosophical turns. Anticipations of historical semantics appear early in McKeon's career, as early as anticipations of philosophical semantics, but not in the form of terminology such as "holoscopic" and "meroscopic" that calls attention to itself. The terminology of historical semantics eventually surfaces in an episode in McKeon's teaching, to be considered later, that prompts Plochmann to identify "selections" as the place where the "Schema" of philosophical semantics in "Philosophic Semantics and Philosophic Inquiry" intersects with the differing subject matters of philosophy (79). "Selections" occur on two levels, subject matter in general and modes of subject matter in particular. Kant, for example, selects the subject matter of "thought" and the mode "transcendental" rather than "reductive," "perspective," or "functional."[10] While "Selection" selects, it is "Principle" that uncovers the ultimate priority in the subject matter that grounds the inferential structure of the philosophy.

When definitions of philosophical turns do appear they update and revise McKeon's long-standing conviction that changes in the subject matter of philosophy undermine any view of the history of philosophy as a linear progression. McKeon recounts the formation of this conviction in one of his autobiographical essays, "A Philosopher Meditates on Discovery." The "discovery" he recounts in detail led to two paradoxes that proved seminar for him: (1) the "truth, though one, has no single

---

10. The semantic profiles McKeon recorded on several note cards include a mode of selection (*On Knowing—Social* 422), but evidently because modes of selection do not appear on all the cards, only modes of principle, method, and interpretation are included in the records listed (*On Knowing—Social Sciences* 360–84).

expression," (2) "the true is sometimes false and sometimes true" (48). This discovery appealed to him, he goes on,

> in spite of the fact that it ran counter to my most fundamental convictions at the time. I should have preferred to think of the development of philosophy, as knowledge, as a progressive evolution in which errors were detected and discarded and truths were accumulated and interrelated. (49, 48, 49).

Similarly, in a 1928 essay on Thomas Aquinas, McKeon insists in his closing paragraph that "the shifts and alterations of the subject of philosophic inquiry suggest, not that we are coming after centuries of inquiry to the truth and that we have at last left the false, but that the philosopher, like the poet and the scientist, takes for his subject what he will" ("Thomas" 444). In other words, philosophy is not an unchanging subject matter that is understood better over time. Rather, philosophy's subject matter changes. The history of philosophy is not linear.

A similar rejection of historical linearity has become widespread in the wake of Thomas S. Kuhn's widely known *The Structure of Scientific Revolutions*, which contends that linear progression of knowledge does not occur even in natural science, where the evidence of linearity would appear to be strongest. Kuhn's term for the linear model is "development-by-accumulation," which he rejects in favor of paradigm shifts entailing changes in subject matter, that is, changes in the conception of "fundamental entities" in the universe and their interactions (2, 4–5). McKeon, in "Philosophy and Method," originally published 1951, suggests that science assumes something of a philosophical character when changes occur of the sort that Kuhn later analyzes as changes in paradigm (184). While questioning of linearity is now widespread, linearity is still sometimes affirmed as in the example of the affirmation by many of Derrida's depiction of himself as the David of deconstruction correcting over two millennia of the Goliath of logocentrism.

McKeon begins the closing paragraph in his Aquinas essay by suggesting that the "philosophical affinities in the flow of history are too strangely mixed to permit over-simple divisions into periods" (444). Here, McKeon questions divisions that his historical semantics will later define. But the passage also suggests that part of what makes historical semantics acceptable for McKeon is that it coexists with philosophical semantics, which covers "affinities" among periods. Regardless of changes in the subject matter of philosophy, philosophies all have principles, methods, interpretations, and selections that have affinities with one another, despite differences in subject matter. A deep study of the applicability of philosophical semantics to the history of philosophy would uncover affinities of this sort. In the present book, as noted earlier, ultimate priorities in different subject matters will be the main exhibit of such affinities.

In 1942, fourteen years after his Aquinas essay, in "Rhetoric in the Middle Ages," McKeon reaffirms his earlier rejection of linearity based on the assumption of an unchanging subject matter. This reaffirmation concludes the essay's introductory section: "if the succession of subject matters and functions can be used to reduce the welter of changes in rhetoric to a significant historical sequence, the theories implicated in the shifts of its subject matter should emerge, not merely as philosophic or sophistic disputes, but in concrete application, each at least defensible and each a challenge to the conception of intellectual history as the simple record of the development of a body of knowledge by more or less adequate investigations of a constant subject matter" (262–63).

Historical semantics continues McKeon's nonlinear view of the history of philosophy, but it also divides history into periods, modifying his earlier skepticism about such division. The development that would lead to these divisions appears to begin in classroom lessons that Plochmann recounts. Plochmann describes these as based on "a 3 x 3 array" in which McKeon would list (1) under "Subject Matters" Things, Thoughts, and Words; (2) under "Philosophic Approaches" different combinations of these three, with each being primary in one, intermediate in another, and posterior in the third; and (3) under "Principal Problems" three questions: "What is metaphysics? Is metaphysics valid? Is metaphysics meaningful?" (79–80). Plochmann indicates that this array first appeared in a winter 1938 course (79). McKeon would later revise the subject matter of words to words and deeds, or language and action. In "Principles and Consequences," where McKeon analyzes the formation of principles in each of these three subject matters, he stresses the interconnectedness of language and action, whereby one can treat, as noted in chapter one, "statements as forms of action" or "purposive forms of action as instances of verbal rules" (395). Principles in this third subject matter relate language and action in some way, implicitly if not explicitly. Any comprehensive account of the linguistic turn would include J. L. Austin's speech-act theory and Kenneth Burke's theory of language as symbolic action. In the philosophizing of the linguistic turn, the term "language" is typically used alone. For the sake of convenience, I will follow that practice, though I will also sometimes emphasize McKeon's combination of language and action as one subject matter that vies with the subject matters of thing and thought in the history of philosophy.

This 1938 appearance of three different orders of priority among "Things, Thoughts, and Words" anticipates the changes in the subject matter of philosophy in historical semantics. But while they are anticipatory, they are still significantly different. When McKeon introduced them in class, he saw them as "Philosophic Approaches," not different periods in a cycle of changes in the subject matter of philosophy.

Plochmann, importantly, makes it clear that while the linguistic approach in this schema was identified with logical positivism, then its heyday, McKeon did not do this out of any sympathy with it. Far from it. Plochmann paraphrases McKeon's lecture thus: "In this linguistic approach, metaphysics is reduced to so slender a role as to consist merely of the assertion that there can exist no metaphysics," adding, "What is left after this impoverishment, McKeon pointed out, is the special sciences, commencing with mathematics and physics, together with the grammars appropriate to them. Being is now nothing more an article of faith for which no demonstration or experiment could possible by forthcoming" (80–81).

McKeon would revise this negative judgment of the linguistic approach in the course of the 1940s when he saw it not as logical positivism applied it, but as a rhetoricizing of philosophy. Initially, in other words, he did not see this approach as rhetorical. "Rhetoric in the Middle Ages" occasioned as we saw a reaffirmation of his rejection of linearity in history. It probably also prompted a reevaluation of his earlier view of rhetoric in his essay on the concept of imitation in antiquity, discussed earlier, and McKeon no doubt drew on it in his later recognition of the rhetoricizing of philosophy. But this is an essay he wrote for the Mediaeval Academy.[11] It does not appear to be involved in McKeon's initial exploration of the prioritizing of language as a "Philosophic Approach."

---

11. Reprintings of "Rhetoric in the Middle Ages" have omitted the footnote at the bottom of p. 1 of its original publication in *Speculum: A Journal of Medieval Studies*, vol. 17, no. 1, January 1942, pp. 1–32: "By way of experimental departure from the customary procedure at meetings of learned societies the following paper will be the subject of discussion at the next meeting of the Mediaeval Academy on April 24, 1942. Rhetoric was chosen as a topic which impinges on many fields of mediaeval study, and an effort is made in the paper to touch, at least, on as many of them as possible. The paper will not be read at

Plochmann indicates that the reservations about this linguistic approach that McKeon presented in class are similar to those in his 1942 essay on G. E. Moore (80), his most extended discussion of a philosopher practicing this approach. McKeon's initial negative judgment of it permeates this essay, which appeared in a volume of essays, *The Philosophy of G. E. Moore*, published in a series called *The Library of Living Philosophers*. After appearing in 1942, this volume appeared in a second edition in 1952. In the "General Introduction" for the series, it is indicated that each volume aims to include "exponents and opponents of the philosopher's thought" (ix). One assumes that McKeon was selected as an "opponent," for it is hard to imagine any other reason for his selection.

McKeon came of age intellectually in the 1920s, the decade of Wittgenstein's *Tractatus*, the formation of the Vienna Circle, and the rise of logical positivism, sometimes also called logical empiricism. Moore along with Bertrand Russell came to be seen as precursors of these developments.[12] The Moore volume, which even gave Moore the opportunity to write responses to all the essays in the volume, testifies to his status during the decades logical positivism enjoyed its heyday before being discredited in later stages of the linguistic turn. But while this Circle was forming in Vienna, McKeon was studying Medieval philosophy in Paris, his dissertation research on Spinoza having "already brought [him] into contact with currents of medieval thought" (*Freedom* 12). In 1928,

---

the meeting but will be considered in informal panel discussion in which it is hoped all members present at the meeting will participate." The passive voice in the second sentence ("was chosen") obscures the role McKeon played in the choice of this topic.

12. Writing in 1959, A. J. Ayer recounts, "The term 'Logical Positivism' was coined some thirty years ago to characterize the standpoint of a group of philosophers, scientists and mathematicians who gave themselves the name of the Vienna Circle. Since that time its reference has been extended to cover other forms of analytical philosophy; so that disciples of Bertrand Russell, G. E. Moore or Ludwig Wittgenstein at Cambridge, or members of the contemporary Oxford movement of linguistic analysis may also find themselves described as logical positivists" (*Logical Positivism* 3). Moore and Russell appear similarly in P. M. S. Hacker's account in *Wittgenstein's Place in Twentieth-Century Analytic Philosophy*: "Both Moore's and Russell's rather different styles of analysis inaugurated twentieth-century analytic philosophy. Though both philosophers were adamant that they were analyzing phenomena, the foundations they laid were readily adaptable to logico-linguistic analysis, once the 'linguistic turn' in philosophy had been taken" (12).

he published *The Philosophy of Spinoza*, which includes a strong chapter, "Spinoza and Experimental Science," that recounts Spinoza's reservations about empiricism in his debates with Boyle, reservations that are likely to have influenced McKeon.

McKeon was thus clearly outside the tradition in which Moore enjoyed a prominent position. It is speculative, but McKeon may have become a candidate for an "opponent" slot in the Moore volume as a result of "word of mouth" connections arising from Rudolf Carnap, a member of the Vienna Circle, coming to the University of Chicago in 1936, where he would teach until 1952.

In the first paragraph of his Moore essay, McKeon observes that while Moore's influential refutation of idealism appeared to signal a welcome turn to realism, Moore ended up "tell[ing] us less about things than about the peculiarities of assertions," so that, the paragraph concludes, "apart from occasional graphic enumerations of samples of its contents, he has not had time to tell us more about the world than simply that it exists" (453–54). McKeon goes on to accentuate repeatedly that Moore's focus on assertions leads to results that amount to little: "his frequent acknowledgement that the questions raised are unimportant and their solutions uncertain" (455); "his philosophic labors seldom yield more than reasons which he grants are inconclusive for beliefs which all or most men share concerning the existence of things" (455–56); "propositions which are shown to be true are seldom important or, if they are important, the reasons for them are inconclusive" (457); "the results of his philosophic analyses . . . disclose dimly the existence, but few other characteristics, of an existent world" (460). In concluding, McKeon concedes that while there may be value in Moore's separation of things, thoughts, and statements, Moore fails to get beyond the separation: "his entire philosophy is devoted, once the separation of the three has been ensured, to a vain effort to find legitimate connections between things, thoughts, and statements" (478). Moore's response to McKeon is exceedingly brief, limited to one paragraph in which he also responds to another contributor to the volume. Without attending in detail to any of McKeon's arguments, Moore remarks simply, "But I can quite understand anyone thinking that the things I have not dealt with are far more important than those I have dealt with" (676).

McKeon's interest in "legitimate connections" among things, thoughts, and statements appears in the classroom lesson Plochman recounts. Instead of connecting them in one way, McKeon connects them in three ways, each a different order of priority among the three. In the linguistic approach, words are "primary," things are "intermediate," and thoughts are "posterior." This schema would appear to revise McKeon's earlier view contrasting being (thought, thing) to appearance (language, action).[13] In this revision, thing, thought, and language are on equal footing, equal footing despite McKeon's initially negative view of this linguistic approach. Why does McKeon do this?

The best explanation is his interest in uncovering the nature of philosophy through a study of the history of philosophy. His commitment to this project was strong enough to motivate him to consider a contemporary episode in this history that challenged his assumption about the centrality of metaphysics, traceable to Gilson's influence. Its centrality for McKeon at the time of the classroom lesson is evident in its inclusion of a list of "Principal Problems," all of which are questions about metaphysics. One of these is clearly prompted by the linguistic approach's challenge to his assumptions: "Is metaphysics meaningful?" (Plochmann 80).

McKeon's would meet this challenge in the course of the 1940s by finding that an important part of the nature of philosophy resides in a cycle of changes in the subject matter of philosophy, changes consisting of different orders of priority, including changes that prioritize language and thereby rhetoricize philosophy. The linguistic approach that McKeon initially saw as negative became positive when he recognized that its underpinnings in rhetoric should refocus it on problems of communication and community, not the negative anti-metaphysics of logical positivism. McKeon himself began to practice this rhetoricizing of philosophy himself and he would find in the history of philosophy, as we shall see, earlier periods when such rhetoricizing of philosophy occurred.

In 1993, the noted rhetorical scholar, Richard Lanham, identified McKeon and Kenneth Burke as "our two greatest rhetoricians," adding that lamentably both are "very hard to understand. Of the two, Burke, the Great Amplifier, is far the easier to follow. McKeon condenses" (165);

---

13. The evidence for this is not conclusive but it is suggestive. Writing in 1982, McKeon recounts his move to the University of Chicago in 1934. He joined a faculty group and was asked to write a paper on the "history and varieties of grammars." He reproduces this paper he wrote in the 1930s but never published. This paper includes a diagram that he explains thus: "The horizontal line connecting statement and action . . . is the realm of appearance, or *phainomena*. The vertical line connecting thought and thing . . . marks the realm of being, or *to on*" ("Criticism" 18, 38).

indeed, a number of McKeon essays should have been expanded into books. It happens that Burke and McKeon were longtime friends.[14] Lanham particularly credits McKeon and Burke with fostering a rhetorical "open-ended experimentality" (24). For reasons that will appear in the remainder of this chapter and especially the next, open-endedness is the essence of rhetoricized philosophy. Rhetoricized philosophy is open-ended in principle.

McKeon's rhetorical turn differs dramatically enough from his early work to prompt Charles Wegener, like Plochmann a McKeon student, to ask whether the relation between early and late McKeon is continuous or discontinuous. A McKeon student in the 1940s, Wegener remembers a McKeon preoccupied with "logical and methodological questions and their close relation to metaphysics," adding, "[O]ne of the persistent items in the student scuttlebutt which always surrounded him was that he had in mind to write—and perhaps had already written in part—a history of logic" (104). Wegener recalls a course McKeon frequently taught in the 1930s called "metaphysics and method" that later "disappeared from his repertory" but that his logical courses might well have used a reversed title "method and metaphysics" (104). Wegener writes this over a decade after McKeon's death, and even in retrospect he wonders, given the McKeon he knew in the classroom, why McKeon turned to rhetoric, as he asks, "Did [McKeon] follow where the argument led? If so, what is the argument?" (109). Wegener leaves his questions unanswered, but he implies that he thinks the answer is "no" to the question of whether McKeon "follow[ed] where the argument led," which erases the second question altogether. For Wegener explicitly leaves explaining McKeon's rhetorical turn to "historians and biographers" (109), which would seem to put the explanation outside the domain of philosophical

---

14. Jack Selzer's authoritative chronology indicates that early in 1917, a few months before turning 20, Burke entered Columbia University and began taking a ferry to classes with McKeon (186), who was three years younger. McKeon was born in 1900; Burke, in 1897. Their correspondence has not been published, but it is accessible in the Burke papers at Penn State University and the McKeon papers at the University of Chicago. They appeared together at the University of Chicago on 13 November 1970, in a debate moderated by Wayne Booth, entitled "Richard McKeon and Kenneth Burke: Rhetoric and Poetic." A transcript of this debate, with commentaries by James Beasley and myself, appears in *KB Journal*, 15.1, Spring 2021, kbjournal.org. See also Wess, "Burke's McKeon Side," and "A McKeonist Understanding of Kenneth Burke's Rhetorical Realism."

argument. With respect to biography, Wegener does include an endnote contrasting McKeon's pluralism to the pluralism "his friend Kenneth Burke was developing" in the 1940s from a rhetorical standpoint (106n2, 246). While this suggests a possible influence in McKeon's biography, Wegener does not make a point of it. With respect to history, he does make a point of noting that McKeon's turn coincides with a widespread growth in the prominence of rhetoric in the last half of the twentieth century (109), which agrees with McKeon's identification of the rhetorical basis of much twentieth-century philosophy. Booth locates the beginning of this historical development in the "mid-fifties" in "The Revival of Rhetoric," published in 1965, four years after the appearance of his seminal *The Rhetoric of Fiction* (10). But Wegener is not interested in assimilating McKeon to history or tracing influences on his work. He is looking for continuity in McKeon based on philosophical argument, and he fails to find it.

But continuity is there and key to it is the emergence in McKeon's ongoing inquiry into the nature of philosophy of historical semantics, which refines McKeon's long-standing argument that the subject matter of philosophy is not constant but changes. Initially, as evidenced in his Aquinas essay, McKeon seems to have thought such changes were arbitrary ("what he will"). Historical semantics finds an order in these changes, another layer in the continuous development of McKeon's pluralism, one tied to subject matter in philosophy. The emergence of historical semantics coincides with the recognition of the emergence of the subject matter that rhetoricizes philosophy, as seen with particular clarity in "The Methods of Rhetoric and Philosophy: Invention and Judgment," to which we shall turn later in this chapter to see McKeon laying out the basis of this rhetoricizing in language and action.

Like Wegener, Plochmann sees McKeon's work on rhetoric as a departure his early work, one that he sees growing out of McKeon's involvement with UNESCO's efforts after WWII to help foster world peace,

> In the late 1960s and 1970s he [McKeon] turned his attention more and more to the uses of rhetoric, which he now called an architectonic art. This may have been owing to his realization that one must use all available means of persuasion if one hopes to win hostile persons or states over to a search for common understanding, peace, and world unity. Not that McKeon grew disillusioned with philosophy; he merely approached it from another side.

This passage appears in a section entitled "Rhetoric in History," where Plochmann claims that this "approached it from another side" exhibits McKeon's "ability to extract from a relatively neglected corner of the history of philosophy a whole program for that discipline and, if carried a step or two farther, a philosophy itself" (151, 154). But Plochmann attributes this rhetorical turn to McKeon's work with UNESCO, whereas "The Methods of Rhetoric and Philosophy," as we shall see, makes it clear that this turn arises from McKeon coming to terms with the emergence of the prominence of language in philosophy in the twentieth century, which would prove to make it a century marked by what came to be called "the linguistic turn." Marking a turn in the history of philosophy, this emergence, McKeon's initial reservations about it notwithstanding, prompted his inquiry into what it might indicate about the nature of philosophy. This inquiry antedates UNESCO.

But UNESCO did add an important dimension to McKeon's inquiry because it posed practical problems that required rhetoric for solutions. In "A Philosophy for UNESCO," McKeon pinpoints the philosophy needed by identifying "a fashion in which philosophy is developed, not by [1] seeking agreement concerning principles on which action may be based, but by [2] seeking agreement concerning actions based on different principles" (578). McKeon illustrates alternative (1) by recounting how Dr. Julian Huxley, UNESCO'S first Director-General, offered a "common philosophy for UNESCO—namely, scientific or evolutionary humanism" (576), explicitly conceived as an alternative to "philosophies based on competing theologies . . . [and] politico-economic doctrines" as well as to "any particular philosophy, such as, existentialism" or any "theory in which State is more important than individual, or which depends on a class theory or a doctrine of racial superiority" (575–76). Nonetheless, "Dr. Huxley was doubtless surprised when his effort to avoid particularisms and rigidities was treated, both at the meeting of the Preparatory Commission and at the First Annual Session of the General Conference of UNESCO, as one more philosophy" (576). Efforts to formulate such a "common philosophy" were subsequently abandoned. Instead, efforts turned to "philosophy conceived as an effort to secure agreement concerning projects and courses of action on the basis of different grounds and principles" (582). Such agreement is rhetorical consensus rather than a consequence of one philosophical principle, even one that aims to be as capacious as Huxley's. It is noteworthy, if only as an aside, that an important work of McKeon scholarship that remains to be written would combine a detailed historical study of the formation of UNESCO with an in-depth analysis of McKeon's role in it. A contribution to such a study is Erik Doxtader's "The Rhetorical Question of Human Rights—A Preface," which draws extensively on a number of McKeon essays that address UNESCO concerns.[15]

---

15. In a 1950 lecture published in 1952, McKeon lists his role in numerous UNESCO activities in the late 1940s, which included membership on "several committees of experts" ("Knowledge" 299). He was one of only two who served on both committees that produced two early UNESCO volumes: (1) *Human Rights, Comments and Interpretations* and (2) *Democracy in a World of Tensions*, one committee for each book. The *Human Rights* committee conceived its work as preparatory for the U.N.'s Universal Declaration of Human Rights, which is among the diverse materials included in the volume (273–80). This committee began its work early in 1947 by sending a questionnaire, an idea originating with McKeon (Doxtader 359), "to the National Commissions of member states, as well as to individual scholars" (McKeon, "Knowledge" 320). Later that year, the committee reviewed replies and, identifying itself as a "committee of experts" (*Human Rights* 258n1), sent a report to "the Commission on Human Rights"; the next year, this committee met again to edit *Human Rights, Comments and Interpretations* ("Knowledge" 320–23). This volume includes the questionnaire (251–57), a selection of the replies (18–249), and the committee's report, completed July 1947, along with a list of committee members: Edward H. Carr, *Chairman*, Richard P. McKeon, *Rapporteur*, Pierre Auger, Georges Friedmann, Harold J. Laski, Chung-Shu Lo, and Luc Somerhausen (258–72). However, the committee's report was "ignored," evidently in part because UNESCO was never authorized to produce it (Morsink 397), and the publication of *Human Rights* was "delayed until after" the U.N. adopted the Universal Declaration of Human Rights (Slaughter 340n33).

McKeon's chapter in *Human Rights*, "The Philosophic Bases and Material Circumstances of the Rights of Man," was later reprinted in *Ethics*, from which I quote. McKeon begins by posing the "paradox" at the center of his pluralistic work for UNESCO: "the resolution of practical problems involves philosophic commitments but agreement concerning actions to be taken need not presuppose philosophic agreement" (180). *Democracy* was edited by McKeon, who contributes a chapter (all the chapters are entitled by the names of their authors) and writes a Foreword recounting the work of the committee of experts (v–xi). In 1948–1949, following the model of the committee for *Human Rights*, the committee for *Democracy* sent out a questionnaire, reviewed replies, and wrote reports to the UNESCO Secretariat, one listing points on which committee members agree, the other listing recommendations for publicizing the committee's work. *Democracy* includes the questionnaire (513-21), a selection of replies (1-512), the reports and a list of committee members, which include two

Watson's study of McKeon's pluralism, referenced in chapter one, extends to a detailed study of his historical semantics, which Watson describes "as three-stage cycles in the history of philosophy" in a user-friendly compilation of texts in which examples appear ("McKeon" 234–35). All but two of these texts appear after 1950. The earliest ex-

---

holdovers from the previous committee, Edward Hallett Carr, *Chairman*, and Richard McKeon, *Rapporteur*, as well as four others: Chaim Perelman, *Vice Chairman*, Sergio Barque de Hollanda, Pierre Ricoeur, and Alf Ross (522–31). There is also a selected bibliography of "Texts on Democracy and Its Role in Ideological Conflicts" (532–36) and a very useful Index organized by topics such as "Western and Eastern Democracy," listing under each topic the authors in the volume who comment on it (537-40).

In addition, beginning in 1950, McKeon served on a committee of a nongovernmental organization within UNESCO, "International Council for Philosophy and Humanistic Studies," which tasked this committee with "the project of a 'Dictionary of Fundamental Terms of Philosophy and Political Thought'" that was not completed but for which McKeon wrote an essay on the term "dialectic" ("Dialectical and Political Thought" 28–29). Plochmann claims that McKeon also wrote for this dictionary an essay defining "power," "Power and the Language of Power," published in 1958, (97, 109), but he does not indicate the basis for this claim. In the essay itself, there is nothing to indicate that it was written for this purpose; the essay includes a reference to the "United Nations and its Specialized Agencies," but only to make the point that they are "not organizations of power, but panels for discussions among representatives of powers" (109).

McKeon's work with UNESCO prompted an exchange with Warner A. Wick, initiated by Wick, that ranges beyond strictly UNESCO concerns to general problems in the nature and dissemination of philosophy. This exchange appeared in *Ethics: An International Journal of Social, Political, and Legal Philosophy*: (1) Wick, "Philosophy in Community and Communication," vol. 62, no.4, Jul. 1952, pp. 282–92; (2) McKeon, "Communication and Community as Philosophy," vol. 63, no.3, Apr. 1953, pp. 190–206; (3) Wick, "A Note on Professor McKeon's Remarks," vol. 63, no. 4, Jul. 1953, pp. 305–07; (4) McKeon, "Thinking, Doing, and Teaching," vol. 64, no.1, Oct. 1953, pp. 52–55.

Considering McKeon's work with UNESCO, Thomas M. Conley limits himself to commentary on this dictionary project, which is marginal to the main work McKeon did for UNESCO. Moreover, Conley mistakenly links this project with *The Idea of Freedom*, a two-volume work produced by Mortimer Adler's Institute for Philosophical Research (Conley 288). As Adler indicates, his Institute was founded in 1952 (92), two years after the launching of the dictionary project, and its work had no connection whatsoever to UNESCO (267–81).

ample, more like a rough than a final draft, appears in "The Philosophic Bases of Art and Criticism," among the McKeon essays that should have been books, which originally appeared in *Modern Philology* in two installments, November 1943 and February 1944, before being reprinted in *Critics and Criticism*. Here is the passage that Watson references in his compilation: "The principles of art have been sought in the nature of things and in the faculties of man as well as in the circumstances of artistic production or the effects of aesthetic contemplation" (*Critics* 476). The cycle appears here as (1) thing, (2) faculties, which constitute thought, and (3) circumstances and effects of art, which are much narrower in scope than language and action. In 1943, in short, the third part of the cycle was underdeveloped. This rough draft comes shortly after the Moore essay and the related classroom project that Plochmann recounts, another indication that the beginnings of the formation of historical semantics in McKeon's pluralism occurs in the years marking the turn from the late 1930s to the early 1940s. But as Watson's compilation suggests, historical semantics does not come fully into its own until the 1950s. "The Methods of Rhetoric and Philosophy" does not appear until 1966, offering by happenstance a valuable perspective on the seminal *The Linguistic Turn: Recent Essays in Philosophical Method*, which McKeon's student Richard Rorty published one year later.

As indicated in chapter one, McKeon typically references historical semantics to contextualize a particular subject under analysis, although he sometimes presents the full cycle of historical semantics in general terms. A valuable supplement to the presentation of the cycle in general terms cited in chapter one appears in *Freedom and History: The Semantics of Philosophical Controversies and Ideological Conflicts*, originally published in 1952, then reprinted in *Freedom and History and Other Essays*. Here, McKeon sketches cycles from Greek antiquity to the present (164–66), each of which takes centuries. In this sketch, the most recent turn to thing occurs in the seventeenth century, followed by the turn to thought in the eighteenth and nineteenth centuries, and the turn to language and action in the twentieth century. In classes, he would sometimes summarize this most recent cycle to identify the distinctiveness of the twentieth century.

In this sketch, McKeon analogizes "fashions of philosophy" in the twentieth century and those in two great ages of rhetoric, (1) "the last century of the Roman Republic and the first centuries of the Roman Empire," and (2) "the end of the Middle Ages and the beginning of the

Renaissance" (165–66).[16] In a similar sketch of cycles in "A Philosopher Meditates on Discovery" (52–54) the analogies are to "the Roman, the Carolingian, and the Renaissance periods" (54). But the analogies to the Roman and Renaissance periods are the most important, as evidenced by their prominence in the McKeon essay known most widely among scholars of rhetoric, "The Uses of Rhetoric in a Technological Age: Architectonic Productive Arts," which originated as the paper he gave at the 1970 Wingspread conference.[17] This conference proved to be epochal in the field of rhetoric, engendering not only a conference volume, which includes McKeon's paper (4463), *The Prospect of Rhetoric*, edited by Lloyd F. Bitzer and Edwin Black, Prentice-Hall, 1971, but also two later books reviewing the conference retrospectively: *Making and Unmaking the Prospects for Rhetoric*, edited by Theresa Enos and Richard McNabb, Lawrence Erlbaum Associates, 1997; *Reengaging the Prospects of Rhetoric: Current Conversations and Contemporary Challenges*, edited by Mark J. Porrovecchio, Routledge, 2010.

A much more detailed recounting of cycles from Greek antiquity to the present appears in "Imitation and Poetry," mentioned earlier as among the McKeon essays that should have been a book. The sketches of cycles in *Freedom and History* and "A Philosophy Meditates on Discovery" are introductory rather than the main object of analysis as in "Imitation and Poetry." In *Freedom and History*, the concern is less with historical semantics as an analysis of cycles of changing subject matters in philosophy than with the role the subject matter historical semantics identifies in any period plays in that period:

> The oppositions of ideas in doctrine and in action depend on a minimum communication and a minimum recognition of common conditions and common problems. The problem of *historical* semantics is not a problem of ambiguity (although *philosophic* semantics tends to turn on questions of ambiguity in those philosophic methods which seek univocal definitions),

---

16. This analogy to Rome also appears in one of his autobiographical essays, originally published in 1952, in McKeon's remark that "under the influence of distaste for his [Cicero's] utilitarian verbalism, the similarity of our own philosophic tendencies to his was overlooked" ("Philosopher" 48).

17. A detailed analysis of this paper appears in my chapter in the forthcoming *Cambridge History of Rhetoric, Volume 5: Modern Rhetoric (from 1900)*, eds. Daniel M. Gross, Steven J. Mailloux, and LuMing Mao, Cambridge UP.

but rather a problem of the persistence, recurrence, and transformation of problems under different verbal forms. Historical semantics is therefore a first step, essential to any effort to place thought and philosophy in the circumstances that condition its forms and development. (181)

An illustration of this passage appears in the next chapter, "The Linguistic Turn," where historical semantics is a "first step," identifying the subject matter of language common to competing philosophies, thereby making them relevant to one another in the "recognition of common conditions and common problems." Because the linguistic turn occurs slowly over many decades, this chapter will be concerned particularly with "the persistence, recurrence, and transformation of problems" as philosophies compete with one another to complete the turn from thought to a new ultimate priority in language. Chapters four and five will differ insofar as each will focus and a single philosopher and his effort to inaugurate a metaphysical turn. McKeon's inquiry into the history of philosophy to discover the nature of philosophy, then, identifies three fundamental subject matters: thing, thought, language and action. McKeon insists, "There is no preestablished priority of being, cause, or rule among things, thoughts, actions, and statements; each in turn may be made fundamental" ("Discourse" 163). Watson's term for the relation among these three is "*reciprocal priority*" (*Architectonics* 10): in each, one is prior to the other two. Thing, thought, language and action appear in all philosophies, but the fashion in which each appears in any philosophy depends on which of the three is prior. Kant's turn, for example, is from the priority of thing to the priority of thought, whereby thing becomes a thing-in-itself inaccessible to thought.

Watson assumes that the turns from subject matter to subject matter proves that the choice of subject matters "cannot be decided by the facts," so that the choice of any subject matter is "arbitrary," like the choice of "units of length" for measuring, the "base for a number system" and so on (10). Using one of his examples, one could first equate reality to that which is to be measured, then equate philosophy to the choice of the unit of measurement. Should it be a meter? A yard? Both work as units of measurement, so that the basis of choice is purely pragmatic. Watson thus reduces to pragmatism alone the philosophical turns combination of realism and pragmatism, discussed in chapter one.

Attention to ultimate priorities offers insight into the cycle's realistic dimension. In philosophic turns from one ultimate priority to another, philosophic debate centers on the "facts" Watson discounts, specifically the facts of the subject matter where the incoming ultimate priority at issue is located. In each subject matter there is an existent that is an ultimate priority. This priority is established by metaphysical argument akin to the argument Williams presents. Again, bear in mind two senses of metaphysics, the strict sense as in the metaphysical turn and the broad sense as in any ultimate priority, even Williams's.

The nature of an ultimate priority's existence is crucial. The consequences that follow from an ultimate priority are based on the characteristics of its existence. From Kant's ultimate priority in thought, for example, follow his three critiques, each ordering mental faculties in different ways, and the three together architectonically ordering mental life as a whole. That such consequences follow from existents that qualify as ultimate priorities explains the different senses in which these existents qualify as real, even if some of these senses depart somewhat from the usual meanings of reality. There is a sense in which Kant's thought is real, as we saw in chapter one and will return to at the end of chapter four. McKeon aims to broaden what can be considered real in a lecture, "Being, Existence, and That Which Is," delivered as the Presidential Address at a meeting of the Metaphysical Society of America, surely an occasion when what qualifies as real is high on the agenda. McKeon no doubt startled some in his audience when he claimed that our notions of what things can be should "include things we say and things we seek" (254).

The cycle of historical semantics thus exhibits modes of reality. The modes are limited to "the subject matters in which philosophers have found their basic distinctions," as McKeon puts it in chapter one's epigraph. In other words, whether a subject matter can qualify as a subject matter for philosophy depends on whether it encompasses an existent that is an ultimate priority, or, more broadly, a cluster of possible ultimate priorities that philosophers sort out in their debates in a philosophical turn from one to another.

McKeon uses the term "metaphysics" in strict and broad senses. Both appear simultaneously when he observes, "Metaphysics is still out [strict], but discourse and culture have assumed the structuralizing functions of metaphysics" [broad] ("Discourse" 172). In the broad sense, he sketches where to look for ultimate priorities, which he calls "principles," in each of the subject matters in the cycle of historical semantics: (1) a "metaphysics of ontology" looks for "principles of being in things," "adapt[ing] the principles of language to the properties and functions of things"; (2) a "metaphysics prepared for or assumed by a critical or experimental examination of forms of thought or associations of ideas makes practical reason or action architectonic, as Kant and Mill do; seeks principles of knowledge in thought or perception; and adapts the principles of language to the categories of thought or the impulsions of emotion; (3) a "metaphysics prepared for by an experimental or existential examination of communication and culture, seeks to discover, to use, and to test principles of production and discourse in communication . . . and adapts the principles of language and the principles of action to each other" ("Future" 299). Williams's "empiricist metaphysic" illustrates (2) in finding an ultimate priority in "perception."

In this passage, metaphysics is as central as it was in the classroom lecture Plochmann recounts, but in a new way. As a result of the discovery of historical semantics, metaphysics now appears as modes of metaphysics. These modes reveal that philosophical turns teach that philosophizing is always based on a subject matter that is real, even if it proclaims to be antirealism. The subject matter may be only a component of reality, such as language, but in some cases a component of reality is enough to be the location in reality of a philosophy's "basic distinctions," its ultimate priority. Furthermore, as chapter three will illustrate more than any other, in a turn to a subject matter, ultimate priority becomes a fundamental issue among the philosophers of the turn as they debate what it is exactly in this subject matter that makes it ultimately prior to the subject matters in other turns.

McKeon's mature view of the twentieth-century's philosophical turn can conclude this chapter and introduce a major theme in chapter three. This view appears in the aforementioned "The Methods of Rhetoric and Philosophy: Invention and Judgment." After its original appearance in 1966, it was reprinted twice, first in *Rhetoric: Essays in Invention and Discovery*, a collection of McKeon essays edited by Mark Backman, Ox Bow Press, 1987; then in 2005, in the text I reference, in *Selected Writings of Richard McKeon*, volume 2. In this essay, McKeon articulates the fashion in which in the twentieth century "rhetoric is transmuted into philosophy" (100).

McKeon begins by treating the twentieth-century's turn to language and action as a philosophical turn, like other turns in the history of philosophy: "Periodical revolutions occur in the history of philosophy which change the perspectives of philosophical inquiry and transform the meanings of philosophic words and the natures of things meant. Kant called the insurrection in which he participated a Copernican revolution" (97). McKeon ends his first paragraph with sentences that merit full attention because they deploy the historical semantics of thing, thought, and language and action to define the distinctiveness of the twentieth-century's philosophical turn. This turn

> exhibited the absurdity of metaphysical statements which purport to be about all things, and idealistic statements which confuse thinking with being. Since it is absurd to seek to base meanings on alleged characteristics of being or on supposed forms of thought, inquiry into what men say and what they do may be used to provide clarification and test of what they say they think and of what they think is the case. Things and thoughts are in the significances and applications of language and in the consequences and circumstances of action. (97)

The chief shortcoming in this twentieth-century turn, McKeon adds in the next paragraph, is that it has failed to develop an "art of rhetoric . . . adequate to the possibilities of communication or to the contents or ends to which communication might be adapted" (97).

Key to this philosophical turn that "transmute[s]" rhetoric into philosophy is the view of language that makes it the subject matter of philosophy, prior to the subject matters of thing and thought. In this chapter's epigraph, McKeon contrasts two views, one in which language is posterior, the other in which it is prior:

> Posterior: "Words may be thought to designate things, signify thoughts, and induce actions, if things, thoughts, and actions are thought to exist apart from and prior to words."

> Prior: "Or words may be thought to be the sources and causes of what things, thoughts, and actions are thought to be, and therefore, are." ("Pluralism" 54)

McKeon adds commentary to which we will return in the final chapter in considering whether the turns themselves offer a basis for preferring one over the others. In the cycle, they are equal, each having its day in the sun, but the final chapter will consider whether there is nonetheless a philosophical basis for preference. McKeon uses his distinction between "posterior" and "prior" to distinguish two rhetorics. Drawing on examples from antiquity, he aligns "posterior" with Aristotle and "prior" with the Sophists.

The distinctiveness of the subject matter in which language is prior is that words are "sources and causes" of everything so that language's inventiveness is dominant everywhere. By virtue of this inventiveness, no formulation can preemptively foreclose future formulations ("Methods" 100). "Rhetoric is an art of invention and disposition," McKeon's sums up in "Philosophy of Communications and the Arts," first published in 1970 and reprinted in *Selected Writings*, volume 2, from which I quote. McKeon goes on, "[I]t is an art of communication between a speaker and his audience, and it is therefore an art of construction of the subject matter of communication, that is, of anything whatever that can be an object of attention. What is, is established by the convictions and agreements of men" (317). This is the sophistic truth about "what is" in the context of the twentieth-century's subject matter of philosophy, but it would be false in the context of other subject matters such as Aristotle's—"the true is sometimes false and sometimes true," to recall the earlier discussion of one of McKeon's aphorisms in his recounting of the "discovery" that proved seminal for him. Existence in rhetorical reality is always open to revision, so that any representation of this rhetorical reality must be open to the new to represent it accurately.

Chapter three will show how the linguistic turn "transmute[s]" rhetoric into philosophy even though it tends not to recognize this because of its preoccupation with antiphilosophical themes, beginning with its therapeutic cure for metaphysics, its labeling metaphysical language "nonsense," and so on. This rhetoricizing of philosophy was nonetheless evident to some observers. In *Rhetoric and Philosophy in Conflict: An Historical Survey*, Samuel Ijsseling finds unrecognized links to rhetoric in strategies used to bring traditional philosophy into question in an array of thinkers including Heidegger, Derrida, and Foucault (5). From Ijsseling's standpoint, the twentieth-century's turn to rhetoric was evident in important work that did not always or fully recognize its own rhetoricality. Eventually, of course, rhetoric enjoyed a historical revival, as Booth and Wegener testify. It is becoming more common to say that "rhetoric is everywhere," William Selinger remarks in 2018 in observing that McKeon, in the early 1960s, anticipated the flourishing rhetoric enjoys today (150). Rhetoric's most recent time in the doldrums no doubt made it company few wanted to keep before its fortunes began rising. Its nadir may be Kant's condemnation of rhetoric in his *Critique of Judgment* (171, Part 1, Book 2, section #53), cited by John Bender and David E. Wellbery as making at the time "the obsolescence of rhetoric explicit" in their 1990 historical account of rhetoric's decline and the formation in the twentieth century of the framework for its revival (18).

Chapters two and three together, then, uncover the rhetorical underpinnings of the linguistic turn not always recognized as such. Notwithstanding Badiou's view that "sophistry," his term for rhetoric, is philosophy's "adversary," albeit one "philosophy must forever endure" ("*Manifesto*" 133), in the twentieth century, "rhetoric is transmuted into philosophy."

3 The Linguistic Turn: A Narrative

> [T]he characteristic of language is that meanings are arbitrary; therefore, any word can mean anything and, in fact, does.
>
> —McKeon, *On Knowing: The Natural Sciences*, 190

Richard Rorty's *The Linguistic Turn: Recent Essays in Philosophical Method* no doubt helped to solidify the "linguistic turn" as a shorthand name for a philosophical epoch. Appearing in 1967, when Rorty was thirty-six, the book attracted enough attention to prompt two subsequent editions, with "Recent" omitted from the subtitle, the last in 1992. 1967 was also Derrida's *"annus mirabilis"* (Lawlor 2), seeing the publication, at age thirty-seven, of his *Speech and Phenomena*, *Of Grammatology*, and *Writing and Difference*; English translations of these would appear, respectively, in 1973, 1976, and 1978. While some, as noted in chapter one, call Derrida one of the linguistic turn's "architects," *The Linguistic Turn* testifies that this turn began long before he exploded onto the scene. Yet, as also noted in chapter one, there is nonetheless a sense in which seeing Derrida as an architect of the linguistic turn contains a grain of truth insofar as he helps it complete its turn to its ultimate priority. This chapter's narrative will culminate in places in Derrida where his antiphilosophy exhibits the rhetoricizing of philosophy, even including the term "rhetoric" in a key cluster of terms, without quite recognizing itself as a rhetoricizing of philosophy. The twentieth century saw both a flourishing of antiphilosophy and a revival of rhetoric. The two, as the century recedes in the rearview mirror of history, may increasingly be recognized as two sides of the same coin. That would confirm McKeon's judgment, discussed earlier, that the twentieth century is analogous to earlier periods when rhetoric was dominant.

Rorty's 1962 essay "Realism, Categories, and the 'Linguistic Turn'" begins with a bird's-eye view of philosophy over the course of the preceding three centuries that "led philosophers away from things to ideas, and away from ideas to words" (307; see also *Philosophy Mirror* 316–17). This recounting of philosophical turns echoes the turns recorded in McKeon's historical semantics. While this opening paragraph includes no reference to McKeon, there is, in a footnote later in the essay, acknowledgement of "studies by Richard McKeon of the history of philosophical controversy" (312–13n11). More importantly, in the first paragraph of his Preface in *Philosophy and the Mirror of Nature*, Rorty identifies McKeon explicitly as one from whom he "learned to view the history of philosophy as a series, not of alternative solutions to the same problems, but of quite different sets of problems" (xiii).

Each of the turns Rorty recounts in echoing McKeon changes the subject matter of philosophy. Differing subject matters distinguish different historical periods, posing "different sets of problems" in each period. The problem of turning to the subject matter of the linguistic turn centers in McKeon's contrast between two views of language, discussed near the end of the last chapter, one in which language is posterior to subject matter independent of language and one in which it is prior. When language is prior, nothing is altogether independent of language. As McKeon puts it, "[W]ords may be thought to be the sources and causes of what things, thoughts, and actions are thought to be, and, therefore, are" ("Pluralism" 54).

Rorty sums up the distinctive problems posed by the linguistic turn in the form of two precepts. First, "One cannot transcend language; that is, one cannot find a point of view outside of all linguistic frameworks from which the world will appear 'as it is.' One can't think without thinking in a language." Second, "[W]e can't penetrate through language to nonlinguistic data which will guide our choice of languages" ("Realism" 310, 311). These two are interdependent: when language is prior, there is no position outside the linguistic from which to access the non-linguistic independently of the linguistic and to thereby see how the nonlinguistic supervises the linguistic. But Rorty saying this in his precepts is one thing, explaining it philosophically is another. The ultimate priority, when explained, can in turn explain Rorty's precepts—an explained explainer if you will. The better the explainer, the better it explains. Finding that best explainer is the core issue in the debates that constitute the narrative of the linguistic turn from the reigning ultimate priority at its beginning to a new one at its end.

To be clear, in each turn, language in the form of philosophical texts is posterior to the ultimate priority that philosophizing seeks to identify. The priority is an existent, and the texts are posterior to the priority they identify and from which they reason philosophically. What is distinctive about the philosophical texts of the linguistic turn is that they are themselves language yet posterior to the ultimate priority in language that they seek to identify. This distinguishing characteristic poses problems of its own that will surface in the course of the present chapter.

Philosophizing in the linguistic turn often enforces Rorty's precepts by deploying some variant of Derrida's famous polemic in *Of Grammatology* against the "idea of the book . . . the signified preexists it, supervises its inscriptions and its signs, and is independent of it in its ideality" (18). The term "signified" is ambiguous insofar as it may be a meaning or a referent, as in Frege's famous distinction between meanings ("evening star," "morning star") and referent (Venus). That in the case of the "book" the signified "preexists" the "inscriptions" and "signs" that it "supervises" indicates that it is a referent. Against "preexists," *Grammatology* claims, "*There is nothing outside of the text*" (158). Nothing is outside because nothing is independent of the "inscriptions" and "signs" that mediate access to it. Erasing "preexists" enforces Rorty's precepts.

Philosophical debates in the linguistic turn are words about words because they aim to explain exactly what it is in language that makes it prior, not subject to the "supervision" of things or thoughts prior to language. Action is ambiguous insofar as it may be seen as apart from language or as a dimension of language itself, as in Kenneth Burke's theory of symbolic action (*Philosophy of Literary Form*) or J. L. Austin's speech-act theory (*How to Do Things with Words*). As we have seen, McKeon observes in "Principles and Consequences" that one may "treat sequential statements as forms of action or . . . purposive courses of action as instances of verbal rules" (395). That the subject matter of philosophy in the linguistic turn is itself language poses a paradox: linguistic turn philosophical texts subject themselves to the "supervision" of language in order to explain why language is not subject to the "supervision" of things, thoughts, and acts conceived as separate from language. Forms of the word "supervise" enclosed in quotation marks are a motif going forward that is positive or negative from the standpoint of the linguistic turn depending on whether language is doing the "supervising" or being "supervised" by non-language.

Problems the linguistic turn repeatedly encounters appear indirectly in a satire of the turn that may help to distinguish stages in the narrative of the linguistic turn as they unfold in the present chapter. In this satire, Paul R. Gross and Norman Levitt imagine people in a windowless room. To facilitate later references back to their satire, I will modify it to the extent of saying it is Gross and Levitt who are in this room. Their satire targets Latour in particular but can easily be generalized beyond Latour to the linguistic turn in general. The specific target is Latour's claim that "settlement" of a dispute among scientists appears in agreement about a representation of nature, an agreement caused not by nature but by resolution of intersubjective interaction and disagreement among the scientists in the social construction of scientific facts in scientific texts.

In this satiric story, a dispute arises over whether it is raining. Gross and Levitt go outside and find various kinds of evidence of rain. They return to their room and agree that it is raining. The satiric point: "Insofar as we are disciples of Latour, we can never explain our agreement on this point by the simple fact that it is raining. Rain, remember, is the outcome of our 'settlement,' not its cause! Baldly put, this seems ridiculous" (58). Rain does not "supervise" the "settlement." Rather, the "settlement" produces the rain.

As satiric arguments go, Gross and Levitt's satire is weak insofar as it grossly oversimplifies the process by which scientists arrive at a "settlement." A good satire should capture more of the substance of the object it targets than this one does. Even everyday language makes distinctions such as "drizzle" and "downpour," suggesting that the reality of rain does not automatically trigger the word "rain," the way the reality of the sun tans the skin of sunbathers, but can instead prompt debates about word choice analogous to scientific debates prior to a "settlement." Among scientists, moreover, "settlement" would no doubt involve instrumental measurements of quantity and intensity of precipitation. Gross and Levitt's "rain" is unimaginative.

Nonetheless, and perhaps because of its unimaginativeness, the satire is simple enough to facilitate extrapolating from it a Rortyian "set of problems." The one that looms largest in the satire centers on the conception of priority. The satire presupposes a causal priority in which the "settlement" is in some sense an efficient cause of the "outcome," the "rain." What could be more absurd than to suggest that the words in the "settlement" cause the rain? Nonetheless, anyone who lived through the heyday of the linguistic turn no doubt encountered variants of this satiric line of critique in hallway conversations that reduce the linguistic turn to linguistic idealism.

To answer this critique, the linguistic turn defines priority not in the terms of the efficient causality presupposed in Gross and Levitt's satire, but in terms of some kind of mediation in which language is prior to that which is mediated through language. One might want to distinguish modes of mediation, such as differences in mediation in science and culture, but these modes would all be inscribed within an architectonic of the linguistic mediation governing access to anything nonlinguistic.

While the mediating word is prior to that which is accessed through the mediation, there is one exception, one that occurs in the philosophical texts explaining exactly what makes language prior. For the explanation of mediation is not itself mediated through these texts. One does not access mediation A through mediation B, and B through C, and so on in an infinite regress that would unfold if one absolutized mediation by insisting that even mediation is mediated, for if one did that, mediation itself would always be out of reach, a mystery beyond explanation. The words doing the mediating are the subject matter of philosophy, and this subject matter "supervises" the words, Derrida's "inscriptions" and "signs," that philosophically explain the mediating process.

This chapter, following this introductory section, will be straightforwardly divided into three titled sections: "The Beginning," "The Middle," and "The End." Untitled subsections appear in each section. Narrative in form, the chapter will recount first the turn from thought to language, then, the turn to the issue of ultimate priority centering in language, an issue debated for decades.

THE BEGINNING

Rorty's intellectual biographer Neil Gross records that Rorty envisioned that *The Linguistic Turn* "would be taught, not as a substitute for, but in conjunction with other similar books that had recently appeared such as Antony Flew's *Essays on Logic and Language* (1951) and *Essays in Conceptual Analysis* (1956), A. J. Ayer's *Logical Positivism* (1959) and Gilbert Ryle's *The Revolution in Philosophy* (1956)" (178). Gross reports that these earlier books prompted the first publisher Rorty approached to reject his proposal because "the market for analytic anthologies was saturated" (178), a judgment that *The Linguistic Turn*'s impact proved wrong.

The Linguistic Turn was part of Rorty's effort to credentialize himself as an analytic philosopher in his ultimately successful bid for tenure at Princeton, where such a credential was necessary in the 1960s (Gross 165–89, 339). In the long run, however, Princeton's commitment to the analytic tradition contributed to Rorty's departure (Gross 227–33, 339–40), following his turn from this tradition (Gross 192–227, 340), in a direction that brought him closer to Derrida.[18] Closer but still far: Rorty is to Derrida as a principle's consequence (Rorty) is to the principle (Derrida).

The beginning of the linguistic turn appears in *The Linguistic Turn* in Part I: "Classic Statements of the Thesis that Philosophical Questions are Questions of Language." The first "classic" is Moritz Schlick's "The Future of Philosophy," based on a paper given at a conference in 1930 (Hacker 42, 285n30), later published in 1932. Around Schlick, philosophers began gathering in 1924 for regular meetings. They called themselves "the Vienna Circle" and became one of the principal forces launching a new philosophical movement that "became known as 'logical positivism'" (Hacker 39).

Much of the time at the Vienna Circle's meetings was devoted to a close reading of Wittgenstein's *Tractatus Logico-Philosophicus*, published in 1921, which became the Circle's fundamental text (Schlick, "Turning" 54). Try as it might, however, the Circle never found a clear interpretation of some passages according to Carnap. Reaching out to Wittgenstein accomplished little, Carnap adds, because Wittgenstein shied away from facing direct questions in dialogue, agreeing to meet with only a select few and even there struggling to answer whenever he finally did answer: "When finally, sometimes after a prolonged arduous effort, his answer came forth, his statement stood before us like a newly created piece of art or a divine revelation. . . . [T]he impression he made on us was as if insight came to him as through a divine inspiration, so that we could not help feeling that any sober rational comment or analysis of it would be a profanation" ("Autobiography" 26). "Oracular" may be the best word to characterize this manner of speaking, as well Wittgenstein's style of philosophizing in short passages connected to one another loosely more often than tightly. The numbering scheme in the *Tractatus* sometimes adds a tightness that would not be there otherwise. It is also easy to imagine how oracular expressions, coming forth regularly, would sometimes be impenetrably opaque, even to the Vienna

---

18. While Gross's fine book reads like a biography, even including separate chapters on Rorty's parents and his relationship with each, Gross is clear that his book is a contribution to "the new sociology of ideas," a "nascent research area." Substantial parts of the book address debates in this area, to which Gross contributes with his thesis of the importance of "'intellectual self-concepts' that thinkers hold: the narratives of self to which they subscribe that characterize them as thinkers of such and such a type, as 'activist' or 'Christian' intellectuals or, in the case of Richard Rorty, as 'leftist American patriot'" (xi, xii).

Circle, and sometimes aphoristically memorable enough to spread out to the wider culture as happened with some of Wittgenstein's utterances. Perhaps one is the price to be paid for the other.

Today, logical positivism is generally seen as that which the linguistic turn turned against, not as that where it began. The present subsection, the longest in the "The Beginning" section, offers an explanation of both why the linguistic turn began with logical positivism and why in later decades logical positivism would come to be seen as the linguistic turn's antagonist rather than as its originator. Following this subsection, two short subsections will consider briefly Frege and a sampling of retrospective views of the *Tractatus* from the standpoint of later stages in the linguistic turn. Concluding "The Beginning," the second longest subsection will take up Wittgenstein's antiphilosophy to uncover its ties to rhetoric, which in turn will lead to the transition to "The Middle" stage in this chapter's narrative of the history of the linguistic turn.

The Vienna Circle came to prefer "Logical Empiricism" to "Logical Positivism," Morton White recounts, when it "realized how bad the odor of the word 'positivism' was for those who associated it with the narrowness of Auguste Comte" (*Age* 204). But "logical positivism" stuck. White himself tends to use "positivism" rather than "empiricism" in *Toward Reunion in Philosophy*, his critique of analytic philosophy. Against this tendency, Richard Creath uses "Logical Empiricism" to entitle his account of this philosophical movement in the Stanford Encyclopedia of Philosophy. Importantly, the term "logical" in either usage signaled the replacement of psychological analysis by logical analysis" (Hacker 283n8). This replacement's significance is the part of logical positivism that tends to get overshadowed by later stages in the narrative of the linguistic turn that depict logical positivism as an antagonist rather than as the turn's originator.

The problem the linguistic turn addressed, Rorty recounts, is that "in the course of the nineteenth century, evolutionary biology and empirical psychology had begun to naturalize the notions of 'mind,' 'consciousness,' and 'experience.'" In the terminology of McKeon's historical semantics, in other words, the naturalizing of these notions clustered around "thought" demoted the existent thought to a position of posteriority to such naturalizing, raising questions about the prioritizing of thought that Kant put in place in his turn from thing to thought. Turning from thought to language for philosophical prioritizing appeared plausible because, Rorty continues, "Language seemed able to avoid relativization to history, for description was thought to be a single indissoluble activity, whether done by Neanderthals, Greeks, or Germans. If one could give *a priori* conditions of the activity of description, then one would be in a position to offer apodictic truths" ("Wittgenstein, Heidegger" 53). Analytic philosophy would see itself avoiding such relativization, and in Michael Dummett's account, "What distinguishes analytical philosophy, in its diverse manifestations, from other schools is the belief, first, that a philosophical account of thought can be attained through a philosophical account of language, and, secondly, that a comprehensive account can only be so attained" (4).

Rorty elaborates further that in its beginnings the linguistic turn "attempt[ed] to retain Kant's picture of philosophy as providing a permanent ahistorical framework for inquiry in the form of a theory of knowledge. The 'linguistic turn' . . . started as the attempt to produce a nonpsychologistic empiricism by rephrasing philosophical questions as questions of 'logic'" (*Philosophy Mirror* 257). This new turn sought, Rorty adds, "to ask Kantian questions without having to trespass on the psychologists' turf by talking, with Kant, about 'experience' or 'consciousness. That was, indeed, the initial motive for the 'turn'" (*Consequences* xxi).

In other words, the turn began with a baby step by continuing what it was turning from on one level but doing so by turning to language on another level, that is, to a new subject matter for philosophy, displacing the subject matter of thought in favor of the subject matter of language. (Analogous baby steps, we shall see in chapters four and five, occur in Meillassoux and Harman.) But turning to this new subject matter of language proved to be far easier than discovering the existent in this subject matter that is its ultimate priority. Discovering that would take decades.

In his introduction to *The Linguistic Turn*, Rorty attributes the coinage of the term "the linguistic turn" to Gustav Bergmann (9n10). Bergmann is sometimes cited as a member of the Vienna Circle (Hacker 39), but he must have been a junior member, perhaps something like a postdoctoral fellow. Born in 1906, which made him twenty-four years younger than Schlick, he earned a PhD in mathematics at the University of Vienna in 1928. Looking back at this time decades later, he remarks, "The logical positivists of the Vienna Circle were my first teachers" (*Metaphysics* x). Subsequently, pursuing an academic career in the 1930s as a Jew, he encountered obstacles to employment, so he took a law degree from the University of Vienna in 1935 and began a new career as a lawyer, but not for long. In 1938, he fled to the United States, where he settled into his career as a philosopher. In short, a precocious start followed by a restart over a decade later because of the misfortune of being a Jew in Vienna in the 1930s.

In his selection of "Classic Statements," Rorty includes with Schlick's essay an abridged 1953 Bergmann essay (63–71) that identifies the beginning of the linguistic turn not with Frege, as Michael Dummett later argues as we shall see, but with Wittgenstein's *Tractatus*. In Bergmann's words,

> The very name, logical positivist, is by now unwelcome to some, though it is still and quite reasonably applied to all, particularly from the outside. Reasonably, because they unmistakably share a philosophical style. They all accept the linguistic turn Wittgenstein initiated in the *Tractatus*. (63)[19]

P. M. S. Hacker similarly identifies the *Tractatus* as the beginning of the linguistic turn (3).

Schlick's "The Future of Philosophy" looks to the history of philosophy to contrast the glories of philosophy that a historian might celebrate to the more sober questions a philosopher asks about what truths philosophies of the past have actually discovered. The history of philosophy, Schlick laments, is marked more by controversies without resolution than by progressive accumulation of knowledge. He thinks philosophy will do better in the future he envisions.

---

19. This essay, "Logical Positivism, Language, and the Reconstruction of Metaphysics," is reprinted in unabridged form in Bergmann's *The Metaphysics of Logical Positivism* (30–77). His coupling of logical positivism and metaphysics in his book's title sounds oxymoronic insofar as hostility to metaphysics is one of logical positivism's trademarks. To understand Bergmann, "reconstruction" is the word to underline in his essay's title. The linguistic turn Bergmann favored aimed to construct an "ideal" language and reconstruct metaphysics in terms of this language: "What the reconstructionists hope to reconstruct in the new style is the old metaphysics" (32; Rorty, *Linguistic Turn* 64). Bergmann describes this direction in his philosophizing as aiming to "free [himself] from Carnapian positivism," but having said that he quickly goes on, "I wish to add . . . that this by now radical dissent has not at all affected either my gratitude or my admiration for Carnap" (*Metaphysics* vi). In "Strawson's Ontology," reprinted in *Logic and Reality* (171–92), Bergmann pits his ideal language philosophy against P. F. Strawson's ordinary language philosophy. These opposed views of language appear as Parts II and III in Rorty's *The Linguistic Turn*.

Schlick's sober philosopher presupposes a linear view of history: the subject matter of philosophy has not changed, but the mistakes about it in the past are now being replaced by correct views of it in the present. In our era, the poster child for such linearity took form in the repeated citations of Derrida's correction of the reign of "*logocentrism*," which is typically depicted as reigning from the "pre-Socratics to Heidegger" (*Of Grammatology* 3).

McKeon offers an alternative view, one in which philosophical turns are signs of cyclical changes in the subject matter of philosophy. A metaphysical turn today presupposes a cyclical return to metaphysics, a return with a difference to be sure, but a difference consistent with bearing a "family resemblance" to metaphysical periods of the past. Meillassoux, as we shall see in the next chapter, has a view of history that is similar to McKeon's insofar as it too is cyclical, although in Meillassoux's view it consists of only two alternating orientations. To see what philosophical turns reveal about philosophy, one must give up, at least tentatively, viewing them as simply corrections of the past and consider them instead as turns that change the subject matter of philosophy, turns, moreover, that can repeat.

Schlick is confident about the future because he sees a change in the relations between philosophy and science. In the past, they were more or less seen confusedly as one, but the great progress of science in recent times shows that it is science not philosophy that accumulates knowledge. Whereas science's job is the "discovery of *truth*," philosophy "has for its object the discovery of *meaning*," that is, "the discovery of sense." In other words, philosophy can correct its past mistakes about its subject matter by seeing its subject matter clearly, seeing that language is what philosophy is about. Drawing a clear line between philosophy and science instead of confusingly merging the two, Schlick envisions the "whole future of philosophy" consisting of breaking with the past by recognizing that past philosophical problems are either "mistakes and misunderstandings of our language" or "ordinary scientific questions in disguise" ("Future" 48, 51).

Creath's "Logical Empiricism" allows one to see Schlick's refocusing of philosophy in a broader context. Creath recounts a process in which science after science exited philosophy to form autonomous disciplines, including by "early in the twentieth century mathematics, physics, chemistry, biology, and the social sciences," then adds that psychology was in the process of separating itself at the dawn of this new century, but as the "logical" in logical positivism suggests, this separating was mutual (section 2: "Background").

In the beginning of the linguistic turn, then, Wittgenstein's *Tractatus* is the pivotal text and the logical positivists are the pivotal group. Language was now to be the subject matter of philosophy. It is easy enough to imagine how those living in the midst of this turn experienced it as revolutionary. Schlick was well qualified to be a leader in this undertaking, until his career was tragically cut short when he was murdered in 1936, at age 54.[20] He completed a doctorate in physics under Max Planck, then turned to philosophy, completing in 1917 a book on the philosophical implications of Einstein's relativity theory, *Space and Time in Contemporary Physics*, and in 1918 a book defending empiricist epistemology, *General Theory of Knowledge* (Hacker 39, 65). Before appearing first in Rorty's volume, Schlick authored four of the seventeen essays in *Logical Positivism*, more than any of the other authors Ayer included in editing this volume.

Bergmann echoes Schlick's linear history by praising "linguistic philosophers," the "linguistic turn," for "talk[ing] about the world by means of talking about a suitable language," while condemning "the paradox, absurdity, and opacity of prelinguistic philosophy [that] stems from failure to distinguish between speaking and speaking about speaking" (*Logic* 177; qtd. in Rorty, *Linguistic Turn* 8–9). Bergmann thus echoes Schlick in turning philosophy away from talking about the world to focus on the prior problem of writing about the words most suitable for talking about the world.

---

20. Schlick's assailant, Johann Nelböck, in 1925 at age twenty-two, took an undergraduate course from Schlick and would later earn a doctorate (Edmonds 170). Nelböck's hostility for Schlick evolved between 1925 and 1936 for a variety of reasons, including Nelböck's own mental instability. Even though Schlick was not Jewish (Edmonds 177), his death was seen through an anti-Semitic lens in some quarters. One news article published a few weeks after his murder declared, "The Jew is a born anti-metaphysician and loves logicality, mathematicality, formalism, and positivism in philosophy, in other words, all the characteristics that Schlick embodied to the highest degree. We would like to point out, however, that we are Christians living in a Christian German state, and that it is up to us to determine which philosophy is good and appropriate" (Edmonds 176). Benefiting from this anti-Semitic context, Nelböck was given a lenient ten-year sentence (Edmonds 178). Schlick's murder was the final straw for a number of his associates, prompting them to move abroad (Edmonds 181–82).

Bergmann's opposition between prelinguistic and linguistic philosophy registers his linear view of history. By contrast, more attuned than Bergmann to philosophical turns in the history of philosophy, McKeon notes in a 1930 essay that philosophical interest in propositions about propositions appears in the fourteenth century's interest in "*insolubilia*" and reappears in early twentieth-century's interest in "the problem of types" ("*De Anima*" 681). Bergmann's linear view helps to explain his neglect of parallels to the linguistic turn in Ockham in his essay, "Some Remarks on the Ontology of Ockham." Bergmann confesses that his knowledge of Ockham is limited mainly to one book, Ernest Moody's *The Logic of William of Ockham*, so much so that he begins by suggesting that a more accurate title for his essay would be "Some Remarks on the Ontology Contained in the Ockham Fragments Selected and Explicated by Moody," even acknowledging, that philosophy has not benefited from "the cautious silence . . . contemporary philosophers maintain about all but a very few of their more remote predecessors" (144). But Bergmann's essay does little to correct this neglect, despite there being in Moody's analysis of Ockham parallels to the linguistic turn, even to Schlick's view of the relationship between philosophy and science. According to Moody, who expresses indebtedness to McKeon in his Preface (vi), "Ockham, as we have already seen, distinguishes logic from the real sciences by the fact that logic states truths [propositions] about forms of discourse [about propositions], while the real sciences use such forms of discourse for the statement of truths about things which are not signs" (44). Ockham's distinction suggests why McKeon sees Ockham in particular and interest in nominalistic logics in general as evidence that as the fourteenth century turned toward the Renaissance there was a turn from epistemology to language and rhetoric ("Philosopher" 53; *Freedom* 165), a turn analogous to the turn from thought to language in the linguistic turn. But Bergmann's linear view of history looks past these parallels. His focus instead, as summarized in his concluding paragraph, is to pinpoint shortcomings in Ockham to show that the "problem of relations was not fully understood until several centuries after Ockham" (154). Ockham's nominalism questioned the reality of universals, including relations, refusing them ontological status. Regarding relations, Bergmann credits Bertrand Russell with finally discovering their reality, a discovery Bergmann elsewhere calls "epochal," part of the reason Bergmann groups Russell with Moore, Husserl, and Wittgenstein as the four greatest philosophers of the twentieth century (*Logic* 240, 239).

This reality of relations deserves comment to avoid confusion about this initial stage of the linguistic turn. The achievement of this stage is the turn from thought to language; the shortcoming, to which we will turn shortly, is the logical positivist theorizing of language that violated Rorty's precepts by allowing direct, not mediated, access to sensory reality. For Russell, without trying to go into the details of his analysis, the importance of relations is that "once their reality is admitted, all *logical* grounds for supposing the world of sense to be illusory disappear" (*Our Knowledge* 59). Russell's reality of relations is thus consistent with logical positivism.

Nonetheless, while Bergmann does not get high grades as a historian of philosophy, he did contribute notably to philosophy's turn from the subject matter of thought to the subject matter of language, and he did give a name that stuck to this turn. It is also notable that while Bergmann locates the beginning of the linguistic turn in 1921, his coinage of "the linguistic turn" occurs at mid-century, a sign that this coinage itself is not the beginning but somewhere in the middle, signaling the linguistic turn's deepening recognition of itself as a distinctive historical epoch, with a discernible beginning.

A correlative contribution is Bergmann's recognition that in the linguistic turn, language becomes "literally a part of the world" (*Logic* 7). Language is often conceived as apart from existence, as in Aristotle's formulation that one can have knowledge only of that which exists, so that while one can "know the meaning of the phrase or name 'goat-stag,'" one cannot have knowledge of a goat-stag because no such creature exists (*Posterior Analytics* 2.7.92b7; *Basic Works* 166). But even in this formulation, "goat-stag" is a linguistic existent.[21] Hence, when the linguistic turn makes language the subject matter of philosophy, language is elevated to existent status where, as in Rorty's precepts, whatever is not language is dependent on language in the sense that it is accessible only through the mediation of language. Language becomes a *conditio sine qua non*. In one sense, the linguistic turn leaves reality to science; in another it makes language the fundamental reality, philosophically prior to all other realities.

Given the "whole future of philosophy" Schlick envisioned, one can see him applauding *Tractatus* 6.53:

---

21. Furthermore, even in Aristotle one can find considerable attention to linguistic existents. See McKeon, "Aristotle's Conception of Language."

> The correct method in philosophy would really be the following: to say nothing except what can be said, i.e. propositions of natural science—i.e., something that has nothing to do with philosophy—and then, whenever someone else wanted to say something metaphysical, to demonstrate to him that he had failed to give a meaning to certain signs in his propositions.[22]

Citing 6.53 as "[p]robably the best-known thesis of the *Tractatus*," G. E. M. Anscombe, Wittgenstein's student and both translator and co-editor of his *Philososophical Investigations*, characterizes this thesis as the source of "the method of criticism adopted by the Vienna Circle and in this country [UK] by Professor A. J. Ayer" (150). Footnoting Anscombe, one might add that Ayer's highly readable *Language, Truth and Logic* stimulated widespread discussion when it appeared in 1936, then became a best seller after the WWII when it reappeared in a second edition, and arguably remains to this day for many "the epitome of logical positivism" (Creath, section 4.1: "Empiricism, Verificationism, and Anti-Metaphysics"). Rorty calls it "the most important manifesto of logical empiricism" ("Untruth" 32). Anscombe, however, does not see this method as altogether faithful to the *Tractatus*. Anscombe's differences with Ayer merit attention, not to determine who was right, but to illustrate differences among logical positivists about how best to turn from thought to language. Debates among positivists about how best to effect the turn evidence the importance of the turn to the positivists.

In stating her reservations about Ayer's and the Vienna Circle's reading of the *Tractatus*, she cites 4.1121, which addresses the problem of displacing psychology from the centrality it enjoys when thought is philosophy's fundamental subject matter. When fundamental, thought is always vulnerable to displacement because it is, in McKeon's words, "impossible to conceive elements, modes, or forms of thought ungrounded in reality, unexpressed in language, and inoperative in action" ("Phi-

---

22. Wittgenstein is omitted from *The Linguistic Turn*, but in its Preface, Rorty does indicate that he would have liked to include sections 89-113 from part I of *Philosophical Investigations*, explaining, "Wittgenstein's literary executors, however, have adopted a firm, and quite understandable, policy of not permitting this work to be excerpted" (Preface, n.pag., footnote 1). Decades later, writing as a full-fledged pragmatist, Rorty describes sections 89-113 "as an unfortunate leftover from Wittgenstein's early, positivistic period, the period in which he thought that '[t]he totality of true propositions is the whole of natural science'" ("Wittgenstein" 164). Here, Rorty quotes from *Tractatus* 4.11.

losophy of Communications" 312). Because of this interdependence, a thought is not absolutely independent and is thus vulnerable to displacement to a dependent position by anything with which it is inextricably connected. By the same token, the interdependence makes displacement difficult. Notably, 4.1121 ends with a recognition of the difficulty of changing priorities:

> Psychology is no more closely related to philosophy than any other natural science.
> Theory of knowledge is the philosophy of psychology.
> Does not my study of sign-language correspond to the study of thought-processes, which philosophers used to consider so essential to the philosophy of logic? Only in most cases they got entangled in unessential psychological investigations, and with my method too there is an analogous risk.

Turning away from this "unessential" is essential, but Wittgenstein sees his method as risking the "entangle[ment]" to be avoided.

In Anscombe's recounting, 4.1121 shows (1) "that Wittgenstein evidently did not think that epistemology had any bearing on his subject-matter"; and (2) that "Wittgenstein is trying to break the dictatorial control over the rest of philosophy that had long been exercised by what is called theory of knowledge—that is, by the philosophy of sensation, perception, imagination, and, generally, of 'experience.'" Evidence that the *Tractatus* did not fulfill Wittgenstein's intention, in Anscombe's view, appears in its influence on logical positivism: "But the influence of the *Tractatus* produced logical positivism, whose main doctrine is 'verificationism'; and in that doctrine a theory of knowledge once more reigned supreme, and a prominent position was given to the test for significance by asking for the *observations* that would verify a statement." I italicized "*observations*" because earlier, to illustrate the "most common view of the *Tractatus*," she quotes a paragraph from Karl Popper summarizing its doctrine in which Popper uses "observed" once and "observation" five times (27, 152, 152 [italics added], 25).

Anscombe is clearly right that the *Tractatus* does not theorize the psychological apparatus informing observations, beginning at the level of sensory experience and moving to higher levels. Its proposition 4, "A thought is a proposition with a sense," by assimilating thought to proposition appears consistent with the linguistic turn's reversal of the relation of thought to language. Anscombe quotes Wittgenstein remarking in a letter, "I don't know *what* the constituents of a thought are but I know *that* it must have constituents which correspond to the words of language. Again the kind of relation of the constituents of the thought and of the pictured fact is irrelevant. It would be a matter of psychology to find out" (28).

But one needs to qualify her judgment that in "verificationism" the "theory of knowledge once more reigned supreme." For Ayer's *Language* explicitly rejects Kant's reliance on psychological processes of thought: "he [Kant] said that the human understanding was so constituted that it lost itself in contradictions when it ventured out beyond the limits of possible experience and attempted to deal with things in themselves." By contrast, Ayer reiterates the linguistic turn from thought to language. For logical positivism, he explains, "the fruitlessness of attempting to transcend the limits of possible sense-experience will be deduced, not from a psychological hypothesis concerning the actual constitution of the human mind, but from the rule which determines the literal significance of language," the "criterion of verifiability," which requires that for a statement to have "literal significance" there must be conditions under which "observations" can determine whether it is true or false (34, 35). Ayer thus turns against thought by turning to and privileging language that references the sensory. He thus shows, as McKeon explains, that a turn to language can borrow epistemology's "critique" of human faculties, such as Kant's critique of "pure reason," and redeploy it in a critique of language ("Philosophy of Communications" 312–13). "Critique" goes hand-in-hand with the centrality of mediation in the philosophical subject matters of thought on the one hand and language on the other.

Departing from the normative "observation" is the target in Gross and Levitt's satire, which presupposes that it is obvious that one "observes" the rainfall and then says, "It is raining," thus exemplifying "verificationism," where "it is raining" is judged to be true because it is verified by the rain outside that one can observe. A sign of the importance of the verification principle appears in extensive debates among logical positivists over its technical fine points.[23] "It is raining" qualifies technically even if Gross and Levitt stay inside their windowless room because it is enough to know that empirical observation can determine

---

23. Useful surveys of these debates appear in Creath and Uebel. When I accessed their online texts in 2014, these surveys appeared in Creath's section 4.1, "Empiricism, Verificationism, and Anti-Metaphysics," and in Uebel's section 3.1, "Verification and the Critique of Metaphysics."

whether "it is raining" is the case and thus whether "it is raining" has meaning, sense rather than nonsense. It is not philosophy's job to do the verifying; as Schlick puts it, "By means of philosophy statements are explained, by means of science they are verified" ("Turning" 56).

Ayer's first chapter, "The Elimination of Metaphysics," carries out the project in Wittgenstein's 6.53, which, as we saw, Anscombe pinpoints as the key link between *Tractatus* and logical positivism.[24] Writing about writing, Ayer's chapter focuses on language to argue that because "no statement which refers to a 'reality' transcending the limits of all possible sense-experience can possibly have any literal significance," metaphysicians striving "to describe such a reality have all been devoted to the production of nonsense" (34). The distinction between "sense" and "nonsense" informs the view of language that Ayer in particular and logical positivism in general wielded in their dismissal of metaphysics and valorization of empirical science. Russell introduced this distinction in his introduction to the *Tractatus*. He defined "nonsense" as in effect a privative insofar it keeps language from enjoying a state of purity: a "logically perfect language ... prevent[s] nonsense"; because the "essential business of language is to assert or deny facts," logic must overcome the "vague[ness]" of ordinary language by determining "the conditions for sense rather than nonsense" (x). One might question whether Russell identifies the "essential business of language" insofar as it relegates most of language to the ash heap of nonsense. Russell actually illustrates McKeon's point, discussed earlier, that early stages of the linguistic turn lacked an "art of rhetoric ... adequate to the possibilities of communication or to the contents or ends to which communication might be adapted" (97). Yes, sometimes the communication of facts is the aim and language must be shaped accordingly. But that does not demote to "nonsense" the use of language to achieve the myriad of other purposes of communication.

While Ayer clearly sees himself in particular and logical positivism in general turning to language, away from psychology, his theorizing of language—with the exception of "analytic" language[25]—(1) inscribes it

---

24. The second edition of Ayer's *Language*, instead of revising the first, discusses modifications of the first in a new "Introduction." "The Elimination of Metaphysics" remains chapter one, but comes after this "Introduction."

25. The exception of "analytic" language in Ayer's *Language*, in the chapter "The *A Priori*," is prompted by a difficulty that any empiricism encounters, namely that "the truths of formal logic and mathematics" have no empirical

in the commonsensical view of language as posterior to what it is about and (2) limits what it is about to the empirical realm "out there." In this theoretical model, observation is the position outside language that enables one to compare language (e.g., "it is raining") to that which is prior to language (e.g., rainfall outside) in order to verify whether the language has subjected itself to the "supervision" of the nonlinguistic. Ayer turns against psychology but keeps language's posteriority, thereby keeping part of the thought orientation that logical positivism turns against. Observation presupposes the standpoint that Rorty, in his precepts, pinpoints as that which the linguistic turn ultimately overturns: adapting Rorty's words to state this presupposition, one would say that observation is, "a point of view outside of all linguistic frameworks from which the world will appear 'as it is,'" so that "nonlinguistic data . . . can guide our choice of language." Comparing the observed nonlinguistic to the linguistic presupposes thought independent of language. Ayer rejects Kant, but keeps a modicum of thought that is enough to inhibit completion of the turn from the priority of thought to the priority of language. Ayer makes a linguistic turn while at the same time incorporating into this turn something from what it is turning against. Ayer rejects Kant in the name of language, but then theorizes language as posterior in presupposing observation in a verification process involving psychological components prior to language in the subject matter of thought.

Ayer's argument is also noteworthy from the standpoint of an ultimate priority's role in changing the subject matter of philosophy. In his critique of Kant, Ayer clearly prioritizes language over Kant's ultimate priority of thought, his "psychological hypothesis," to a significant degree, albeit not completely. But language is clearly posterior to thing in Ayer's "criterion of verifiability," where whether the sensory "supervises" a statement determines whether the statement has "literal significance." As discussed in chapter two, a new ultimate priority in a philosophical turn has to be prior not only to the ultimate priority in the subject matter it is turning from, in this case thought, but also to the ultimate priority in the other possible subject matter, in this case thing.

---

basis and "appear to everyone to be necessary and certain." Logical positivism's solution resides in the claim that "the truths of logic and mathematics are analytic propositions or tautologies" (72, 77). That tautologies, by saying nothing beyond themselves, slide out from under the umbrella of language as posterior is not Ayer's concern, but it does indicate why this part of his logical positivism departs from his general theorizing about language.

Ayer makes some progress in the prioritizing of language over thought, but none at all in prioritizing language over thing.

Ayer becomes vulnerable to critique in later stages of the linguistic turn because of his shortcomings in prioritizing in the directions of both thought and thing. Prioritizing in the direction of thing becomes central because if language is prior to thing, there is no way for Ayer's "observation" to occur. This is easy to see in retrospect, but the issue of ultimate priority explains why the critique of logical positivism played out that way.

As noted earlier, McKeon taught Rorty to see "the history of philosophy as a series, not of alternative solutions to the same problems, but of quite different sets of problems" (xiii). One set of problems emerges in a philosophical turn changing the subject matter of philosophy in direction X; another set emerges in a turn changing this subject matter in direction Y. However different the problems from turn to turn, the problems always derive from finding what is needed to establish in the subject matter one is turning to an ultimate priority that is prior to the other possible subject matters and thus to ultimate priorities in those subject matters. The distinctive set of problems posed in a turn to language explains why the critique of logical positivism took the form it did.

Attention to the problem of ultimate priority may often supply a needed corrective to interpretations of philosophy. A corrective is needed when interpretations presuppose that the subject matter of philosophy is unchanging and that one should judge a philosophy based on how close it comes to stating truths about this unchanging subject matter. Philosophic turns provide the needed corrective by showing that philosophies debating one another are engaged in changing the subject matter of philosophy. These changes are not haphazard, the product of a century's whim. Rather, these changes take their form from the limited number of ways to establish an order of priority among thing, thought, language and action.

To be clear, logical positivism consists of words in philosophical texts that are about words conceived as the subject matter of philosophy, just as in later stages the linguistic turn would continue to consist of words in philosophical texts about such words. Throughout, the words in the texts are posterior to the subject matter of words that they are about. The change that occurs in the history of the linguistic turn is in the view of words. Logical positivists, at the beginning of the linguistic turn, conceived words on the commonsensical model as posterior to the nonlinguistic, specifically the empirical nonlinguistic, whereas later, in accord with Rorty's precepts, the linguistic turn conceived words as prior to the nonlinguistic. Explaining the priority of words to the nonlinguistic becomes the fundamental philosophical problem that would take the linguistic turn decades to solve.

Because Ayer's "verification" principle so clearly presupposes observation independent of language, his text is an exemplary illustration of turning from thought to language on the one hand while nonetheless retaining something from thought on the other hand. Nonetheless, Ayer is close to Wittgenstein, where analysis—"A proposition has one and only one complete analysis" (3.25)—is the analogue to Ayer's verification with its component of observation. Analysis is not absent from Ayer insofar as it is involved in determining whether a statement's reference makes the statement verifiable, but analysis is more prominent in Wittgenstein, where analysis divides a proposition into simples, that is, elementary propositions (*Elementarsätze*): "It is obvious that the analysis of propositions must bring us to elementary propositions which consist of names in immediate combination" (4.221). That analysis aims for elementary propositions follows from the *sine quo non* of "sense": "The requirement that simple signs be possible is the requirement that sense be determinate" (3.23). A combination of simples results in a "picture" in the *Tractatus*'s picture theory of representation that was not destined for a long life. "Sense," needed for determinate meaning, is thus arrived at by an analytic process: "If we know on purely logical grounds that there must be elementary propositions, then everyone who understands propositions in their unanalyzed form must know it" (5.5562).

Anscombe accentuates the difference Wittgenstein's emphasis on analysis makes in her paraphrase: "the elementary propositions have not the role of simple observation statements. . . . [Rather,] the character of inference, and of meaning itself, *demands* that there should be elementary propositions" (28). Even so, a modicum of observation is inescapable even in Wittgenstein's *Tractatus*: "In a proposition a thought finds an expression that can be perceived by the senses" (3.1). This ingredient marks the overlap between Ayer's verification and Wittgenstein's analysis.

But whatever the differences between Wittgenstein and Ayer, they are alike privileging "sense" against "nonsense," perhaps the principal legacy of logical positivism. The privileging of "sense" comes with the privileging of the empirical that went with logical positivism's alliance with science. The metaphysician's failure "to give a meaning to certain signs in his propositions," as *Tractatus* puts it at 6.53, results in "nonsense," the term Wittgenstein uses in his Preface to the *Tractatus* to label whatever is on the other side of language's "limit" (3), this limit itself defined as "sense" in 4.5: "It now seems possible to give the most general propositional form: that is, to give a description of the propositions of *any* sign-language *whatsoever* in such a way that every possible sense can be expressed by a symbol satisfying the description."

What is notable for the history of the linguistic turn is that this distinction between sense and nonsense presupposes the commonsensical view of language as posterior rather than as prior. In Ayer's and Wittgenstein's "sense," the word is posterior to something, whereas in "nonsense," it is posterior to nothing. One sign of commitment to this view of language is puzzlement whenever language appears to reference that which does not exist. "What is mysterious about negation," Anscombe reflects, "is that something's *not* being the case should be capable of being something that *is* the case," adding in a footnote that this "problem is the ancient one of how a false proposition makes sense" (70). By contrast, Burke responds differently to what is "mysterious" for Anscombe. Inspired by Bergson's consideration of the negative, Burke reflects that about any "X," one could go on indefinitely saying "X is not this," "X is not that," etc., a phenomenon of language that appears to him to be not a mystery but a basis for speculation in "A Dramatistic View of the Origins of Language" that the negative, which appears posterior to nothing, is at the heart of the origins of language and its priority (*Language* 419–79).[26] In Burke's account of these origins, the hortatory negative is prior to the propositional negative that Anscombe considers. Burke's speculation registers a concern with the "genesis of language" that Claire Colebrook sees as generally more characteristic of continental than analytic philosophy (286–87). Not an analytic philosopher but an American, Burke is an exception to this generality.

Leaving aside the mysteries of "do not" or "not," one can distinguish false from nonsense within an empirical framework fairly easily. The verification principle does not require that one actually verify, only that one determine what counts as "sense" by what can be verified empirically. "It is raining" has "sense" regardless of whether in particular circumstances it is true or false. Either way, Gross and Levitt can look outside to check. Wittgenstein's *Tractatus* determines whether a proposition is determinate so that "[t]he agreement or disagreement of its sense with reality con-

---

26. For my commentary on "Dramatistic View," see *Kenneth Burke*, pp. 228–34.

stitutes its truth or falsity" (2.222). By contrast, "nonsense" cannot be tested empirically so that it is neither true nor false.

In sum, and in short, logical positivism consists of words about words, the mark of the linguistic turn according to Bergmann. But by conceiving words as posterior, as in commonsense, logical positivism preoccupied itself with distinguishing words that have an empirical referent ("sense") from words that do not ("nonsense"). This view of language would become the antagonist that later stages of the linguistic turn would polemicize against.

While Bergmann locates the beginning of the linguistic turn in the *Tractatus*, Dummett locates it in Frege's "analysis of thought by means of the analysis of language" (25). Bergmann's location deserves precedence because Bergmann also gave the turn its name, but Frege, among those who influenced Wittgenstein, can be credited with anticipating the beginning. Dummett observes that Frege turned to language for an alternative to the psychologizing of number, a turn that illustrates McKeon's point that arguments against the subject matter of thought include that this subject matter "psychologizes the objects of thought" ("Philosophy of Communications" 311). Dummett identifies the reversal of the relation of thought and language with such pinpoint accuracy that he confidently locates Frege's linguistic turn in section #62 of his early *The Foundations of Arithmetic* (Dummett 5), which begins, "How, then, are numbers to be given to us, if we cannot have any ideas or intuitions of them? Since it is only in the context of a proposition that words have any meaning, our problem becomes this: To define the sense of a proposition in which a number word occurs" (Frege 73^e). Dummett's focus on this reversal of the relation of thought and language provides an analogue to the Kantian reversal of the relation of thing and thought. Beginning with language foregrounds the communal formation of usage. As Dummett puts it, "The accessibility of thoughts will then reside in their capacity for linguistic expression, and their objectivity and independence from inner mental processes in the *common* practice of speaking the language, governed by agreement among the linguistic community on standards of correct use and on criteria for the truth of statements" (25). In usage, in short, thought is objective in the sense that it is independent of the psychology of "inner mental processes." What is inherently subjective in the individual body, where these mental processes occur, is thus displaced by the usage produced by verbal communication among bodies. Dummett, if not Frege, recognizes McKeon's point about the need for a turn to language to get to the level of communication.

While the linguistic turn made language the subject matter of philosophy, as Bergmann stresses, reliance on the commonsensical view of language inhibited the inquiry into language needed to complete the turn from thought to language. Given the centrality of Wittgenstein's *Tractatus* at the beginning of the turn, it is not surprising that one finds theorists in later stages of the narrative of the history of the linguistic turn looking back at the *Tractatus* to try to pinpoint exactly where it went wrong. Daniel D. Hutto is one example. By happenstance, Hutto uses rainfall, Gross and Levitt's example, to distinguish (1) "It is raining" from (2) "'It is raining' is a proposition." The *Tractatus*, Hutto observes, consists of propositions like (2) to explain (1), although concrete illustrations like "It is raining" appear rarely. The *Tractatus*, in other words, is a philosophical text about the subject matter of language. The shortcoming Hutto sees in what it says about language surfaces in section 6.54, where Wittgenstein says that if you understand him you will recognizes the propositions in his text "as nonsensical." Language about language, in short, is nonsense. Hutto attributes this judgment to *Tractatus*'s "impoverished view of the function of language": Wittgenstein "had limited means of characterizing its remarks. They were *meant* to be elucidations, but he was pushed by his own understanding of sense to regard them either as statements of fact or as mere nonsense" (99, 102), a disjunction that Russell echoes in his "Introduction," as noted earlier. Eventually, Hutto goes on, Wittgenstein would go beyond the limiting commonsensical "idea that all propositions are essentially representative of facts"—that is, that language is posterior to the nonlinguistic—but in the *Tractatus* he was not there yet. "By the Tractarian criterion," Hutto sums up, "there is no doubt that 'It is raining' *says* something, as it pictures a possible state of affairs in the world. . . . But what exactly is being said that is of a merely factual nature when it is remarked that '"It is raining" is a proposition'? What merely possible state of affairs does this picture?" (109, 99). "'It is raining' is a proposition" is a statement but what it references is not to be found in the sensory world. The statement is "nonsense" when one is limited to the distinction between "sense" and "nonsense." That is why Wittgenstein says that his statements in the *Tractatus* are "nonsensical."

Similarly concerned with words about words, Thomas Ricketts offers a criticism similar to Hutto's in his consideration of the example of "A is," where "A" is a name and "A is" is understood as affirming the existence not of what "A" names but of the name "A" itself. In other words, the name "A" is both the referent of the proposition and the subject in the proposition claiming that this referent exists. Such sentences are not only words about words, or in this example words about a word, a name, but words about themselves where the self-reference makes them self-evidently true. Ricketts goes on, "But for this very reason, the admission of such sentences violates Wittgenstein's understanding of truth as agreement with facts. Sentences are pictures of reality that are true or false in virtue of their agreement or disagreement with reality." Two passages Ricketts cites to support his point are 2.223 ("In order to tell whether a picture is true or false we must compare it with reality") and 2.224 ("It is impossible to tell from the picture alone whether it is true or false"). Ricketts concludes, "Wittgenstein's view thus rules out representations that presuppose their own truth. For to admit a representation that presupposes its own truth is to admit a representation whose truth does not consist in its agreement with reality, a picture whose truth can be recognized without comparing it to reality" (86–87, 87). *Tractatus*, then, even though it is largely words about words would, in Ricketts's account, disallow instances of words about words that violate the commonsensical view that language is posterior to the nonlinguistic that it is about.

Hutto and Ricketts thus offer analyses suggesting that the distinction between "sense" and "nonsense" impedes overturning the commonsensical view of language by aborting inquiry into words themselves, the necessary focus in inquiry into how words are prior rather than posterior to the nonlinguistic. This inquiry is essential to completing the linguistic turn's turn to its ultimate priority. Evidence that this distinction proved to be an impediment is that later stages of the linguistic turn would abandon it.

Before turning the middle stage in this chapter's narrative of the linguistic turn's history, it is necessary to consider this turn's posture of antiphilosophy, the posture that inhibited its recognition of its rhetoricizing of philosophy. An exemplary statement of sympathy with this posture begins Cora Diamond's seminal "Throwing Away the Ladder: How to Read the *Tractatus*," first published as an article in 1988, then reprinted as chapter six (179–204) in her 1991 *The Realistic Spirit: Wittgenstein, Philosophy, and the Mind*:

> Whether one is reading Wittgenstein's *Tractatus* or his later writings, one must be struck by his insistence that he is not putting

> forward philosophical doctrines or theses; or by his suggestion that it cannot be done, that it is only through some confusion one is in about what one is doing that one could take oneself to be putting forward philosophical doctrines or theses at all. I think that there is almost nothing in Wittgenstein which is of value and which can be grasped if it is pulled away from that view of philosophy. (179)

This claim that philosophy "cannot be done" presupposes that antiphilosophy is the order not just of the day but for all time, while philosophy is the smoke of illusion that one should avoid. In this sense, antiphilosophy presents itself as therapeutic.

For Diamond, the key passage for antiphilosophy in the *Tractatus* is not the 6.53 central for logical positivism but 6.54. Whereas Hutto finds in 6.54 a sign of Wittgenstein's limitations, Diamond sees it as the key to the antiphilosophy that her "Throwing Away the Ladder" celebrates. Diamond takes her title from the famous parenthetical aside at the end of 6.54's first paragraph:

> My propositions serve as elucidations in the following way: anyone who understands me eventually recognizes them as nonsensical, when he has used them—as steps—to climb up beyond them. (He must, so to speak, throw away the ladder after he has climbed up it.)
>
> He must transcend these propositions, and then he will see the world aright.

Diamond asks what is left after throwing away the ladder. Referencing "the logical form of reality" as representative of the *Tractatus*'s subject matter, Diamond asks, "Are we going to keep the idea that there is something or other in reality that we gesture at, however badly, when we speak of 'the logical form of reality,' so that *it, what* we were gesturing at, is there but cannot be expressed in words? *That* is what I want to call chickening out" (*Realistic* 181). To not chicken out is to say that there is no "*it*," that notions such as "logical form of reality" reference nothing.

Reviewing *Realistic Spirit*, Warren Goldfarb notes that a shortcoming of the term "chickening out" is that it has "no graceful opposite," so that it leaves one without a good positive term to characterize Diamond's reading. Goldfarb proposes to substitute "*irresolute*" for "chickening out," which makes Diamond's reading "*resolute*" (64). Responding to Goldfarb, Diamond "appreciate[s]" his irresolute/resolute distinction, adding that "irresolute" not only captures what she meant by "chickening out" but "emphasizes also another element, a kind of dithering" ("Realism" 78). Diamond's reading thus acquired the name "resolute" that subsequently evolved into "resolutism," a reading of Wittgenstein's corpus emphasizing a 'therapeutic' continuity between what are traditionally seen as his 'early' and 'late' periods" (*Beyond the* Tractatus *Wars* 1).

My aim here is not to step into the thicket of debates fostered by this resolute reading of *Tractatus*.[27] Rather, it is to counter antiphilosophy's claim that philosophy cannot be done with the claim antiphilosophy rhetoricizes philosophy without realizing it.

Resolutism does not realize this either. But when it looks back at the *Tractatus*, it does not repeat the usual arguments against logical positivism that became commonplace in later stages of the linguistic turn. Instead, it finds signs of the rhetorical without recognizing their provenance in the rhetoricizing of philosophy.

Diamond writes in the name of realism, but not the realism of logical positivism. She spells out her realism in chapter one of *The Realistic Spirit*, "Realism and the Realistic Spirit" (39–72). When philosophical realism purports to identify timeless truths, thus fixing the future forever, it is rejected by Diamond's "realistic spirit." But when realism becomes equivalent to openness to new possibilities, as she illustrates with a passage from Wittgenstein, from *Remarks on the Foundations of Mathematics* (66–70), it becomes equivalent to the "realistic spirit." Diamond's realism, in other words, is a realism of openness to future innovation. What Diamond misses is twofold: (1) "timeless truths" are to "openness to future innovation" as philosophy is to rhetoricized philosophy; (2) "openness to future innovation" is rhetoricized philosophy's "timeless truth."

This realism of openness is affirmed energetically in Rupert Read's "Throwing Away 'The Bedrock.'" Read explicitly presents himself as "tak[ing] forward" the rejection of an ineffable something in the *Tractatus* in the "Diamond/Conant reading of Wittgenstein" (89), referencing the close association between James Conant and Diamond, as evidenced in Conant's acknowledgement in "The Method of the *Tractatus*," a major essay to which we will turn shortly, "My most pervasive debt is to Cora Diamond, with whom—at some point or other over the past thirteen years—I have discussed every idea in this essay." Regarding the ineffable, Conant concedes that there are passages in the *Tractatus* refer-

---

27. For a review of these debates, see Silver Bronzo. "The Resolute Reading and Its Critics."

encing what can only be shown, not said, but to see these as affirming an ineffable something beyond words "is to mistake the target of the work for its doctrine" (425,381). Or, in Diamond's more colorful language, to affirm an ineffable something is to "chicken out."

Read asks, "What words *can* be absolutely relied on here, unproblematically taken at face value, in philosophy?" His answer is absolute: "None. . . . True philosophy is never taking any frame indefinitely or absolutely for granted." Read's "true philosophy" is rhetoricized philosophy. Read argues that philosophizing tends to give terms technical meanings that fossilize into "bedrock." One must be ready, Read insists, to allow any term to be "thrown away" (96, 97). Conant, we shall see, illustrates Read's point dramatically.

That any term can be "thrown away" exemplifies Diamond's realism of openness to the new. Whereas Dummett's analysis of Frege's turn from thought to language focuses on Frege's reliance on conventions of usage, Diamond's resolute reading of Wittgenstein focuses on novelty. Commenting in *The Realistic Spirit* on Wittgenstein's trademark notion of meaning as "use," Diamond stresses the liberation that comes from acquiring the ability to look at "use without imposing on it what one thinks must already be there in it. The notion of use itself and what is meant by giving or presenting it thus also changes" (33). The reason for this is that, she explains, "use can be seen only as belonging to the spatial, temporal phenomenon of language," so that it is subject to the capacity for innovation inherent in language: What is characteristic of language, of using words, is that we do new things." Various examples appear in *Realistic Spirit*. "Shirley Temple," for example, started as a name, then later became a drink (33, 99). In her example of "use," Diamond recognizes that, because of this characteristic of language, a meaning of use put forward as "the" eternal truth about use may turn out to be exposed as merely "a" meaning when displaced by a new meaning at a later date, one that will turn out in the long run to be another "a" rather than "the." Because of this characteristic of language, when language becomes the subject matter of philosophy, philosophy should turn to rhetoric, as we saw McKeon contend in chapter two.

But the distinction between Dummett's focus and Diamond's is really a distinction without a difference: a convention begins as a novelty; a novelty is potentially a new convention. Both are properties of rhetoric. McKeon's "Philosophy of Communications and the Arts," as we saw in chapter two, defines rhetoric as "an art of communication between a speaker and his audience, and it is therefore an art of construction of the subject matter of communication, that is, of anything whatever that can be an object of attention" (317). An "object of attention" begins as a novelty and may become a convention in what Rorty calls "normal discourse," to be considered later in this chapter.

When philosophy is rhetoricized, philosophy's ultimate priority guarantees Diamond's realism of openness to the new. No "timeless truths" except the timeless truth of openness to innovation, to the new. In other words, rhetoricized philosophy makes closure, a final word, impossible. Put paradoxically, closure is closed. In ordinary experience, the closure of closure appears in linguistic usage, which consists of conventions overturned by novelties that become new conventions, a reality of openness to the new charted in the many volumes of the *Oxford English Dictionary*.

Usage is notably central in Claire Colebrook's thesis in the first paragraph of her account of the linguistic turn. After this turn, Colebrook claims, "It would no longer be legitimate to establish the true meaning or essence of an identity, and then correct ordinary usage, for meaning and identity are established through linguistic usage" (279); Colebrook's "identity" established by usage is equivalent to McKeon's "object of attention."

Put in the form of what Burke calls "perspective by incongruity" (*Permanence* 88–92) the philosophical closure of closure is "the tyranny of the new." That which enthrones this tyranny is the argument that no word can be the final word except the word that says no word is final. In other words, that which enthrones this tyrant in none other than antiphilosophy, the deconstruction of supposed final words such as the supposed "timeless truths" of "*logocentrism*."

Convention and novelty are qualities of the tyranny of the new, considered as an object of inquiry. These qualities answer one of the fundamental questions that Aristotle poses at the beginning of the second book of *Posterior Analytics*, namely, how is the object of one's inquiry qualified? This answer, in turn, poses the question of "why?" that needs to be answered to explain these qualities. To answer this question is to identify the ultimate priority in the linguistic turn, the priority that completes the turn that logical positivism started but did not complete. Establishing this ultimate priority rhetoricizes philosophy, on which Read unwittingly relies in his readiness to see putative bedrocks "thrown away."

Conant's "The Method of *Tractatus*" is nearly 100 pages long, somewhere between an essay and a book. Among other things, it offers a veritable compendium of meanings for the terms "nonsense" and "elucidation" that Wittgenstein uses in 6.54. Conant explicates these instead of throwing them away, but a by-product of Conant's analysis calls attention to one claim in the *Tractatus* that merits attention here, even though it is dwarfed by the *Tractatus*'s distinction between "sense" and "nonsense," because it is a sign of an emergent rhetoricizing of philosophy beneath the antiphilosophy of the *Tractatus* at the beginning of the narrative of the linguistic turn.

"Caesar is a prime number," Conant's most illustrative example in his analysis, is not from the *Tractatus*, but Conant does connect this illustration to what is arguably the *Tractatus*'s most important example of "nonsense": "Socrates is identical" (5.473, 5.4733). "Caesar is a prime number" appears obviously nonsensical, but Conant cautions that one needs to distinguish "substantial" from "austere" conceptions of nonsense, a distinction important for resolutism. A "resolute" reader of the *Tractatus*, Conant affirms the "austere" against the "substantial." The "substantial" conception distinguishes two forms of nonsense: "Mere nonsense is simply unintelligible—it expresses no thought. Substantial nonsense is composed of intelligible ingredients combined in an illegitimate way—it expresses a logically incoherent thought." "The austere conception," by contrast, "holds that mere nonsense is, from a logical point of view, the only kind of nonsense there is" (380, 381).

From the standpoint of the "substantial" conception, "Caesar is a prime number" contains two intelligible ingredients, "Caesar" and "is a prime number," that do not go together logically. The "austere" conception, by contrast, sees "mere nonsense," as it questions the putative intelligibility of these ingredients, because it views the sentence from the standpoint of one of Frege's three core principles, each of which, Conant argues, "is reworked and plays a central role in the *Tractatus*"; the relevant one here is "never to ask for the meaning of a word in isolation, but only in the context of a proposition" (384). From this contextual viewpoint, "Caesar is a prime number" is nonsensical because the words in this sentence do not have meanings compatible with one another. In this respect, "Caesar is a prime number" is equivalent to Chomsky's famous "Colorless green ideas sleep furiously" (15).

Conant produces his illuminating illustration by proposing, "We could assign a meaning to 'Caesar' that would allow us to treat 'Caesar' as the kind of logical element that symbolizes a number; or, alternatively, we could assign a meaning to 'prime number' that would allow us to treat it as the kind of element that symbolizes a predicate which applies to persons. So there are two natural ways of making sense of this string" (419). Words such as "Caesar" and "prime number" incarnate novelty and convention. Any word can be given any meaning (novelty) and any new meaning can become common usage (convention). Conant's proposal builds on the openness to innovation inherent in language.

Meanings contextually compatible with one another, in other words, articulate logical relations. The problem is always specifying meanings, not logic. As Wittgenstein says in 5.473: "In a certain sense, we cannot make mistakes in logic," like the illogic the "substantial" conception sees in "Caesar is a prime number." Both of Conant's revisions find meanings that produce logic, meanings that overturn conventions of usage to produce novelty. Nonsense occurs on the level of signs such as "Caesar is a prime number," not on the logical level that signs symbolize (cf. 4.4611). But the logical level has no existence independently of signs that symbolize it. This conception of the relation of logic to verbal signs, it seems to me, is analogous to Aristotle's analysis in *Metaphysics*, book seven, chapter eight, of a bronze sphere. The spherical form (= logic) is actualized in the bronze sphere (= words), guiding the actualization yet having no existence apart from this actualization, finally actualized because bronze has the potential to actualize this form. To be clear, I'm not suggesting an Aristotelian influence, only an analogy that may clarify the Conant example.

Conant's analysis of "Caesar is a prime number" clarifies his analysis of Wittgenstein's "Socrates is identical": "Wittgenstein says in this passage that the nonsensicality of the string ['Socrates is identical'] is due not to an impermissible employment of a symbol, but rather to our failing to make a determination of meaning" (411). Or, as Wittgenstein puts it, "The proposition is nonsensical because we have failed to make an *arbitrary* determination" (5.473; italics added), that is, an arbitrary determination of meaning like those in Conant's analysis of "Caesar is a prime number."

Carnap would appear to go even further when he extends the combination of convention and novelty to logic itself. He records that during his time in the Vienna Circle the "most important insight" he gained from Wittgenstein centered on logic as consisting of tautologies: "Logical statements are true under all conceivable circumstances; thus their truth is independent of the contingent facts of the world. . . . [I]t follows that these statements do not say anything about the world and thus have no factual content" ("Autobiography" 25). This divorce of logic from factual reality is even more striking in the *"Principle of Tolerance"* that Carnap proposes in *The Logical Syntax of Language*: *"In logic, there are no morals*. Everyone is at liberty to build up his own logic, i.e. his own form of language, as he wishes. All that is required of him is that, if he wishes to discuss it, he must state his methods clearly, and give syntactical rules instead of philosophical arguments" (51, 52). The introduction of something totally new into the world is the specific consequence of the priority of language that Carnap's *"Principle of Tolerance"* authorizes, a principle Carnap later says might better be called "the principle of conventionality'" (*Introduction* 247). But there is nothing here to indicate the philosophical principle from which this consequence derives. Search for "philosophical arguments" for such a principle, that is, for the enthronement of the tyrant in the tyranny of the new, is instead discouraged.

Carnap's principle of conventionality also appears in Morton White's *Toward Reunion in Philosophy*, first published in 1956. "In recent years it has become more and more evident," White observes, that the logical positivist's theory of meaning used "in his attempt to discredit traditional metaphysics is also the product of a decision to speak in a certain way rather than a factual description of scientific language" (19). Implicit in "speak in a certain" way is a criterion that White clarifies by analogizing the logical positivist to the moralist: "The moralist says that acts of stealing ought not to be committed; the theorist of meaning says that 'thing-in-itself' ought not to be called meaningful"; White adds, "The point is that we set up a rule which allows us to give as a reason for calling an expression meaningful the fact that it is observable, just as a moral rule allows us to give as a reason for saying that something ought not be done the fact that it is an act of stealing" (109; see also 160, 162–63, 195). White's analogy here of the moralist to the logical positivist suggests the logical positivist's verificationist test was a cover for something closer to a test for proper linguistic usage. What is different is that instead of basing proper usage on social and grammatical criteria, the positivist bases it on scientific rectitude. White's critique, then, is that whereas logical positivists thought they were testing words against empirical existents, stating facts purely, they were really imposing rules governing linguistic usage to valorize such facts. White thus departs from the typical critique of logical positivism in later stages of the linguistic turn by in effect depicting them as engaged in establishing a McKeonist "object of attention."

Burke does something similar to what White does, but takes a step beyond White insofar as he revises what counts as empirical. The similarity appears when he argues that facts cannot be divorced from values absolutely so that any presentation of facts necessarily entails "a *choice of stylization*." By this logic, the purer one's statement of facts, the more one valorizes facts, the purity registering a distinctive stylization. "To the logical positivist," Burke insists, "logical positivism is a 'good' term" (*Philosophy* 126, 150). The revision of what counts as empirical begins when he registers an attitude toward logical positivist philosophizing that was common in areas of the broader culture, (1) "one could, if he wished, maintain that all theology, metaphysics, philosophy, criticism, poetry, drama, fiction, political exhortation, historical interpretation, and personal statements about the lovable and the hateful—one could if he wanted to be as drastically thorough as some of our positivists now seem to want to be—maintain that every bit of this is nonsense"; (2) then, Burke underlines that even words of nonsense are existents: "Yet these words of nonsense would themselves be real words, involving real tactics, having real demonstrable relationships, and demonstrably affecting relationships"; finally, Burke concludes, (3) "[E]ven when statements about the *nature of the world* are abstractly metaphysical, statements about the *nature of these statements* can be as empirical as the statement, 'This is Mr. Smith,' made when introducing Mr. Smith in the accepted manner" (*Grammar* 57–58).

Here, Burke relocates empirical from what is "out there" to linguistic "communications." Even words of "nonsense" can communicate between speaker and hearer, establishing between them a shared McKeonist "object of attention." Communication is an existent and as such can be an empirical object, something than can be investigated just as readily as empirical objects of sensory perception. Whatever one may want to say about words for the supernatural, Burke observes, such words "are real so far as their nature their nature as sheer words is concerned." More broadly, Burke adds, "[O]f all situations having to do with language, the only time when something can be discussed wholly in terms of itself, is when we are using words about words. Insofar as nonverbal things are discussed in terms of words (or symbols generally), they are necessarily discussed in terms of what they are not" (*Language* 374, 375).

Importantly, the Burkean empirical registers the shift from the beginning to the middle stage in the history of the linguistic turn because it turns away from the positivist assumption that language is posterior to the empirical objects of sensory perception. Turning away from that assumption puts the linguistic turn on the road to discovery of that which makes language prior rather than posterior to thing, the step needed to get to the ultimate priority that is prior to both thought and thing and to thereby establish language and action as the subject matter of philosophy. The Burkean empirical strategically relocates the empirical to direct attention to language first and to what language is about second, redirecting inquiry into what makes language prior, an inquiry that becomes the preoccupation of theory in the later decades of the twentieth century. Language's priority becomes the first reality, prior to non-linguistic reality. McKeon characterizes this first reality thus: "What we do and what we say are not mere channels to reality but the specifications and embodiments of the real. We treat facts when we act and speak, and the analysis of action and language is the analysis of what is and of what it is" ("Flight" 229). Insofar as language is part of the world, its grounding is part of the ontology of the world, an unalterable component of the world, potentially if not actually insofar as its actuality anywhere demonstrates that it is a potentially that can become an actuality somewhere if not everywhere.

The "middle" part of the narrative of the linguistic turn establishes the Burkean sense of the empirical as the object to be explained. The "final" part finds the ultimate priority that interrelates words and deeds to explain why language is prior to what language is about.

The Middle

The advance from the beginning to the middle of the linguistic turn evidences itself most clearly when language becomes the object of empirical observation in Burke's sense. Examples of linguistic behavior becoming the focus of empirical observation appear in Wittgenstein and Quine. The Wittgenstein example is notable because it marks the turn from the early to the later Wittgenstein. But the Quine example is more important for our purposes for reasons we will turn to shortly.

Wittgenstein's *Philosophical Investigations* begins with Wittgenstein presenting Augustine's commonsensical view that words are names for things. Then, section #2 presents an anecdote introduced as an illustration of Augustine's view: "Let us imagine a language for which the description given by Augustine is right. The language is meant to serve for communication between a builder A and an assistant B." This language is limited to four words: "block," "pillar," "slab," and "beam." This anecdote will remain the main focus for the next twenty sections. It is consistent with Augustine insofar as it consists of names conceived as posterior to non-linguistic things, but empirical attention is paid mainly to the use of these words in communications between builder and assistant, not to the relation of the names to the empirically viewed things.

While Wittgenstein's turn to communications is important, his main concern continues to be antiphilosophy, as Goldfarb shows convincingly in "I Want You to Bring Me a Slab: Remarks on the Opening Sections of the *Philosophical Investigations*," an essay Diamond applauds for its demonstration of "the misconceptions that accompany the beginnings of our philosophizing" (*Realistic Spirit* 37n10). Goldfarb shrewdly uncovers the philosophizing aspirations of Wittgenstein's implicit interlocutor by showing how even the simple language in the communications between builder and assistant defeats what Goldfarb considers attempts to philosophize language.

Goldfarb's main illustration is Wittgenstein's extensive consideration of "Slab" and "Bring me a slab" in hypothetical communications between builder A and assistant B. Insofar as the longer "Bring me a slab" explains the elliptical "Slab" more than the latter explains the former, "the interlocutor concludes that the shorter sentence depends on the longer one," a conclusion that amounts to "an inchoate conception of 'full sense,'" a conception on the way to "a philosophical picture of the essence of language" (275). But as Goldfarb shows, Wittgenstein rejects such privileging of one over the other.

Quine's turn to the Burkean empirical appears in his theory of translation. Quine calls his theory "*radical* translation, i.e., translation of the language of a hitherto untouched people." Here, translation occurs between two languages that do not share any linguistic and cultural conditions, so that all the linguist doing the translation "has to go on are the forces that he sees impinging on the native's surfaces and the observable behavior, vocal and otherwise, of the native" (*Word* 28). In "radical" translation, then, intercultural traditions are absent, leaving translator and native speaker sharing nothing beyond a mixture of positivist and Burkean empiricals, which exist in dramatic tension in

Quine's theory. In the end, the theory resolves the tension in favor of the Burkean empirical.

This drama occupies most of "The Middle," the remainder of which takes two additional steps. First, a brief section presents a decisive theoretical step that Donald Davidson takes beyond the positivist empirical, one that Quine verges on taking but in the end does not take because, while he subordinates the positivist to the Burkean empirical, he cannot bring himself to discard the positivist empirical altogether. Second, Quine is shown to exemplify the philosophical exemptionalism mentioned in chapter one.

The importance of the empirical to Quine, even in this shift to the Burkean empirical, signals that he is as committed as the logical positivists to philosophy's cooperation with science. His differences with logical positivism center in the conception of language he thinks one needs to understand this cooperation. This complication in language that requires careful conceptualization appears in one of his favorite examples of radical translation, a thought experiment wherein the appearance in a natural setting of a small, furry creature prompts the response "gavagai" in the native speaker of the language being translated and "rabbit" in the language of the linguist doing the translating. In a manner consistent with Saussure, Quine cautions against yielding to the temptation to equate "gavagai" to "rabbit," that is, to see them as alternative positive terms for the same thing.

> For, consider "gavagai." Who knows but what the objects to which this term applies are not rabbits after all, but mere stages, or brief temporal segments, of rabbits? . . . Or perhaps the objects to which "gavagai" applies are all and sundry undetached parts of rabbits. . . . When from the sameness of stimulus meanings of "Gavagai" and "Rabbit" the linguist leaps to the conclusion that a gavagai is a whole enduring rabbit, he is just taking for granted that the native is enough like us to have a brief general term for rabbits and no brief general term for rabbit stages or parts. (*Word* 51–52; for other discussions of this example, see *Word* 29–46, 71–72; "Meaning" 464–65; "Speaking" 1–6; "Ontological Relativity" 30–35, 39, 40, 45, 47–48)

Different languages, in other words, consist of different differences. Analogously, a translator for whom Gross and Levitt's language is foreign might respond to the stimulus that prompts their "it is raining" with "rainever," a term for a time of year, the rainy season, rather than for the happenstance event of rainfall on a particular day.

This example presents the core drama in Quine's theorizing. On one side, language is posterior to the sensory empirical stimulus to which native speaker and translator respond. On the other side, language is prior in the different languages informing the responses "gavagai" and "rabbit," of native and translator, the difference that impedes simply equating "rabbit" and "gavagai." In this drama, language as prior eventually outweighs language as posterior, prompting Quine to turn to pragmatism, away from positivist certainty that "sense" can be distinguished from "nonsense."

Quine uses this "gavagai" example so often that Ian Hacking jokes that Quine "dwell[s] on translation involving imaginary explorers encountering natives who live in jungles populated by fauna unknown to any real jungle, namely, rabbits" (*Social Construction* 45). While in one sense Hacking's joking probably registers a response to Quine's repetitiveness shared by others. Would not an occasional new example be more imaginative? In another sense it goes over the top insofar as it is unfair to Quine. First, Hacking gives no indication of why Quine would trouble himself with translation of the language of imaginary jungle peoples in the first place, even though Quine indicates explicitly that he takes this trouble because of what radical translation entails.[28] Second, while Quine does sometime speak of a "jungle linguist," or a "jungle-to-English" dictionary, the term "jungle" disappears in places, so that Quine may make a revision that Hacking ignores.[29] In any case, Quine is never concerned with the reality of a jungle language, only the reality of translating a language when one is limited to empirical observation of the native speaker of the language using words in concrete situations.

---

28. Perhaps it is significant that in "Ontological Relativity," a later text, Quine appears defensive when he characterizes his gavagai/rabbit example as "contrived" and "perverse" (35), even while continuing to use it as the linchpin of his argument; such characterizations do not appear in "Meaning and Translation," which I believe is where the example is first used. In this later text, he also uses new examples, albeit from French and Japanese, which depart from the rules of "radical" translation, the French example more so than the Japanese.

29. Evidence on this point may be inconclusive. A passage in *Word and Object* (29) follows closely a passage in "Meaning and Translation" (148), with change from "jungle linguist" to "linguist" being among the revisions. But "jungle linguist" and "jungle-to-English" appear elsewhere in *Word* (e.g., 32, 70).

As Hacking's response suggests, moreover, Quine's theorizing of translation is not incidental, appearing briefly and then gone for good, but a central feature of his work in multiple texts such as *Word and Object*, "Meaning and Translation," "Speaking of Objects," and "Ontological Relativity," the title essay of *Ontological Relativity and Other Essays*. These texts appear during roughly a ten-year period from the late 1950s to the late 1960s.

What does Quine's use of translation indicate about his view of language? Radical translation exhibits sharply contrasting linguistic responses to the same nonverbal stimulus. Crucially, moreover, the contrasting responses are not simple alternatives, two ways of saying the same thing. "Translation and Meaning," a long chapter in *Word and Object*, begins with Quine's promise, "In this chapter we shall consider how much of language can be made sense of in terms of its stimulus conditions [language as posterior], and what scope this leaves for empirically unconditioned variation in one's conceptual scheme [language as prior]" (26). One may ask whether this combination of posteriority and priority is possible, but it is best not to try to answer until seeing all that is at stake for Quine in this combination. Quine never quite rises to the level of the ultimate priority that appears in "The End" of the narrative of the history of the linguistic turn. But the ultimate priority in Quine's philosophy is centered on language and thus pointed in the direction of the final stage in this narrative.

Insofar as Quine views language in terms of this stimulus side, he continues logical positivism's view of language as posterior, but as we shall see, it becomes harder and harder in Quine's philosophizing to find immediate contact with nonlinguistic stimuli. With this stimulus side, Quine combines the notion of a "conceptual scheme." In the translator's scheme, the stimulus prompts "rabbit," conceived as "a whole enduring rabbit," whereas the same stimulus prompts "gavagai" in the native speaker, conceived not necessarily the same way but possibly in any of a number of different ways. At this conceptual level, language is prior rather than posterior insofar as it conceptualizes the stimulus and different schemes may conceptualize the same stimulus differently. It is at the level of different conceptualizations that one sees the priority of, as Quine puts it, "empirically unconditioned variation in one's conceptual scheme" (*Word* 26).

Quine's conceptual scheme is akin to Thomas Kuhn's paradigm. Paradigms are "models from which spring particular coherent traditions of scientific research," but these models differ because they are informed by different answers to fundamental questions that guide scientific research: "What are the fundamental entities of which the universe is composed? How do these interact with each other and with the senses? What questions may legitimately be asked of such entities and what techniques employed in seeking solutions?" Answers differ because "[a]n apparently arbitrary element, compounded of personal and historical accident, is always a formative ingredient of the beliefs espoused by a given scientific community at a given time" (10, 4–5, 4). Such an "arbitrary element" similarly informs the conceptual schemes of Quine's native speaker and translator, so that even though they respond to the same sensory stimulus, they respond to it through the lens of different conceptual schemes. Unlike logical positivism's division between sense and nonsense, Quine thus divides language into two interdependent levels, sensory and conceptual, of a holistic structure that registers, insofar as it accords with Rorty's precepts, the beginnings of the reversal of logical positivism's commonsensical view of language. Sensory stimulus is no longer unmediated, as in the verification procedure, but is instead mediated through a conceptual scheme. The functional interrelationship between the conceptual and the sensory is where Quine looks for his ultimate priority, which is a step in the linguistic turn's philosophical turn from one ultimate priority to a new one.

This functional interrelationship, in Quine's view, informs science, as in this illustration:

> [T]he power of a nonverbal stimulus to elicit a given sentence commonly depends on earlier associations of sentences with sentences. And in fact it is cases of this kind that best illustrate how language transcends the confines of essentially phenomenalistic reporting. Thus someone mixes the contents of two test tubes, observes a green tint, and says "There was copper in it." Here the sentence is elicited by a nonverbal stimulus, but the stimulus depends for its efficacy upon an earlier network of associations of words with words; viz., one's learning of chemical theory. (*Word* 10–11)

"There was copper in it" thus combines response to the nonverbal stimuli of the green mixture with the conceptual scheme of chemical theory that predicts when green indicates the presence of copper. By contrast, the logical positivist is limited to the statement that the mixture of these contents is green. Ayer's sensory observation can verify the green color and Wittgenstein's analysis can unpack the determinate sense of the statement, but that is only part of the story from Quine's holistic standpoint. Sensory intuition, moreover, cannot comprehend this holistic structure. Comprehending it requires intellection.

That there was copper in the green test tube is a particular that exemplifies the functional interrelationship between sensory and conceptual levels of Quine's holistic structure of language. To show how something is "organized to function, its capacities and functionings and the interrelations among those capacities and functionings," as Putnam puts it in chapter two, is to identity the form that is comprehended by the mind, not seen by the eye. To examine closely Quine's analysis of the interrelationship between the two levels of his holistic structure is to watch Quine's intellectual comprehension of the form of this structure and the ultimate priority from which it derives.

From Quine's holistic standpoint, the logical positivist's focus on the individual statement to determine whether it is sense or nonsense, by the test of either verification or analysis, becomes in his seminal "Two Dogmas of Empiricism," a "dogma of reductionism . . . in the supposition that each statement, taken in isolation from its fellows, can admit of confirmation or infirmation," a dogma he rejects in favor of the view "that our statements about the external world face the tribunal of sense experience not individually but only as a corporate body" (41). The green color of the test tube mixture tests the conceptual scheme that predicts it. Merely one or two failures of prediction are likely to prompt not revision of the scheme but blame for the failure on "a mistake in observation or a result of unexplained interference" (*Word* 18–19). Only repeated failures force consideration of whether the scheme needs revising. Quine captures his view of how science progresses in a metaphoric narrative of a boat that one rebuilds plank by plank (revision by revision) while staying afloat (*Word* 3; see also "Identity" 78–79).

This departure from logical positivism, however, is not where Quine stops. While this departure takes a step beyond logical positivism toward the completion of the linguistic turn, it is a small step, one that a positivist might even be persuaded to join Quine in taking. Quine takes a much larger step, one that would shock a positivist, when in "Two Dogmas" he makes a pragmatic turn, insisting dramatically that empiricism itself is a conceptual scheme depending on physical objects as "posits comparable, epistemologically, to the gods of Homer" (44), preferable only because pragmatically more effective, at least so far: "The myth of physical objects is epistemologically superior to most in that it has proved more efficacious than other myths as a device for working a manageable structure into the flux of experience" (44; see also "Ontological Relativity" 34–35). This pragmatic turn is an indication that in the functional interrelationship in Quine's holistic structure, the conceptual dominates. Other indications of this dominance appear the more closely one examines Quine's philosophizing about language, both translation from language to language and language by itself. In both, he takes steps to magnify the importance of nonverbal stimuli, which is consistent with his commitment to the cooperation of philosophy and science. But this magnification, ironically, leads back to pragmatism as the ultimate priority that functions as arbiter, as in the choice of the "myth of physical objects" over Homer's gods.

"Meaning and Translation" initially appeared in a volume devoted to translation.[30] This essay includes methodological considerations of how a translator could put yes/no questions to a native informant to determine exactly which features of the furry creature prompt "gavagai" ("Meaning" 461; see also *Word* 29). If, for example, the rabbit that prompted "gavagai" was white, the translator could present a black rabbit to the native informant and ask, "gavagai?" A "yes" would eliminate white as a relevant factor; black or white, it is still "gavagai." Quine's analysis is even careful enough to suggest procedures whereby his translator could discriminate behavior, vocal or otherwise, that means "yes" from that that means "no" (*Word* 29–30). Here is a procedure for analysis of the Burkean empirical insofar as the aim is to determine not the empirical "out there," but the empirically observable words native speakers use in specific circumstances. One can imagine how a translator using these procedures could accumulate enough knowledge to predict what native speakers would say in any given circumstances. But this knowledge, Quine stresses, would be limited. "I have urged," Quine insists in "Speaking of Objects," "that we could know the necessary and sufficient stimulatory conditions of every possible act of utterance, in a foreign language, and still not know how to determine what objects the speakers of that language believe in" (11). In other words, the translator could use yes/no questions to know the "stimulatory conditions" of "gavagai"

---

30. *On Translation.* Edited by Reuben A. Brower, Harvard Studies in Comparative Literature 23, Harvard UP, 1959. 148-72. My quotations from "Meaning and Translation" are from a later reprinting.

well enough to be able to predict when "gavagai" will be uttered, without knowing exactly what "gavagai" conceptualizes.

Quine would, of course, not deny that a translator who was a bit of an anthropologist could also begin to unpack the native speaker's conceptual scheme. But for Quine that only leads to indeterminacy, or more precisely as we shall see shortly, greater indeterminacy. Analogies between conceptual schemes permit approximate translation of one into another, but Quine observes that "the analogies weaken as we move out toward the theoretical sentences, farthest from observation," fostering an illusion of a shared subject matter beyond the level of nonverbal stimuli, where what is shared is real ("Meaning" 477). Quine terms attempts to map one system onto another "analytical hypotheses," concluding that "rival systems of analytical hypotheses can conform to all speech dispositions within each of the languages concerned and yet dictate, in countless cases, utterly disparate translations . . . translations each of which would be excluded by the other system of translation" (*Word* 73). Translation is indeterminate. "Meaning and Translation" concludes, "What is really involved is difficulty or indeterminacy of correlation. It is just that there is less basis of comparison—less sense in saying what is good translation and what is bad—the farther we get away from sentences with visibly direct conditioning to nonverbal stimuli and the farther we get off home ground" (478).

Another suggestive perspective on the indeterminacy of translation appears in a comment on Chomsky's positing of "innate-structures" in the mind to explain language-learning. Quine agrees that such structures are needed to explain how "the child [gets] over this great hump that lies beyond ostension, or induction. If Chomsky's anti-empiricism or anti-behaviorism says merely that conditioning is insufficient to explain language-learning, then the doctrine is of a piece with my doctrine of the indeterminacy of translation" ("Linguistics" 58). In other words, if languages were the result purely of empirical conditioning, they would tend to be similar insofar as empirical reality is pretty much the same everywhere. Indeterminacy evidences the incompatible conceptual schemes in different languages, schemes that can explain the empirical but cannot be grasped by solely by "ostension, or induction."

What exactly, then, is the evidence for "there was copper in it"? One could observe the mixture turning green and the scientist uttering "there was copper in it," correlating the two so that one could predict when this utterance would occur just as Quine's translator could predict when "gavagai" would occur, without knowing chemical theory, that is, the conceptual scheme conceptualizing the green mixture as evidence of copper. "Now if objective reference is so inaccessible to observation," Quine asks in "Speaking of Objects," "who is to say on empirical grounds that belief in objects of one or another description is right or wrong? How can there be empirical evidence against existence statements?" (11). What is the evidence for the existence of copper, of rabbits, of gavagai? Quine answers, "If we then go on to assign the sentence some import in point of existence of objects, by arbitrary projection [of a conceptual scheme] in the case of the heathen language or as a matter of course in the case of our own [conceptual scheme], thereupon what has already been counting as empirical evidence comes to count as empirical evidence for or against the existence of the objects" (11). In other words, the stimulus conditions prompting "gavagai" and "rabbit" can also settle what counts as evidence for the associated conceptualized objects. Translation at this nonverbal stimulus level is less indeterminate than at the levels that move away from this one, but it is still indeterminate.

In the case of the example of "gavagai" and "rabbit," then, Quine's view means that one nonverbal stimulus can count as evidence for different objects in different conceptual schemes, that is, different ontologies, since for Quine "[o]ne's ontology is basic to the conceptual scheme by which he interprets all experiences, even the most commonplace ones" ("On What" 10). On the one hand, then, "gavagai" and "rabbit" are elevated in the functional interrelation between nonverbal stimuli and conceptual scheme because they exhibit, as quoted above, "visibly direct conditioning to nonverbal stimuli." But on the other hand, "visibly direct conditioning to nonverbal stimuli" can count as evidence for different conceptual schemes." The best nonverbal evidence one can get can support different conceptual schemes.

In other words, the best evidence supports the pragmatic turn because it does not dictate the choice of conceptual scheme. Pragmatic testing is the ultimate arbiter. Insofar as Quine relies on pragmatic tests, he is close to Rorty's view of knowledge not "as a matter of getting reality right, but rather as a matter of acquiring habits of action for coping with reality" (*Objectivity* 1). For Quine, translation elevates the importance of nonverbal stimuli, but this elevation, in turn, ends up reinforcing his pragmatic turn.

Indeterminacy of translation thus edges on the tyranny of the new insofar as it leads Quine to an open-ended view of ontology. There is no single ontology, only ontologies, "cultural posits" such as empirical objects and Homer's gods. One may prefer one to another, but only for pragmatic reasons comparable to reasons for preferring one set of conventions over another.

Quine begins *Word and Object* with the claim that what we know ultimately results from the effects that physical things "induce at our sensory surfaces" (1). Again, nonverbal stimuli are elevated in their functional interrelationship with the conceptual, elevated in a way that reminds one of Williams's "empiricist metaphysic," discussed in chapter two. But this elevation also turns out to be more apparent than real. The difficulty is that sensory experience by itself is too transitory and chaotic so that we need language, learned under "conspicuously intersubjective circumstances" (1), to bring things into focus: "Linguistically, and hence conceptually, the things in sharpest focus are the things that are public enough to be talked of publicly, common and conspicuous enough to be talked of often, and near enough to sense to be quickly identified and learned by name; it is to these that words apply first and foremost" (1). The intersubjectivity Quine sees in language is equivalent to earlier references to "usage" (Colebrook) and "standards of correct use" (Dummett). This intersubjective emphasis on usage informs Quine's critique of the second of the dogmas he overturns in "Two Dogmas," namely, as we saw in Ayer, the exempting of "analytic propositions or tautologies" from the demand for verification on the grounds that they exemplify "truths of formal logic and mathematics." One of Quine's arguments in his critique is that a tautology such as "No bachelor is married" is based on usage: if the lexicographer "glosses 'bachelor' as 'unmarried man' it is because of this belief that there is a relation of synonymy between those forms, implicit in general or preferred usage prior to his own work" (24). A change in usage could dissolve the tautology, which calls into question Ayer's view of what tautology exemplifies.

The more closely Quine attends to the nonverbal, the more he ends up subordinating it to the linguistic. "A visual stimulation," for example, "is perhaps best identified, for present purposes, with the pattern of chromatic irradiation of the eye," yet looking "deep into the subject's head would be inappropriate even if feasible, for we want to keep clear of idiosyncratic neural routings or private history of habit formation. We are after his socially inculcated linguistic usage, hence his responses to conditions normally subject to social assessment" (*Word* 31). Surely "neural routings" are involved in the physiological causal connections that would appear to lead Quine to seeing sensory experience as the avenue to knowledge, yet these are dismissed as idiosyncratic (because a bit different every time they occur?) and habitual (because while repetitious relative to individuals, habits may vary from individual to individual?). The "linguistic usage" trumps the physiological.

However much the physiological level would appear to be essential for an observer to see empirical reality unencumbered by language and thus be in a position to judge whether a statement of this reality is "supervised" by it adequately, Quine rejects this level in favor of a level in which the observer observes though the lens of language intersubjectively created, that is, through the lens of linguistic usage in the pragmatic domain of the tyranny of the new. In Quine's view, two men, one with normal color vision and the other color-blind, have different neural routings but, nonetheless, "both men are pretty good about attributing 'red' to just the red things" (*Word* 8). Quine sums up his view with a metaphor that privileges intersubjective usage over physiological processes: "Different persons growing up in the same language are like different bushes trimmed and trained to take the shape of identical elephants. The anatomical details of twigs and branches will fulfill the elephantine form differently from bush to bush, but the overall outward results are alike" (*Word* 8). In "Epistemology Naturalized," Quine contrasts the "meager input" on the physiological level to the "torrential output" on the intersubjectively formed language one learns in one's culture (83).

Such formulations make it harder to see the nonverbal stimulus supposedly shared by the native who says "gavagai" and the translator who says "rabbit," for the stimulus would seem to be transformed by the differing intersubjective usages of these words.[31] Quine concedes that usage

---

31. Going into more technical detail, one would want to clarify that Quine's use of the notion of meaning presupposes his analysis in "On What There Is" wherein "meaning," conceived as an abstract entity that exists in some sense, is dismissed in favor of "meaningfulness," conceived as a mode of behavior (11; see also "Speaking" 14, *Word* 33). Meaningfulness manifests itself behaviorally in (1) saying "red" (verbal behavior) in response to sensory stimulus of red ("those distinctive photochemical effects which are wrought in one's retina by the impact of red light" [*Word* 6]) or (2) saying "yes" (intersubjective verbal behavior) confirming someone else's verbalization "red." Early in "On What There Is," before this distinction between meaning and meaningfulness, Quine also disassociates meaning from objects of reference, using the example of the mythological Pegasus to argue that equating meaning to a referential object would require finding a referential object for the word "Pegasus" to give the

can transform even color: "Color words are notoriously ill matched between remote languages, because of differences in customary grouping of shades" (*Word* 41). How would this impact "green" evidencing "copper"? White questions whether Quine is altogether clear on how the sensory retains enough independence to legitimate his reliance on the test of predictability (*Toward Reunion* 274).

Quine's theorizing of language, on the level of conceptual scheme, is in accord with Rorty's precepts. "We can improve our conceptual scheme, our philosophy," in Quine's view, "but we cannot detach ourselves from it and compare it objectively with an unconceptualized reality," so that (1) "it is meaningless . . . to inquire into the absolute correctness of a conceptual scheme as a mirror of reality" while (2) it is meaningful to test a conceptual scheme by a "pragmatic standard" of "efficacy in communication and in prediction" ("Identity" 79; see also "Two Dogmas" 46). In other words, on the level of conceptual scheme, we cannot stand outside language to compare the nonlinguistic with the linguistic to see if the latter subjects itself to the "supervision" of the former. But given Quine's view of the way the intersubjectivity of language mediates even our experience of nonlinguistic stimuli such as color, his holistic structure interrelating sensory and conceptual would appear to be in accord with Rorty's precepts. Quine's opening sentences in "Meaning and Translation" appear to stake out a position outside language: "Empirical meaning is what remains when, given discourse together with all its stimulatory conditions, we peel away the verbiage [to step outside language]. It is what the sentences of one language and their firm translations in a completely alien language have in common" (148). But the closer one looks at Quine's theorizing of the intersubjectivity of language, the harder it is to see how the last vestige of verbiage could ever be peeled away. In this intersubjectivity of language, there is the interplay of convention and novelty in the tyranny of the new.

---

word meaning, a search that ends in dead-end puzzles over "nonbeing" (1–2). "Pegasus is not" states a truth, yet if the meaning of "Pegasus" resides in an object of some sort, this object must exist for there to be the meaning, but its existence would seem to contradict this truth. Such puzzles disappear when meaning is dissociated from object. In sum, stimulus meaning resides in behavioral/verbal response to stimulus, which is sufficient for Quine's empirical purposes. "Observational" is a species of "occasional": "in behavioral terms, an occasion sentence may be said to be the more observational the more nearly its stimulus meanings for different speakers tend to coincide" (*Word* 43).

While Quine, whether he realizes it fully or not, may toll the bell for the death of the commonsensical view of language in the linguistic turn's turn from the priority of thought to the priority of language, it is arguable that Donald Davidson heard this death knell more clearly than did Quine himself. The putative distinctiveness of the sensory level, as Davidson explains in "Coherence Theory of Truth," "springs from the obvious thought: sensations are what connect the world and our beliefs, and they are candidates for justifiers because we often are aware of them," but that there is such a connection, he contends, "is just another belief" (142). In other words, Davidson sees no way to "draw the line between observation sentences and theoretical sentences" (149), precisely the line that distinguishes the two levels in Quine's holistic structure. Hearing the bell clearly, Davidson dissolves the distinction between Quine's two levels.

The full force of Davidson's seemingly offhanded "just another belief" is easy to miss. In the long empirical tradition that established itself in the seventeenth and eighteenth centuries, as we saw in Putnam's recounting in chapter two, the immediacy of sensory experience appeared to distinguish it sharply from the intellection of belief. Open your eyes and you see, uncover your ears and you hear, and so on, all automatic, intuitive, by contrast to the intellectual activity of weighing alternatives in deciding which to believe. This immediacy finds poetic expression in Wordsworth's "Expostulation and Reply":

> The eye—it cannot choose but see;
> We cannot bid the ear be still;
> Our bodies feel, where'er they be,
> Against or with our will.

This immediacy made sensations "candidates for justifiers," as Davidson puts it, and one might add that, judged by the standard of the empirical tradition's influence, they became very successful candidates indeed. Immediate experiences registered in "observation sentences" became the "justifiers" of "theoretical sentences" produced by the intellect. But the "obvious thought" that "sensations are what connect the world and our beliefs," Davidson suggests, is just that, a "thought," "just another belief," another product of intellection.

Instead of contrasting sensory experience to intellection, Davidson thus proposes that turning "sensations" into "justifiers" actually presupposes intellection. In "On the Very Idea of a Conceptual Scheme," Davidson overturns the "third dogma" of empiricism, insisting that

> any dualism of scheme and content, of organizing system and something waiting to be organized, cannot be made intelligible and defensible. It is itself a dogma of empiricism, the third dogma. The third, and perhaps the last, for if we give it up it is not clear that there is anything distinctive left to call empiricism. (189).

In the narrative of the linguistic turn, then, Davidson's rejection of any scheme/content dualism may be said to complete the displacement of logical positivism's empiricism in favor of the Burkean empirical that distinguishes the middle from the beginning of the linguistic turn.

When Quine remarks early in *Word and Object* that he will "ponder our talk of physical phenomena as a physical phenomenon" (5), he accentuates Bergmann's point that the linguistic turn foregrounds the sense in which language is a component of reality. Elsewhere, Quine adds, "I am not suggesting a dependence of being upon language. What is under consideration is not the ontological state of affairs, but the ontological commitments of a discourse. What there is does not in general depend on one's use of language, but what one says there is does" ("Logic" 103; see also "On Carnap's" 205). Being does not depend on language, but positivist empirical objects and Homer's gods depend equally on the discourses that claim they exist. Language and action, words and their use in making claims, thus becomes the portion of reality where Quine's ultimate priority is located.

Throughout the history of the linguistic turn, philosophical texts are about language, but there is a notable change when the attention of these texts shifts to the Burkean empirical. The analyses of Hutto and Ricketts discussed earlier identify difficulties the linguistic turn encountered in writing about language when it presupposed the commonsensical view of language. But these difficulties disappear in the "middle" of the narrative of the linguistic turn as texts appear, such as Quine's, that analyze language to show that it is omnipresent in the sense, as defined in Rorty's precepts, that one cannot step outside language to see directly whether the linguistic subjects itself adequately to the "supervision" of the nonlinguistic.

But as these earlier difficulties disappear, new ones emerge as the linguistic turn tries to complete the turn from the priority of thought to the priority of language. The texts Quine writes presuppose that the nature of language "supervises" his writing in these texts, because his texts claim to state the nature of language accurately. But while these texts claim to be "supervised" by language, they claim that language itself is not "supervised" by the nonlinguistic but instead is prior to the nonlinguistic, mediating access to it. Language is prior except in the case of the philosophical texts that subject themselves to the "supervision" of this priority and are thus posterior to it. Because of this difference in the relation of prior and posterior in the two cases, any text defending the commonsensical view of language is shown to be wrong because language is prior, ultimately prior, mediating access to the nonlinguistic, but the text showing this is itself posterior to language, the reality where Quine finds his ultimate priority. Quine accesses this reality directly, not indirectly through the mediation.

Perspectivism may clarify this difference between when direct access is and is not possible, particularly because it is a close analogy to writing. Quine's "conceptual schemes" have even been equated to "points of view from which individuals, cultures, or periods survey the passing scene" (Davidson, "On the Very Idea" 183). Even more, this perspectival ingredient in Quine's thought has been equated to Nietzsche's well-known perspectivism (West 251).

The notion of perspective is easy to understand, so easy that talk of perspective typically looks past the sense in which this talk is not itself a perspective. Reflecting on perspectives on a penny, Russell charts how multiple eyes seeing one side of the same penny see it perspectivally in multiple ways (*Our Knowledge* 98). Depending on the distance between eye and penny, the penny varies in size; depending on the angle from which the eye views the penny, the penny will appear somewhere on a spectrum ranging from circular to oblong. Flip the penny over, and repeat. But now focus on Russell. With his eyes, he cannot see simultaneously what all these eyes see from their varying perspectives. But by explaining the concept of perspective, he can explain these many perspectives, distinguishing for each what is seen and what is not seen. Explaining the characteristics of a perspective, one can infer from these characteristics what eyes will see depending on their relation to the penny. The explanation of the concept becomes the explainer of the multiplicity of perspectives. But this explained explainer is not itself a perspective.

To repeat, the thing to emphasize in this example is that Russell's explained explainer of perspectives is not itself a perspective. Similarly, Quine's conception of language explains how the speaker of "gavagai" and the speaker of "rabbit" articulate reality in different perspectives. Not itself a perspective, Quine's concept of language explains perspectives such as those in these two speakers.

The difference between Russell and Quine is a difference between eye and language. The eye is, like music, a universal language, so that Russell can easily imagine what each of multiple eyes can see and not see, whereas Quine cannot put himself as easily inside multiple perspectives. But his explained explainer can conceptualize the possibility of multiple conceptualizations of the world, distinct from one another, but all the same in their reality as linguistic existents.

Returning to the holistic "myth of physical objects," one needs to view it two ways. On the one hand, Quine is claiming that positivist empiricism is a mediated construct in which reality appears as physical objects. This "myth of physical objects" may be pragmatically more successful than any other mediation, but it is a mediation nonetheless, a perspective. On the other hand, there is no mediation in Quine's explanation of how a holistic structure, combining levels of conceptual scheme and words for nonverbal stimuli, is, to recall Putnam's paraphrase of Aristotle, "organized to function" as a mediation.

This holistic structure, like Russell's explained explainer, is Quine's ultimate priority, from which derives his explanation of the different instantiations of it in the speakers of "gavagai" and "rabbit." As his ultimate priority, it is the reality that Quine accesses directly, intuitively, like Williams's intuition of the order of priority in his "empiricist metaphysic." The different instantiations mediate access to the same furry creature, excluding in principle the possibility of one true access. By sharp contrast, there is one true, direct, non-sensory, intuitive access to the reality of Quine's ultimate priority.

Quine is exemptionalist in exempting himself from the rule he imposes on others when he rejects their claim to have direct access to reality, like the logical positivist's claim to have direct access to sensory reality, on the ground that this access is mediated, mediated by the "myth of physical objects" in the case of the logical positivist. Quine exempts himself from this rule when he claims direct access to the reality of his ultimate priority.

This exemptionalism becomes normative in the linguistic turn's theorizing about language as its history progresses: (1) philosophizing explains more and more how language is "organized to function," to repeat Putnam's phrase, as mediation (2) in philosophical texts claiming to have unmediated access to language to whose "supervision" they subject themselves.

This exemptionalism tends to go unnoticed, though Latour is an exception to this tendency insofar as criticizes those who are "simultaneously constructivist where nature is concerned and realist where society is concerned" (*We* 27). In other words, they access nature through a social constructive process but they access this process directly, without mediation.

Quine's holistic structure explains mediation, which in turn explains his pragmatism. Because there is no direct access to "out there," there is no way for what is "out there" to "supervise" one's choice of the "myth of physical objects" over Homer's gods. By contrast, Quine's holistic structure is not a pragmatic choice. Quine's grasp of it is unmediated, direct, though not immediate in the sense in which sensory intuition is immediate. Rather, it is Quine's intellectual intuition of how the interrelationship between the sensory and the conceptual is "organized to function" as mediation.

Prioritizing language, one ends up with a philosophy of mediation, a mode of skepticism. From the standpoint of the problem of ultimate priority, Quine's prioritizing of language establishes itself by denying direct access to both thought and thing. But this denial of direct access is based on Quine's direct access to his prioritized language.

What exemptionalism conceals is that philosophical turning changes the subject matter of philosophy. What remains the same is not the subject matter but direct access to the subject matter whatever it is, more precisely, direct access to the ultimate priority that grounds the inferential structure of a philosophy. This sameness in inferential structure is the focus in McKeon's philosophical semantics.

The denial of direct access has been the standard way that philosophies of mediation, based either on prioritizing thought or language, have prioritized themselves above the metaphysics that claims direct access to thing. Recognition of changes in the subject matter of philosophy corrects this denial that informs various truisms that derive from Kant's claim that the thing-in-itself is inaccessible, a claim that Kant himself does not hold to consistently, as we shall see at the end of chapter four.

McKeon corrects this denial implicitly by using the term "metaphysical" in reference to each of the three subject matters in the passage quoted near the end of chapter two. McKeon's use of this term signals direct access to reality, the reality of all three possible subject matters.

In sum, on the level of sameness, the unchanging, a philosophy accesses directly an ultimate priority in a subject matter. On the level of philosophical turning, the changing, ultimate priority poses the "set of problems" that need solution to complete the turn to the new subject matter. At this level of turning, ultimate priority corrects the mistaken assumption that subject matter of philosophy is unchanging.

That it is direct access that is unchanging, not subject matter, will be an important consideration in the final chapter. If the denial of direct access is unfounded by which mediating philosophies prioritize themselves over metaphysical direct access to thing, then what bearing might that have on answering the question of whether the evidence of the turns themselves is a basis for a preferential order among the turns?

The End

Charting inferential chains that follow from an ultimate priority requires two fundamental things of the priority. First, it must exist because the inferences based on it presuppose its existence; that "gavagai" and "rabbit" mediate the nonlinguistic differently, for example, presupposes that language is an existent with mediating capacity. The ultimate priority's distinctive characteristics authorize distinctive inferences. That is why one ultimate priority, authorizing inferential chains of one kind, can displace another one that authorized different inferential chains. McKeon envisions different existents authorizing different inferential chains in different historical periods. Second, it must be possible to state this existence directly, not indirectly through a mediation, to explain how it is "organized to function."

Davidson's rejection of the "dualism of scheme and content" marks the turn from the "middle" to the "end" of the turn from the priority of thought to the priority of language. What is "out there" remains antecedent to language in one sense, for it would be an extreme linguistic idealism to claim that language creates the world, as in Gross and Levitt's satiric implication that Latour sees the words "it is raining" creating the rainfall. But the focus on language in the Burkean empirical led to the theoretical consensus, as exemplified in Quine, that language, while it does not literally make what is "out there," does in some sense construct it in mediating access to it. This priority poses the philosophical question of what exactly it is in language that is the ultimate priority that endows language with this constructive, mediating power. To identify this "what" is to identify that which becomes the ultimate priority in linguistic turn.

Glimpsing without quite articulating the relation of antiphilosophy to the rhetoricizing of philosophy, Colin Koopman observes,

> A methodological focus on linguistic usage promises to fulfill the first positive desideratum insofar as it provides [A] a field of philosophical reflection that refers purely to our linguistic practices of justifying our beliefs to one another with reasons. This dispenses with [B] the old foundational need for an appeal to super-linguistic realities or idealities which our sociolinguistic justifications are answerable to. (71)

[B] is what antiphilosophy rejects. [A] is rhetoric, although Koopman does not use the term and may not see it for what it is. But Koopman does glimpse the interdependence of the two, though he appears to see the turn to [A] as dispensing with [B], whereas it is [B], beginning with Wittgenstein's *Tractatus*, that cleared the way for [A]. Furthermore, "focus on linguistic usage" is descriptive rather than explanatory because it does not identify the "what," that is, the priority that produces the explanation of why "linguistic usage" becomes the "focus."

Explaining this interdependence also fulfills chapter-two's promise to explain McKeon's identification of rhetoric as what the linguistic turn needs to turn to complete itself. At the core of this explanation is the "what" that produces the inferential chain that transforms putative antiphilosophy into a step on the road to the philosophizing of rhetoric. One irony in the history of the linguistic turn is that this interdependence has tended to be inhibitory rather than revelatory insofar as antiphilosophers have tended to see themselves erasing philosophy when they were actually rhetoricizing philosophy. This tendency will be examined in this section, "The End," in Rorty first, then in Derrida.

This tendency proves to be stronger in Rorty than Derrida. Rorty comes close to identifying the linguistic turn's ultimate priority, but does not, as we shall see, get beyond the descriptive "*languages* are made rather than found," introduced in *Contingency, Irony, and Solidarity* (7), to the explanation of why this is the case. Failing this fundamental job of philosophy, Rorty sees himself in his later work drifting away from philosophy to considerations of culture in general.

Derrida surpasses Rorty. He insists that he is a philosopher first and foremost, despite his deconstruction of "*logocentrism*," philosophy's paradigmatic model because of its privileging of "presence." His penetrating analysis of the priority of language in his deconstructive demonstration that "presence" is posterior rather than prior takes him to the edge of the linguistic turn's ultimate priority. The key is Derrida's uncovering the linguistic priority of invention, essential to the tyranny of the new. He identifies this moment of invention with a cluster of terms that includes "rhetoric." This cluster might be considered metaphorically as the bridge from antiphilosophy to rhetoric.

Characteristics of rhetoric are abundant in Rorty's work, the term "rhetoric" even sometimes appearing honorifically (*Contingency* 53), albeit in passing rather than at center stage as in McKeon. But Rorty's commitment to antiphilosophy above all else, which in his work takes the form of antifoundationalism, inhibits his philosophizing. This inhibition is similar to one that appears in Jacques Bouveresse's "Reading Rorty: Pragmatism and Its Consequences." Bouveresse thinks that Rorty, despite his reservations about Derrida, is too "charitable" toward Derrida, explaining that he never understood how Derrida "could claim to have escaped onto-theological metaphysics," while at the same time claiming that *différance* is, in Derrida's words, "the common root of all conceptual oppositions that mark our language, such as, to take only a few examples, sensible/intelligible, intuition/signification, nature/culture, etc." (134, quoting Derrida, *Positions* 9). For Bouveresse, and for Rorty too, any antifoundational escape from "onto-theological metaphysics" cannot at the same time be a foundation of "all conceptual oppositions." In other words, the inhibition Rorty and Bouveresse share arises from a binary opposition between foundational and antifoundational that is absolutely pure, excluding any sense in which the antifoundational can clear the way, as Koopman suggests, to a grounding of "all conceptual oppositions" in a rhetoricized philosophy, which is what *différance* actually does.

Rorty's antifoundationalism appears in *Philosophy and the Mirror of Nature*, published in 1979, a book that helped to popularize antifoundationalism. In this book, Rorty depicts himself extending the "holism and pragmatism" that he sees Quine sharing with Sellars and Wittgenstein

(10). This extending continues in the later *Contingency, Irony, and Solidarity*, where attention to language increases, evidently because during the decade between these books Rorty came to "think of Donald Davidson's work as deepening and extending the lines of thought traced by Sellars and Quine" (*Objectivity* 1).

Rorty characterizes the foundationalist as one who wants to get "beyond argument to compulsion from the object known, to a situation in which argument would be not just silly but impossible, for anyone gripped by the object in the required way will be *unable* to doubt or see an alternative. To reach that point is to reach the foundations of knowledge." Rorty adds that foundationalism is thus "a desire for constraint—a desire to find 'foundations' to which one might cling, frameworks beyond which one must not stray, objects which impose themselves, representations which cannot be gainsaid" (*Philosophy Mirror* 159, 315).

Rorty's language—"objects which impose themselves," "gripped," "compulsion"—appears to presuppose the positivist empirical. In recounting the empirical tradition, Rorty depicts Locke as playing a crucial role in conceptualizing knowledge "as a relation between persons and objects rather than persons and propositions," adding that Locke gravitates toward a purely mechanical causality in which the mind "is something like a wax tablet upon which objects make *impressions*" (*Philosophy Mirror* 142), akin presumably to Wordsworth's "The eye—it cannot choose but see." Rorty seems similarly to propose such mechanical causality in his language of "compulsion."

He insists, moreover, that Kant's account is equally causal: "It may seem shocking to call Kant's account 'causal,' but the notion of 'transcendental constitution' is entirely parasitical on the Descartes-Locke notion of the mechanics of inner space, and Kant's self-deceptive use of 'ground' rather than 'cause' should not be permitted to obscure this point" (*Philosophy Mirror* 151n31). The "neo-Kantian consensus," Rorty concludes, "thus appears as the end-product of an original wish to substitute *confrontation* for *conversation* as the determinant of our belief" (*Philosophy Mirror* 163). It is the object whose representation "cannot be gainsaid" that is confrontational, foundational, appearing "with some unimaginable sort of immediacy which would make discourse and description superfluous" (*Philosophy Mirror* 375).

For Rorty, then, the term "representation" in his text references words that are thought to be posterior to nonlinguistic "objects which impose themselves," such that one is "gripped" by them, so that a representation of them "cannot be gainsaid." In the later *Contingency*, he cites "Red wins" and "Black wins" at a roulette table as seeming to confirm that "some nonlinguistic state of the world . . . 'makes a belief true' by 'corresponding' to it'" (5).[32] Positivist concentration on such isolated propositions is what Quine calls, as we saw earlier, the "dogma of reductionism." Like Quine, Rorty insists that one must instead view "vocabularies as wholes," explaining, "When the notion of 'description of the world' is moved from the level of criterion-governed sentences within language games to language games as wholes, games which we do not choose between by reference to criteria, the idea that the world decides which descriptions are true can no longer be given a clear sense. . . . [T]he fact that Newton's vocabulary lets us predict the world more easily than Aristotle's does not mean that the world speaks Newtonian" (*Contingency* 5–6).

Rorty proposes an antifoundational alternative akin to the view he finds in Sellars, namely, that "knowledge is inseparable from a social practice—the practice of justifying one's assertions to one's fellow-humans. It is not presupposed by this practice, but comes into being along with it" ("Introduction" 4). Similarly, Rorty observes that "we can think of knowledge as a relation to propositions, and thus of justification as a relation between the propositions in question and other propositions from which the former may be inferred" (*Philosophy Mirror* 159).[33] Conceiving knowledge thus, Rorty continues, "[W]e will see no need to end the potentially infinite regress of propositions-brought-forward-in-de-

---

32. Rorty's point is clear even though his roulette table example is not purely nonlinguistic. Colors are nonlinguistic, explainable in terms of physics and physiology, but when they are capable of "winning," they are part of a language game.

33. In "The Absence of Rhetorical Theory in Richard Rorty's Linguistic Pragmatism," Robert Danisch sees Rorty arriving at "the precipice of rhetorical theory" when he valorizes "an ability to 'utter sentences with the intention of justifying the utterance of other sentences'" (161, quoting *Philosophy and the Mirror of Nature*, p. 182). But Danisch contends that Rorty does not get past this precipice to rhetorical theorizing of "the language arts [as] a vehicle for acts of citizenship, public deliberation, and the improvement of sociopolitical conditions" (158). Leaving aside whether this contention is accurate, I think Danisch's view of rhetoric is too constricted. When Rorty is at this "precipice," he is already in a rhetoricized philosophy, even though he never manages actually to rhetoricize philosophy himself insofar as his antipathy to "foundations" keeps him from ever recognizing the ultimate priority from which the rhetoricizing of philosophy follows.

fense-of-other-propositions. It would be foolish to keep conversation on the subject going once everyone, or the majority, or the wise, are satisfied, but of course we *can*" (159).

One sign of the rhetoricity of this "conversation" appears in the determination that it pauses when "the majority, or the wise, are satisfied," an indication that a McKeonist "object of attention," introduced in chapter two, has formed rhetorically. But the conversation may resume at any time—"of course we *can*"—leading to the rhetorical formation of a new "object." No such object can foreclose the possibility of its displacement by a future object, precisely because such objects depend on the variability of human attention and belief. In the rhetoricizing of philosophy, the tyranny of the new is impregnable.

It is worth noting, if only in passing, that rhetoric's tyranny of the new evidences itself in a notable form of critique that Rorty devises. This tyranny appears in the reason Rorty gives for saying Proust succeeds where Hegel, Nietzsche, and Heidegger's fail. The latter three challenged this tyrant in their efforts to be the "last philosopher," that is, to produce something that could not displaced, could not "become an element in anybody else's beautiful pattern, one more little thing," whereas Proust accepted this tyrant's rule, "content to think that he might serve as an element in other people's beautiful patterns. It pleased him to think that he might play for some successor the role which one of his own precursors—say, Balzac or Saint-Simon—had played for him" (*Contingency* 106). Later, Rorty congratulates Derrida for matching Proust's success (*Contingency* 137); elsewhere, he adds that Derrida's "great theme is the impossibility of closure" ("Deconstruction" 8).

Writing in the context of the subject matter of the linguistic turn, Rorty writes words about words, where words are the Burkean empirical, a transformation of the empirical Rorty notes in commenting on a sense in which language is empirical ("Feminism" 218). Rorty's contrast between foundational and anti-foundational appears to presuppose, then, a contrast between the sensory (positivist empirical) and the nonsensory (Burkean empirical). There is a sensory component to language, of course, but it is secondary. Comprehending language involves a kind of reverse engineering that needs to go beyond the sensory to something akin to the intellectual intuition that the heyday of the empirical tradition discredited. Davidson, as we saw, discredits the sensory, depicting its putative power to connect us to the world as a belief, that is, a form of intellectual intuition. Rorty reaffirms Davidson's discrediting of "the distinction between scheme and content" ("Derrida Philosophical Tradition" 331). The difference between sensory experience and intellection, then, may inform the difference Rorty sees between foundational and antifoundational. The sensory eye may be "gripped" (foundational, positivism) but not the mind's eye (antifoundational). The rhetoricizing of philosophy occurs on the level of the mind's eye, but that does not make the ultimate priority from which it derives any less foundational.

Rorty fleshes out his antifoundationalism in additional detail later in *Philosophy and the Mirror of Nature* when he rewrites Thomas Kuhn's distinction in *The Structure of Scientific Revolutions* between "normal" and "revolutionary" science as a distinction between "normal" and "abnormal" discourse. Normal discourse "is conducted within an agreed-upon set of conventions," whereas abnormal discourse sets reigning conventions aside, producing sometimes empty "nonsense," at other times "intellectual revolution" that leads to a new normal discourse (320). In Rorty's first essay on Derrida, published in 1977, he depicts Derrida as an "abnormal" philosopher ("Derrida Language" 679–81). Seven years later, he singles out Derrida's "différance" as a term that had by then become so familiar that any "literary theorist" displaying ignorance of it "would be out on his ear" ("Deconstruction" 18), presumably a sign that Derrida's discourse was now "normal."

This interplay of normal and abnormal, Rorty proposes, occurs within "*conversation* as the ultimate context within which knowledge is to be understood" (*Philosophy Mirror* 389)—ultimate context, but not ultimate priority. In this conversation, rhetoric is embodied as an existent, just as it is in Burke's image of history as an "unending conversation" (*Philosophy* 110), not an existent that is a fixed object, but one that undergoes continual change in forming McKeonist "object of attention" after "object of attention." "To see keeping a conversation going as a sufficient aim of philosophy, to see wisdom as consisting in the ability to sustain a conversation" Rorty proposes, "is to see human beings as generators of new descriptions" (*Philosophy Mirror* 378).

Importantly, like predecessors in the history of the linguistic turn, Rorty sees language as an existent, a reality, "a fairly small portion of reality" (*Philosophy Mirror* 261), but it is a reality nonetheless, one that he considers "as natural as the beaver's teeth" ("Response McDowell" 123), presumably because it is as pragmatically essential to humans as extraordinary strong teeth are to beavers. This linguistic reality is that to whose "supervision" Rorty's philosophical texts subject themselves.

This linguistic reality poses problems that distinguish the linguistic turn as a distinctive philosophical epoch. As we saw early in this chapter, Rorty follows McKeon in seeing philosophy in different historical periods posing "different sets of problems." Rorty, however, tends to see the linguistic turn as dismissing problems wholesale, whereas it would be more McKeonist to be cautious enough consider the extent to which new problems may be transformations of old ones, no less new for being transformations, but nonetheless revelatory and accurate to see as transformations.

Notable among the problems Rorty dismisses is the erasure of the distinction between reality and appearance. He proposes that "the distinction between the past and the future can substitute for all the old philosophical distinctions—the ones which Derrideans call 'the binary oppositions of Western metaphysics.' The most important of these oppositions is that between reality and appearance. Others include the distinctions between the unconditioned and the conditioned, the absolute and the relative, and the properly moral as opposed to the merely prudent" (*Philosophy Social* 24). Dismissal of the reality/appearance distinction occurs repeatedly (*Philosophy Social Hope* 47, "Remarks" 14, "Response Critchley" 43). Rorty notwithstanding, his centering of his philosophizing on the portion of reality that is language transforms this "most important" distinction instead of erasing it, as seen particularly in *Contingency, Irony, and Solidarity*, where a transformation of this distinction appears in plain sight as Rorty's representation that "cannot be gainsaid," even though Rorty thinks he erases it.

In this book, words about words appear notably in Rorty's representation of language with the statement "*languages* are made rather than found" (7). To explain this thesis, Rorty contrasts "correspondence" and "redescription." Correspondence is to the foundational as redescription is to the antifoundational. The difference between correspondence and redescription appears in Rorty's commentary on Galileo. The "positivist sees Galileo as making a discovery—finally coming up with the words which were needed to fit the world properly, words Aristotle missed" (*Contingency* 19). In the correspondence model, the words that "fit the world properly" are "found" not "made." Aristotle did not find them; Galileo did. By contrast, "the Davidsonian sees him [Galileo] as having hit upon a tool which happened to work better for certain purposes than any previous tool. Once we found out what could be done with a Galilean vocabulary, nobody was much interested in doing the things which used to be done . . . with an Aristotelian vocabulary" (19).

Rorty presumably here sees himself substituting a distinction in time, Aristotle being Galileo's past, for the distinction between reality and appearance, but this obscures Rorty's fundamental point. For the positivist, reality is to appearance as Galileo is to Aristotle. That gets it wrong from the standpoint of the transformation of the appearance/reality distinction that Rorty produces but does not recognize. From the standpoint of Rorty's transformation, appearance is identified with the positivist for mistakenly seeing words as corresponding to nonlinguistic reality, "finding" rather than "making" reality. "Red wins" and "Black wins" appear to correspond to nonlinguistic reality but the reality is that they are words in a holistic language game that is a "redescription." Galileo's words are a "redescription" that replaces Aristotle's words, which themselves were a "redescription." The reality of language consists of "redescription" succeeding "redescription." Correspondence is appearance, whereas redescription is reality. Furthermore, because Rorty's text "fits" this reality of redescription, it does not make it but instead finds it.

In the linguistic turn, the distinction between reality and appearance is thus transformed, not erased. The distinction between past and future is a secondary effect of Rorty's fundamental reality, deriving from the fact that redescription follows redescription in time. In one of his earliest essays on Derrida, Rorty recognizes words about words in the form of texts commenting on other texts (*Consequences* 95–96). Commenting on this Rorty essay, David Couzens Hoy paraphrases Rorty as seeing "writing as not the attempt to represent properly the representational relation between language and the world, but simply as reinterpretive writing about writing."[34] Representation is exposed as appearance by the reality of redescription. This reality is the closure on the foundational level that guarantees the openness of the tyranny of the new.

"[L]*anguages* are made" is thus Rorty's ultimate priority. It is an ultimate priority both because it exists in the reality of redescription displacing redescription and because it inaugurates the inferential chain

---

34. Before its reprinting in *Consequences of Pragmatism*, this essay, "Philosophy as a Kind of Writing: An Essay on Derrida," appeared as one of a cluster of essays on "Literary Hermeneutics" in *New Literary History*, vol. 10, 1978, pp. 141-60. When *New Literary History* publishes such clusters, it typically asks someone to comment on all the essays in the cluster. In this case, it asked Hoy, whose comment on Rorty appears on p. 164 in his commentary "Hermeneutic Circularity, Indeterminacy, and Incommensurability," pp. 161–73.

that explains, for just one example, why Galileo's work is a redescription of Aristotle's, which is itself a redescription, and so on. Rorty's variant of the exemptionalism we saw in Quine's is concentrated in the double meaning of "*languages* are made": they mediate and they are real. Because "*languages* are made," they are "organized to function" as redescriptions, that is, as mediations, rather than as representations. But Rorty's language exempts itself from this rule because it represents the reality of "*languages* are made." Redescriptions mediate but Rorty's account of redescription succeeding redescription in the tyranny of the new is unmediated, a "representation" that "cannot be gainsaid" of the reality of his ultimate priority. Comprehending language intellectually, Rorty intuits that it functions as redescription rather than as representation. Redescription mediates, whereas this mediation is real. From the foundational reality of the ultimate priority of redescription, Rorty derives his "conversation," his "ultimate context."

Rather than recognize this philosophical foundation, even more, rather than inquire more deeply into this foundation to determine exactly why language is a making, an invention, Rorty depicts himself instead modifying his antifoundationalism by broadening it from language in particular to culture in general, moving from philosophy rather than inquiring into the ultimate priority of his philosophy. This broadening appears in characterizing redescription as rising up against an orthodoxy by "redescrib[ing] lots and lots of things in new ways, until you have created a pattern of linguistic behavior which will tempt the rising generation to adopt it. . . . [I]t works holistically and pragmatically." Modifying his initial use of his tool analogy, Rorty observes that whereas the maker of a new tool knows its purpose, the creation of a new vocabulary becomes "the creation of a new form of cultural life . . . [that] will have its utility only explained retrospectively" (*Contingency* 9, 55).

Seeing language in particular and culture in general thus intertwined, Rorty cites approvingly Davidson's erasure of the "boundary between knowing a language and knowing our way around in the world generally" when he writes "Twenty-Five Years After," a retrospective essay included in the 1992 edition of *The Linguistic Turn* (373, quoting Davidson, "Nice Derangement," 107). This erasure occurs because a redescription is a use of language that is or is not pragmatically successful in getting around in the world. Language is subject to this pragmatic test because it is in essence a making that may be useful rather than a finding that is the one true representation of a nonlinguistic reality.

Davidson's erasure marks the difference Rorty traces between his views in the 1960s and 1990s. In the 1960s, he viewed the problems of philosophy as problems of language, but he now thinks that the only truth there is in that view is antiphilosophy's rejection of foundationalism, that is, the "truth . . . that the particular problems *about representation* which philosophers have discussed were pseudo-problems, created by a bad description of human knowledge, one that turned out to be optional and replaceable." In the 1990s, by contrast, he no longer sees philosophy itself as "anything unified, continuous, or structured" (*Linguistic Turn* 372, 374). Perhaps the interdependence of antiphilosophy and the rhetoricizing of philosophy better explains the difference Rorty sees between his 1960s self and his 1990s self, but that he cannot quite recognize rhetoricized philosophy as philosophy with a structure, the tyranny of the new, ordered by an ultimate priority.

Finally, because "*languages* are made," they are contingencies. While the idea of contingency might have prompted a deeper exploration of Rorty's ultimate priority, it actually prompts some odd passages. Rorty speculates that "genuine novelty can, after all, occur in a world of blind, contingent, mechanical forces," where novelties occur such as "a cosmic ray scrambl[ing] the atoms in a DNA molecule, thus sending things off in the direction of the orchids or the anthropoids," where even seminal ideas found in Aristotle, Saint Paul, and Newton "for all we know, or should care . . . were the results of cosmic rays scrambling the fine structures of some crucial neurons in their respective brains" (*Contingency* 17). While these remarks are speculative, from the standpoint of "*languages* are made rather than found," one wonders if they are speculative findings or speculative redescriptive makings. Galileo's account of motion may be viewed as a redescription displacing Aristotle's redescription, but is this attribution of seminal ideas to "cosmic rays" a redescription of a previous redescription or a speculative representation?

In any case, Rorty sees contingency everywhere when he defines "'naturalism' as the view that *anything* might have been otherwise" (*Essays* 55). Does "*anything*" really mean anything, even contingency itself? Meillassoux, as we shall see in the next chapter, construes Rorty as saying even contingency is contingent, a view Meillassoux rejects in espousing "the necessity of contingency" as the subtitle of *After Finitude*. If even contingency is contingent, then it may give way to necessity at any moment. Contingency is forever only if it is itself necessary, the impregnable tyrant in the tyranny of the new. Meillassoux reaffirms this tyranny but finds it in the cosmos rather than in language.

Derrida has a prominent place in twentieth-century antiphilosophy even while insisting, "I maintain that I am a philosopher and that I want to remain a philosopher, and this philosophical responsibility is something that commands me," giving as his reason his recognition of the "necessity of posing transcendental questions in order not to be held within the fragility of an incompetent empiricist discourse" ("Remarks" 81). While the linguistic turn begins on the positivistic empirical level and later moves to the Burkean empirical, Derrida takes it to a transcendental level beyond the empirical in general.

The basis of Derrida's antiphilosophy is an ultimate prioritizing of language that simultaneously rhetoricizes philosophy. Whether Derrida ever recognizes this simultaneity is not altogether clear, but as we shall see, he does theorize invention, which is fundamental in rhetoric's openness to the new. He also considers examples of invention in later essays such as "Declarations of Independence" and "Psyche: Inventions of the Other."[35]

Meanwhile, others did see what Derrida may see only belatedly. Newton Garver, for example, in his "Preface" to Derrida's *Speech and Phenomena*, begins with the novel idea that consideration of twentieth-century philosophy of language might be approached most profitably from the standpoint of the medieval trivium: grammar, logic, and rhetoric (ix). From this standpoint, Garver proposes, one can see that Derrida radically turns tradition upside down because he "regards logic as derivative from rhetorical considerations" (xxii). Garver offers a narrative of the twentieth-century's philosophizing of language that moves from logic to rhetoric. Habermas echoes Garver when he observes that "Derrida is particularly interested in standing the primacy of logic over rhetoric, canonized since Aristotle, on its head," adding that while there are protests to this canonization within the tradition, these are not recognized by Derrida (187). Marshall McLuhan found even more than a protest when in his dissertation research on Thomas Nashe he discovered that "the sixteenth century was nothing if not an age of rhetoric" after unexpectedly encountering "the wealth of rhetorical doctrines and the varied and self-conscious exemplification of those doctrines at every level of expression which the sixteenth century exhibits, not only in England,

---

35. For a consideration of Derrida's "Declarations of Independence" from the standpoint of Burke's theory of rhetoric, see Wess, *Kenneth Burke*, pp. 158–67.

but, perhaps, more fully in Italy, France, and Spain, and Germany [sic]" (5). Nonetheless, in Derrida's texts, the David of deconstruction takes on a Goliath of *logocentrism* who has enjoyed uninterrupted rule for over two millennia.

Rorty, by giving extensive, though sometimes unsympathetic, attention to Derrida, breaks ranks with most American philosophers. Joining others who contrast Derrida's focus on language in his early writings to his attention to broader social and political issues in later writings, Rorty sometimes favors the later Derrida over the earlier (e.g., *Contingency* 123–25; *Essays* 113n8, 128). Derrida, however, rejects this view, emphatically insisting that (1) "there never was in the 1980s or 1990s, as has sometimes been claimed, a *political turn* or *ethical turn* in 'deconstruction,' at least not as I experience [sic] it," then (2) adding the crucial theoretical point, "The thinking of the political has always been a thinking of différance and the thinking of différance always a thinking *of* the political, of the contour and limits of the political" (*Rogues* 39). This interdependence, as we shall see, is inseparable from the rhetoricizing of philosophy. Rorty himself, in a 1993 symposium, concedes, "I have, in the past, made too much of the difference between the earlier and later Derrida" ("Response Critchley" 41). (Note: *différance* is sometimes italicized, sometimes not; it also sometimes appears without the acute é. In quoting, I reproduce what appears in the source. Speaking in my own voice, I use the acute é and italics)

Rorty describes himself as returning to Derrida "over and over again, always unable to get a clear synoptic view of his intent, but always fascinated" (*Truth* 12–13). Perhaps his failure to get a "synoptic view" arises from his blind spot about "*différance*," second in renown only to "deconstruction" in the cluster of terms associated with Derrida. Rorty returns to *différance* repeatedly in varying contexts, usually to fault it but occasionally to find value in it.

Late in his career, Rorty points to *différance* as the reason for placing Derrida among those

> still convinced that there is something "out there" to be gotten right—something, for example, that Heidegger was trying to get right when he talked about the *die ontologische Differenz,* and that Derrida was still trying to get right when he talked about *différance.* They still believe in something like a fixed, ahistorical, framework of human existence that philosophers

should try to describe with greater accuracy. (*Philosophy Cultural Politics* 128–29)

This passage appears in the revised version of a 2003 paper included in *Philosophy as Cultural Politics*, published in 2007. Earlier, in a 1989 paper, Rorty was tentative. Defining transcendental argument as claiming that "something is a condition of the *possibility* of something else—a *noncausal* condition," he proposes as a hypothetical that Derrida "is just one more metaphysician" if he uses "transcendental arguments . . . to infer the existence of such quasi entities as 'différance," "trace," and "archi-writing" (*Essays* 112). Rorty's tentativeness in 1989 thus disappears in 2007.

Rorty's location of *différance* "out there" risks blurring the distinction that would reserve "out there" for the nonlinguistic, as for example Rorty appears to presuppose when he remarks, "Logocentrists believe that language sometimes accurately represents something nonlinguistic" (*Essays* 130). Rorty adds to this risk when he suggests *différance* is an "entity," albeit "quasi." *Différance* is thing-like, "out there," insofar as it is ahistorical, something humans must live with, not something they can alter, but it is not a pure thing, wholly apart from humans, like "the *absolute* outside of pre-critical thinkers" that Meillassoux invokes in calling for a return to the "*great outdoors*" (*After Finitude* 7). This "*absolute*" is "out there" in a sense in which *différance* is not.

Rorty evidently takes these risks because he both sees *différance* as foundational and associates foundations with "out there" and "entity." But while *différance* is foundational, it is foundational of the antifoundationalism of antiphilosophy. Derrida insists that "[i]t is not a being-present, however excellent, unique, principal, or transcendent one makes it. It commands nothing, rules over nothing, and nowhere does it exercise any authority" ("Differance" 153). But it commands nothing in two senses, one in the sense of antiphilosophy, the other in the sense of the rhetoricizing of philosophy in the tyranny of the new. *Différance* is like the well-known rabbit-duck image that appears to be a rabbit viewed one way and a duck viewed another way. Viewed one way, *différance* is antiphilosophy, and it is this view that dominates Derrida's pages. But viewed another way, it philosophizes rhetoric. This view can also be gleaned from Derrida's pages, but it is not foregrounded or possibly even fully recognized.

Differences between Rorty and Derrida are perhaps all traceable to their different views of language, differences that surface dramatically in

Rorty's response to Derrida's claim that *différance* is neither a word nor a concept. Reading this claim while looking at what looks like a word on Derrida's page, Rorty throws up his arms in dismay in one place, exclaiming that "Derrida sometimes goes in for word magic" (*Contingency* 124n6). In another place, he insists that Derrida's claim is "not true," amplifying, "The first time Derrida used that collocation of letters, it was, indeed, not a word, but only a misspelling. But around the third or fourth time he used it, it had *become* a word. All that it takes for a vocable or an inscription to become a word, after all, is a place in a language game. By now it is a very familiar word indeed"; then adding, "As to concepthood, we Wittgensteinian nominalists think that to have a concept is to be able to use a word. Any word that has a use automatically signifies a concept" (*Essays* 102–03).

It is easy to share Rorty's dismay, but Derrida's point is clear. A straightforward explanation appears in commentary on a passage in "Saussure where it interests us," as Derrida puts it in referencing Saussure's notion of language as a system of differences without positive terms ("Differance" 140, quoting Saussure 120). The clarification is that the "possibility" of concepts and words, as distinct from actual concepts and words, arises from the "play of differences" (140). "The difference that Saussure speaks about," Derrida concludes, "is neither itself a concept nor one word among others" (140).

Whereas Derrida thus sees two levels, one level of words and concepts, the other level being the transcendental level, beyond the empirical, that makes words and concepts possible, Rorty sees only the level of the Burkean empirical. What he means by "language game" in dismissing Derrida's claim is equivalent to what he means by "normal discourse" elsewhere. Both terms reference the level of speakers and hearers, where usage and convention govern, subject to the supreme rule of the tyranny of the new, which Rorty recognizes in effect, as we saw earlier in considering his critique of philosophers who purport to speak the final word instead of being content, like Proust, to accept displacement down the road. Rorty resists two levels because he resists transcendental argument.

Because of this resistance, Rorty does not grasp exactly what installs the tyranny of the new. What installs it is the ultimate priority of the linguistic turn. The closest Rorty comes to this priority is his claim that "*languages* are made," discussed earlier. In the reality of Rorty's argument, "*languages* are made" is the "something [that] is a condition of something else," this something else being the consequences of this condition that he traces in his analyses. He uses two levels in spite of himself, which perhaps partly explains why his "condition" is inadequate. What is the existent in language that explains why it is made, invented, not "supervised" by any existent external to language? The mere assertion that "*languages* are made" is not sufficient as an explained explainer because it is itself unexplained.

For Derrida, as Habermas observes, "Writing counts as the absolutely originary sign, abstracted from all pragmatic contexts of communication, independent of speaking and listening subjects" (178). As absolute origin, writing enthrones the tyrant who insures the reign of newness in pragmatic contexts of communication. Rorty sees only these pragmatic contexts, where words are existents in language games, where three or four uses of a new "vocable" (phonemes) or "inscription" (graphemes) are enough usage for it to "*become* a word." This becoming occurs in communication, the realm of rhetoric, where persuasion establishes conventional usage as in McKeonist "objects of attention." Rorty sees in the case of *différance*, prior to language games, only a misspelling not yet a word, leaving unaddressed the question of whether a misspelling presupposes a word. Rorty sees something prior to the game insofar it was not until the "third or fourth" use that *différance* became a word in a game, but dismisses this something, no doubt because of his suspicion of transcendental argument in general, not just the transcendental argument in *différance*.

Différance, Derrida's ultimate priority, is the condition of oppositions. As Derrida puts it: "the movement of *différance*, as that which produces different things, that which differentiates, is the common root of all the oppositional concepts that mark our language, such as, to take only a few examples, sensible/intelligible, intuition/signification, nature/culture, etc." (*Positions* 9). Indebted to Saussure's conception of "language as a system of differences without positive terms," Derrida outpaces Saussure in pursuing the consequences of this conception. Saussure claims that "*the linguistic sign is arbitrary*," explaining, "I mean that it is unmotivated, i.e. arbitrary in that it actually has no natural connection with the signified" (67, 69). Saussure's reasoning thus presupposes a reality that "supervises" an opposition between natural and arbitrary connections. Imagine, for example, a sunbather spending hours on a beach under a sunny sky, then subsequently sporting a deep tan. In this case, there is a "natural connection" between the sunny sky and the tan. Onomatopoeias are language's closest approximations to such connections, but as Saussure notes, these are only "conventional imitations" (69). "Sizzle" imitates the sound coming from the frying pan, but the connection between the sizzling frying pan and the word "sizzle" is not natural, like the sunbather's tan. "Sizzle" is arbitrary, like all linguistic signs, conventionalized by cultural rules of usage. Derrida explicitly revises Saussure by insisting that "the rupture of that 'natural attachment' puts in question the idea of naturalness" (*Grammatology* 46). For Derrida, in other words, *différance* invents Saussure's opposition: whereas Saussure presupposes an ontology consisting of natural and arbitrary components, *différance* invents the distinction between natural and arbitrary, this distinction becoming a mediating lens through which connections are classified as one or the other. This invention mediates access to what is "out there." There is no disputing that there is something "out there." The claim is that the only access to this something is through the mediating opposition.

Consequently, "[i]n marking out differance," Derrida observes in a summarizing overview, "everything is a matter of strategy and risk" ("Differance" 135). For example, the nature/nurture distinction, analogous to the nature/arbitrary distinction, is strategic, deployed for purposes that are political in the broad sense, thereby incidentally illustrating Derrida's point, quoted earlier, that *différance* is inherently political. Nature/nurture debates expose the strategies involved in defending different lines between the two and the risks of drawing it here rather than there. The point about "strategy and risk" is that distinctions are not subject to the "supervision" of an authoritative, self-evident reality, but are instead pragmatic strategies for living in an actual world. Derrida insists, as we shall see, that there is a sense in which he is concerned with truth, but it is a pragmatic truth posterior to invention.

It is in this "strategy and risk" that Rorty finds in *différance* a pragmatic ingredient that appeals to him. In his construal, "*Différance* is the name of the situation which the dialectical philosopher starts from—the wish to revolt against the eternalization and cosmologization of the present vocabulary by creating a new vocabulary which will not permit the old questions to be asked" (*Consequences* 103). This new vocabulary aspires to be a new "normal discourse" informed by a new "strategy" for coping with reality, one that carries distinctive risks. Rather than attend to the technicalities of *différance*, however, Rorty views *différance* merely as an "abbreviation" for the "familiar Peircean-Wittgensteinian anti-Cartesian thesis that meaning is a function of context, and that there is no theoretical barrier to an endless series of recontextualizations" (*Essays* 125). This "endless series" is the tyranny of the new, but Rorty looks past the distinctive way that *différance* installs this tyrant in a moment in which antiphilosophy and the rhetoricizing of philosophy coalesce.

In "Difference," Derrida adds that *différance* itself is a "matter of strategy and risk" as he proposes that "strategically" it is suited to treat "what is most characteristic of our 'epoch'" (135–36). But "strategy and risk" at this level differs from the "strategy and risk" at the level of an opposition like nature/nurture. This difference

becomes clear in the last part of this essay, where Derrida considers variants of difference in Nietzsche, Freud, Levinas, and, especially, Heidegger. Debate among variants is about the best formulation of how the tyrant of the new tyrannizes. In this debate, each formulation may be seen as involving the "strategy and risk" inherent in venturing a formulation. Derrida defends his formulation against these other candidates.

Différance combines difference and deferral ("Difference" 129). Derrida's reservations about difference by itself are explicit. Difference presupposes unity, "some organic unity, some primordial and homogeneous unity, that would eventually come to be divided up"; even worse, "Above all, formed on the verb 'to differentiate,' this word would annul the economic signification of detour, temporalizing delay, 'deferring'" ("Differance" 143). The combination of differ and defer is "organized to function" in a way that produces not only binary oppositions, but more importantly oppositions in which neither of the opposed terms is prior to the other. It is philosophy that hierarchizes these terms. But from the standpoint of the ultimate priority of *différance*, this hierarchizing is not "supervised" by nonlinguistic reality, as philosophy thinks, but is, instead, a linguistic invention that mediates access to nonlinguistic reality.

In Derrida's explanation of *différance*, deferral undergoes a transformation, appearing first in the commonsensical model of language that Derrida overturns, then reappearing later as a crucial part of the overturning. In this commonsensical model, defer appears in a form that mistakenly claims that language is posterior to what it is about. Derrida rehearses this claim thus: "Let us begin with the problem of signs and writing. . . . We ordinarily say that a sign is put in place of the thing itself, the present thing—'thing' holding here for the sense as well as the referent. . . . The sign would thus be a deferred presence" ("Differance" 138). This deferral is satirically cancelled at Swift's Academy of Lagado, where Gulliver observes "Sages" who dispense with words altogether and simply carry things, even at the cost of walking around weighed down with heavy loads of things in order, upon encountering anyone, to converse without the customary deferral of presence. In this commonsensical model, deferral occurs in a time that is continuous, designating the relation of one moment in time to another. It is assumed that the sign is "supervised" by the thing, temporarily standing in for the thing so that one will not have to walk around with a bag of things.

For Derrida, it is important to bear in mind, presence is a big tent, encompassing modes of thought as well as the things in Swift's satire. It encompasses "presence of the thing to sight as *eidos*, presence as substance/essence/existence [*ousia*], temporal presence as point [*stigmè*] of the now or of the moment [*nun*], the self-presence of the cogito, consciousness, subjectivity, the co-presence of the other and of the self, intersubjectivity as the intentional phenomenon of the ego, and so forth" (*Grammatology* 12: Derrida's brackets). Consciousness is particularly important in Derrida's early targeting of Husserl. Exploring this targeting carefully, Joshua Kates details how in *Speech and Phenomena* Derrida treats *différance* "at length for the first time" to critique the self-presence of consciousness in Husserl and to replace it with a "differential relation to self" (140). Similarly, Gasché pinpoints this relation as the condition of self-presence in Husserl (194). *Différance* thus inaugurates Derrida's variant of the turn from thought, the turn characteristic of the linguistic turn from its beginnings.

"Logocentrism" sees "the being of the entity as presence" (*Grammatology* 12). As such, "logocentrism" is the target of Derrida's antiphilosophy. Thomas Baldwin summarizes the standard view that "presence" presupposes "an account of objective knowledge on the foundation of some immediate intuitive relationship between a person and something else," that is, "the knowing subject is presented immediately with an object that is thereby understood for what it is. So the logocentric conception of presence is one according to which the possibility of objective knowledge is thought to be founded on the immediate cognitive presence of an object to a subject" (108–09).[36] This "immediate cogni-

---

36. It happens that Baldwin taught Derrida at Cambridge University in 1991, then in 1992, witnessed the "Derrida affair," in which, as he recounts, Cambridge awarded Derrida an honorary degree in the face of an "extraordinary public debate about Derrida's work in which several distinguished philosophers with no knowledge of Derrida's writings denounced him as an intellectual charlatan" (107).

tive presence," note, collapses Aristotle's distinction, discussed in chapter two, between what is better known to us [sensory immediacy] and what is better known in being [cognitive intellect]. The deferral that Derrida rejects, in other words, presupposes the collapse of Aristotle's distinction.

Derrida is exemptionalist in intellectually comprehending how differ and defer are "organized to function" in *différance*, thereby exempting himself from the rule he imposes on logocentrism in denying its claim to such intellectual comprehension on the ground that the presence that logocentrism thinks it accesses directly is actually a mediation produced by the operation of *différance*. In his deconstruction of logocentrism's claim that presence is immediate, Derrida shows that "presence is announced," as he puts it in the interviews collected in *Positions*, which Gasché calls Derrida's "most exhaustive account of the formal features of differance" (195). "What defers presence," explains Derrida in answering one question, "is the very basis on which presence is announced or desired in what represents it, its sign, its trace" (*Positions* 8). This deferral is key to binary oppositions in which each of the opposed terms is dependent on the other, so that neither term is prior to the other.

Producing opposed terms in which neither is prior to the other is how *différance* is "organized to function." The key to this organization appears is Derrida's seemingly gnomic formulation: "As a common root, *différance* is also the element of the *same* (to be distinguished from the identical) in which these oppositions are announced" (*Positions* 9). In the announcement, in other words, the terms are paradoxically different in one sense and the same in another. This paradox arises because these oppositions are not subject to the "supervision" of reality. They are inventions that mediate access to reality in the form of opposed terms in which neither is prior to the other because each is dependent on the other. In their mutual dependency they are the same, yet not identical because they are different in being opposites.

Precedent for this characteristic of *différance* appears in Aristotle's analysis of opposites in which there is no relation of priority of one term to the other: "opposites are always simultaneous by nature. . . . [F]or in all such cases the essential being is the same as a certain relation to something, so that it is impossible to understand the one term without the other, and accordingly in the definition of the one the other too must be embraced" (*Topics* 142a23–32). One can sense this mutual dependency is a simple opposition such as that between the terms "hot" and "cold," opposites that are the "same" insofar as each involves the other, yet not "identical" insofar as "hot" differs from "cold." Derrida explains *différance*, his explainer, thus:

> Differance is what makes the movement of signification possible only if each element that is said to be "present," appearing on the stage of presence [e.g., hot], is related to something other than itself but retains the mark of a past element and already lets itself be hollowed out by the mark of its relation to a future element. This trace relates no less to what is called the future than to what is called the past, and it constitutes what is called the present by this very relation to what it is not [e.g., not cold], to what it absolutely is not; that is, not even to a past or future considered as a modified present. ("Differance" 142–43)

Presence is not an antecedent reality with "supervising" authority, as logocentrism thinks, but is rather "constitute[d]," invented, "announced" in a temporal process. This process, however, is not a continuous time in which past and future are "modified present[s]" and deferral is a relation of one moment to another as in the deferral in the commonsensical view of language. As Gasché puts it in his precise analysis, "[D]ifferance as time points at an 'absolute past,' a past that is no longer a modification of a present, no longer a present-past, but a past to which, according to the logic of the archetrace, a present moment must refer in order to be what it is" (197).

Hot and cold are related in continuous time in the case of a body that is first cold, then warmed up and made hot, or vice versa. Here, hot and cold are "modifications of a present." But as meanings, "hot" and "cold" are simultaneous, not related in continuous time, but each referring to the other to mean what it means, "to be what it is." For Derrida, the meanings in discontinuous time mediate access to the realities in continuous time. The logocentric presence of hot is produced by the linguistic "hot" that is what it is by its simultaneous deferral of "cold." "The structure of 'presence,'" *Grammatology*'s translator sums up, "is thus constituted by difference and deferment" (Spivak xliii).

Introducing *différance* as combination of differ and defer, Derrida aligns differ with "nonidentity" and defer with "order of the *same*," so that together there is "*sameness* which is not identical" ("Differance" 129): "sameness" insofar as the meaning of "hot" is simultaneous with the meaning of "cold," "not identical" insofar as "hot" and "cold" are opposites. In sum, opposites that are the same are not in a hierarchical relationship in which one is prior to the other.

Derrida's "announced presence" is thus "never present in itself, in an adequate presence that would refer only to itself" ("Difference" 140). Hot never refers only to itself. Writing thus brings "announced presences" into existence. Deconstruction exposes logocentric "presence" as an appearance by showing the realities of the effects of *différance* that produce "announced presence." This exposure overturns the commonsensical model, enshrined in logocentrism, of writing as posterior to what it is about, that is, "supervised" by what it is about, replacing it with a model in which writing is prior.

Viewing philosophy through the lens of his theorizing of binary oppositions, Derrida sees philosophy hierarchizing binary oppositions, that is, hierarchizing what cannot be hierarchized, in what he calls the "metaphysical decision":

> Metaphysics, in its most traditional form reigns over the Austinian heritage.... Two indications bear witness to this: 1. The hierarchical axiology.... 2. The enterprise of returning "strategically," ideally, to an origin or to a "priority"... in order *then* to think in terms of derivation, complication, deterioration, accident, etc. All metaphysicians, from Plato to Rousseau, Descartes to Husserl, have proceeded in this way, conceiving good to be before evil, the positive before the negative, the pure before the impure, the simple before the complex, the essential before the accidental, the imitated before the imitation, etc. And this is not just *one* metaphysical gesture among others, it is *the* metaphysical exigency. (*Limited* 93)

In Austin's case, "hierarchical axiology" appears in the subordination of fiction to reality, as in the subordination of saying "I do" in a marriage ceremony performed on stage in a theatrical performance to saying "I do" in a marriage ceremony in real life. Such hierarchizing "decisions," Derrida stresses, may not be recognized as such: "The more confident, implicit, buried the metaphysical decision is, the more its order, and calm, reigns over methodological technicity" (*Limited* 93). But buried or not, such hierarchies are each an effect of a "metaphysical decision" informed by valuation (axiology) rather than "supervision" by hierarchical existences beyond language. Furthermore, each "decision" is posterior to the binary opposition it presupposes.

Derrida's tracing of hierarchies to axiological preference rather than foundational realities proved popular in a context of widespread interest in challenging hierarchies based on gender, race, class, colonialism, sexual orientation, and so on. But simply overturning a hierarchy fails to take into account that the meanings of the paired terms in Derrida's summary view of "the metaphysical decision" are simultaneously constituted in the operation of *différance*. Simply overturning a hierarchy replaces one with another.

An example of sensitivity to this issue appears in Dominic Head's joining of the concerns of ecocriticism and postcolonialism in an interpretation of J. M. Coetzee's *Life and Times of Michael K*. Michael K is the colonial subject, who frees himself to become the novel's center. In other words, a figure hierarchically subordinated achieves a hierarchical reversal. But Head adds a qualification in proposing that in Michael K "a new, provisional platform of judgment is installed in a qualified recentering" (28). This qualification bespeaks a Derridean influence. In the reversal of the hierarchy, the new center cannot simply become a center without qualification. That would be to substitute one hierarchy for another. To speak of a "provisional" center, however, is to risk trying to have your cake and eat it too. In other words, it is to risk having a center while trying to call it something else.

For Derrida, the reversal is only preparation for the second stage, which aims to displace both hierarchies as equally effects of *différance*, which precludes reference to extra-textual reality to justify preference for one hierarchy over the other. Each hierarchy "announces presence" but they do so in opposite ways. Derrida summarizes the deconstructive process thus:

> Very schematically: an opposition of metaphysical concepts (e.g., speech/writing, presence/absence, etc.) is never the confrontation of two terms, but a hierarchy and the order of a subordination. Deconstruction cannot be restricted or immediately pass to a neutralization: it must, through a double gesture, a double science, a double-writing—[sic] put into practice a *reversal* of the classical opposition *and* a general *displacement* of the system. (*Limited* 21)

Deconstruction thus returns one to the binary opposition produced by *différance* prior to the "metaphysical decision" that transforms the opposition into a hierarchy. Deconstruction is antiphilosophy in the sense that it takes up a philosophical text purporting to be subject to the "supervision" of a hierarchy fixed in thing (metaphysics) or thought (epistemology), then shows that this text actually results from a "metaphysical decision" that transforms a binary opposition, produced by *différance* in which neither term is prior to the other, into a hierarchical order. Deconstruction antiphilosophically transforms such hierarchized binary oppositions by returning them to their origins in *différance*, a "non-originary origin" (Biesecker 120).

In a 1988 interview, included in *Limited Inc*, Derrida corrects a number of what he considers mistaken views. One correction begins, "I have never 'put such concepts as truth, reference, and the stability of interpretive contexts radically into question' if 'putting radically into question' means contesting that there *are* and that there *should be* truth, reference, and stable contexts of interpretation" (150; Derrida quotes words from the interviewer's question). What he sees himself having actually done is different: "I have—but this is something entirely different—posed questions that I hope are radical concerning the possibility of these things, of these values, of these norms, of this stability (which by essence is always provisional and finite)" (150).

Derrida elaborates that by "possibility of these things" he means that in "pragmatically determined situations" one "must submit (in large measure: I will explain later this qualification, which may seem strange) to the norms of the context that requires one to prove, to demonstrate, to proceed correctly, to conform to the rules of language and to a great number of other social, ethical, political-institutional rules, etc." (*Limited Inc* 150–51). This promised "qualification" introduces the transcendent level that manifests itself in the difference between the unconditioned and the conditioned. A given context is conditioned and imposes rules to which one must "submit," but with the qualification "in large measure," because no context is final. One must "submit" to reigning norms, but such submission is "in large measure," not absolute, because there is always openness to the new that can lead to a new context with new norms.

What is unconditioned is that there must be a context, not that there must be any particular context:

> it [unconditionality] is independent of every context. . . . It announces itself as such only in the *opening* of context. Not that it is simply present (existent) elsewhere, outside of all context; rather it intervenes in the determination of context from its very

inception, and from an injunction, a law, a responsibility that transcends this or that determination of a given context. (*Limited Inc* 152)

The unconditioned is not an existent antecedent to all contexts. Its independence of every context resides not in an independent existence but in the "*opening* of context," not any context in particular but any context in general. The unconditioned, in other words, guarantees that no context is "supervised" by anything independent and prior to it, so that every context is a new thing, framed by a binary opposition that is an effect of *différance*, vulnerable to displacement by a later instance of *différance*. The context's hierarchizing of the binary is posterior to *différance*.

Transcendent, this unconditioned "*opening* of context" is the place of the invention of context, irreducible to "supervisory" antecedents, with a "frame" or "border" that "always entails a clause of nonclosure" (*Limited Inc* 152), because no context closes off openness to the possibility of a new context. The unconditioned enthrones the tyrant enforcing the tyranny of the new.

This "*opening* of context" is "the moment of strategies, of rhetorics, of ethics, and of politics" (*Limited Inc* 152), as Derrida puts it in almost recognizing that his antiphilosophy is actually a rhetoricizing of philosophy. The invention that occurs in this "*opening*" is rhetorical in the sense that it is not creation *ex nihlio*, but is rather invention, occasioned by multiple antecedent circumstances, including ethics and politics, but irreducible to them. This invention deploys antecedent discursive materials in new ways, transforming them to invent something that has no antecedent. In "Psyche: Inventions of the Other," Derrida observes, "An invention always presupposes some illegality, the breaking of an implicit contract; it inserts a disorder into the peaceful orderings of things, it disregards the proprieties" (25).

Antiphilosophy's *modus operandi* is critique, exposure of the mere provisionality of what a philosophy considered a foundational and permanent principle, without consideration that its account of provisionality in this critique is itself grounded in a foundational and permanent principle in the form of the tyrant in rhetoric's tyranny of the new that guarantees the rule of provisionality. Perhaps the closest Derrida comes to recognizing this tyrant, in effect rather than in actuality, occurs when he remarks that the foundational status of *différance* may be recognized only upon the condition of immediately putting it under erasure (*Grammatology* 23–24). Antiphilosophy requires the erasure, but the erasure deflects attention from antiphilosophy's rhetoricizing of philosophy. This practice of putting under erasure, which became common in the heyday of deconstruction, exemplifies McKeon's remark, "Yet the principles employed for these purposes [of critique] are seldom stated as clearly as the principles detected in assumptions about the nature of consequences which are shown to be erroneous or fallacious" ("Principles" 395). In short, the rhetoricizing of philosophy is ignored to spotlight antiphilosophy's critique.

Différance invents oppositions that frame englobing contexts in each of which there is "truth, reference, and the stability of interpretive contexts," but only provisionally. At the same time, *différance* does "supervise" the words in Derrida's text that represent what *différance* does, even what it is:

> *The (pure) trace is différance.* It does not depend on any sensible plenitude, audible or visible, phonic or graphic. It is, on the contrary, the condition of such a plenitude. Although it *does not exist*, although it is never a *being-present* outside of all plenitude, its possibility is by rights anterior to all that one calls sign (signified/signifier, content/expression, etc.) concept or operation [sic], motor or sensory. (*Grammatology* 62)

Moreover, *différance* is permanent, not provisional. It is the permanent tyrant in the tyranny of the new.

Différance's permanence, it should be noted, appears indirectly. Writing or, better, archi-writing, as theorized by *différance*, is prior to "any sensible plenitude, audible or visible." Archi-writing does not depend on the sounds of speech or the visible marks of writing, but they depend on it to stand out as speech rather than noise or as writing rather than random visible shapes. But the sensible plenitudes appear in the multitude of different languages, each embedded in a history that produced it. Archi-writing is the ultimate priority independent of history. When one speaks or writes, one is "always already" posterior to the *différance* that makes speaking and writing possible.

This "always already" exemplifies the claim that the linguistic turn can make in McKeon's cycle of turns to being prior to the subject matters of thing and thought. Philosophies in which the ultimate priority is found in thing or in thought necessarily appear in language. Hence, there is a specific sense in which that which makes language possible is that which makes these philosophies possible. This specific sense presupposes an ontological order that justifies the claim, quoted in chapter two's epigraph, that "words may be thought to be the sources and causes of what things, thoughts, and actions are thought to be, and therefore, are."

The issue of the linguistic turn's ultimate priority appears in McKeon's opposition, referenced earlier, between those "who propose to treat sequential statements as forms of action or to treat purposive courses of action as instances of verbal rules" ("Principles" 395). Burke views language as action, locating the tyrant in the tyranny of the new in the act in his pentad of act, agent, scene, agency, and purpose: "there could be *novelty* only if there were likewise a locus of motivation within the act itself, a newness not already present in elements classifiable under any of the other four headings" (*Grammar* 65). The act constitutes the rules, this constitutive operation theorized in "The Dialectic of Constitutions," in the third and last part of his *A Grammar of Motives*.[37] By contrast, for Derrida rules are "norms" put in place by the invention of a contextualizing philosophic opposition in accord with the rule of *différance*. *Différance* is the one thing not vulnerable to displacement. It is the tyrant, the rule of rules, the one rule that cannot be broken, the rule instantiated in the "strategy and risk" in the discursive action of proposing a new *différance*.

Descending from the level of ultimate priority common to all principles in McKeon's philosophical semantics, one finds, as noted in chapter two, distinctions among four principles. Three of these are based on assumptions about varying hierarchical relations among wholes and parts. The fourth, which McKeon calls "actional principles," refuses all such hierarchizing based on "the assumption that all distinctions are initially arbitrary" ("Philosophic Semantics" 211). This assumption is what *différance* presupposes in producing binary oppositions in which neither of the opposed terms is prior to the other.

The ontological arbitrariness of the word is not an idea invented by a human mind, but the discovery of a reality that is intelligible. Such a discovery occurs in Davidson's "A Nice Derangement of Epitaphs," a title inspired by Mrs. Malaprop's use of "epitaphs" for "epithets" (103).

---

37. For analyses of Burke's theoretical model, see Wess, (1) "Burke's 'Dialectic of Constitutions,'" and (2) *Kenneth Burke*, pp. 142–48. For a contrast between Austin's reliance on conventions such as those determining what counts as a marriage and Burke's reliance on a constitutional model that explains how conventions come to be, see Wess *Kenneth Burke*, pp. 139–42. In this sense, Burke's constitutional model is prior to Austin's performative model.

Davidson's study of malapropisms prompts his discovery of the arbitrariness at the heart of language: "There is no word or construction that cannot be converted to a new use by an ingenious or ignorant speaker" (100). This discovery is something Diamond also glimpses, as discussed earlier. What Davidson discovered in language, in other words, is traceable ultimately to the rhetorical tyranny of the new inherent in language. As Paul de Man puts it, "Rhetoric radically suspends logic and opens up vertiginous possibilities of referential aberration" (10),

Davidson's discovery prompts him to conclude with the half-truth "that there is no such thing as a language, not if a language is anything like what many philosophers and linguists have supposed," because the capacity for innovation inherent in language exhibited in malapropisms shows that there is no "clearly defined shared structure which language-users acquire and then apply to cases. . . . [W]e should give up the attempt to illuminate how we communicate by appeal to conventions" (107). The whole truth is that the arbitrary and the conventional are interdependent. Any novelty may become a convention and any convention began as a novelty.

McKeon, in this chapter's epigraph, identifies arbitrariness as the defining characteristic of language. Considered ontologically as a component of reality, a word is simultaneously an act and a rule. However much circumstances may call for a new word, they do not cause it. A new word is an invention, an act. At the same time, however much a word is an act, it is also a rule exemplified in the use of it by multiple agents in multiple circumstances to mean the same thing. One can say X means Y, but X can mean Y only if others agree. But such rules are conventions; any conventionalized word can become a new word at any time, as Davidson discovered. Communication depends on words both as acts and rules to produce a McKeonist "object of attention," just as "*différance*," a neologism, became a widespread "object of attention." As first noted in chapter one, McKeon joins language and action because one can treat equally "statements as forms of action" and "courses of action as instances of verbal rules." The ontological arbitrariness of words grounds the rhetoricizing of philosophy, the tyranny of the new.

4 Meillassoux: Metaphysical Turn as Chaotic Pragmatism

> [I]f we are in direct contact only with what we do and say and make, with language and with operations, we come ultimately to the problem of the relation of what we say or make—artifacts, institutions, sciences—to what we do not say or make.
>
> —McKeon, *Thought, Action, and Passion*, p. 186

As suggested in chapter one, the emergent metaphysical turn, based on evidence in the work of Meillassoux and Harman, may repeat the linguistic turn's decades-long search for its ultimate priority. For this new turn, like the linguistic turn, may be getting off to a slow start. Just as in its beginnings the linguistic turn drew on ingredients of what it was turning from in retaining, as quoted in chapter three, "Kant's picture of philosophy as providing a permanent ahistorical framework for inquiry in the form of a theory of knowledge," Meillassoux and Harman draw on ingredients from the linguistic turn as will appear intermittently in this chapter and the next. They transform these ingredients just as the linguistic turn transformed Kant. But in both cases, a tie to what is turned from remains to be overcome. That took decades in the case of the linguistic turn.

As also noted in chapter one, Meillassoux contributed notably to this emergence by identifying in the term "correlationism" a common antagonist for philosophies otherwise divided, thereby turning disparate philosophers into participants in a philosophical movement. Meillassoux defines this term in chapter one of his influential *After Finitude*, "[T]he central notion of modern philosophy since Kant seems to be that of *correlation*. By 'correlation' we mean the idea according to which we only ever have access to the correlation between thinking and being, and never to either term considered apart from the other." Because of correlationism, he goes on, "[C]ontemporary philosophers have lost the *great outdoors*, the *absolute* outside of pre-critical thinkers: that outside which was not relative to us . . . existing in itself regardless of whether we are thinking of it or not" (5, 7; italics in quotations are in the text's quoted unless otherwise noted). While Meillassoux uses the phrase "*great outdoors*" without any evident ecological concerns, it captures ecophilosophical interest in a return to realism, albeit a realism, as we shall see at the end of this book's final chapter, that may need to affirm his "*absolute* outside" in one sense while departing from it in another.

In McKeonist terms, this "*great outdoors*" is a variant of the subject matter of thing. Meillassoux's project aims to turn philosophy to thing from correlationism, which makes thought primary in limiting access to what is beyond thought to that which is mediated through thought. Meillassoux refers to correlational mediation as a "wall" and breaking through it as an "aperture" in the wall (*After Finitude* 63, 64), a metaphor that proves to be apt. Meillassoux goes beyond correlationism from within correlationism, like carving out an aperture to escape from an enclosed space, a move not everyone applauds, as we shall see, because it paradoxically seems to depend on correlationism to get beyond correlationism. This dependency helps to explain why Meillassoux turns from thought rather than language and action; more on this later.

No doubt because of the explosive influence of *After Finitude*'s critique of correlationism, commentary on Meillassoux has tended to focus mainly if not exclusively on this critique, even though Meillassoux stresses that *After Finitude* is a part of "a forthcoming work in which we hope to develop the theoretical positions that we are merely sketching here, as well as their ethical consequences: *L'inexistence divine. Essai sur le dieu virtual* [*Divine Inexistence: An Essay on the Virtual God*]" (*After Finitude* 132n15; Meillassoux's brackets). Seconding Meillassoux, Alain Badiou, in the Preface he writes for *After Finitude*, calls the book a "fragment" of a larger philosophical "enterprise" (vi).[38] Harman reports that *Divine*

---

38. Badiou's praise for Meillassoux's project in his Preface to *After Finitude* matches his supportive comments in *Logics of Worlds* (119, 512, 564). What Badiou and Meillassoux say about each other, Harman declares, "contain almost limitless stakes for both" (*Quentin* 112). The relation between the two is well worth detailed study. While the most widely known connection between them is no doubt their shared interest in mathematics, Meillassoux's *The Number and the Siren: A Decipherment of Mallarmé's "Coup de dés"* (2012) signals another shared interest as well as a point of difference. Regarding this difference, Meillassoux recounts receiving a letter from Badiou that defines it succinctly: Meillassoux "believes in a necessity of contingency," whereas Badiou "upholds a contingency of necessity" (Interview Harman 218). Meillassoux points to this difference in "Badiou and Mallarmé: The Event and the Perhaps," while also

Inexistence may expand to three volumes, which adds to the evidence of its importance to Meillassoux (*Quentin* 140).

An additional reason commentary has tended to focus on *After Finitude* alone rather than on it and *Divine Inexistence* together is that the two works appear to go in opposite directions. On the one hand, chapter two of *After Finitude* argues that insofar as philosophy has limited rational thought to that which is found within the contours of the correlation of subject and object, it not only has left itself no basis to criticize irrational thought that wanders freely beyond these contours, but also has arguably even thereby unintentionally encouraged such thought. On the other hand, *Divine Inexistence*, by admonishing us to believe in "*God because he does not exist*" (Harman translation 238), would seem to qualify as precisely the kind of irrational thought that *After Finitude* discourages.

A book that goes in the opposite direction is Christopher Watkins's *Difficult Atheism: Post-Theological Thinking in Alain Badiou, Jean-Luc Nancy, and Quentin Meillassoux*. Watkins offers an extensive analysis of *Divine Inexistence*, while correlationism gets relatively little attention on a handful of pages.

Nonetheless, asking whether *After Finitude* and *Divine Inexistence* relate to one another coherently is essential to evaluating and understanding Meillassoux. Consideration of the two works together is hindered, of course, by *Divine Inexistence* being a work in progress. Beginning as Meillassoux's 1997 doctoral thesis, it has to date appeared only in a few translated fragments, Graham Harman's and Nathan Brown's. But themes from *Divine Inexistence* also appear in a number of articles. The available material is no substitute for a completed work, but it is considerable enough to inquire into the sense in which *After Finitude* is a "fragment" of what Meillassoux's larger "enterprise" is up to philosophically. Harman remarks that "despite the term 'fragment,' the pages of *After Finitude* are nowhere to be found within those of *Divine Inexistence*" so that "it would be better to describe both works as fragments of a longer philosophical trajectory" (*Quentin* 139). That may be the case, but connections between the two are discernible. Some are even obvious.

---

recounting Badiou's decades-long interest in Mallarmé, possibly the source of his own interest in him (35). This essay considers the "contingency [event] of necessity [truth]" evident in Badiou when he alludes to Mallarmé's *Coup de dés*, then crosses out the crucial "perhaps" near this poem's end: "perhaps" must go because "there are truths" (*Logics* 4). But not for Meillassoux, whose defense of "perhaps" exemplifies his "necessity of contingency."

Consequently, rather than treat *After Finitude* as more or less a stand-alone book, the present chapter will consider it in the context of *Divine Inexistence*, ending rather than beginning with Meillassoux's critique of correlationism. *Divine Inexistence* moves comprehensively from theory to practice, while *After Finitude*, as Meillassoux puts it, is "merely sketching" some "theoretical positions" in need of more development. Consideration of *Divine Inexistence* enables one to see that Meillassoux's project is what this chapter calls "Chaotic Pragmatism." Seeing his critique of correlationism in this broader context reveals what is at stake in it for Meillassoux's project.

Metaphysics, Speculation, Speculative Materialism

The characteristic of thing, as exemplified in Meillassoux's *"great outdoors,"* is its independence of the human. *Différance* is thing-like insofar as it is a linguistic operation that humans cannot alter the way that they can change the meaning of a word. In this sense, it is independent of the human. But it is nonetheless an impure thing insofar as it is activated through human activity. It may, Derrida suggests, have an origin prior to the human ("And Say" 135), which would increase its independence, but whether that would increase it to the level of the *"great outdoors"* remains unclear. In any case, its thing-likeness is what enables it to operate as an ultimate priority. That it operates through human activity contributes to the inferences following from it, distinguishing them from the inferences following from the ultimate priorities in other philosophical subject matters. The possibility of such thing-likeness is the reason that McKeon argues "for a broader use of the term 'things' to include things we say and things we seek as well as the things we know" ("Being" 254–55). The ultimate priorities in the subject matters of thing, thought, and language are distinct because of the differences in these subject matters. But each functions as a thing in being the foundation in reality of an inferential structure, thereby making the term "metaphysical" applicable to each, as we saw earlier.

The metaphysical turn finds its ultimate priority in thing in the purest sense. In initiating this turn, Meillassoux depicts himself, in his 2012 Berlin lecture, swimming upstream against an entrenched tradition of anti-metaphysics: "My main concern . . . comes down to saying that thought is capable of the 'absolute,' capable even of producing something like 'eternal truths'; and this despite the various destructions and deconstructions that all traditional metaphysics have undergone over the last century and a half" ("Iteration" 1).[39] Commenting on this proclamation, Harman remarks, "By this stage no one will be fooled by the scare quotes, since we know Meillassoux *literally maintains* that his philosophy can deduce absolute eternal truths. This is what makes his philosophy both so refreshing and so appealing a target for critical engagement" (*Quentin* 98). In *Divine Inexistence*, Meillassoux affirms that the "project of metaphysics ought to be restored in its legitimacy" (Harman translation 280).

At other times, however, Meillassoux rejects metaphysics in the name of speculation. All metaphysics is speculation, he explains, but speculation need not be metaphysical. Speculation includes all philosophies that "accord to thought the capacity to accede to an absolute" but in metaphysics this absolute is a necessary entity of some kind "constrain[ing] things to being thus rather than otherwise," whereas in speculation that is not metaphysical, the absolute "constrain[s] them to being able not to be how they are," that is, to being contingencies, capable of changing at any time for no reason ("Spectral Dilemma" 274–75; see also *After Finitude* 34, "Immanence" 445–46). In *After Finitude*, Meillassoux even conflates metaphysics with ideology, charging that both are equally guilty of "the illusory manufacturing of necessary entities. . . . [T]his God, this world, this history, and ultimately this actually existing political regime necessarily exists and must be the way it is" (34; see also "Potentiality" 227). It should be noted that the awkward expression "constrain[s] them to being able not to be how they are" appears more

---

39. "Berlin lecture" has become shorthand for Meillassoux's actual title, "Iteration, Reiteration, Repetition: A Speculative Analysis of the Meaningless Sign." Harman reports that this lecture was part of a series, spread out over a few months, designed to repeat in a different form the 2007 Speculative Realism workshop by having Brassier, Grant, Harman, and Meillassoux lecture in Berlin on different dates, with the addition of a fifth, Marin Häaglund (*Quentin* 97–98). Harman adds that Meillassoux did not want his lecture to go beyond the lecture room because it is incomplete, as the text makes clear. Nonetheless, the lecture was pirated and circulated, acquiring enough notoriety in the process to become known by its shorthand title. The difficulty in heeding Meillassoux's wish is that this Berlin lecture updates *After Finitude* in specific ways, including the addition of a new term, "subjectalism" (3), and a theorizing of language intended to demonstrate the capacity of mathematics to describe the world scientifically. Hence, while one hesitates to ignore Meillassoux's wish, if one ignores this lecture, one will leave out widely known updates.

concisely in *After Finitude*'s subtitle: *"An Essay on the Necessity of Contingency."* In embracing speculation, Meillassoux sometimes also identifies himself as a materialist, a speculative materialist. His materialism, however, does not presuppose any material entities such as atoms that typically underwrite materialism. Instead, his speculative materialism presupposes the possibility of thinking *"what there can be when there is no thought"* (*After Finitude* 121). This materialism, then, presupposes existents in a world in which thought does not exist, as depicted in "Ancestrality," *After Finitude*'s memorable first chapter, which includes reference to the earth before humans appeared.

While Meillassoux distinguishes speculation and metaphysics, he also finds "constraint" in both. Considering that the linguistic turn, in the course of its unfolding, discovered the need to find that which makes language prior, one might consider, if only tentatively, whether the ultimate priority of the metaphysical turn will be marked by its imposing constraint of some kind. Constraint is implicit, for example, in Harman's remark, to be considered in the next chapter, that he makes his basic distinction between real and sensual objects because "something in the world itself is requiring [him] to do that" ("Propositions" 51). In any case, Meillassoux sees in metaphysics and speculation both a difference and a similarity, so that while he prefers the term "speculation," he nonetheless sometimes uses the term "metaphysics" approvingly. This chapter prefers "metaphysics," seeing Meillassoux's speculation as a mode of metaphysics. His turn to thing a la speculation is a turn to contingency, the *"Necessity of Contingency."*

Historical Cycles

Like McKeon, Meillassoux sees a cycle in the history of philosophy, although his cycle consists of two turns, metaphysical turns to the *"great outdoors"* and skeptical turns from the *"great outdoors."* "Metaphysics and skepticism," he proposes, "are always like two enemies fighting against each other, but it is always in skepticism that we discover how to realize metaphysics. Montaigne's skepticism was the key to Descartes' new metaphysics, because it discovered a new way of thinking" ("Presentation" 437). Meillassoux does not elaborate, but Ann Hartle, in *Montaigne and the Origins of Modern Philosophy*, probably identifies at least part of what he has in mind when she describes Montaigne's *Essays* as presenting "a man who must achieve his own mind within the world of inherited opinion" (51). In any case, as we shall see, Meillassoux's Montaigne is Rorty.

This particular turn from Montaigne to Descartes, from McKeon's standpoint, is part of the turn from the priority of language in the rhetorical age of the Renaissance to the priority of thing in the metaphysics of the seventeenth century. As we saw in chapter two, McKeon sees the linguistic turn as another rhetorical age, an age that rhetoricizes philosophy. Meillassoux similarly analogizes the Renaissance to the twentieth century in analogizing Montaigne to twentieth-century postmodernity ("Immanence" 450).

While Meillassoux's looking to skepticism to find something to realize his metaphysics conforms to his view of the history of philosophy, this chapter suggests that it may prove as counterproductive as the linguistic turn's initial reliance on the commonsensical view of language as posterior proved to be. Most dramatically, as we shall see, by looking to skepticism to realize his metaphysics, Meillassoux may unwittingly embrace a new form of skepticism, one that may appear in "Ancestrality," though with rare exception this possibility goes unnoticed.

Before turning to *Divine Inexistence*, it is worth noting that Meillassoux adds refinements to his theorizing of correlationism that bring him closer to McKeon. He is farthest from McKeon when he treats correlationism as continuous from the eighteenth century to the present, as in this snapshot: "[E]ver since Kant to discover what divides rival philosophers is no longer to ask who has grasped the true nature of substantiality, but rather to ask who has grasped the more originary correlation: is it the thinker of the subject-object correlation, the noetico-noematic correlation, or the language-referent correlation?" (*After Finitude* 6, see also 121; "Presentation" 427). In this snapshot, Meillassoux collapses the distinction McKeon makes between the subject matter of thought and the subject matter of language and action. Meillassoux moves closer to McKeon when he acknowledges that philosophies in the twentieth century resisted correlationism: "Philosophies of the twentieth century, even when they tried to escape correlationism . . . denigrated realism, which was identified with naïve or dogmatic realism" ("Presentation" 434). Here, Meillassoux moves closer to McKeon by distinguishing a period of correlationism from a period that resists it while still continuing its antirealism. He thus distinguishes two periods without distinguishing the basis of the antirealism in each. Correlationism," Steven Shaviro summarizes, presupposes that "our very experience of the world can take place only under conditions of our own making" (6). But there is a difference between identifying these conditions with thought on the one hand or with language and action on the other. In yet another formulation, Meillassoux contrasts "two principal versions of correlationism: a transcendental one, which claims that there are some universal forms of the subjective knowledge of things, and the postmodern one, which denies the existence of any such subjective universality" ("Time" 1).

The real issue between Meillassoux and the linguistic turn centers on the relation between subject and object that defines correlationism. For Derrida, *différance* produces this relation. But Meillassoux cannot accept this demotion of correlationism to the level of posteriority because his critique of correlationism depends on correlationism. Interviewed by Harman, Meillassoux explains that he conceives the term "correlation" broadly to encompass any philosophy that insists upon an "uncircumventible correlation between a subjective pole and an objective pole, both understood in the broadest sense of the term" (213; see also "Time" 1). Meillassoux concedes that Derrida exemplifies a "sickened correlationism," but remains within correlationism nonetheless insofar as "it is always *for* a subject that there is an undecidable event or a failure of signification" (Interview Harman 215). This is debatable. Derrida insists, "The 'subject' of writing does not exist if we mean by that some sovereign solitude of the author" (*Writing* 226). Settling this debate, however, is less important here than simply noting Meillassoux's strategy for squeezing Derrida into the correlation of subject and object, while recognizing it is a tight ("sickened") squeeze.

The key point: because Meillassoux's critique of correlationism depends, as we shall see, on the agency of the subject of correlation, Meillassoux cannot fully recognize the sense in which the linguistic turn, in its culminating phase, goes beyond correlationism. Meillassoux turns against thought rather than language, notwithstanding his use of Rorty.

Throughout this history of correlationism, regardless of whether one sees it as one period or divides it into two, the "*great outdoors*" was assumed to be a whole containing humans with their capacities for thought and language. Only an idealism, such as the linguist idealism in the Gross and Levitt's satiric motif in chapter three, would claim that thought or language could constitute the whole of things. In this context, a standard form of argument became critique in which claims of unmediated access to the "*great outdoors*" were exposed as mediated, with the exposure giving a detailed account of the mediating operations, be they in thought or in language. As noted in chapter three, McKeon calls attention to the way that critiques of human faculties of thought could easily be redeployed as critiques of human language ("Philosophy of Communications" 312–13). Critiques could shift from one context to the other because of the extent to which the two contexts shared antirealist underlying assumptions. Such exposures were often characterized as demystification or negative hermeneutics.

Meillassoux aims to find the "aperture" in the "wall" of correlational mediations and thus to open a path to the *great outdoors*," thing in the purest sense. In this pure sense, thing is independent of human thought and language, while it still contains humans. What changes is that thought and language cease to be ultimate priorities that erect a mediating wall. In Meillassoux, as we shall see, this piercing is achieved through intellectual intuition. Piercing this wall, Meillassoux also rejects demystification, even though in *After Finitude*, in rejecting metaphysics, as we saw earlier, he seems to have in mind the familiar negative hermeneutics of ideology critique. But in *Divine Inexistence*, he dismisses the "mocking enterprise of demystification that only allows our species a few mediocre projects compared with what we are capable of envisaging. It is a sarcasm of humans toward humans, and thus a hatred of oneself" (Harman translation 283).[40]

WORLDS IN A NON-WHOLE WORLD

The term "contingency" marks the relation Meillassoux sees between himself and Rorty as he enacts what he sees as his variant of the cyclical turn from skepticism to metaphysics. In the passage marking this relationship, Meillassoux also uses a term closely related to "contingency," namely, "facticity."[41] If everything that exists is a contingent fact, something that is here today but may be gone tomorrow, then that universal cannot itself be a fact: "the facticity of everything cannot be thought as a fact" (*After Finitude* 79). "Contingency" and "facticity" are almost

---

40. Meillassoux's view on this point is anticipated in Burke's *Attitudes toward History*, where Burke offers a "comic corrective" to demystification in the form of debunking (166).

41. Harman makes a point of stressing that Meillassoux's use of the term "facticity" should not be confused with Heidegger's use of it to designate "the specific situation of humans in a world at any moment" (*Quentin* 21).

interchangeable terms: what exists are facts and facts are contingent, but facticity is not a fact and contingency is not contingent.

Meillassoux uses Rorty's variant of the linguistic turn's skeptical rejection of absolutes, which parallels the correlationist rejection of absolutes. Rorty's linguistic turn, in other words, becomes a stand-in for Kantian correlationism. Meillassoux ignores Rorty's view of language, "*languages* are made," which grounds Rorty's rejection. Instead, he insists that while one must applaud Rorty's rejection of absolutes, one must go beyond Rorty to recognize the sense in which his rejection depends on an absolute:

> using the Rortian tactic of saying that it is contingent: "Give me the reason why it should be a universal discourse, a universal truth, a universal reality—give me the reason. It's not possible to give a reason." . . . [C]ontemporary skepticism, the contemporary correlationism, shows us where to look for the absolute. You can pursue contingency, but you can't say that facticity is a fact. If you say facticity is a fact, that even contingency is contingent, what are you saying? ("Presentation" 437; see also "Time" 9, and *Divine Inexistence*, Brown translation 28–29)

Here, Meillassoux exemplifies his point that "what has been called 'the end of metaphysics' is the very condition of an authentic access to the absolute" ("Immanence" 445; see also 446–47). He depicts Rorty using contingency to skeptically challenge absolutes, thereby ending metaphysics. He then takes Rorty's contingency and absolutizes it to claim that the principle of contingency cannot itself be a contingency. He implies that this is the point that Rorty misses, that Rorty may think contingency itself is contingent. Meillassoux references no passage in Rorty to support his claim. But the last chapter did reference one that could do so, namely, Rorty's definition of "'naturalism' as the view that *anything* might have been otherwise." Meillassoux's claim in effect construes "*anything*" as including contingency itself.

Importantly, Meillassoux turns from skepticism to his own metaphysics first by identifying the contingency that Rorty deploys in his skepticism, then by identifying the point at which Rorty takes his skepticism one step too far. For if contingency is itself contingent, then contingency can disappear, displaced by necessity. Meillassoux's metaphysical turn absolutizes contingency in a Burkean "paradox of purity," or "paradox of the absolute" (*Grammar* 35).[42] Meillassoux makes contingency itself the one necessity, as in *After Finitude*'s subtitle: *An Essay on the Necessity of Contingency*.

While "contingency" becomes Meillassoux's dominant term, it is equivalent in a few texts to the term "advent *ex nihlio*." By this term, Meillassoux is not claiming that being arose from nothingness. Rather, he is pinpointing an "advent" or effect that is "*ex nihlio*" in the sense that it exceeds its cause, so that such an effect has "no reason at all for its advent, and hence nothing (no law) can limit it." This absence of limitation, moreover, ironically means "a world that is capable of everything ought *also* to be capable of not accomplishing those things of which it is capable" (*Divine Inexistence*, Harman translation 226, 227; see also "Potentiality" 226). Nothing happening proves the point as much as something happening, a line of argument Burke calls "Heads I Win, Tails You Lose" and suggests is more pervasive than one might think (*Attitudes* 260–63).

The principle of contingency informs a cosmos that Meillassoux describes as "an overturned Platonism": it "consists in taking the side of a purely intelligible chaos against the illusory fixity of the phenomenon" ("Contingency" 326; see also "Spectral" 273). This cosmos is structured in *Divine Inexistence* by means of a group of terms clustered around the term "world," which includes a distinction marked by the difference between lowercase "w" and capital "W." In this cluster, the basic distinction is between "world" and "World," with "Universe" sometimes synonymized with "World." Contingency governs the "non-Whole world" that contains "Worlds." As Meillassoux explains, "I reserve the term 'world' with a lowercase 'w' to designate the non-Whole of what is" (Harman translation 238). Within this "non-Whole world," a "World" can appear "suddenly. . . . [t]he *improbabilizable advent of a new constancy*" (Har-

---

42. Burke proceeds mainly by a broad range of examples to make his point, but he does offer a formula: "a transcending of one term [e.g., contingent existent] by its other [e.g., contingency qua universal], and for the reversed ambiguous derivation of one term from its ancestral principle" (*Grammar* 38). Paradoxes arise from the assimilation of a particular to the universal that encompasses it. For example, a particular escape assimilated to the universal idea of escape becomes caught forever in the transition from prison to escape: "For in freeing oneself *perpetually*, one would in a sense remain perpetually prisoner, since one would never have definitively escaped" (*Grammar* 36). Analogously, contingency appears in particulars that come and go, but assimilated to the universality of contingency, contingency is forever and thus necessary.

man translation 238). In this inverted Platonism, then, the "non-Whole world" beyond "Worlds" is chaotic, where one contingent "World" can displace another at any time for no reason; Meillassoux elaborates on the philosophical signification of this point in *After Finitude* when he denies the principle of sufficient reason (60). Contrastingly, a "World" contains phenomenal "constancy," chartable by science, fixed until displaced by another "World" with new "constancies." "Worlds" are instances of advent *ex nihlio*. They "have a right to a majestic capital letter . . . because there is more in a World than in the world, since there is more in what ensues than there is in the origin (more in the 'effect' than in the 'cause')" (Harman translation 238).

Divine Inexistence's "Worlds" recall the end of chapter one, where we saw McKeon, in the 1960s, envisioning a revolutionary turn to metaphysical problems of parts and wholes. Ordered relations between part and whole appear in the "constancy" of a "World." But "Worlds" are posterior to "non-Whole world," the priority of contingency that displaces one "World" for another. Analogously, Derrida's *différance* is prior to the binary oppositions that it invents and that the "metaphysical decisions" of philosophers turn into hierarchized orderings. From the standpoint of McKeon's philosophical semantics, as distinct from historical semantics, both Meillassoux and Derrida assume that distinctions, in Meillassoux's "Worlds" and in Derrida's "metaphysical decisions," are "initially arbitrary," an assumption characteristic of "[a]ctional principles" ("Philosophical Semantics" 211, 215). "Worlds" result from arbitrary contingencies; "metaphysical decisions" hierarchize arbitrary binary oppositions invented by *différance*. But from the standpoint of historical semantics, Meillassoux's "non-Whole world" and Derrida's *différance* are radically different, because they are in different subject matters, in the "*great outdoors*" where humans play no role (thing) and in binary oppositions where *différance* activates human discourse (words and acts).

Because a "World" exists in an "inverted Platonism," it paradoxically is and is not compatible with science. Because a "World" possesses "constancy," science can chart it. Because a "World" can be displaced by another one at any time for no reason, this "constancy" is not constant. Harman translates this possibility into the speculative example of a vase falling today because of the present law of gravity but flying upward or hovering tomorrow if "the law of nature changed suddenly and without warning" (*Quentin* 62).⁴³ Meillassoux's authorization of such chaotic change provides opportunities for arguments that his philosophy is incompatible with science (Gratton, *Speculative Realism* 48).

Meillassoux himself anticipates such arguments in recognizing that elimination of predictability would end science as we know it, but questions whether that consequence by itself is enough to guarantee the ontological necessity that predictability presupposes (*After Finitude* 86, 93–94). He anticipates criticism of his work, like Adrian Johnston's, that he could not distinguish scientific error from contingent change from "World" to "World." Did Newton make an error, Johnston asks, or was the "World" Newtonian before suddenly "becoming post-Newtonian at some arbitrary instant of time at the start of the twentieth century" ("Hume's Revenge" 100)? Meillassoux uses the same contrast between Newton and Einstein to contrast Popper (no change in the laws of nature; Einstein falsified Newton) to Hume (one cannot be sure) (*After Finitude* 85–86).

Hume's famous billiard ball anecdote, quoted at length in *After Finitude* (88), is an important text for Meillassoux both in *After Finitude* and in later work. Peter Hallward even suggests, "The simplest way to introduce Meillassoux's general project is as a reformulation and radicalization of what he on several occasions describes as 'Hume's problem'" (131). Meillassoux formulates "Hume's problem" thus: "is it possible to prove that, in the future, the same effects will follow from the same causes, all other things being equal, ceteris paribus?" ("Contingency" 322; see also *After Finitude* 85). Hume's answer, of course, is "no." Meillassoux agrees but adds that "no" may be the right answer for different reasons: (1) there is a necessary or probable connection between cause and effect but it is impossible to prove; (2) there is no necessary or probable connection in the first place, thus there is nothing to prove. Hume's "no," Meillassoux contends, presupposes (1) rather than (2) ("Contingency" 323, 325). Contrastingly, Meillassoux affirms (2) because it illustrates a key claim in *Divine Inexistence*: "To say that becoming is rational means that

---

43. Harman may take this vase example from Meillassoux's example of a vase falling in an empty house (*After Finitude* 19). Meillassoux's example is part of his rejection of the claim that spatial distance inhibiting observation challenges correlationism as much as the temporal distance Meillassoux features in "Ancestrality." Harman made this claim in reviewing *After Finitude*, "Quentin Meillassoux: A New French Philosopher." Meillassoux's rejection does not mention Harman, but may nonetheless be a response to Harman. This rejection will be examined in a consideration of "Ancestrality" later in this chapter.

becoming can actually produce everything that is thinkable (i.e., noncontradictory)" (Harman translation 227). Hume's billiard ball (cause) hitting a second ball (effect) contrasts the expected effect to a variety of effects, all noncontradictory, like Harman's example of a vase rising or hovering instead of falling, and thus thinkable, therefore, possible. Rather than privilege the expected effect, Meillassoux proposes, one should privilege the thinkable and therefore the possibility of Hume's array of possibilities. It is not that thought is incapable of grasping a necessary connection that is there; rather, it is "a capacity of thought to intuit *a priori*, in the real itself, the effective absence of the reason of things as laws, and the possibility of their being modified as any moment" ("Spectral Dilemma" 273). "Hume has convinced us," Meillassoux concludes, "that we could *a priori* (that is to say without contradiction) conceive a chaotic modification of natural laws" ("Spectral Dilemma" 273).

Meillassoux extends his speculation about science into science fiction to propose a new subgenre, "extro-science fiction." This extension appears in his *Science Fiction and Extro-Science Fiction*, which includes as an appendix an Isaac Asimov story, "The Billiard Ball." The Asimov story qualifies as science fiction. It is consistent with natural science because it is a physical law, remaining in place throughout the narrative, that in the end explains the resolution of the plot. By contrast, extroscience fiction presupposes the possibility of changes in physical laws, like the change from a Newtonian to an Einsteinian "World." The challenge for extro-science fiction is to devise narratives that incorporate such changes in physical laws. Meillassoux surveys examples in specific fictions that suggest possible directions for this new genre. This survey concludes with what Meillassoux considers a genuine "prototype," René Barjavel's *Ravage*, where the change in physical laws centers in changes in the workings of electricity. One character is quoted who sounds like Meillassoux: "We live in a universe that we believe to be immutable because we have always seen it obey the same laws, but nothing rules out that it can abruptly start to change, that sugar become bitter and that the stone float up instead of falling when you drop it" (51–52). *Ravage* addresses one question that Johnston asks in his criticism: if a change of "Worlds" separating Newton from Einstein occurred, how would one recognize such an "intervention of hyper-chaotic temporal contingency?" ("Hume's Revenge" 100). In *Ravage*, change is signaled dramatically so that in its narrative the issue Johnston poses does not arise.

Harman poses a different problem, one focusing not on science but on the structure of Meillassoux's cosmos, specifically its two tiers, with "non-Whole world" at the top and "Worlds" at the bottom, which reminds Harman of the split in pre-Galilean physics between the "superlunary" and the "sublunary." Harman adds, more importantly,

> What makes this dangerous is that it allows him [Meillassoux] to transfer all key ontological problems over to the question of the sudden changes of laws. Rather than raising the question of why there should be laws at all, he simply questions whether laws are eternal and whether they have any reason for existing. (*Quentin* 66; see also 39)

Brassier observes similarly that Meillassoux "has not explained why reality should exhibit the constancy it seems to, given its absolute contingency" (*Nihil Unbound* 82).

This shortcoming is profitably viewed from the standpoint of the difference, charted in McKeon's historical semantics, between Rorty's and Meillassoux's different subject matters. What is not a problem for Rorty becomes a problem for Meillassoux. In a Rortian world, discourses are contingent, but this contingency is discursive rather than cosmic. Discourses arise in Rorty's philosophical "conversation," have their day in the sun of normalcy, then undergo displacement in the face of an abnormal discourse becoming the new normal. Whether a discourse achieves normalcy depends on whether it passes the pragmatic test of facilitating human coping with the realities of living. For Quine, as we saw in the last chapter, the "myth of physical objects" is pragmatically more successful than other myths such as Homer's gods at "working a manageable structure into the flux of experience" ("Two Dogmas" 44). Rorty's "conversation" thus explains both the innovations introducing new discourses to be put to a pragmatic test and the process by which consensus forms to stabilize discourses into norms of acceptable argument. By contrast, Meillassoux's metaphysical contingency explains the chaos of the "non-Whole world," but not the "constancy" of a "World." Evidencing sensitivity to the problem that Harman's criticism identifies, Meillassoux revises his thinking about "*hyper-Chaos*" to solve it. Introducing "*hyper-Chaos*" in *After Finitude*, Meillassoux comments that "far from guaranteeing order, it guarantees only the possible destruction of every order" (*After Finitude* 64). That would explain change from "World" to "World," but not "constancies" within a "World." A later revision corrects that deficiency when Meillassoux explains, "Hyper-chaos is very different from what we call usually 'chaos.' By chaos we usually mean disorder, randomness, the eternal becoming of everything. But these properties are not properties of Hyper-chaos: its contingency is so radical that even becoming, disorder, or randomness can be destroyed by it, and replaced by order, determinism, and fixity" ("Time" 10). Just as contingency explains why something or nothing happens, Hyper-chaos explains why there is order or disorder. In connection with this revision Meillassoux even adds a terminological revision, "That's why I now prefer to use the term *surcontingence*, supercontingency, rather than contingency" ("Time" 10). Later, he adds the term "*Surchaos*" ("Immanence" 446). Meillassoux finds similar explanatory power in time. Asking himself, "What is facticity once it is considered as an absolute, rather than as a limit?," he answers, "*time*—facticity as absolute must be considered as time," adding, "Things are so contingent in Hyper-chaos that time is able to destroy even the becoming of things. If facticity is the absolute, contingency no longer means the necessity of destruction or disorder, but rather the equal contingency of order and disorder" ("Time" 10), a point he notably repeats in "Potentiality" (232}. These later revisions, it should be noted, may be seen as elaborations of a sentence in *After Finitude* about time: "It is a Time capable of destroying even becoming itself by bringing forth, perhaps forever, fixity, stasis, and death" (64). But here the fixity of order is associated with the negativity of death. The later elaborations, however, eliminate negative associations to stake out a neutral position between order and disorder. That an occurrence has to occur at a time appears to turn time into a neutral agency that causes the occurrence of both order and disorder. One commentator, Jon Roffe, construes Meillassoux as wanting to subordinate time to the principle of unreason at the heart of contingency, the essence of facticity. But in the end, Roffe contends, one cannot have contingency without time, without a before and an after (63).

While the "non-Whole world" appears to enjoy the absolute freedom of contingency, a limitation of this freedom surfaces in Meillassoux's consideration of the trio of matter, life, and thought. This trio appears in both *Divine Inexistence* and later texts. For Meillassoux, these three are distinct "Worlds," "which are actually coexistent, despite every evident indication that they succeed one another in time" ("Immanence" 461). Meillassoux clarifies this distinctiveness in "Potentiality and Virtuality." Potentiality is change consistent with "constancies" in a "World": "*Po-*

tentialities are the non-actualized cases of an indexed set of possibilities under the condition of a given law." Contrastingly, "*virtuality* [is] the property of every set of cases of emerging within a becoming which is not dominated by any pre-constituted totality of possibles" (231, 232). A virtuality, in other words, is an "advent *ex nihlio*," an effect, or "possible," that exceeds its cause, a "World" thus distinct from what precedes it even if it coexists with it.

The "World" of matter, however, would not appear to qualify as an "advent *ex nihlio*" because there is nothing prior to it. It cannot be an effect that exceeds its cause if there is no cause. Meillassoux addresses this problem by distinguishing matter from nature. Nature is a "constancy" characteristic of a "World," whereas "matter is a primordial ontological order: it is the fact that there must be something and not nothing—contingent beings as such" (Interview Dolphijn and van der Tuin 8). In other words, contingency presupposes something rather than nothing, which would appear to introduce a necessity akin to some kind of entity, despite Meillassoux's resistance to any such necessary entity in his preference for speculation over metaphysics. Brassier poses the problem by contrasting two claims. The "weak" claim is that if something exists it must exist contingently, whereas the "strong" claim is that "it is absolutely necessary that contingent entities exist" (*Nihil Unbound* 71). The weak claim would allow for the possibility that there could someday be nothing. That would mean that contingency was not necessary, that it could someday disappear, that contingency is itself contingent. The strong claim preserves the necessity of contingency, but limits contingency by tying it necessarily to matter. Contingency is free to do anything except abandon matter. Meillassoux's distinction between "matter" and "nature," then, presupposes that while there is one "matter" that is always with us, there can be different "natures," that is, different "Worlds," with different "constancies."

"May-being" and Chaotic Pragmatism

While careful analysis is required to detect the exact differences between life and thought that make each a distinctive "advent *ex nihlio*," little to no analysis is needed to see the difference most important to Meillassoux:

> We know that the eternal truth of contingency is the foundation of an immanent theory of being qua being. . . . Now, how can we demonstrate that this life itself possesses the dimension

of immortality? The demonstration (and herein lies its great strangeness) is *without difficulty* given what has been established. The factial is an ontology that allows us to think immortality directly as one possibility *among others*, but as a *real* possibility (since it is noncontradictory) of advent *ex nihlio*." (*Divine Inexistence*, Harman translation 236–37)

Nothing could be more clearly different than the difference between the "Worlds" of mortality and immortality.

After affirming that immortality is a real possibility, Meillassoux adds an additional affirmation that must surprise anyone who reads *Divine Inexistence* after having read *After Finitude*:

> *the sole possible novelty surpassing humans just as humans surpass life would be the recommencement of the human*. That is why the fourth World ought to be called the World of justice: for it is only the World of the rebirth of humans *that makes universal justice possible, by erasing even the injustice of shattered lives*. (Harman translation 239; see also "Immanence" 462)

After Finitude draws on Cantor to conclude, "What the set-axiomatic demonstrates is at the very least a fundamental uncertainty regarding the totalizability of the possible" (105). This uncertainty also appears in *Divine Inexistence*, though it is not theorized as thoroughly as in *After Finitude*, when Meillassoux, using "Universe," a synonym for "World," asserts that because "possible universes cannot be recorded in a list as possible cases of a Universe of Universes," "we obtain the theoretical weapons needed for the idea *of a true novelty*, given that the result of the advent of a Universe of hidden cases is no longer reducible to the simple manifestation-actualization of an eternally fixed reservoir of possibilities" (Harman translation 228). Any such list would be prior to contingency, limiting contingency's options. In the absence of a fixed list of possibilities, how could this "fourth World" be "*the sole possible novelty*"?

While *Divine Inexistence* itself thus contains a passage that corrects "*sole possible novelty*" by erasing "*sole*," it leaves firmly in place the "*possible novelty*" of "rebirth" and "immortality" in a "World of the rebirth of humans." By the logic of contingency, Johnston quips, the possibility for which Meillassoux hopes is as likely to be realized as the deity of the "flying spaghetti monster" ("Hume's Revenge" 112), an apparent reference to the Church of the Flying Spaghetti Monster. Johnston is right, but his point is beside the point from Meillassoux's standpoint, because

Meillassoux merges theory and practice in what he defines as philosophy's final and most important challenge, *"not being, but 'may-being.'* For the may-be unites within itself the true heart of every ontology (the absoluteness of factual possibility) and the deepest aspirations of ethics (the universal fulfillment of justice)" ("Immanence" 463; see also "Time" 11 and *Divine Inexistence,* Harman translation 236). The divorce of possibility from probability is a distinguishing feature on the theory side of Meillassoux's merger. Harman speculates that of Meillassoux's ideas the one on which his "future reception" may depend is his untethering of "philosophical speculation . . . from the laws of probability" (*Quentin* 200; see also 173).

"May-being" is the ultimate priority in Meillassoux's metaphysical turn. *"May-being"* exhibits Meillassoux's derivation of metaphysics from skepticism by his own account. *"May-being"* transforms the linguistic tyranny of the new into a cosmic tyranny of the new in which nothing can ever stop the possibility of "World" displacing "World." *"May-being"* is a metaphysical mirror image of that from which it turns. But that from which it turns is in the subject matter of language and the mirror is in the subject matter of the cosmos. Whether this mirroring relationship says much about that to which the metaphysical turn ultimately turns depends on how the metaphysical turn develops in future decades.

In its merger of theory and practice, *"may-being"* takes the form of what this chapter calls "Chaotic Pragmatism." In Quine's pragmatism, it is a human decision that concludes that to cope with reality the myth of physical objects is pragmatically better than the myth of Homer's gods. Chaotic pragmatism takes this decision out of human hands and puts it in the hands of the chaos in which contingent "World" displaces contingent "World" in a "non-Whole world." One "World" may be pragmatically better for humans than another, but human preference has nothing to do with bringing it about and may even be counterproductive. The Soviet Union erred, Meillassoux pronounces with Olympian assurance, in failing to recognize that Marx's promised "end of politics is that which proceeds from an ontological uprising that is independent of our action" ("Immanence" 477).

Meillassoux's reasons for affirming the real possibility of a "World of the rebirth of humans" appear in concise form in "The Spectral Dilemma." Appearing in 2008, this essay offered at that time, as Harman notes, "the Anglophone readership its first taste of the major themes of the unpublished *L'Inexistence divine*" (*Quentin* 86). Meillassoux states the dilemma that concerns him from the standpoint of the dead. He defines "spectre" as a "dead person who has not been properly mourned, who haunts us, bothers us." The preeminent examples are those who suffered "terrible deaths" ("Spectral Dilemma" 261, 262). Meillassoux thinks more broadly elsewhere when he faults communism for "renouncing the eschatological hope of a universal equality of the living and the dead," because this renunciation fostered "sacrifice of the present generation to future generations, who would be the only beneficiaries of the revolution to come" ("Immanence" 453–54).

The dilemma that inhibits mourning exists when the only alternatives are atheism and religion ("Spectral Dilemma" 265): atheism leaves no hope for the dead and religion's existent God is the one who permitted the deaths in the first place, thus hardly a proper basis for mourning. For a cure, look to "divine inexistence": against atheism, it offers the possibility of resurrection; against religion, it offers a God not yet here and thus untainted by the blood of history. "For if God does not exist," Meillassoux insists, "everything becomes fragile, even death. If God does not exist, things become capable of anything: whether of the absurd or of reaching their highest state" (Interview Harman 221). That is why one should believe in God because he does not exist. Yes, maybe the absurdity of a spaghetti monster, but maybe also the possibility of immortality. In Meillassoux's chaotic pragmatism, death is not final. Death does not erase the possibility of rebirth. We will return to this crucial point later, in the context of the critique of correlationism.

However unlikely, because this possibility is a real possibility, it can, Meillassoux proposes, "enhance, *in our own world*, the subjectivity of human beings living in our day by profoundly transforming the private lives of those who take seriously such a hypothesis [of the reality of this possibility]" ("Immanence" 462–63]. One is protected from the charge of empty wishful thinking by the rationalism of becoming: "To say that becoming is rational means that becoming can actually produce everything that is thinkable (i.e., noncontradictory)" (*Divine Inexistence*, Harman translation 227). This possibility is "noncontradictory" because it follows from the ultimate priority of *"may-being."*

"The goal of every philosophy," Meillassoux proclaims, *"must be the immanent inscription of values in being"* (*Divine Inexistence*, Harman translation 244). But humans do not do the inscribing in Meillassoux's chaotic pragmatism, a point underlined in his rejection of sophistry, which may be construed as a rejection of the linguistic turn: "The inscription of val-

ues in the world opposes philosophy to sophistry in primordial fashion. The sophist is the one for whom value is nothing more than a profitable social convention. . . . Value is sheer invention, a simple artifice created by humans whose sole aim is that everyone should live well" (245). An arguably Nietzschean variant would be the view that even though "the accord between the world and any particular value is a matter of illusion," one can nonetheless "*make that illusion itself into a value*" (253–54). Such social conventions and illusions are contingent, but they are Rortian contingencies, not contingencies from the "non-Whole world." Meillassoux also rejects "the religious person who inscribes value in the world through the irrational means of a revelation, a tradition, an authority" (245). The disqualifier here is "irrational": "every position that consists in limiting the exercise of reason is religious" (279). This is religion via fideistic limitation of reason, again, far from the "non-Whole world."

Meillassoux pinpoints three past "*inscription[s] of values in being*," calling them three great "Symbols," defined as ontological links "between being and value": (1) in antiquity, eternal justice in celestial world; (2) in Rousseau, eternal goodness in childlike being, prior to society; (3) in Hegel and Marx, communitarian ideal in teleological narrative (*Divine Inexistence*, Harman translation 246, 249–51). All three, however, from the standpoint of Meillassoux's "speculation," make the mistake of presupposing a necessary entity, so that all of them eventually suffered the pain of disillusionment. This is another argument against reliance on the necessary entities of metaphysics, but is Meillassoux's alternative any better? Instead of disillusionment, "*may-being*" may displace a good contingency by a bad one.

In the "*inscription of values in being*," contingency (being) is the common denominator in all "Worlds," whereas value distinguishes "World" from "World." As Meillassoux explains, "It is not the eternal which has value for the eternal is *only* the blind, stupid, and anonymous contingency of each thing"; in other words, each particular contingency partakes of the universality of contingency. In "may-being," "Value is inserted into a reality no longer identified with a determinate and perennial substance, but rather with the possibility of lawless change" (*Divine Inexistence* 260, 255).

While this lawlessness would seem to encourage passive quietism, Meillassoux thinks that it encourages activism for two reasons. The first one arises directly from "*may-being*," as distinct from unchanging being. Instead of coming to terms with something unchanging, one needs to concern oneself with "before" and "after," that is, "*the contradiction between the present ethics* that awaits the fourth World, *and the ethics to come* that would follow the advent of such a world" (*Divine Inexistence*, Harman translation 256). A clear example appears in "The Immanence of the World Beyond" in his critique of the USSR. Meillassoux contrasts two "types of militants": one loves the political struggle above all else, the other engages in the struggle but values above all else life without politics (476). The militant who loves political struggle above all else is likely should the struggle succeed to yield to "the temptation of nihilism" (472), whereas the militant who loves life without politics will fare better. Meillassoux aligns the USSR with the lover of struggle in failing to recognize, as we saw earlier, that the "end of politics is that which proceeds from an ontological uprising that is independent of our action" (477). The USSR missed this truth in thinking "that the end of politics could be a politics" (477). Politically, then, Meillassoux appears to place himself in the tradition that in the twentieth century spent considerable intellectual energies figuring out why the revolution that was supposed to be inevitable did not happen. He both adds another explanation and finds in "*may-being*" another reason to keep revolutionary hope alive.

The second reason deploys an analogy with Kant's "*as if*" (*Prolegomena* 106): "Kantians see in beauty the sign of a possible existence of God." Analogously, just as the Divine appears to cause beauty in nature without actually doing so, activism can appear to cause the "fourth World" to come without actually doing so. For if this "World" were to come, such activism would be viewed "as if" it caused it (*Divine Inexistence*, Harman translation 268, 269). In this sense, the activism would be part of the realization of the contingency. Harman captures this reasoning concisely and penetratingly: the "World" of Justice is "*causally independent* of our actions . . . [but] *non-causally dependent*, related intimately to our thought without being caused by it" (*Quentin* 160). Without recognition of this mode of dependency it is easy to see why one would mistakenly think passive waiting would be just as good as activist advocacy (e.g., Gratton, *Speculative Realism* 83).

Meillassoux's reasoning has a possible historical analogue in Puritan belief in predestination. Even though what one did had no bearing on one's predestined fate, Puritans found in their virtues evidence that they were the fortunate ones among the elect. Meillassoux inverts this model: instead of proving that one is among the predestined elect, one insures that one is on the right side of history should the "fourth World" come to be.

Ancestrality

"Ancestrality," *After Finitude*'s first chapter, is widely known. Perhaps less widely known is that there are two versions of it. One section (pages 18–26) appears for the first time in the English translation before being added to later French editions (Harman, *Quentin* 40; see also Brassier, *Nihil Unbound* 53). Harman suggests in 2011 that this new section may be in part in response to one of his arguments in his 2007 review of the French edition of *After Finitude* ("Meillassoux's Virtual Future" 82). While Meillassoux does not mention Harman by name in this new section, he does restate one of Harman's arguments in detail in rejecting it. Consideration of pages 18–26 will conclude this section's consideration of "Ancestrality." Prior to that the focus will be the first of the two versions.

Reminding one of the cosmic scope of *Divine Inexistence*'s "non-Whole world," "Ancestrality" features a memorable cosmic sequence: first the origin of the universe, then the accretion of the earth, then the origin of life on earth, and finally the emergence of humans with their correlationism, which appears to be a puny cocoon in this cosmic context. Correlationism seems overwhelmed after reading just a handful of pages.

But "Ancestrality" is not a refutation of correlationism, though that may be easy to miss while under the spell of its power in a first reading. Harman confesses that he missed it in his first two readings, not realizing his misreading until his third reading (*Prince of Networks* 164). No doubt he is not alone. Affirming that "Ancestrality" aims at less than might appear initially, Meillassoux explains in later texts (1) that "the problem of ancestrality is not—not at all—intended as a refutation of correlationism" ("Time" 5); (2) that "Ancestrality" aims only to show correlationist readers that "there could be a problem in correlationism" ("Presentation" 439).

What poses this problem is the "arche-fossil," defined as existents "anterior to terrestrial life" (*After Finitude* 10). These existents from a time when there was no thought are what make Meillassoux's speculative materialism a materialism, a thinking of an existence in which thought and thus the correlational was absent. By existing prior to humans, the arche-fossil is by definition an existent that is independent of any correlationist fusion of subject and object. "There is no possible compromise between the correlation and the arche-fossil," Meillassoux observes, "once one has acknowledged one, one has thereby disqualified the other" (*After Finitude* 17).

The arche-fossil, Meillassoux suggests, exposes every variant of correlationism "as an extreme idealism, one that is incapable of admitting that what science tells us about these occurrences of matter independent of humanity effectively occurred as described by science" (*After Finitude* 18). While this sounds like a refutation, it is misleading insofar as Meillassoux's actual refutation is very different, as we shall see. Rather than lump all variants together as one kind of thing, Meillassoux discriminates among variants, pitting one against another to see which, in effect, is strongest, the one that must be refuted to refute correlationism.

Meillassoux references briefly the basis of the scientific dating that produces the dates of the stages in his cosmic sequence. Scientists "generally rely upon the constant rate of disintegration of radioactive nuclei, as well as upon the laws of thermoluminescence—the latter permitting the application of dating techniques to the light emitted by stars" (*After Finitude* 9). This sounds straightforward. No doubt both the sequence and its basis in this science of measurement are usually taken at face value, especially on a first reading. This passage looks different, however, in the light of later chapters. But even before this passage there is a discussion of scientific objectivity that raises the possibility that it is not as straightforward as it appears.

Among the effects of the Kantian philosophical turn, Meillassoux observes, is a change in what counts as objectivity. "From this point on," he explains, "*intersubjectivity*, the consensus of a community, supplants the *adequation* between the representations of a solitary subject and the thing itself as the veritable criterion of objectivity, and of scientific objectivity more particularly" (*After Finitude* 4). In the linguistic turn, this intersubjectivity is in language. This is Quinean pragmatic "objectivity," not the objectivity that would meet the standard of the "*great outdoors.*"

The deeper problem emerges in the introduction of contingency and factiality in later chapters. These introduce the logic of the "non-Whole world." Scientific dating measures matter, but as we have seen, for Meillassoux, matter appears in different natures. When did the nature appear that is measured to arrive at the dates in Meillassoux's cosmic sequence? Ciprian Jeler sums up the issue precisely: "the principle of factiality doesn't tell us that the radioactive decay rates *really did change* in the last Y years, but it tells us that is it *impossible* to assume that they didn't" (25; see also Gratton, *Speculative Realism* 73 and "After the Subject" 71).

Meillassoux confirms Jeler and Gratton when later in *After Finitude* he returns to the topic of the decay of radioactive material. Meillassoux describes the premise of his reasoning as "a Cartesian thesis, viz., *that whatever is mathematically conceivable is absolutely possible*" (*After Finitude* 117). This would appear to update *Divine Inexistence*'s claim that everything thinkable (noncontradictory) is possible by substituting "mathematical" for "thinkable." Meillassoux does not mean that reality itself is mathematical such that reality and mathematics are a Pythagorean oneness. Rather, "the absoluteness of that which is mathematizable . . . [is] the possibility of factial existence outside thought—and not: the necessity of existence outside thought" (117). Possible, but not necessary, since necessity "would be contrary to our ontology" (117). It is possible to mathematize the rate of radioactive decay, but this rate is a "constancy" in "a World," not "the World." Mathematizing this rate can date an object, but whether the date is accurate depends on how long this "constancy" has been in effect. An object that survives from one "World" to another "World" would be subject to different "constancies." The dates in the ancestral argument in *After Finitude*'s first chapter are possible but not necessary. Meillassoux derives his "non-Whole world" from the contingency he finds in Rortyian skepticism, but he ends up with a skepticism of another kind.

This role of the mathematizable, it is important to add, points in the direction of Meillassoux's later work. His Berlin lecture, a work in progress, suggests the direction in which he is going to develop the line of argument sketched in *After Finitude*. Ironically, in this development, he appears to be going forward by returning even more deeply to the linguistic turn. The Berlin lecture has two main parts, with the first updating his critique of correlationism, most notably with the addition of the term "subjectalism," applied among others to Harman ("Iteration" 7), a topic to be considered in the next chapter. The second, "Essay on the Derivation of Galileanism," begins,

> I now come to the principal subject of this paper. It concerns the attempt to obtain a factial derivation that would legitimate *the absolutizing capacity of modern science*—that is to say, *Galilean science*, science that proceeds via the mathematization of nature. For what preoccupies me is the rediscovery of a Cartesian rather

> than a Kantian conception of experimental science. . . . [I]t is a matter of establishing that it at least makes sense to suppose that a scientific theory can identify a true property of reality, independently of our existing to think that reality. (18)

Meillassoux distinguishes two senses of "absolute": the "*primo*" sense is the familiar absolute of contingency or facticity; the secondary sense encompasses the natural sciences, which absolutize not in the "*primo*" sense but in the sense that they identify properties independent of thought in our "World," with its particular "constancies" (18). Because the lecture does not reach this secondary level, Meillassoux explains at the end, the lecture project is incomplete: the lecture shows "that to produce an empty sign, one must have access to the eternity of contingency," but it has not "shown that the empty sign allows, in turn, the description of a world independent of thought" (37; see also "Time" 12). This incompleteness, one suspects, is among the reasons Meillassoux never authorized the public circulation that the essay has undergone (Harman, *Quentin* 98).

The key advance in the lecture, then, resides in its linkage of the empty sign and contingency, a linkage Meillassoux forges by returning to Saussure and revising him along Derridean lines. The arbitrariness of signs is an analogue to the arbitrariness of "Worlds." Just as meaning "X" of a sign can replace meaning "Y," "World" can replace "World." The details of Meillassoux's analysis are subtle.[44]

---

44. Meillassoux's demonstration of the sign's relation to contingency divorces the sign from the sensible. Meillassoux explains, "This point is essential for our undertaking: for sensible plurality (let's say *diversity*) does not escape correlation (I cannot absolutize it, it belongs to the sphere of our relation to the world)" ("Iteration" 34). Escaping correlationism, this suggests, is a matter of escaping the sensible whereby everything thinkable is in some sense thinkable "for us." This escape is charted by the lecture's trio of key terms: repetition, iteration, and reiteration (the order of the terms in the title does not appear to be consistent with the order of their importance in the demonstration). Tied most closely to the sensible, repetition is illustrated with melody (time) and architecture (space), series of differences limited to a finite order (31-32). Iteration is a series of marks that do "not differ sensibly in any way" and that is without limitation, hence not ordered in any way (32). Reiteration is the decisive third step. Meillassoux's notion of reiteration depends on a modification of Saussure's principle of the arbitrariness of the sign (Saussure 67). Such arbitrariness, as the last chapter argues, is at the heart of the linguistic turn's ontology, the truth this turn took decades to discover. Whereas Saussure focuses on the arbitrary

Meillassoux introduces the new section in "Ancestrality" added for the English translation as "two correlationist rejoinders to the ancestral objection," each of which he reviews and refutes. The first is the one that appears to respond to Harman's contention, in reviewing the original French edition of *After Finitude*, that spatial distance, in the form of objects currently existing but inaccessible to humans, challenges correlationism as much as the arche-fossil in "Ancestrality" extending back to a time before humans existed. Harman's examples of spatial distance include "events unfolding right now in the core of Alpha Centauri" ("Quentin" 107). Meillassoux's examples include "[a]n event occurring in an immensely distant galaxy, beyond the reach of every possible observation" (*After Finitude* 18). Spatial distance, Meillassoux counters, "invokes an event and a consciousness which are considered as synchronic," so that, however great the distance, the event could nonetheless conceivably be witnessed and is thus "recuperable," something that could be given, that is, could be a correlate and thus would pose no challenge to correlationism (20–21). Even if this event occurs on a planet with no life, it would not qualify as an arche-fossil because it would be "recuperable" by consciousness on earth. Indeed, we do live in a time when such spatial distance is overcome routinely. What was long impossible to witness now regularly turns up on our computer screens as some vehicle in outer space sends back pictures from great distances of things never witnessed heretofore, at least by eyes on earth. Because consciousness on earth was synchronous with these distant things, these things were always potentially "recuperable" and thus did not qualify as arche-fossils. By contrast, temporal distance is diachronous. The arche-fossil is "*prior to givenness in*

---

relation between signified and signifier, such that the same signified could be signified by different signifiers in different languages (67–68), Meillassoux is "interested in the signifier *before* its link to the signified . . . in an arbitrariness of the sign defined independently of its relation to meaning" ("Iteration" 27). Meillassoux's sign is empty, meaningless. Meillassoux explains that the difference this makes is that "*any sensible mark*" can serve as an empty sign (27). In reiteration, Meillassoux's principle of arbitrariness appears in the recodability of any series of signs at the level of iteration; any series can be recoded by another series (36). Such recoding, Meillassoux appears to reason, presupposes the standpoint of contingency beyond the finite standpoint of the sensible, for recoding is analogous to changes from "World" to "World" in the "non-Whole world." Such change would appear to be the essence of contingency in that any "World," with its "constancy," is subordinate to its contingent essence, by virtue of which it is vulnerable to displacement.

its entirety" (21). Givenness is a correlate that did not exist until humans appeared so that correlations between objects and humans could occur. The arche-fossil, existent before humans, testifies to a time when there was no givenness, and unlike spatial distance, it is not "recuperable" in the absence of the time machines of myth.

This contrast between space and time appears to clarify Meillassoux's thinking on givenness better than anything else. Take a rock as an example of an arche-fossil. For a time it existed in the absence of humans and their correlations, but when humans appeared, it became a correlate, potentially if not actually, because it could now be witnessed, examined, dated. But before humans appeared, there was no possibility of a correlate, whereas with a synchronic consciousness and a thing spatially distant, a correlate is always possible, no matter how great the distance.

Although Meillassoux's argument appears persuasive, it actually calls into question the arche-fossil's existence. Meillassoux even offers the argument that calls it into question, although he evidently does not realize it. When Meillassoux considers synchrony between consciousness on earth and "[a]n event occurring in an immensely distant galaxy," he fails to consider that such synchrony can work in two directions, not only from consciousness on earth to events in outer space, but possibly also from consciousness in outer space to events on earth. Meillassoux's earth-centeredness stifles his philosophical imagination. In other words, during the time arche-fossils existed on earth prior to correlations on earth, there may have been consciousness in other galaxies, hence synchronicity between that consciousness and earth's arche-fossil. If there were such a distant consciousness during the time of the arche-fossil, then it would not be an arche-fossil because it would be "recuperable" for that consciousness. For all we know, a consciousness on a faraway goldilocks planet with advanced surveillance technology actually did witness it before any human appeared on earth. In such a case, the arche-fossil would exist in a time prior to correlation on earth, but it would not exist in a time prior to correlation in the cosmos. Meillassoux's reasoning in his argument against spatial distance thus boomerangs, leaving in doubt whether there ever was an arche-fossil.

A final irony is that the possibility of such an extraterrestrial consciousness does surface at one point, but Meillassoux does not see it, so he calls it a "counterfactual": "[I]f a consciousness had observed the emergence of terrestrial life, the time of the emergence *of* the given would have been a time of emergence *in* the given" (*After Finitude* 21). To view this emergence, this consciousness would have to be extraterrestrial. The "given" is correlational, fusing subject and object. Viewing the emergence of life and the given fusing subject and object on earth would be "*in* the given" in the sense that it would be in the fusion of subject (the extraterrestrial consciousness viewing) and object (the emergence of terrestrial life and the correlational on earth). Meillassoux sees that as a counterfactual that proves his point that no one could see the emergence of the given; only after this emergence could there be a given. Prior to this emergence, there was the arche-fossil in the absence of the given. But if one assumes the possibility that the consciousness viewing this emergence is extraterrestrial, the counterfactual disappears along with the arche-fossil, the object in the correlation with the extraterrestrial subject. There is no way to know for certain whether there ever was an arche-fossil on earth, at least not until we have the technology to determine the location and history of every consciousness in the cosmos.

The second rejoinder argues that Meillassoux fails to distinguish between bodies, which do exist at specific times and locations in space, and the conditions of knowledge, which do not: "these transcendental conditions of cognition, they cannot be said to arise or to disappear—not because they are eternal but because they are 'outside time' and 'outside space'—they remain out of reach of scientific discourse about objects because they provide the forms of this discourse" (22–23). Consequently, while the "recuperable" in space requires the simultaneous coexistence in time of a consciousness and an object, the "recuperable" in time does not depend on such simultaneity. It is the subject of science, the "transcendental conditions of cognition," not the physically existent body of scientist, who determines the age of rocks based on scientific laws and mathematical measurements, whereby a correlational relation comes to be between the rocks in their ancient-hood and the subject of science.

Meillassoux concedes that the transcendental does not exist the way in which objects exist. Nonetheless, he argues, the transcendental is indissociable from the body. Meillassoux's argument for this indissociability is that

> there can only be a transcendental subject on condition that such a subject *takes place.*
>
> What do we mean by "taking place"? We mean that the transcendental insofar as it refuses all metaphysical dogmatism, remains indissociable from the notion of a *point of view*. Let us suppose a subject without a point of view on the world—such

> a subject would have access to the world as a totality. . . . But such a subject would thereby violate the essential finitude of the transcendental subject. (*After Finitude* 24)

But does not Meillassoux claim access to the "non-Whole world," the nontotality from which "Worlds" derive. His ultimate priority of "*may-being*" encompasses all that has happened and all that will happen. A better example of a philosophy that comes closer to staying within the limits of "the notion of a *point of view*" appears in the next chapter, but even Harman stays within these limits only by going beyond them in one crucial respect.

CORRELATIONISM

Returning to Meillassoux's term "aperture" puts us on track to his refutation of correlationism. This apertural piercing entails a dependency on correlationism that troubles some commentators. Paul J. Ennis, for example, contends that while there "is no doubting that Meillassoux has prompted an intensive reflection upon correlationism," there nonetheless "remain distinct concerns that he himself remains implicated in both transcendentalism and correlationism" (34). Similarly, Gratton contends that Meillassoux "works his way out from the correlationist circle and thus must take the reality of that circle as the hidden premise of his argument" (*Speculative Realism* 41). True, but this is hardly "hidden." Meillassoux puts what he does in the light of day in this statement in his "Presentation" at the 2007 Speculative Realism Workshop:

> I can access a speculative realism which clearly refutes, but no longer disqualifies, correlationism. I think an X independent of any thinking, and know it for sure, thanks to the correlationist himself and his fight against the absolute, the idealist absolute. (432; see also "Time" 9)[45]

Further, there is for Meillassoux no question that the correlational relation between subject and object is real, part of the history of the "non-Whole world" recounted in "Ancestrality." Meillassoux can "think an X

---

45. Meillassoux devotes pages to surveying modes of disqualification such as "replacing the discussion with the correlationist with an exposition of his motivations" ("Presentation" 423). He dismisses all these modes, insisting that if one wants to reject correlationism, one must refute the correlationist's argument.

independent of any thinking, and know it for sure" because the correlationist thinks an X that is not a correlate of thought, but is rather a non-correlate in the *"great outdoors,"* independent of the correlational relation of subject and object. The correlationist thus does what correlationism deems impossible, thereby refuting correlationism. *After Finitude* shows the correlationist doing this to defeat the "idealist absolute." This argumentative strategy is indirect in its reliance on the correlationist to do the heavy lifting. "Presentation" explains the development of this strategy.

Before turning to "Presentation," we need to recall that at the beginning of this chapter, we saw Meillassoux indicate that *After Finitude* is part of his larger project of *Divine Inexistence*. In focusing on correlationism, *After Finitude* takes up what he sees as the hegemonic tradition in philosophy in recent centuries, the correlationism that bars access to the *"great outdoors."* What is at stake in *After Finitude* is whether in fact correlationism refutes itself in a way consistent with the contingency of *"may-being"* in the *"great outdoors,"* Meillassoux's ultimate priority. Can what *After Finitude* shows the correlationist doing happen in the "non-Whole world"?

Importantly, Meillassoux's "think[ing] an X independent of any thinking" is his solution to the problem McKeon poses in this chapter's epigraph: "if we are in direct contact only with what we do and say and make, with language and with operations, we come ultimately to the problem of the relation of what we say or make—artifacts, institutions, sciences—to what we do not say or make" (*Thought* 186). Meillassoux's solution deploys his distinctive variant of intellectual intuition, which he names, "*intuition dianoétique*, 'dianoetic intuition.' I mean by these words, the essential intertwining of a simple intuition and of a discursivity, a demonstration—both being entailed by the access to factuality" ("Presentation" 433). Dianoetic intuition encapsulates Meillassoux's clarifying analysis in "Presentation" of the strategy informing the philosophical argument in *After Finitude*. Meillassoux appears to align such intuition with Aristotle's *nous* in a passage that indicates that it refines the meaning of term "intellectual intuition" used in *After Finitude*: "We have a *nous* unveiled by a *dianoia*, an intuition unveiled by a demonstration. This is why I called it an intellectual intuition: not, of course, because it is an intuition which creates its object, as Kant defined it, but because it is an intuition discovered by reasoning" ("Presentation" 434).

Meillassoux distinguishes his view from Kant's, at least in part, because Brassier takes his view of intellectual intuition from Kant and judges Meillassoux's view accordingly in the concluding section of the chapter in *Nihil Unbound* that he devotes to Meillassoux. Their differing views of intellectual intuition mark their sharpest difference. For Kant, Brassier explains, "intellectual intuition actively creates its object," something beyond the capacity of humans, for only an intellect "unburdened by sensibility—such as God's—possesses this power to produce its object" (92). Humans can do no better than idealism. For Brassier, Meillassoux's "referent 'absolute contingency' is exclusively determined by the sense of the contingently existing thought 'everything that is, is absolutely contingent'" (93). Assuming that Kant has delivered the final word on intellectual intuition, Brassier turns to Laruelle's posited real for an alternative and finds in it "unilateralization," summarizing it thus: "It is no longer thought that determines the object, whether through representation or intuition, but rather the object that seizes thought and forces it to think it, or better, *according* to it" (149). This object, notably, is not pure, independent and indifferent like Meillassoux's "*great outdoors.*" Rather, Brassier's object is like a helicopter parent who "seizes" thought and shakes it into obedient "*accord[ance]*." Unilateralization is magical thinking.

In *After Finitude*, Meillassoux credits intellectual intuition with grasping the contingency principle because "contingency is neither visible nor perceptible in things and only thought is capable of accessing it" (82). Here, intellectual intuition is defined by contrast to sensory intuition. Dianoetic intuition refines this by stressing that the intellectual takes the form of "discover[y] by reasoning." "Presentation" clarifies this discovery process.

This clarification centers on the sequence in *After Finitude* from the correlationist's self-refutation to the passage introducing Aristotle's anhypothetical principle:

> It seems we have reached our goal, which was to identity the faultline in the correlationist circle that would allow us to cut through it towards an absolute. . . . What we have here is a *principle*, and even, we could say, an *anhypothetical* principle . . . in the Aristotelian sense. By "anhypothetical principle," Aristotle meant a fundamental proposition that could not be deduced from any other, but which could be proved by argument. This proof, which he called "indirect" or "refutational," proceeds not by deducing the principle from some other proposition—in which case it would no longer count as a principle—but by

pointing out the inevitable inconsistency into which anyone contesting the truth of the principle is bound to fall. (60–61)

Meillassoux first considers this principle in *Divine Inexistence*, where a separate section, pages 30–38 in the Brown translation, is entitled "The Principle of factuality as anhypothetical principle." *After Finitude* revises this principle under the influence of Aristotle, but this revision does not alter its purpose. "Anhypothetical" means "not" hypothetical, just as anharmonic is not harmonic and anarchy is not archy, that is, government rule, as in monarchy, oligarchy. Meillassoux introduces this principle in *Divine Inexistence* to proclaim his ambition to avoid beginning by positing: "what we call hypothetical reason designates the conception according to which the beginning of reason can only be *posited*—as an axiom, postulate, thesis, hypothesis, etc." (Brown translation 31). Meillassoux's continuing resistance to beginnings based on positing evidences itself in "Presentation" in his criticism of Laruelle for relying on a "*posited* Real" ("Presentation" 433). In *Divine Inexistence*, the "advent *ex nihlio*," discussed earlier, theorizes beginnings that defeat the hypotheses of "experimental rationality" because one cannot, for example, formulate a hypothesis for the advent of life that could be tested experimentally (Harman translation 232; see also 236). Rejecting positing, then, has always been fundamental for Meillassoux. He may have reasoned that because positing instantiates thought, he must reject it to avoid tying himself inextricably to correlationism. What he found in Aristotle is an alternative to "advent *ex nihlio*."

"Presentation" clarifies the argumentative strategy in *After Finitude* with the help of the notion of pragmatic contradiction, which Meillassoux defines as "contradicting the content of a sentence by enunciation of this very sentence. . . . For example: 'I don't think'" ("Presentation" 411). Sometimes he reserves the term "performative" rather than "pragmatic" for a "public enunciation" such as "I don't exist" ("Iteration" 1), but not always (see "Time" 9). "I don't think" would appear to qualify as "performative" but he calls it "pragmatic." In any case, pragmatic contradiction is the core logic that the anhypothetical principle transforms into the drama of indirect or refutational proof that consists of "pointing out the inevitable inconsistency into which anyone contesting the truth of the principle is bound to fall." The "speculative philosopher," who stands in for Meillassoux, engages in such "pointing out" in the debate Meillassoux stages in *After Finitude* (56–59).

In looking for the best strategy to combat correlationism, Meillassoux stresses the "exceptional *strength*" of the correlational argument, which he spells out thus: "No X without givenness of X, and no theory about X without a positing of X. If you speak about something you speak about something that is given to you, and posited by you" ("Presentation" 409). An example is the correlational argument against realism: "If you think X, then you *think* X. That is what I called the 'circle of correlation,' the first argument of every correlationism which claims that realism is necessarily a vicious circle, a denial of its very *act*" ("Presentation" 413). Restated in the drama of the anhypothetical principle, imagine the realist contesting the correlational principle by positing a real beyond the correlation, then the correlationist pointing out the inconsistency of a realism that depends on positing, a thought. The correlationist thus upholds the correlational principle but does so indirectly by exposing the realist's inconsistency, the inconsistency that is in effect a self-refutation. Positing is the core problem for Meillassoux: to "think X" is real is to "*think* X," that is, to presuppose thought's positing of X. The strategy Meillassoux chooses, as he explains in "Presentation," is to do to correlationism what correlationism does to realism: "I can refute the correlationist refutation of realism, grounded as it is on the accusation of pragmatic contradiction, because *I* discover in correlational reasoning a pragmatic contradiction" (432; see also "Time" 9). Among the commentators sensitive to Meillassoux's reliance on correlationism to refute correlationism, Harman relies heavily on the imprecise lens of metaphoric characterizations to identify the effects of Meillassoux's deployment of this strategy. Examples: "he turns it upside-down," "turn it against itself," "radicalizing the correlate from within rather than leaping naively into a reality beyond it," "overturning," (*Quentin* 14, 21, 21, 22).

Meillassoux sums up his strategy by contrasting it to Laruelle's, contending that Laruelle has no defense against the correlationist, whereas the correlationist has no defense against him. There is positing in both Laruelle and in Meillassoux's strategy, but there is an important difference between the two:

> Why do I think that Laruelle fails to escape correlationism? It is because he doesn't begin by refuting correlationism but by positing an axiom, a Real supposed to precede any position. If you begin with the Real, you can't refute the objection of the circle—that is, the Real is a *posited* Real. . . . I believe, on the contrary, that you must begin with correlationism, then show

that correlationism must itself posit the facticity of the correlation, and demonstrate in this way that this facticity is absolute contingency. Then, finally, you will accede to an independent Real. ("Presentation" 433)

In both cases, what is posited is an "independent Real." But in Laruelle's case, the positing serves his interests, whereas in the correlationist's case, the positing is against the interests of correlationism. This positing of an "independent Real," a noncorrelate, refutes correlationism.

Why would the correlationist do this? For the complete answer to that, one must turn to the analysis in *After Finitude*. But Meillassoux does add here one additional crucial point: "Hence, the only way to the Real, according to me, is through a proof, a *demonstration*. . . . The simple intuition of facticity is transmuted by a *dianoia*, by a demonstration, into an intuition of a radical exteriority" ("Presentation" 433). Unlike Aristotle's intellectual intuition of the form informing how a thing is "organized to function," as Putnam puts it in chapter two, Meillassoux's dianoetic intuition is a demonstrative proof, a reasoning process that forces the correlationist to reason against correlationism under the watchful eye of Meillassoux's "speculative philosopher." The Aristotelian model Meillassoux follows here is the one in which Aristotle imagines facing the denier of the law of noncontradiction. The denier who refuses to speak is "no better than a vegetable," while the one who says "something which is *significant* both for himself and for another" reasons in accord with the law he purports to deny (*Metaphysics* 4.4.1006a15–22, *Basic Works* 737–38). Similarly, the correlationist reasons against correlationism.

This method of indirect refutation relies on the agency of the one being refuted, an agency that refutes itself. Both Aristotle and Meillassoux deploy this agency in the interests of a metaphysical turn to thing. Aristotle deploys it to achieve this turn by refuting the prioritizing of language. Aristotle's depiction of this agency of self-refutation includes the sophists; Protagoras is singled out by name at one point (*Metaphysics* 4.5.1009a6, *Basic Works* 743). What is at stake in Aristotle's refutation is the difference that McKeon, as we saw earlier, records between the Aristotelian view that language is posterior to reality and the sophist view that language is a distinctive component of reality that is prior to reality in general. This distinctive component centers in the reality that X, a thing, does not cause whatever word one uses to refer to it. The word is an act, an invention. One is free to say both that "X is a precipice" and that "X is not a precipice." Aristotle agrees that X does not cause the word that references it, but he counters that *"significant"* language requires recognition, implicitly if not explicitly, of the law of noncontradiction whereby X cannot be and not be in the same respect, at the same time, in the same place. Aristotle includes among his many arguments that one who walks near a precipice regularly is always careful to avoid falling (*Metaphysics* 4.4. 1008b15–18; *Basic Works* 742–43). One may say that "X is a precipice" and that "X is not a precipice," but the reality prior to language is always one or the other.

Notably, Meillassoux ignores the guidance Aristotle offers for turning against the linguistic turn. His correlationist agency of self-refutation refutes not the prioritizing of language but the correlationist subject, the subject of epistemology who prioritizes thought. His agency of self-refutation refutes the priority of thought to turn to a prioritizing of thing.

But before implementing his strategy of exposing a pragmatic contradiction in correlational reasoning, Meillassoux must select his target from among the variant forms of correlationism. He acknowledges that correlationism comes in more than one variant early in *After Finitude* when he indicates that there are "two types of correlationist thought," the first conceiving the correlational as "eternal" (10), but the second turns out in Meillassoux's analysis to encompass multiple subtypes. Sensitive to Meillassoux's discrimination of multiple variants, Harman construes this as an invitation to look for more, adding "Very Strong Correlationism" (*Quentin* 14), and suggesting additional discriminations are possible.

The key to Meillassoux's solution to the problem of identifying the right target appears when he tells us that he examines variants to find "the most rigorous," what one might consider the "king of the hill" if you will, the one that defeats all other variants. But if this variant achieves final victory by means of a pragmatic contradiction, it falls too, joining all the other variants it defeated. That, as we shall see, is the basic design of Meillassoux's refutation. The correlationist's victory is a fall because to win the correlationist must think a noncorrelate, "an X independent of any thinking," as Meillassoux puts it in a passage quoted earlier.

Harman construes thus Meillassoux's moves from variant to variant, "With each step in the series . . . Meillassoux becomes increasingly sympathetic to the position described, while remaining somewhat dissatisfied" (*Quentin* 18). While "dissatisfied" adds a helpful qualification, "sympathetic" is still misleading because Meillassoux is looking for the "king of the hill," not the variant that is closest to his views. He appears to be on the side of the variant that triumphs over a different variant only because he is looking for the one that defeats all the others. The use of "sympathetic" is nonetheless understandable because of Meillassoux's great skill at presenting arguments with which he profoundly disagrees. This skill is what I admire most in his work. Dialogue is out of fashion as a mode of philosophizing, which is unfortunate, for Meillassoux appears ideally suited to write great dialogue. But this skill can make it difficult for the reader to distinguish when Meillassoux speaks for himself from when he mimics a position with which he disagrees.

Harman's mistaking mimicking for sympathy leads Harman astray when he attributes to Meillassoux the view that *"we cannot think things-in-themselves without thinking them, and thereby turning them into correlates of thought"* (Quentin 213; see also 3, 9, 21, as well as 10 and 16, where he quotes *After Finitude* 27). This view is, of course, the pragmatic contradiction that the correlationist uncovers in realism. Meillassoux is sympathetic with it in the sense that he considers it a strong argument, so much so that it inspires him to turn the tables and find the pragmatic contradiction in correlational reasoning. That kind of sympathy is not the sympathy Harman has in mind.

To determine the "king of the hill," Meillassoux looks for the variant that addresses most effectively issues that arise at both ends of "the correlation between thinking and being" (*After Finitude* 5), which rules that neither "thinking" nor "being" can be considered apart from the other. Issues arise over whether this rule is broken in a particular case.

Focusing on the "being" end, Gratton asks and answers, "Is his refutation of the correlationist as knockdown as Meillassoux argues. In a word, no. . . . Kant isn't asserting that the in-itself doesn't exist, but rather that what we know can't simply be accounted for by some unmediated access to the in-itself" (*Speculative Realism* 46). Gratton cites no text, but here is one that may serve to pose key issues at the "being" end:

> Kantian transcendentalism could be identified with a "weak" correlationism. . . . It proscribes any knowledge of the thing-in-itself . . . but maintains the thinkability of the in-itself. According to Kant, we know *a priori* that the thing-in-itself is noncontradictory and that it actually exists. By way of contrast, the strong model of correlationism maintains not only that it is illegitimate to claim that we *know* the in-itself, but *also* that it is illegitimate to claim that we can at least *think* it. (*After Finitude* 35)

Contrary to Gratton's reading, Meillassoux does not question that Kant claims the in-itself exists. The claim, rather, is that because he claims it exists, his correlationism is "weak." Perhaps Gratton misconstrues this demotion of Kant as a questioning of Kant's claim.

Meillassoux sides here with the "strong model" against Kant. But this is a particularly interesting case, for while he sides with it in his search for the "king of the hill," it is clear that he disagrees with it. Elaborating on the strong model's claim, Meillassoux's focuses sharply on the thinkability of contradiction. Leaving aside the knowability of in-itself, can we think it in the sense that we think it is noncontradictory? Can we assume, in other words, that anything that exists is noncontradictory? Strong correlationism says "no," asking, "For by what miraculous operation is Kantian thought able to get out of itself in order to verify that what is unthinkable for us is impossible in itself?" (*After Finitude* 35). Strong correlationism agrees with Kant that what is thinkable for us is what is noncontradictory, but it rigorously refuses to go beyond the correlation of "thinking and being" in any way, even to assume that the contradictory is not only unthinkable for us but also that it does not exist outside the correlation as well. Strong correlationism thus stays within the limits of the correlation more rigorously than does the Kant's weak correlationism. About anything beyond the correlation, strong correlationism is agnostic. Maybe the law of noncontradiction holds outside the correlation as well as inside, but maybe it does not.

On this issue, while Meillassoux sides with the strong against the weak in his search for the "king of the hill," he disagrees with the strong when instead of mimicking the strong, he speaks for himself. For he agrees with Kant that a contradictory entity is impossible. Such an entity

> could never become other than it is, since it already *is* this other. As contradictory, this entity is always-already whatever it is not. . . . Consequently, we know . . . why noncontradiction is an absolute ontological truth: because it is necessary that what is be determined in such a way as to be *capable of becoming* and of being subsequently determined in *some other way*. (*After Finitude* 69–71)

This view appears to mark a crucial stage in Meillassoux's development. He reports that Hegel and Marx inspired a "love of dialectic" that consumed him in his youth until he "understood the profound reason why there could never be *contradictions* in reality" (Interview Harman 217).

Strong correlationism's agnosticism is not limited to the law of non-contradiction. It also disqualifies any affirmation or denial of any X outside correlation, thus rendering philosophy powerless to say "yes" or "no" to any X beyond correlation that anyone puts forward no matter how bizarre or contradictory. Meillassoux's deep reservations about this self-imposed limitation on philosophy appear in chapter two of *After Finitude*.

Even though Meillassoux thus disagrees with strong correlationism profoundly, he can nonetheless side with it in his search for the "king of the hill" because it rigorously stays with the limits of the correlation of "thinking and being." Reading Meillassoux thus requires discriminations in his views that can sometimes be difficult.

While Kant loses in the debates that center on the "being" side of the "thinking and being" correlation, he comes out on top in the debate Meillassoux stages between him and Hegel, which centers on the "thinking" side. Whereas in Hegel's "speculative idealism" one could "*deduce*" forms of thought, in Kant's "transcendental idealism," one can only "*describe*" them: "Kant maintains that it is impossible to derive the forms of thought from a principle or system capable of endowing them with absolute necessity" (*After Finitude* 38). In Kant, one can describe the forms involved in the "thinking and being" correlation, but not deduce them from a principle outside the correlation. Meillassoux cites no textual support for this point, but clear support does appear when Kant disavows the possibility of any such deduction, explaining in a passage quoted earlier, in chapter one, "This peculiarity of our understanding, that it can produce *a priori* unity of apperception solely by means of the categories, and only by such and so many, is as little capable of further explanation as why we have just these and no other functions of judgment, or why space and time are the only forms of our possible intuition" (*Critique of Pure Reason* B145–46). Kant does not go as far as Meillassoux in envisioning the possibility of these forms changing as "World" displaces "World" in the "non-Whole world," but he does agree that one cannot deduce these forms from a principle with "absolute necessity"

In sum, strong correlationism is agnostic in the internal, subjective direction of "thinking" as well as the external, objective direction of "being." Meillassoux does not identify most of the variants of correlationism that he distinguishes with individual philosophers, but one might venture that it is Meillassoux himself who best defends strong correlationism even though this defense is ironically designed not to espouse it but ultimately to find where to defend itself it must pragmatically contradict itself.

Meillassoux's narrative of warring variants culminates with strong correlationism debating subjectivist metaphysics, which absolutizes the correlation, judging that "the correlation is the only veritable in-itself." While strong correlationism is rigorously agnostic about what is outside the correlation, the correlational idealist insists that there is absolutely nothing outside the correlation itself. The idealist turns even the arche-fossil into a correlate by "eternaliz[ing] the Self or the Mind" who witnesses it (*After Finitude* 52, 11). Of the two types of correlationism identified early in *After Finitude*, the subjectivist metaphysician is the first type, the idealist who conceives the correlation as all-encompassing and "eternal," whereas the strong correlationist is the subtype of the second type that defeats the other subtypes. Among the more baffling criticisms of Meillassoux is the claim that he "has counter-arguments against nonabsolutist correlationism but not against an 'absolutization of the correlate'" (Johnston, "Hume's Revenge" 98). One may debate whether the argument against the idealist absolute is successful, but not whether it exists.

In this culminating confrontation, it is the strong correlationist who becomes "king of the hill," but does so by affirming a noncorrelate, that is, by a pragmatic contradiction. Strong correlationism thus ironically wins by losing, that is, by refuting correlationism. What motivates strong correlationism to do this, Meillassoux contends, is that while correlationism targets both realism and absolutism, it is best viewed not as "an antirealism but [as] an anti*absolutism*. Correlationism is the modern way to reject all possible knowledge of an absolute: it is the claim that we are closed up in our representations—whether conscious, linguistic, or historical—with no sure access to an eternal reality independent of our specific point of view" ("Presentation" 427; see also *After Finitude* 11). Of the two, absolutism is the tougher antagonist: "If strong correlationism can easily rebuff the realist who figures as its 'external' adversary, it is altogether more difficult for it to defeat the 'subjectivist' metaphysician who is its 'internal' adversary" (*After Finitude* 38).

The culminating confrontation appears in a dialogue (*After Finitude* 55–59), albeit one in which Meillassoux summarizes the views of the participants instead of depicting them speaking for themselves, with the exception of the "speculative philosopher," the last to arrive on scene, who speaks for Meillassoux himself. What is surprising is that this dialogue begins with an atheist and a Christian expressing their views about death, views that are well-known but seemingly not relevant to the opposition between the strong correlationist and the idealist who absolutizes the correlation. But these views are relevant to the concerns of "The Spectral Dilemma" and *Divine Inexistence*. Here, in other words, is where the two sides of Meillasoux's project intersect, although it is left to the reader to do most of the intersecting. From the standpoint of "The Spectral Dilemma," we recall, when it comes to mourning the dead, both the atheist and the Christian have serious shortcomings, especially when compared to the "*may-being*," which rationalizes believing in a God who does not exist. From the standpoint of correlationism, there is a contrast between correlation and death central to this dialogue. If death were a correlation such as redness, which depends on both perceiver and perceived, it would never occur. "[T]o think of myself as a mortal, I must admit that death doesn't depend on my thinking about my death," Meillassoux reasons, for otherwise, "I could be dying indefinitely, but I could never pass away, because I would have to exist to make of death a correlate of my own subjective access to it" ("Presentation" 430–31).

The third to join the dialogue is the strong correlationist, here simply the correlationist, in effect identifying in advance the one destined to be the "king of the hill" who speaks for correlationism. The correlationist quickly puts atheist and Christian under the umbrella of "a strict theoretical agnosticism" (*After Finitude* 55). Later, on the same page, the idealist absolutist appears and quickly refutes in one fell swoop the atheist, the Christian, and the correlational agnostic on the idealist ground that there is nothing outside the correlation in which one exists: "my mind, if not my body, is immortal." The atheist and the Christian remain silent, so the ball is back in the correlationist's court. Now faced with atheism and two forms of immortality, the Christian's and the idealist's, the correlational "agnostic can recuse all three positions as instances of absolutism" (56).

It is at this point that the fifth and final figure enters the dialogue, the one who speaks for Meillassoux, the "speculative philosopher" (56). From this point on, he lectures in accord with the anhypothetical principle to establish Meillassoux's absolute indirectly by exposing the correlationist's pragmatic contradiction. This exposure instantiates Meillassoux's dianoetic intuition. The contradiction establishes indirectly Meillassoux's absolute.

Speaking through this philosopher, Meillassoux begins with what the correlationist established presumably without realizing it, or short of that without fully realizing it. The absolute is not what the atheist, the Christian, or the idealist think. Rather, the absolute is

> *simply the capacity-to-be-other as such, as theorized by the agnostic.* ... But this possibility is no longer a "possibility of ignorance"; viz., a possibility that is merely the result of my inability to know which of the three aforementioned theses is correct—rather, it is the *knowledge* of the very real possibility of all of these eventualities, as well as of a great many others. (56)

The addition of "a great many others" alludes to the ontology of "*may-being*," which authorizes an indefinite if not infinite number of possibilities. That is beyond the scope of anything the correlationist said, but the shift from "ignorance" to "*knowledge*" is implicit in the correlationist's agnosticism. While this agnosticism claims not to know what is outside the correlation, it does claim something is outside the correlation in opposing the idealist who claims nothing is outside the correlation.

After beginning with these claims, Meillassoux asks and answers, "How then are we able to claim this capacity-to-be-other is absolute—an index of knowledge rather than of ignorance? The answer is that it is the agnostic herself who has convinced us of it." It is at this point, to show how she did this, that Meillassoux asks and answers again to explain how the correlationist refutes the idealist by the pragmatic contradiction of thinking a noncorrelate. How does the correlationist

> go about refuting the idealist? She does so by maintaining that we can *think* ourselves as no longer being; in other words, by maintaining that our mortality, our annihilation, and our becoming-wholly-other in God, are all effectively thinkable. But how are these states conceivable as possibilities? On account of the fact that we are able to think—by dint of the absence of any reason for our being—a capacity-to-be-other capable of abolishing us, or of radically transforming us. But if so, then *this capacity-to-be-other cannot be conceived as a correlate of our thinking, precisely because it harbours the possibility of our own non-being.* In order to think myself as mortal, as the atheist does—and hence as capable of not being—I must think my capacity-not-to-be as an absolute possibility, for if I think this possibility as a correlate of my thinking, if I maintain that the possibility of

> my not-being only exists as a correlate of my act of thinking the possibility of my not-being, then I *can no longer conceive the possibility of my not-being*, which is precisely the thesis defended by the idealist. (*After Finitude* 56, 56–57)[46]

This last sentence is so important to Meillassoux that he goes on to restate it three times in the next three sentences.

Hence, when Meillassoux says, as quoted earlier, "I think an X independent of any thinking, and know it for sure, thanks to the correlationist himself and his fight against the absolute, the idealist absolute," the "X" is the noncorrelate, the "*capacity-to-be-other.*"[47] It is independent of correlational thinking in which thinking is always part of the correlation. Thinking the noncorrelate is a different kind of thinking, for the thinking is not part of the noncorrelate, which is an independent real. The correlationist's thinking of this noncorrelate is the correlationist's pragmatic contradiction. This thinking is Meillassoux's dianoetic intuition. In Meillassoux's version of intuition, it matters who does the thinking. The correlationist's intuition is credible because it refutes correlationism. The correlationist is not self-serving but rigorous in recognizing that death is a noncorrelate.

The correlationist thinking of this noncorrelate originates Meillassoux's turn from the priority of thought to the priority of thing. The noncorrelate is the key. In the prioritizing of thought, in Kant's famous formulation, philosophy explains how thing conforms to thought rather than how thought conforms to thing in intuiting how a thing is "organized to function." In this Kantian mode of philosophical explanation, there is no way to get beyond what is in the mind to directly access what is in the thing. By contrast, to think a noncorrelate is to access a thing directly. This direct access differs from Brassier's magical "unilateralization," where the mind is passive and the thing imprints itself on it. Brassier modifies his view significantly in "Concepts and Objects," to be

---

46. Meillassoux's argument from death, Jussi Backman argues, departs from Heidegger in seeing mortality as "transgress[ing] the correlational realm of phenomenal meaning into an absolute noncorrelational realm" (286). See also Gratton's brief comment, limited to the constraints of a footnote, comparing Meillassoux's argument from death to Heidegger's being-towards-death ("After the Subject" 68–69).

47. Meillassoux depicts the correlationist as male in this passage from "Presentation" and female in *After Finitude*.

considered in the final chapter, coming closer to Meillassoux but stopping short because of his dogmatic denial of intellectual intuition.

The *"capacity-to-be-other"* is the essence of what it means to be contingent. As Meillassoux puts it, "the contingency of the correlation, which correlationism needs in order to refute absolutist subjectivism, cannot itself be thought as a correlate of thought. Thus there is necessarily contingency, whether I think it or not" (Interview Harman 214; see also "Time" 8–9). Contingency is the *"great outdoors . . . existing in itself regardless of whether we are thinking of it or not"* (*After Finitude* 7).

In sum, the correlationist's thinking of the noncorrelate of the *"capacity-to-be-other"* instantiated in death would thus appear to endorse the ontology of *"may-being"* and to thereby bring together *After Finitude* and *Divine Inexistence*.

What should give one pause, though, is Meillassoux's turn to the atheist in the climatic passage above: "In order to think myself as mortal, as the atheist does—and hence as capable of not being—I must think my capacity-not-to-be as an absolute possibility." No death is more absolute than the atheist's in the sense that no death is more permanent. But there is no permanent death in *Divine Inexistence*: "The negative knowledge of our mortality thus refers to the positive knowledge of our possible rebirth" (Harman translation 260). In Meillassoux's "non-Whole world," a "World" of atheistic death is possible, but it may be displaced at any time by a "World" of rebirth and immortality. In Meillassoux's argument from death, atheistic death in a "World" stands in for contingency in the "non-Whole world" of *"may-being."* The correlationist's thinking of the noncorrelate of the *"capacity-to-be-other"* in death may bring together *After Finitude* and *Divine Inexistence*, but it does so provisionally at best. For *"may-being"* allows for the possibility of everything but the permanence of nothing except for itself.

Meillassoux staked his metaphysical turn on the correlationist thinking a noncorrelate. This is a turn, however, as depicted in *After Finitude*'s argument from death, that is relative to a "World" characterized by atheistic death. If this noncorrelate were the *"capacity-to-be-other"* of contingency in the "non-Whole world," it would be the ultimate priority of *"may-being"* that constitutes the ontology of the "non-Whole world." But a noncorrelate relative to a "World" falls short of that; atheistic death demonstrates the contingency of humans in the sense that they might become extinct, not the broader contingency that authorizes an indefinite number of possibilities, including the possibility of immortality.

Chaotic pragmatism insists on the impermanence of death. Insofar as Meillassoux's metaphysical turn depends on atheistic death, he is at an impasse. Time will tell if he finds a way beyond it.

KANT'S NONCORRELATE

Meillassoux's critique presupposes that we are enclosed with the cocoon of correlation in need of discovering a "aperture" to find our way out. This view needs correcting because this enclosure is not as airtight as Meillassoux thinks. Consider Kant closely. It is a truism that he bars access to the noumenon, the thing-in-itself, a noncorrelate. We cannot know the noumenon, but we can think it as that which appears in experience as phenomenon. "[O]therwise," as he puts it, "we should be landed in the absurd conclusion that there can be appearance without anything that appears" (*Critique of Pure Reason* 27, Bxxvii). The phenomenon is the way the noumenon beyond experience appears in experience. From this standpoint, one can disqualify any claim to access a noumenon directly, to intuit how it is "organized to function." In the correlation that the *Critique of Pure Reason* explains, the correlation connecting perceiver to the phenomenon perceived mediates access to the noumenon. Direct access to the noumenon is ruled out. But this correlation between perceiver and perceived in Kant's explanation should not be confused with the noncorrelational relation between Kant, the explainer, and this correlation, the explained. Here, Kant stands outside the correlation that Meillassoux thinks is an enclosure that can only be escaped from the inside. The relation of explainer to explained is informed by the inferential structure grounded in Kant's ultimate priority.

Like the exemptionalism we saw in chapter three, itself akin to Meillassoux's pragmatic contradiction, Kant does exempt himself from his rule disqualifying direct access when the noumenon is the human being, unique in being subject to nature's law of causality on one level and the subject of teleological causality on another level: "Now we have in the world only one kind of beings whose causality is teleological, i.e. is directed to purposes.... The being of this kind is man, but man considered as noumenon, the only natural being in which we can recognize, on the side of its peculiar constitution, a supersensible faculty (*freedom*) and also the law of causality" (*Critique of Judgment* 285, section 84; Kant's italics; see also *Foundations* 70). Whereas Meillassoux looks to atheistic death to find a way the correlationist thinks a noncorrelate, Kant thinks a noncorrelate in accessing directly the human being as a noumenon, a thing-in-itself. In this direct access, there is no correlational mediation on the phenomenal level. Kant accesses directly the noumenon, the thing-in-itself, beyond the phenomenon.

As we saw in chapter one, Johnston and Gabriel both insist that Kantian epistemology should not obscure the ontological reality of the subject of epistemology on which it is grounded. Quoting Gabriel again, "The subject with its conceptual capacities actually exists; it is part of the world." In *Critique of Pure Reason*, Kant fleshes out in great detail how this existent, the noumenon of the human subject, is "organized to function" as a thing-in-itself in the epistemological process.

> Man, however, who knows all the rest of nature solely through the senses [correlational mediations], knows himself also through pure apperception; and this, indeed, in acts and inner determinations which he cannot regard as impressions of the senses [unmediated, noncorrelational direct access]. He is thus to himself, on the one hand phenomenon, and on the other hand, in respect of certain faculties the action of which cannot be ascribed to the receptivity of sensibility, a purely intelligible object. We entitle these faculties understanding and reason. (472, A546–47/B574–45)

Reason corresponds to the teleological side of the human subject, understanding to the side of nature's causality. By contrast to the correlational mediated access to empirical objects, Kant here has direct access to how these two faculties are "organized to function" in the human subject, an "intelligible" thing-in-itself. Kant goes on, explaining that reason governs ethics, "reason has causality. . . . '*Ought*' expresses a kind of necessity and of connection with grounds which is found nowhere else in the whole of nature" (472–73, A547/B5575). The *a priori* structure of understanding processes sensory experience, producing correlations that do not go beyond phenomenal appearances: "The understanding can know in nature only what is, what has been, or what will be. . . . This '*ought*' expresses a possible action the ground of which cannot be anything but a mere concept; whereas in the case of merely natural action the ground must always be an appearance" (473, A547–48/B575/76).

Fichte, Meillassoux suggests, saw this failure to explain this noncorrelational access as Kant's failure to "explain how it was possible to write the *Critique of Pure Reason* ("Presentation" 417). Rorty explains this failure by remarking that Kant was never troubled by the question of how we could have apodictic knowledge of the mind's "constituting activities," because "Cartesian privileged access was supposed to take care of that" (*Philosophy Mirror* 137–38). That we think and speak can seduce us into assuming we have privileged, immediate access to these realities. But these realities are as difficult to comprehend as any other reality. Derrida's *difference* is a constituting activity but there is no sense in which we have "immediate access" to it. Access is possible by means of Derrida's intuition of how it is "organized to function."

McKeon's pluralism finds characteristics in thing, thought, and language and action that endow each with a basis for claiming that it is prior to the others. These competing claims of priority evidence themselves in philosophical turns from one subject matter of philosophy to another. In these turns, accessing ultimate priorities in these subject matters is direct, intuitive, not mediated. When this direct access is also an exemptionalist pragmatic contradiction, the question arises, to be addressed in the final chapter, of how to evaluate it. Such evaluation may help to determine if turns themselves offer reasons for preference among them.

5 Harman: Metaphysical Turn as Perspectivalism

> Principles are conceived metaphysically when knowledge is treated as a relation of consequences established in thought to consequences encountered in things.
>
> —McKeon, "Principles and Consequences," 388

Harman is extraordinarily prolific. Books, articles, interviews, reviews, videos and audios of lectures, blogs, and so on—you name it, he produces it, often frequently. As one writes about him, he is doubtless producing something new. Hence, allow me to qualify everything I say about him with "to the best of my knowledge," conceding from the outset that at every point he might be producing something that might prompt me to revise what I say.

In this prolific output, however, there is something of a paradox that makes writing about Harman a little less daunting than might otherwise be the case. For Harman tells us that his huge body of work is at bottom about one "central thought," in a passage that merits full quotation given its importance:

> At some point in your life, if you are lucky, one central thought or one fascinating problem will come to stand at the center of your thinking. You will remain devoted to that thought, quite apart from all of your shifting opinions about the various issues of the day. In my own case, it was the rather surprising realization that objects withdraw from all contact yet somehow make contact anyway, so that the world is dominated by *indirect* forms of contact. This is the paradox I wake up thinking about every day, and all of my philosophical work is an attempt to grapple with this problem. It hardly matters that many others don't even see it as a problem, since that is often the case with what is deepest in one's own work. It is my mission, not theirs, to wrestle with this problem and generate whatever spinoff ideas are needed to address it successfully. Maybe at some point they

will see the problem, or maybe they will at least find some of the spinoff ideas useful. ("On Landscape Ontology"; Harman's italics throughout unless noted otherwise).

This "central thought" appears, of course, in different forms: different terminologies for it, different applications of it, different critiques based on it, and so on. There is plenty of variety to go with this one thought.

This variety notwithstanding, there is not in Harman anything comparable to the problem in reading Meillassoux of putting together parts, *Divine Inexistence* and *After Finitude*, that do not appear to go together. For in reading Harman, while where one starts determines the form of his "central thought" that one first encounters, having encountered it, one can move to other works and quickly see variants of the same thought. One can thus get a good grasp of Harman's philosophy without having to read his works in a particular sequence. Peter Gratton, for example, in his *Speculative Realism: Problems and Prospects*, relies principally on *The Quadruple Object* in his often illuminating chapter on Harman. This book, appearing almost a decade after Harman's first one, benefits from Harman having by that time restated his "central thought" many times in varying ways. Harman tells us in its Preface that he challenged himself to time his writing, "discover[ing] that the final draft of *Quadruple Object* took 86 hours and 34 minutes to complete" (2).

While one could thus start anywhere in Harman, the starting point I recommend is *Tool-Being: Heidegger and the Metaphysics of Objects*, his first book, and in my judgment still his philosophically most rigorous work. By now, I suspect many readers begin with later books that are easier going, benefiting from the simpler formulations Harman produces in moving from variant to variant of his "central thought." But *Tool-Being* provides the originary form of this thought. From the standpoint of this book, one can thus see how later formulations transform this originary form and unpack its implications.

By contrast to Meillassoux, Harman's metaphysical turn to thing is a turn not to pragmatism on a cosmic scale but to realism, or so Harman claims. Harman's notion of realism is sometimes unconventional. Consider, "If we are nevertheless inclined to call Kant a 'realist'—as I am so inclined—then this clearly has nothing to do with his pursuit of the transcendental categories of experience, but only with what escapes such categories: namely the infamous *Ding an sich*, or thing-in-itself" ("Realism" 102). Leaving aside Harman's questionable assumption that he joins a crowd ("we") in seeing Kant as a realist, one might ask how this realism differs from skepticism. Skeptics may presuppose that something is "out there," like the thing-in-itself, in claiming that we simply can never have knowledge of it; skepticism is not solipsism. Harman follows Kant insofar as he offers a skeptical explanation of why we can have no knowledge of the "thing-in-itself."

McKeon's prediction, quoted at the end of chapter one, was that a metaphysical turn would feature "a choice between parts and wholes." In Meillassoux, there is a choice of a whole in the form of pragmatic *"may-being"* in which one "World" may displace an existing "World." In Harman, by contrast, there is no "totality of the world" ("Presentation" 400), only parts in the sense of objects scattered throughout the mundane world that are at most in indirect contact with one another. Scattered rather than hierarchized, these objects constitute a "flat ontology," which Harman celebrates for "prevent[ing] any premature taxonomies from being smuggled into philosophy from the outside," like the "implausible taxonomy between human thought on one side and *everything else in the universe* on the other" (*Object-Oriented Ontology* 55, 56).

This chapter will argue that form is where to look to find the fundamental realist ingredient in Harman's metaphysical turn. Harman alerts us to the importance of form in a passage that merits more attention than it tends to receive: "I am attracted to formal causes because of my suspicions about the existence of matter. Where is this matter supposedly located? Where on earth can we find formless matter? Since there is no such thing we ought to pay attention to forms" (DeLanda and Harman 18). Harman does not think he is alone, moreover, claiming, "Formal causation is where all the action's happening in philosophy" ("Presentation" 406). Definitely no formless matter, then, but it is unclear if there is matterless form. In any case, a fundamental form consistent with his "central thought" would combine contact and no contact in the form of indirect contact. Since this combination is common to all things, it takes the notion of universality about as far as it can go.

The Heidegger Connection

Notably, in having this "central thought," Harman considers himself "lucky." It was Heidegger's view, Harman recounts, "that every great thinker has a single great thought," adding that in Heidegger's case, as noted in chapter two, this thought was *"being is not presence"* (*Heidegger* 1). Harman typically links his philosophy to Heidegger, nowhere more so that in *Tool-Being*, where he forges his initial formulation of his "central thought" through his reading of Heidegger's famous tool analysis, which features a hammer and its breaking. In later work, while not disavowing this linkage to Heidegger, he sometimes offers alternatives. In one place, he suggests that even though his philosophy "comes out of Heidegger, [it] can be linked to Kant most easily perhaps" ("Propositions" 24). The reason for this will become clear later.

But even in *Tool-Being*, Harman makes it clear that his "goal is *not* to reconstruct Heidegger's own understanding of the tool-analysis," even conceding that Heidegger "would revile much of what [he has] to say" (15). There is ambiguity insofar as it is not always clear if Harman sees himself uncovering implications of the tool analysis that Heidegger missed or correcting mistakes that Heidegger made. Harman even suggests that misunderstanding Heidegger "sometimes afflicts Heidegger himself" (*Quadruple* 35; see also "On Vicarious Causation" 192, *Speculative Realism* 93). From the standpoint of philosophical turns, Harman turns against Heidegger's turn from the priority of thought.

Harman begins on *Tool-Being*'s first page by proposing that his tool analysis "gives birth to an ontology of *objects themselves*," but that to see this one must recognize that it is about "objects insofar as they withdraw from human view into a dark subterranean reality that never becomes present to practical action any more than it does to theoretical awareness," a recognition, Harman concedes, that goes against the grain of the usual reading of this analysis as about "the difference between theory and praxis" (1). This difference, fundamental in Heidegger's turn, becomes secondary in Harman's turn to thing, informed by his "central thought."

In presenting his "tool-being," Harman proposes to "abandon the stale example of the hammer and consider a basic piece of infrastructure: a bridge" (21). This sounds innocent, but more is involved than simply substituting a fresh for a stale example. To say that "stale" is a subterfuge may be too strong, but it is not far off the mark. The point of Harman's bridge is not the point of Heidegger's hammer. From the standpoint of philosophical turning, Harman's bridge manifests his metaphysical turn from Heidegger, whereas Heidegger's hammer manifests his turn from the subject matter of thought to the practical subject matter of action. Each of these turns is achieved by a change in the order of what is prior to what.

To sketch Heidegger's turn, one can begin with McKeon's observation, also quoted in chapter three, that thought's claim to priority is vulnerable to displacement because it is impossible to conceive thought "unexpressed in language, and inoperative in action" ("Philosophy of Communications" 312). Exploiting thought's inextricable ties to action, Heidegger prioritizes action by beginning on the practical level of hammering, where the hammer is "ready-to-hand," used routinely without reflective thought in some process. When the hammer breaks, however, there is a shift to "presence-at-hand," at which point thought emerges. When the hammer is viewed "'in a new way' as something present-at-hand," it is heavy or light, "a corporeal Thing subject to the law of gravity" (*Being and Time* 412). Seeing it as subject to the law of gravity operative everywhere and thus nowhere in particular presupposes what Dewey critiqued as the spectator theory of knowing, redescribed by Harman as a "Spock-like emotionless observer" (*Heidegger* 43). But by virtue of Heidegger's turn, this "spectator" is posterior to the prior action that occasions it, not transcendent but posterior to this action. Heidegger thus turns from thought by turning to action, by contrast to logical positivism's turn to language to turn from thought.

Heidegger marks this step from "ready-to-hand" action to "presence-at-hand" thought with the metaphor "lit up"—I count nine uses of the metaphor on pages 102–07 of *Being and Time*. What is "lit up" is a second sense of the word "used," not "used" in "ready-to-hand" actions in everyday living, but "used" in the sense of "assignment," "in-order-to," "towards-this," not "used" unreflectively, but "used for," thus "lighting up" the "totality": "But *when an assignment has been disturbed*—when something is unusable for some purpose—then the assignment becomes explicit" (105, Heidegger's italics). In other words, the broken hammer prompts a shift from the practical level of routine hammering to theoretical reflection on the hammer's "assignment" in the total process, reflection that can lead to designing a different kind of hammer or reconsideration of the hammering function in the total process. But this theoretical thought, is posterior to the prior practical level of action that occasions it.

Heidegger's demotion of thought from prior to posterior is promised in the last sentence of the chapter in *Being and Time* that precedes the chapter containing the tool analysis, "The Worldhood of the World": "Knowing [thought] is a mode of Dasein founded upon Being-in-the-world. Thus Being-in-the-world, as a basic state, must be Interpreted *beforehand*" (90; Heidegger's italics and capitals "B," "D," and "I").

Knowing occurs, but its occurrence is posterior to the practical concreteness of "Being-in-the-world."

For Heidegger, any piece of equipment is always part of a totality in which it performs its function as equipment: "ink-stand, pen, ink, paper, blotting pad, table, lamp, furniture, windows, doors, room"—each needs the others to be the equipment it is. Similarly, "room" is encountered "not as something 'between four walls' in a geometrical spatial sense, but as equipment for residing." The room "in a geometrical spatial sense" is the room "present-at-hand" that is posterior to the prior "ready-to-hand" room wherein "being-in-the-world" occurs; if the room burns down, one concerns oneself with the "presence-at-hand" of geometrical space in rebuilding it, but this is a "presence-at-hand in what is ready-to-hand" (97, 98, 104), that is, a "presence-at-hand" that derives from a prior "ready-to-hand." This "presence-at-hand" is thus viewed by a concrete "being-in-the-world" located somewhere, not by a spectator located nowhere.

Harman's metaphysical turn from Heidegger identifies an "is" that is prior to Heidegger's "ready-to-hand" equipment: "Equipment is not effective 'because people use it'; on the contrary, it can only be used because it is *capable of an effect*, of inflicting some kind of blow on reality. In short, the tool isn't 'used'—it *is*" (*Tool-Being* 20).[48] In other words, a hammer's "use" depends on the prior existence of that out of which the hammer is produced with the capacity to hammer. The "is-ness" of this "that" makes possible the hammer with its capacities.

In accord with Harman's "central thought," then, the hammer marks a point of "*indirect*" contact with this "is," in contact with part of "is," not in contact with the rest of "is." The hammer is in effect one of many possible perspectives on the prior "is," each of which would realize a possible "use" of this "isness."

This counterpoint of "is" to "use" is representative of much of Harman's engagement with Heidegger in that it both (1) identifies a specific text in Heidegger and (2) offers a comment on the text that appears to differ from Heidegger's meaning. A thorough study of Harman's engagement with Heidegger would require close attention to all of the contacts between Heidegger and Harman centered on specific texts in Heidegger. An exhaustive study of these contacts appears in Peter Wolfendale's *Ob-*

---

48. This distinction between "use" and "is" is anticipated in a 1999 lecture in which Harman uses for the first time the phrase "object-oriented philosophy" (*Toward Speculative Realism* 98, 93).

ject-Oriented Philosophy: The Noumenon's New Clothes. This book is thus a useful starting point for such a study despite his uncharitable reading of Harman. Wolfendale acknowledges that Harman says Heidegger would disagree with his reading, but counters, "Harman's reading cannot be an interpretation of the substance of Heidegger's ideas—even one that Heidegger himself would disagree with" (48). Wolfendale's uncharitable reading leads to a reading of Harman's contrast between "use" and "is" that oddly gets the point in one sense while disallowing it in another sense. He gets the point when he recognizes that Harman is saying that "successful reliance upon a thing demands that it possess the causal capacity to produce the effect relied upon," but then adds that the point "is questionable precisely insofar as it is metaphysical rather than phenomenological" (50). The implication is that Harman's metaphysical turn departs from phenomenology so radically that "it cannot be an interpretation of the substance of Heidegger's ideas."

Harman's evidence for an "is" prior to "use" thus becomes the basis for his turn from Heidegger. Whereas for Heidegger the practical is prior to the theoretical, for Harman the practical and the theoretical are equally perspectives that have indirect contact with an "is" in different ways. Neither is prior to the other; both are posterior to the perspectivist form of indirect contact in Harman's "central thought." In the simpler formulation in the later *The Quadruple Object*, Harman concedes that "some things are consciously in mind while others are unconsciously used," but insists that this distinction between conscious and unconscious is secondary to the "truly important rift [that] lies between the withdrawn reality of any object and the distortion of that object by way of both theory *and* practice" (42–43; see also "Presentation" 371, "On Vicarious Causation" 193, "Well-Wrought Broken Hammer" 196, *Speculative Realism* 93). Theory distorts the withdrawn thing one way; practice distorts it another way. Both are subordinate to the prior perspectivist form of indirect contact in which the contact is "distortion" because it is combined with no contact with whatever there is in the object outside this contact. Harman thus revises, as he promises on the first page of *Tool-Being*, the customary view of the relation of theory and practice in Heidegger. This revision entails Harman's shift from hammer to bridge.

Harman's Bridge: Surface View

This bridge appears early in *Tool-Being* and reappears later in a dramatic reversal that makes one see it differently insofar as the form it serves to introduce penetrates it more deeply than one initially thought. Like Heidegger's hammer, the bridge is "equipment" that is "used," but whereas the hammer is used by a single agent, the bridge is used by multiple agents, each with its distinctive perspective.

This bridge exhibits perspective as the originary form of Harman's "central thought." Perspective is a form that encapsulates the combination of contact and no contact that appears in indirect contact, as in the Russell's analysis of multiple perspectives on a penny, considered in chapter three. There is a contact with the penny in the perception of the penny from a particular location combined with no contact with the parts of the penny that cannot be perceived from this location. The perceiver's contact with the penny is direct in the perception, which changes with each change in the perceiver's location relative to the penny, and indirect in the sense that regardless of the perceiver's location, there is no contact with the parts of the penny outside the perceptual contact. Paraphrasing a similar analysis in Husserl of this combination of contact and no contact in perspectivist contact, Timothy Morton, a subscriber to Harman's philosophy, recounts that "[n]o matter how many times you turned around a coin, you never saw the other side as the other side. The coin had a dark side that was seemingly irreducible," so that, "If you thought this through a little more, you saw that all objects were in some sense irreducibly' withdrawn" (*Hyperobjects* 11); Morton later applies the same coin example to OOO (150–51), the acronym Harman settles on for his philosophy, as recounted in chapter one.

Fundamental in Harman is this combination of contact and no contact that appears in the indirect contact exhibited in perspectivist form. This form is the site of major developments in Harman, culminating in *The Quadruple Object*, each development penetrating this form more deeply. Harman's bridge inaugurates these developments:

> [T]he bridge as a whole is not a self-evident, atomic finality; rather, it functions in numerous different equipmental ways, swept up into countless larger systems. Usually it enacts an official plan of efficiency, shaving ten minutes from the drive around a bay. But in certain regions of the world, separating hostile factions, it is monitored by snipers. The bridge can be the unforgettable site

of a fateful conversation (nostalgia-equipment), the location of a distant relative's suicide (memorial-equipment), or perhaps it is simply stalked in a troubling insomnia. It is an object of study for architectural critics or material for sabotage by vandals. In the lives of seagulls and insects, it takes on altogether different aspects. . . . The tool gives birth to one particular world of unleashed forces, and no other—even if that world is mirrored in an indefinite number of *perspectives*. (*Tool-Being* 23, my italics; see also *Towards Speculative Realism* 96)

The nexus of multiple perspectives, the bridge connects the perspectives to form a kind of "world," but the perspectives are all independent of one another, sweeping up the bridge into "countless systems." The term "perspective" in the passage reappears in varying ways in *Tool-Being*, especially in its later stages (e.g., 208, 225, 227, 252, 255, 257, 259, 267, 271), where the bridge's most important reappearance occurs.

In addition to introducing perspective, this bridge underlines an important point for Harman in its inclusion of "seagulls and insects" as well as humans in its array of perspectivist relations with the bridge. Going even farther, Harman sees this perspectivist combination occurring even in "the collision of mindless rocks," which "do not encounter each other in direct presence, but only as a kind of caricature or objectification—the rock did exist beforehand, but never quite in the way in which the rock objectifies it, which requires the *perspective* of this other rock" (*Tool-Being* 208; see also the "collision of inanimate clods of dirt" at *Quentin* 183). This broadening of the scope of perspective has precedent in Nietzsche.[49]

---

49. In *The Will to Power*, #616, Nietzsche says that the "idea permeat[ing] [his] writings" is that "interpretations have been perspective valuations by virtue of which we can survive in life, i.e., in the will to power, for the growth of power." In this context, he entertains the thought "that other interpretations than merely human ones are perhaps somewhere possible." One can go beyond this "perhaps" by extrapolating from his declaration: "To begin with, a nerve-stimulus is transferred into an image: first metaphor" ("On Truth" 82); he adds a second metaphor to get to sound, but his first metaphor is enough for present purposes. Nietzsche thus equates sensory stimulation registered in the physiology of the body to a metaphor, an indirect contact with that sensory object that stimulates the nerve, an indirect contact, moreover, that would differ among animals with differing sensory capacities. Sensory experience, conceptualized this way, is an interpretation, a perspectivist indirect contact. Because such "nerve-stimulus" occurs in non-human bodies as well as human bodies, such

It is such broadening that invites Meillassoux's charge that Harman is a "subjectalist." We need to recall that Meillassoux invents the term "subjectalism" to encompass "all forms of idealism and all forms of vitalism, so as to contest the apparent opposition between these currents—in particular in the twentieth century; and so as to emphasize instead their essential relatedness and their original antimaterialist complicity." Materiality for Meillassoux, as in the example of the arche-fossil, is "external to thought and in itself devoid of all subjectivity" ("Iteration" 7, 3, 2). Subjectialism includes not only the subjectivity of idealism, which is obvious, but also the subjectivity of vitalism, which appears in Harman when he represents rocks having perspectivist caricatures on other rocks.

Harman magnifies his response to this charge by contending that his difference with Meillassoux on this issue is about nothing less than the "*very foundation of philosophy*" (*Quentin* 107). Addressing this charge is nothing new for Harman insofar as he earlier was charged with subscribing to panpsychism, a charge he flatly rejected in *Guerilla Metaphysics* (84), his second book, published in 2005. Subsequently, however, his position softened. In *Prince of Networks*, published in 2009, he says, "As for the term 'panpsychism' itself, I have recently been warming to it. In *Guerilla Metaphysics* I was negative toward the term"; he explains that he shares common misgivings about the term but that they are "outweighed" by the extent to which such misgivings reinforce human-centeredness, so that his "tactical sympathies have shifted toward the panpsychist insight that human cognition is just a more complicated variant of relations already found amidst atoms and stones" (212). In the 2015 second edition of his book on Meillassoux, however, Harman reframes the issue. "I will not contest," he concedes, "that there are apparently great differences between how humans react to raindrops and how the roofs of houses react to them." But these differences are now secondary. The more fundamental difference is between two oppositions: (1) thought and matter, (2) pre-relational and the relational. In (2), sometimes there is thought and sometimes there is no thought. Of the two, (2) is the more fundamental: "the fundamental distinction is that between the pre-relational character of all entities (human or otherwise) and their caricatured models as found in any relation. The difference between relational and nonrelational is much deeper than that between

---

contact extends beyond the human realm. Harman extends it even further, all the way to rocks, his notion of "caricature" performing a function analogous to Nietzsche's metaphor.

thought and matter, and thus is a much better basis for philosophy" (*Quentin* 107; see also *Towards Speculative Realism* 206, *Art* 20). Harman thus rejects the taxonomy of thought and matter, which divides the universe into two ontologies, one of them human-centered. Instead, thought and matter are subordinated to the prior no contact (pre-relational) and contact (relation) in the indirect contact in the perspectivist form of Harman's "central thought." For Harman, then, it is perspectivist forms all the way down, not turtles. This proves true of the bridge too when Harman returns to it later in *Tool-Being*.

These two sides of Harman's philosophy, perspectivist form and its universalization, are what Harman has in mind when he remarks that it is easier to link his philosophy to Kant than to Heidegger. He explains that Kant's philosophy also has two sides and that he can link it to his philosophy by reversing one side and reaffirming the other, albeit in a new way. Here is the one he reverses: "in Kant's framework you can't talk about the interaction of two inanimate entities. All you can talk about is *how humans comes to perceive that collision between two entities* [matter] *in terms of the categories of the Understanding and space and time*" [thought] ("Propositions" 24). In other words, like Meillassoux, Kant makes fundamental the division between thought and matter, humans and everything else, that Harman subordinates. In this respect, Harman reverses a lot of philosophers, including Heidegger (*Towards Speculative Realism* 100). Here is the side Harman reaffirms in his way: "there are things in themselves that can be thought but not known, and so philosophy becomes a mediation on the conditions of human access to the world instead of about the world itself" ("Propositions" 24). Harman's conditions of access differ but perspectivist indirect contact functions similarly, as stressed in *Guerilla Metaphysics*: "The important thing is that any object, at any level of the world, has a reality that can be endlessly explored and viewed from numberless perspectives without ever being exhausted by the sum of these perspectives" (76). No totality of perspectives, in other words, is ever able to access the object. In "Realism with a Straight Face," Harman illustrates with the concrete example of a house: "[t]he thing-in-itself is something we *deduce* from the fact that . . . no number of views of a house suffice to add up to a house" (105). For reasons that will appear later, this italicized "*deduce*" should also be underlined, for it is an inference from Harman's ultimate priority, to be defined in a later section.

There is another notable point that follows from Harman's combination of reversal and reaffirmation. Kant traces the inaccessibility of "things-in-themselves" to limitations in human faculties, which means that, as Harman stresses in quoting Kant, "you can't talk about the interaction of two inanimate entities." Kant's skepticism is based on limitations in the human faculties in the epistemological process. By contrast, the skepticism in Harman's philosophy turns from thought to thing. This metaphysical skepticism limits the accessibility of a house to a human viewer as well as the accessibility of one rock to another in a collision of the two. As we saw, rock A colliding with rock B can do no better than a perspectivist view of it, and vice versa. For Harman's "central thought" all things in the nature of things exist in relations combining contact and no contact in indirect contact. In this combination of reversal and reaffirmation, then, there is a philosophical turn from the subject matter of thought in Kant to the subject matter of things in Harman, a turn that focuses on a formal dimension of the subject matter of things, namely, their existence in relations of indirect contact. This focus is consistent with my earlier claim that form is where to find the realist ingredients in Harman's metaphysical turn.

The first but far from the last development of perspectivist form reinforces the analogy to Kant. It is anticipated in a passage that distinguishes "two separate facets to equipment" such as the bridge: "(1) its irreducibly veiled activity, and (2) its sensible and explorable profile" (*Tool-Being* 22). What is "irreducibly veiled" corresponds to the Kantian noumenon, while the "sensible" corresponds to the phenomenon. In this first development of perspectivist form, the "sensible" point of perspectivist contact becomes the "sensual object" and the "veiled activity" that eludes such contact becomes the "real object." Consistent with his prioritizing of form, Harman later adds, "Only form exists, though for me it comes in two varieties: the real (which exists in its own right) and the sensual (which exists only as the correlate of some real entity that encounters it" (DeLanda and Harman 24). These two varieties will be fleshed out later in this section, when we turn to Harman's use of Husserl. They are to be distinguished from the architectonic form defined in Harman's "central thought," where indirect contact is the form that explains why the real and the sensual are in contact in one sense and not in contact in another sense. These later developments come to fruition in *The Quadruple Object*, where Harman deduces from the relations among these three forms all the relations in the cosmos.

The notion of "sensual object" broadens the notion of objecthood beyond the formulation on the first page of *Tool-Being* that limited it to withdrawal "into a dark subterranean reality." There are problems with this notion of withdrawal, problems that prompt Harman even to propose an alternative term, but these can be addressed later. For now, it is enough to contrast real objects to sensual objects. The interdependence of the two derives from the indirect contact of Harman's "central thought." Returning to the penny example, the sensual object is what one sees in perspectivist viewing of the penny. This object is fully present to the viewer. But no view sees the whole penny, nor do any collection of views. There is always something in the penny, the real object, that escapes sensual objects. The difficulty with the term "withdraw," as we shall see, is that it implies that the real object exercises agency in escaping perspectivist views, whereas the agency in the process is in that which produces the sensual object, the one who views the penny.

One also needs also to remember that the viewer who creates the sensual object, whether it be a human or a seagull viewing the bridge, is itself an object that may in turn be in multiple sensual objects from multiple perspectives. In other words, on the one hand, objects produce sensual objects and, on the other hand, they appear in sensual objects produced by other objects. In one formulation, Harman refers to real objects that neither produce sensual objects nor appear in the sensual objects produced by others as "*dormant* entities" ("Time" 15; see also *Towards Speculative Realism* 207), which implies that to be awake is to be in a relation, either producing sensual objects or appearing in sensual objects. Harman remarks that "touching sensual objects is exactly what real objects do" this touching appearing in two forms (*Speculative Realism* 98).

Sensual objects are "fully present," Harman stresses in "The Return to Metaphysics," a 2011 lecture reprinted in *Bells and Whistles* (25), adding on the same page the importance of Husserl in his theorizing of all that is present in sensual objects. *Quadruple Object*'s chapter, "Sensual Objects," traces the phenomenological context of Harman's development of *Tool-Being*'s "sensible and explorable profile" into Husserlian "sensual objects." Harman puts aside phenomenology's notion of intentional objects "to speak instead of *sensual* objects as a synonymous phrase," explaining that compared to "intentional objects," "the phrase 'sensual objects' is more effective at conveying that we do not speak here of the real world beyond human access where only real objects belong" (26).

Despite this change in terminology, intentionality is still the mode of causality involved: "any given intentional act *is itself a new reality*"

(*Dante's Broken Hammer* 12). Real objects, when they produce sensual objects, are the agency of such acts. To illustrate an especially important feature of Husserlian sensual objects, a feature Harman spotlights in numerous places, Harman imagines Husserl, a real object, viewing not a penny but a "water tower at a distance of one hundred meters, at dusk, in a state of suicidal depression," such that the tower appears in a "variety of different perceptions" as he moves around it (*Quadruple Object* 24). These perceptions are sensual objects; they combine visualizations of the tower in the dusk and Husserl's mood, factors in perception that are discussed in *Guerilla Metaphysics* (25–26).

Here in *The Quadruple Object*, the important development in the conceptualization of the sensual object is the distinction between object and qualities: "In all phenomenal experience, there is a tension between sensual objects and their sensual qualities" (26). As Husserl walks, his perception of the tower, the sensual object that his intentionality causes, remains the same, but its qualities change as he views it from different angles, some brighter, some darker, some perhaps affected by changes in mood. This combination of unchanging object and changing qualities is key to Harman's preference of Husserl to Hume. Whereas in Husserl the object is independent of its changing qualities, in Hume it is reduced to its qualities, so that, strictly speaking, the object changes as the qualities change from moment to moment (*Object-Oriented Ontology* 76–77).

Harman, furthermore, sees Husserl's model as "basically the same thing as substance vs. accident in Aristotle, but at the phenomenal level" (DeLanda and Harman 51). In Husserl's sensual object, then, Harman finds the form, mentioned earlier, of the sensual object. The form of real object, also mentioned earlier, is similarly analogous to this Aristotelian model. In *The Quadruple Object*, Harman finds all the relations in the cosmos (1) by using the architectonic form of indirect contact in his "central thought" to relate the real object and its qualities (RO, RQ) and the sensual object and its qualities (SO, SQ), and (2) by then examining all possible relations between RO, RQ, SO, and SQ.

Because Husserl is the model for the sensual object, however, Husserl's idealism means that the sensual object's existential status is ambiguous. "The unified tree that I witness through my experience," Harman acknowledges, "might be a sheer illusion" ("Time" 8). It may turn out "that the tree was in fact a gallows, so that its surface qualities now shift into a far more sinister key" (*Quadruple Object* 103). Sensual objects thus may or may not be illusory, but when they are not illusory they can put one real object, Husserl, in relation to another real object, the tower. A real object such as Husserl generates many sensual objects in a day; real objects are dwarfed in number by sensual objects. We will see Harman directing attention away from withdrawal to the formal relation between the real and the sensual that becomes more important.

Harman's Bridge: Deep View

In its initial appearance, the bridge appears as what Harman calls "a simple 'black box,'" defined as "a unitary object which has an obvious integrity apart from any use to which it is put, *and* whose own ambivalent internal parts can safely be ignored as irrelevant" (*Tool-Being* 257). A different view appears when Harman takes us inside the bridge. "The way in which bolt and nail and trestle are mutually arranged, contacting one another *as* something specific," Harman claims, "is *ontologically* no different from the way in which I myself confront the bridge" (*Tool-Being* 260; see also 258–59, *Guerilla Metaphysics* 85). In other words, just as perspectivist form informs Harman's contact with the bridge, perspectivist form informs the contact of bolt, nail, and trestle with one another. Bolt and nail and so on, all exist in indirect relations of contact and no contact with one another, a "perspectival drama" that others, Harman suggests, mistakenly limit to the human realm (*Tool-Being* 252; see also *Prince of Networks* 215). Ontologically, this "drama" is a "formal cause" (*Tool-Being* 260).

Harman observes that contemporary philosophy tends to see objects as sets of relations against the traditional view of objects as substances with essences. He reaffirms this view insofar as "every entity is already made up of a set of relations" and *"every set of relations is also an entity."* But he qualifies this reaffirmation by refusing to turn everything into the "total system of relations" he sees in Whitehead. "Contemporary philosophy," Harman metaphorizes for dramatic effect, "has turned everything into an infinite system of conspiratorial relations," wherein "[i]ndividual things have lost their privacy completely, as though their phones were tapped and their essences bugged by the system as a whole" (*Tool-Being* 260, 233, 261).

Harman sees a variant such totalizing in Heidegger's view that any tool performs its function in relation to other tools in a totality of relationships, such as desk, ink-stand, pen etc., all of which work together in the process of writing. Tools in such relationships nonetheless break.

Harman construes breakage as evidence that tools are not absorbed completely by the relations of which they are a part. Breaking is evidence of an independent "is" prior to its "use." The tool would not break if it were not an independent reality but constituted solely by the totality of relations in which it was enmeshed. In short, "*all* beings are broken equipment" (*Tool-Being* 46).

A variant of this reasoning appears in a 1999 lecture, notable for its title, "Object-Oriented Philosophy," Harman's first use of this term (*Towards Speculative Realism* 93), which became the first name for his philosophy (*Tool-Being* 1). Near the end of this lecture, Harman imagines a "chunk of plutonium" abandoned in a desert, existing in relations to sand, weeds, and so on. Here is an object embedded in a system of desert relations. But if something living suddenly were to appear near enough to this plutonium to get a lethal dose, it "would be killed in minutes," thus showing that "there is an additional reality in this strange artificial material that is in no way exhausted by the unions and associations in which it currently happens to be entangled" (*Towards Speculative Realism* 103).

These examples can help one make sense of passages in which Harman's language makes real objects appear to be veritable black holes. For example, "In a certain sense, the tool-being of a thing exists in a vacuum-sealed isolation, exceeding any of the relations that might touch it" (*Tool-Being* 287). The key in this sentence is "a certain sense." Absolute isolation is impossible. The plutonium stranded in the desert has a relation with the sand on which it sits, just as the sand has a relation with the plutonium sitting on it. What exists in "vacuum-sealed isolation" is what eludes such relations, which in the case of the plutonium is its potential lethality.

While Harman here in his first book finds in "broken equipment" evidence of an independent "is" against Heidegger's view of varying pieces of equipment as related to one another in a totality, he later argues more broadly that if things were constituted by their "current and actual state of relations with everything else," then "[r]eality would be exhaustively deployed in its present state, with no hidden surplus or reserve that might surge forth and generate novelty" ("Undermining" 47). Nothing would break. Whether stasis or continual motion would be the result of everything being connected is debatable, but not for Harman, who sees change as evidence of an "is" independent of its connections with other things in a complex of relations.

Positioning himself in the vanguard, Harman claims that a great challenge in "the next several decades" is to establish "firewalls that protect every entity from its neighbors" without "relapsing into a conservative version of substances," that is, "a limited set of privileged durable units" (*Tool-Being* 257, 276). Harman builds such firewalls by reviving the notion of essence: "the term 'essence' is salvageable. . . . It at least does the work of not reducing a thing to its current relations and effects" (DeLanda and Harman 49). This revival prompts his interest in Xavier Zubiri's *On Essence*. Harman gives Zubiri extensive attention in the last part of *Tool-Being*, but concludes that "Zubiri's mistake was to try to locate essences at *discrete* points in the world, confining them to particular natural places in the hierarchy of beings. He did not want to believe that essences are ubiquitous." Harman counters that "either *every* being has an essence or *no* being does" and that "to choose the latter option would be to reduce a thing to its perspectival reality [the sensual point of contact], its existence here and now in the total network of meaning," so that "to establish a being of things that withdraws from any of their relations, we are left with only the first option" (*Tool-Being* 258, 255).

The term "meaning" in "network of meaning" is puzzling because what is at issue is not meaning but existent relations. Leaving that aside, the important thing is that Harman broadens the scope of essence by suggesting that seemingly random objects in random relations could have an essence, giving as an example objects on a table in his bedroom while living in Chicago: a stapler, two computers, five pens, three pencils, a wallet, sunglasses, eleven dimes, and six nickels, then asks, "Does this chaotic grouping of entities have its own unique essence?" (*Tool-Being* 256). He leaves this question unanswered, indicating only that something that turned this grouping into a whole would be an essence.

Harman's enlarging of the scope of essence includes his contestation of Leibniz's limitation of this scope. Leibniz's remark that one could not possibly see the Dutch East India Company as having a substantive essence appears to have inspired Harman to write a short book to show the opposite, that this Company is indeed a substance (*Immaterialism* 37). A shorter example appears in *Tool-Being*, one based on a rewriting of a passage in Leibniz's correspondence, where Leibniz addresses a variant of the classical distinction between a substance and a mere heap, that is, a mere aggregate of things in the absence of a substantive essence. Referencing two diamonds famous in his day as possessions of two eminences, the "Grand Duke" and the "Great Mogul," Leibniz argues that these can never be more than a heap no matter how closely they might be brought together. Harman paraphrases Leibniz, "Finally, even if we fuse them together with some sort of glue, they will are still not a single substance." In line with the unimportance of physical durability in his theory of objects, Harman counters, "What if instead of a physical combination, we ask about the possible *functional* union of two distinct substances?" Such a union would occur, Harman suggests, if Leibniz's aristocratic employer were kidnapped and the kidnappers demanded the two famous diamonds as ransom? That would be enough for Harman to see the two as forming "a single unit (ransom-machine)" (285). This example also suggests that Harman sees the formation of essences as a contingent affair. All that is essential is that something occasions formal causation that puts components in a functional relationship, even something as contingent as a kidnapping. This example is notable enough to merit additional attention later in this chapter.

Summing up his examples, Harman insists that no matter how "absurd," they "are formal systems that exceed any set of parts" (*Tool-Being* 286). For Harman, then, formal causation, regardless of what triggers it, produces objects by organizing what would otherwise be unorganized. Kidnappers are the trigger in the Leibniz example, while the Chicago example awaits a trigger that may or may not occur. "Really, universally, relations stop nowhere," Henry James once observed in claiming that "the exquisite problem of the artist is eternally but to draw, by a geometry of his own, the circle within which they shall happily *appear* to do so" (5). By contrast to James, in Harman they can actually "do so." Formal causes entitize relations into objects that endure like substances, but unlike substances they endure only for varying stretches of time.

Harman enforces this view in later work with a cluster of fallacies: "undermining" reduces objects to simple parts such as atoms in classic materialism, whereas in Harman there is nothing smaller than perspectivist relations like those in the components of the bridge; "overmining" reduces objects to external relations, whereas in Harman the broken tool evidences an independence of external relations always ready to assert itself; "duomining" does both.[50] "Undermining" underlines Harman's

---

50. Harman recounts in "Undermining, Overmining, and Duomining: A Critique," published in 2013, that his use of the term "undermining" originated in a 2009 lecture. This 2013 essay introduces the term "duomining," borrowed from computer science, to define the fallacy of combining both undermining and overmining. Harman claims modern science commits the duomining

commitment to formal causes and his suspicions about the independent existence of matter.

Harman's distinctive variant of perspectivist form, then, transforms both the contact and the no contact in perspectivist indirect contact. Contact becomes a sensual object, and the real object eluding direct contact becomes a quasi-substance with an essence and essential qualities, however transitory. Both objects have form and matter to be considered in detail later, distinct from the perspectivist form that orders their relationship. While the prominence of the terms "sensual object" and "real object" in later works displaces the prominence of "perspective" in *Tool-Being*, perspectivist form remains as the formal cause, fundamental for Harman, that orders the relation between these objects.

Harman's transformations of perspectivist contact and no contact add an additional level of complexity as the conventional idea of perspective becomes a translation of one object with a distinctive form into another object with a distinctive form. "At the heart of OOO," Harman states clearly, "is the idea that the real object undergoes *translation* into a sensual one, so there is no isomorphy between the two; the form itself changes between one place and another" (*Skirmishes* 125). The implications of this combination are worked out in greatest detail in *The Quadruple Object*, as analyzed below, a book written with great speed, perhaps because in it everything comes together.

Attention to this "*translation*" might prompt more attention to sensual objects, which appear to get less attention than real objects, perhaps because sensual ones are fully present, whereas real ones supposedly withdraw, a more popular idea after decades of critiques of presence, culminating in Derrida. One important thing about sensual objects appears in a consideration of whether to treat possibilities as real and if so in what sense. In this context, Harman indicates, "I don't think hypothetically considered scenarios (such as the boiling and freezing points of currently liquid water) are real," explaining that these "are sensual objects, since they exist only as a correlate of the hypothesis-maker." Real boiling and freezing water would be analogous to the lethality of plutonium. Con-

---

fallacy because it "aims both to reduce objects downward to the most basic constituents *and* to claim that these things are, in principle, knowable through mathematization." Harman also indicates that this 2009 lecture was later published in 2011 under the title "On the Undermining of Objects: Grant, Bruno, and Radical Philosophy" (43n2, 46, 43n2). While this title features "undermining" alone, "overmining" is also introduced in the essay (24).

sider boiling: water sits in a pot on a stove, like the plutonium sitting on sand in the desert; heating the water, it turns to steam, just as the plutonium turns lethal in the presence of life. But a hypothetical possibility is different. Harman elaborates, explaining that he solves the problem that worried Quine, namely, that to treat possibilities as real, such as "the possible fat man in the doorway," would proliferate real objects unduly. But for Harman, that is not a worry. For him, an object is either "real here and now (real object) or must be present here and now in the experience of some real object (sensual objects). The possible fat man in the doorway only exists for the brief period that Quine considers the possibility" (DeLanda and Harman 65, 71).

The Latour Connection

In his first book on Latour, *The Prince of Networks*, Harman remarks both that Heidegger "badly needs Bruno Latour to help him develop his model of objects" and that "one of the aims of the present book is to join Latour with Heidegger" (137, 146). Debating Latour in public, Harman avows that while Heidegger occupies one side of his head, Latour occupies the other. Considering that Harman is over two decades younger than Latour, this avowal might be construed as a gesture of polite deference at a public event. But Harman goes beyond mere politeness when he adds, a touch over-dramatically, that this public debate occurs ten years after he became a "Latourian" in February 1998, which itself occurred ten years after he became a Heideggerian in 1988 on a day in late February (*Prince Wolf* 25). (Harman turned twenty in 1988.) Elsewhere, he says that he began reading Latour in February 1998 (*Towards Speculative Realism* 67), so by his own account he became a "Latourian" the month he began reading him. Evidently he was the reader of Latour's dreams. Latour's actor-network theory (ANT) even makes it into Harman's epigraph at his blog: "Object-Oriented Philosophy: The centaur of classical metaphysics shall be mated with the cheetah of actor-network theory."[51]

Amazingly, Latour receives these high marks, even though Harman thinks he is guilty of "overmining" because ANT reduces objects to their

---

51. There is a literary quality to Harman's writing that prompts me to ponder his contrast between "prince" in the title of the Latour book and "cheetah" in the blog epigraph. Is the contrast designed to honor Latour as the inventor of actor-network theory and self-depreciate himself as a follower? Or is "cheetah" simply a poetic counterpart to "centaur"?

relations, specifically effects, leaving no room for a withdrawn dimension independent of relations (*Quadruple Object* 12). Whether this shortcoming actually exists is debated extensively in *The Prince and the Wolf*, a transcript of their public debate, where Harman makes his case and Latour appears unpersuaded. Harman himself took the opposite side on this issue in his first essay on Latour, where he argues that Latour, despite his preoccupation with networks, nonetheless theorizes an object that retains "a certain degree of genuine independence" (*Towards Speculative Realism* 91; see also 81). But Harman changes his mind, settling into his later view by the time he finishes *Tool-Being* (224, 312n50), although he does not coin the fallacy of "overmining" until after he completes *Prince of Networks*.[52]

There are a few references to Latour in *Tool-Being*, but only a few, evidently because Harman did not begin reading Latour until he was well along in the research that informs *Tool-Being*. He defended his dissertation proposal in June 1995 and the dissertation itself in March 1999 ("On Landscape Ontology"), specifically March 17 (*Towards Speculative Realism* 44).[53] But his interest in Latour evidences itself a month after defending his dissertation when he delivers a lecture on Latour, "Bruno Latour, The King of Networks"; at the suggestion of one of his professors at DePaul, he sent a copy to Latour and met him later that year (*Towards Speculative Realism* 67, 93). He frequently defends Latour as one of the most important philosophers of the day despite the relative lack of at-

---

52. In his first book on Latour, *Prince of Networks*, Harman criticizes Latour for overmining without using this term (e.g., 111), evidently because he finished the book before he began using the terms "undermining" and "overmining" in 2009, as discussed in an earlier note. *Prince of Networks* appeared in 2009, but Harman says the "initial manuscript" was completed by February 2008 and was the basis for a day-long symposium on the fifth of that month (*Prince of Networks* 3). This symposium featured a debate between Harman and Latour and was later published under the title *The Prince and the Wolf: Latour and Harman at the LSE*.

53. That Harman took almost four years to complete his dissertation is surprising considering his record of producing multiple books quickly. Part of the reason for the delay, maybe the only reason, is that while working on his dissertation he wrote 143 articles, "most of them fairly long," for a sporting news company. He was good enough to be offered a permanent job, but he turned it down. He credits the experience with teaching him how "to write large quantities of text, on deadline, and in an engaging style that keeps your readers interested" ("On Landscape Ontology").

tention Latour receives among philosophers. These widely contrasting views of Latour manifest themselves in the sharpest differences between Harman and Manuel DeLanda in their exchanges in *The Rise of Realism* (DeLanda and Harman 132–42).

Harman thinks that Latour's *Irreductions* puts one on the road to "object-oriented philosophy" *(Prince Networks 14)*. Latour's contribution to Harman's view of the formation of objects centers in ANT's "actant." (ANT is not to be confused with Latour's later AIME, *An Inquiry into Modes of Existence*). To be an actant is to be real by producing an effect on another actant. Actants range from human to inanimate, so humans are not central, a point that appeals to Harman greatly. In producing effects, actants form relations and in doing so form what Harman sees as objects when constellations of relations acquire an essence, as in his Leibniz example. Harman's difference from Latour occurs at the point that relations become an object, entitized by virtue of an essence, so that even while existing in relationships, they are nonetheless independent of relations, capable of actions like the plutonium's lethality.

In writing *Prince of Networks* in the 2007–2008 period, Harman evidently found answers to questions Brassier posed at the 2007 Speculative Realism Workshop that he could not at the time answer to his satisfaction. Brassier asks how Harman would distinguish things that exist objectively from merely subjective imaginings. Referencing Brassier's presentation at the Workshop, Harman remarks, "[Y]ou heard his objections to me earlier about the hobbits, and he's mentioned the tooth fairy to me before. These are good objections," then adds interestingly, "Since I diverged from Heidegger, Latour was one of the first life preservers I grabbed on to, since he treats all objects on an equal footing, and I like that part of him. But I think there is a problem" ("Presentation" 378–79; see also 391, 401–02).

Harman solves this problem in *Prince of Networks*. One example proposes that atoms are more real than ghosts, but not because of Brassier's distinction between objective and subjective: "What makes an atom more real than a ghost is not that the former exists as a real state of affairs and the latter only in our minds. Instead, what makes the atom more real is that it has more allies." Both are actants that produce effects, but the atom's effects secure more allies than the ghost's. "Experiments testify to the atom's existence," transforming the scientific profession and the education of children, whereas "the ghost has only a paltry number of allies bearing witness to its reality, such as hysterical children and a few old legends" (110–11). But the atom's allies might one day abandon it, so that this present difference in the degree of realness in atoms and ghosts is not fixed. But Harman's example may stack the deck. If one substitutes Santa Claus for ghosts, Santa Claus might turn out to be more real than atoms by Harman's criterion.

In any case, Harman responds directly to Brassier with another example, one that modifies his commitment to Latour's "equal footing." This one contrasts cats he cares for to a monster he imagines. Both are actants that produces effects on Harman. Both will vanish when Harman falls asleep but, Harman adds, "unlike the monster, the cats will remain autonomous forces unleashed in my apartment despite my lack of awareness of their activities" (*Prince Networks* 190). While this second example seems to restore Brassier's dualism of subject and object, Harman's dualism is not limited to humans but extends to all objects, even rocks. The dualism of subject and object goes hand-in-hand with the taxonomy of thought and matter that Harman subordinates to perspectivist form in responding to Meillassoux's charge that he is a "subjectalist." The dualism of sensual object and real object is informed by the priority of the combination of contact and no contact in the indirect contact of perspectivist form that for Harman is prior to the taxonomy of thought and matter.

"Derridean Tyrannies"

Harman depicts himself escaping "the Derridean tyrannies of [his] student years" (*Prince Networks* 121). This depiction presupposes his view of the history of philosophy, which, as we shall see, differs from Meillassoux's, which was considered in the last chapter, as a struggle (1) in which skepticism and metaphysics alternate in turning against one another and, (2) in the case of metaphysical turns, metaphysics ironically finds in skepticism a way to turn against skepticism. Point (2), however, as the example of Meillassoux suggests, may say less about a complete philosophical turn than about a tendency in the infancy of a turn to rely on analogues to what is turned against, analogues with a difference to be sure but analogues nonetheless. A variant of this tendency appears in Harman despite his different view of the history of philosophy.

When Harman began suffering under these "tyrannies," however, is not clear, for Harman indicates retrospectively that not until December 1997, two and a half years after he defended his dissertation proposal, did he become committed to a "*full blown realism*" (*Toward Speculative Realism* 14). Before this commitment, Derrida's antirealism would presumably not have been experienced as a tyranny even if Harman questioned realism for different reasons.

Furthermore, in a lecture he gave before this commitment, on Halloween in 1997 to be exact (*Toward Speculative Realism* 22), Harman actually aligns himself with Derrida in proposing the possibility of "turning the results of Derrida's *Speech and Phenomena* against Heidegger's self-understanding," without, however, identifying specifically which "results" or indicating exactly how they might be used against Heidegger. Even more notably, elsewhere in this lecture there is a passage that appears to anticipate the perspectivist form presented in *Tool-Being*: "There is nothing that could ever make the dark underground of the object's secret life [no contact] congruent with the perceptible hammer apparition that now hovers before our eyes [contact]. These are incommensurable realities, different worlds. In more familiar terms, the hammer-effect can never come to full presence" (*Toward Speculative Realism* 32, 31). Back in 1997, could these "more familiar terms" be construed as anything other than an allusion to Derrida's deconstruction of "presence," especially in the context of the explicit alignment with Derrida against Heidegger in the same lecture? Possibly, then, Derrida is actually the original inspiration for the perspectivist form conceptualized in *Tool-Being*, published in 2002. If so, Harman would confirm Meillassoux's view of the history of philosophy.

In 2005, moreover, in *Guerilla Metaphysics*, Harman congratulates himself for making a metaphysical turn without "reviving the old style of metaphysics of presence criticized so vehemently by Heidegger, Derrida, and their various heirs. After all, the implication of tool-analysis is that objects *never* become present—not even by means of some sort of gradual, asymptotic approach" (74). Here, Harman reminds one of Morton's remark, "I backed into OOO through deconstruction" ("Here" 166). Harman's turn, by questioning the "metaphysics of presence," joins the "various heirs" on the bandwagon of questioners.

At the same time, Harman's view of the history of philosophy suggests that at some point he would sense the danger of staying on a bandwagon too long. Whereas Meillassoux sees metaphysical turns borrowing from antecedent skepticisms, Harman sees all turns turning against their predecessors. "Philosophy is historic," in his view, "because any statement can turn into a platitude once the surrounding conditions have changed, and philosophy is more about outflanking platitudes than about making eternally true propositions," adding that "every statement is doomed to become an empty platitude someday" ("Marginalia"). During its day in the sun, a statement is a Rortyian "normal" discourse, but it becomes a platitude when displaced by an upcoming "abnormal" discourse, something that is inevitable. This is a formula for rhetoric's tyranny of the new, a theme in chapter three. In his 1997 reference to "more familiar terms," Harman engaged in the customary practice of strengthening one's argument by aligning it with a "normal" discourse, but by the same token Derrida's discourse was "normal" for decades. At some point, by seeing "familiar" as a "platitude," Harman may have seen the possibility of an emergent "abnormal" discourse, in his case, one that continued the questioning of the "metaphysics of presence" but in a new way, one that did not rely exclusively on linguistic analysis.

In this "outflanking platitudes" version of the history of philosophy, sensitivity to the winds of change of the sort Harman articulates in his second book, *Guerilla Metaphysics*, becomes key: "there is one extremely powerful hidden force working in favor of a guerrilla metaphysics: namely, the fact that the generally educated public secretly hungers for its triumph, or the triumph of something like it. Nobody outside of the professional guilds feels much enthusiasm for the arid and narrowly self-reflexive style of much philosophical discourse today" (75).

It is worth digressing briefly to note that what is implicit in Harman is explicit in Levi Byrant. Suggesting that philosophical "innovations" occur less by refutation of existing positions than by shifts in "questions and problems" that stimulate interest, Byrant observes, "In many respects, object-oriented ontology, following the advice of Richard Rorty, simply tries to step out of the debate altogether," so that if "this is not good enough for the epistemology police, we are more than happy to confess our guilt and embrace our alleged lack of rigor and continue in harboring our illusions that we can speak of a reality independent of humans" (*Democracy* 29). Byrant and Harman thus appear to see the history of philosophy as consisting of philosophical turns based on assumptions underlying the linguistic turn. Meanwhile, their philosophies turn against the linguistic turn.

Harman comes to distinguish himself from Derrida by claiming that Derrida, unlike himself, "does not try to escape presence by pointing to a withdrawn absent reality" ("Well-Wrought Broken Hammer" 196). Here, Harman utilizes a common misreading of Derrida. Derrida's deconstruction exposes "presence" as a linguistic construction and thus illusory. In exposing presence as an illusion, Derrida is claiming not that there is nothing beyond words, but that whatever is there is inseparable from the linguistic hierarchizing of binary oppositions framing philosophies that foster the illusion of the presence while actually mediating access to whatever is there. This inseparability defines the sense in which "[t]here is nothing outside the text" (*Of Grammatology* 158). Harman joins those who mistakenly claim that Derrida denies the existence of anything outside language.

The linguistic turn's prioritizing of language makes everything dependent on language, not in the sense that language causes everything, à la the Gross and Levitt satire, but in the sense that language mediates access to everything. Derrida insists that *"there is nothing outside the text"* does not mean "that all referents are suspended, denied, or enclosed in a book, as some people have claimed, or have been naïve enough to believe and to have accused me of believing" (*Limited Inc* 148). Harman is among these accusers.

While Harman questions Derrida, in his book on Lovecraft, *Weird Realism*, his analysis of language in this book surprisingly approximates Derrida's view of linguistic mediation, albeit without anything to rival Derrida's elaborate technical theorizing of this mediation. What he approximates, to be clear, is the real Derrida, not the Derrida he joins others in accusing of enclosing referents in a book. Harman explains that the title *Weird Realism* signals his opposition to the view that "philosophical realism is 'representational' in character. Such theories hold not only that there is a real world outside all human contact with it, but also that this reality can be mirrored adequately by the findings of the natural sciences or some other method of knowledge" (51). Harman proposes that his analysis of "the interaction between style and content" in Lovecraft shows, "No reality can be immediately translated into representations of any sort. Reality itself is weird because reality itself is incommensurable with any attempt to represent or measure it. . . . When it comes to grasping reality, illusion and innuendo are the best we can do" (51). Harman even echoes Derrida's view, discussed in chapter three, that truth appears in normative regimes that are provisional rather than permanent when he contends that because language cannot represent reality transparently, "[t]here is no reason to think that any philosophical statement has an inherently closer relationship with reality than its opposite, since *reality is not made of statements*. Just as Aristotle defined substance as that which can support opposite qualities at different times, there is a sense in which reality can support different truths at different times" (14).

While Harman's view here would seem to retreat to the linguistic turn, one can assimilate it to his philosophy with his statement that objects in Derrida "are *sensual*, never real ones," thus limited to the sensual objects that theorize the point of contact in perspectivist form, never getting to "the OOO option: that signs do have an ultimate signified [real object] whose nature is precisely *not* to become present" (*Object-Oriented Ontology* 203, 206). One has contract with the phenomenon of language just as one has contact with the phenomenon of the empirical objects.

One must conceive the sensual object more broadly, in line with the earlier discussion of how Harman broadens Kant's skepticism dramatically, tracing this skepticism not to human faculties of thought but to relations among things as captured in Harman's "central thought." Hence, while the notion of sensual object may bring most readily to mind the Kantian experience of phenomena, as distinct from noumena, Harman's sensual object includes such experience but goes beyond it in two directions. In one, it goes to the sensual object that takes the form of the perspectivist caricature in a collision of rocks. In the other direction, it encompasses Derrida's sensual objects.

In short, the sensual object is Harman's mediator. It is larger in scope than the mediators of thought and language. It appears at the point of indirect contact that relates two objects that cannot relate in any other way. It can be illusory, as when what appears to be a tree turns out to be a gallows. Going even farther, presumably it can be as illusory as an hallucination. It is the ultimate in a metaphysical skepticism that sees Kantian skepticism receding in its rearview mirror. It remains to be seen how well Harman's metaphysics as metaphysical skepticism will stand up in debates in coming decades among philosophers of the metaphysical turn.

Harman might have used his "outflanking" metaphor, discussed earlier, to focus not on outflanking platitudes but on outflanking the turns to thought and language. He might have read Derrida from the standpoint of his principle of "hyperbolic reading," that is, reading not to find fault with a philosophy but to "concede all or most of its claims" to determine, having read it in the most charitable way possible, the value of what it has to offer (*Quentin* 202). Reading Derrida that way, Harman could concede that Derrida's exposure of presence as a linguistic construct has value from the standpoint of perspectivist form. Harman could then add that this perspectivist form outflanks Derrida because it is instantiated not only in human language but also in non-human and inanimate agencies, that is, in things in general.

Such outflanking appears in effect in a 1999 lecture that begins with a retrospective on philosophy in the twentieth century. Harman suggests that the one commonplace that appears regularly in such retrospectives is that "the great philosophical achievement of our century lies in its 'linguistic turn,'" explaining, "Instead of an aloof human subject that merely observes the world while managing to keep its fingers clean, the human being now appears as a less autonomous figure, unable to escape fully from a network of linguistic significations and historical projections." Harman then outflanks the linguistic turn by vivid evocation of realities it ignores, realities marked by interactions akin to his example of mindless rocks having caricatured perspectives on one another as they collide:

> Even as the philosophy of language and its supposedly reactionary opponents both declare victory, the arena of the world is packed with diverse objects, their forces unleashed and mostly unloved. Red billiard ball smacks green billiard ball. . . . While human philosophers bludgeon each other over the very possibility of "access" to the world, sharks bludgeon tuna fish and icebergs smash into coastlines. (*Towards Speculative Realism* 93, 94)

Harman generalizes his outflanking strategy in another formulation. In response to a question asking why he focuses "on objects rather than on 'language, social change, sexuality, or animals,'" Harman answers that "philosophy is obliged to be global in scope," explaining, "If philosophy were to give one of these other entities a starring role, it would have to reduce the rest of the universe to them. 'Language is the root of everything.' Here, you are choosing one specific kind of entity to be the root of all others, and there is no basis for this. . . . Only philosophy can be a general theory of objects" ("Interview"), as in Harman's title, *Object-Oriented Ontology: A New Theory of Everything*.

Harman's "language is the root of everything" is ambiguous. Harman seems to intend his remark as a reductio ad absurdum: what could be more absurd than to see language as the root of everything? But "language is the root of everything" can also mean that language is about everything in the sense that it mediates access to everything. One might rephrase Harman's point as an issue opposing narrowing to broadening. Reducing everything to consideration of the linguistic mediating process that limits access to everything is narrow compared to Harman's sensual object, which mediates access in multiple ways, not just the linguistic.

A question for the final chapter: Can this distinction between narrowing and broadening help to evaluate philosophical turns?

While the term "withdrawal" figures prominently in Harman's efforts to distance himself from Derrida, the term has, as noted earlier, nonetheless proven problematic in the absence of any method to replace Derrida's deconstructive exposure of presence as an illusion. In *Speculative Realism*, published in 2018, Harman reviews the "frequent hostility" this term provokes:

> Many critics of OOO seem to think it sufficient to mock this term with sarcastic quotation marks, forgetting that the point is to mark an unrepayable debt to Heidegger.... But perhaps the most important critique of the term, however ill its intentions, came from a supercilious professor of design who archly questioned me in public as to why objects should "withdraw" in the first place, and who seemed to enjoy repeatedly calling it "just a simple question" even after it was answered successfully on the first try.

Leaving aside the "unrepayable debt," which seems to be little more than an unphilosophical appeal to authority, and tabling temporarily this supposedly successful answer, I will add here that Harman himself undercuts this answer when he proposes to substitute a new term for "withdrawal," "I have recently begun to use the term 'withheld' instead of withdraw; time will tell which is better" (105, 106). In subsequent pages, however, Harman uses "withdraw" rather than "withheld." Make of that what you will.

The term "withdraw" is philosophically imprecise. The claim is that an object is unknowable, like Kant's thing-in-itself, because it withdraws. But that claim attributes agency to the object and thus a degree of knowledge of it. Having given up Derrida's exposure of presence as illusory, Harman lapses into imprecision in looking for an alternative. This attribution naturally prompts the question of Harman's interlocutor. "Withhold" differs from "withdraw" mainly by implying that presence is an existent and is purposely withheld from view, whereas "withdraw" might be from a threatening possibility rather than an actual existent. Both terms suffer from the same problem of expressing knowledge when they are supposedly doing the opposite in order to point "to a withdrawn absent reality."

Notably, Harman's discomfort with "withdrawal" appears not only in his search for an alternative but also in occasional downplaying of the importance of withdrawal in his philosophy, as in this passage at the beginning of "Aesthetics and the Tension in Objects":

> Object-Oriented Ontology (OOO) is probably best known for its thesis that objects "withdraw" from direct interaction with one another, a term drawn from Martin Heidegger's emphasis on the withdrawal (*entziehen/Entzug*) of Being from all presence to human Dasein. While it is certainly not inaccurate to stress OOO's concern with this topic, to do so marks an artificial restriction of a wider problem. A more fitting way to characterize OOO would be to say that it holds the world to be made up of two types of objects (sensual, real) and two types of qualities (sensual, real). (11)

This chapter is consistent with this passage insofar as from the beginning it saw the key to Harman not in withdrawal but in perspectivist form and its progeny sensual and real objects. The distinction between real and sensual objects was the first development of perspectivist form. In this passage, Harman goes on to sketch the second and culminating development, which appears in *The Quadruple Object*, part of which appeared in the earlier discussion of Husserl and the rest of which will be considered later. In this development, multiple relations between and within real and sensual objects are mapped by the shorthand, mentioned earlier, of RO, RQ, SO, and SQ.

Ultimate Priority

Harman rejects Husserl's elevation of the intellectual over the sensual, subscribing instead to Heidegger's insistence "that the difference between the intellect and the senses is simply not that important, given that both reduce entities to presence before the mind" (*Art* 22). Nonetheless, Harman claims that he "distinguish[es] between real objects that withdraw and sensual ones that don't" because "something in the world is requiring me to do that" ("Propositions" 51). Here, this "something" is a "presence before the mind" of Harman. One can square these two passages if one recognizes that in the first, "entities" (e.g., person, house, rock) are what is not present, whereas in the second, what is present before Harman's mind is a form in which real objects and sensual objects combine in the indirect contact of perspectivist form, precisely the form that limits accessibility to real objects. This "requiring me" is Harman's intuition of his "central thought," quoted at the beginning of this chapter. Form is fundamental for Harman, as we saw earlier, even to the point of questioning whether matter exists. Attending to Harman's consideration of objects in relation to form is generally more profitable than his consideration of objects independently of form.

Harman's "requiring me" passage opposes the view that if you distinguish real and sensual objects, "you need to first reflect on the human conditions of access that allow us to make that very distinction"; Harman opposes this view because he considers it "just an attempt to give philosophy back to epistemology" ("Propositions" 51). Harman's "requiring me" is metaphysical realism, a realism of form. It does not involve any concepts that Harman brings as a subject of epistemology. Rather, it is a form in reality that Harman accesses directly, intuitively. Thing prior, thought posterior.

This intuition in Harman parallels the correlationist's intuition in Meillassoux when the correlationist, to gain final victory in the battle among correlationists, must affirm a reality beyond and independent of the correlation of subject and object. That is the correlationist's "requiring me" moment. These instances of metaphysical realism are important steps in the metaphysical turn. Metaphysical realism will be an important consideration in the final chapter's answer to the question of whether there is a preferential order among the turns.

This parallel between Meillassoux and Harman coexists with a significant difference. Meillassoux develops a theory of intellectual intuition for his moment of metaphysical realism, but in the end, it seems applicable only in the limited case of the correlationist that Meillassoux dramatizes in his dialogue about death. There is no such limitation in Harman, but Harman does little to develop the theory of intellectual intuition in his moment of metaphysical realism. These moments of intuition in Meillassoux's and Harman's metaphysical realism are important but significantly limited, albeit in different ways.

This "requiring me" passage is to lead to follow to find Harman's fundamental subject matter, his ultimate priority. Harman, however, often poses the problem of knowledge as a problem of knowing objects such as persons, houses, rocks, and so on. Posed this way, Harman finds no solution. Harman rejects "there is a real world, and it can be known" in favor of "there is a real world, and it cannot be known" ("Fear" 140). This denial of knowledge is in tension with the display of knowledge of his ultimate priority.

Before following the lead of "requiring me," one needs to note where Harman crosses the path of Aristotle's intellectual intuition. One is where he contends knowledge is impossible via the reductio ad absurdum that knowledge, say, of a tree would entail actually becoming a tree, growing roots, bearing fruit, shedding leaves, etc. Harman concedes that while no one subscribes to this reductio explicitly, there are those who subscribe to it implicitly: "[I]f someone holds that there is an isomorphic relationship between knowledge and reality, such that reality can be fully mathematized, then it also follows that a perfect mathematical model of a thing should be able to step into the world and do the labor of that thing" ("I Am" 788–89). What is Aristotelian in this tree example is Harman's focus on tree functions: growing roots, bearing fruit, shedding leaves, and so on. There was in the earlier Leibniz example similarly attention to functioning, triggered by a hypothetical kidnapping, as key to object formation. In both, knowledge of the object is knowledge of how it is "organized to function." But in the tree example, such knowledge is deemed possible only by becoming the materiality of a tree. Making knowledge dependent on materiality in this way is surprising insofar as it departs radically from Harman's insistence that form is fundamental, that matter may not even exist. Harman's account of capacities and functionings independent of matter is where to look for his exercise of intellectual intuition, something he does extensively in *Quadruple Object* in analyzing how the formal relationships among RO, RQ, SO, and SQ are "organized to function."

Harman references Aristotle's intellectual intuition in answering his insistent interlocutor on the question of withdrawal. The point of withdrawal, Harman claims, is that one thing cannot replicate the "form or structure" of the other. "It is not," Harman explains, "as if a giraffe, for example, were simply a form inhering in matter, so that I could extract that form and bring it into my mind without also bringing the matter along—one of least convincing features of Aristotle's philosophical tradition." Here, Harman forgets that in his "requiring me" passage, he extracts the form of the relation between real and sensual objects without "bringing the matter" along of a single real or sensual object.

Harman continues, "Instead, the giraffe-form that I think does not coincide with the giraffe-form in the giraffe itself. If that were not the case, then perfect mathematical knowledge of a giraffe would itself be a giraffe" (*Speculative Realism* 105). While Harman here implicitly equates Aristotle's form to mathematical knowledge, elsewhere he says the opposite: "I would say the Aristotelian forms are not mathematical formalisations. They are substantial forms" ("Presentation" 384). Leaving that aside, one notes again the assumption that knowing a form, "giraffe-form," entails being in the material that the form informs, the actual "giraffe." Harman says the opposite not only in the "requiring me" passage, but also when he proposes, consistent with his insistence on the primacy of form, that one way to recognize the "independent reality of a thing" is to "imagine that it were composed of different elements. Coining a new term, we can call these ''" ("Undermining" 50). In other words, "countercompositional" presupposes knowing a form apart from its matter so that one can imagine the form "composed of different elements." A "countercompositional" response to the ancient "Ship of Theseus" question would be that the ship is the same even after all its material components are changed because the form is the same.

Again, it is more profitable to attend most closely to what Harman says about objects in relation to form, especially the form in his "requiring me" passage. "Only form exists," Harman insists in a passage quoted earlier, "though for me it comes in two varieties: the real (which exists in its own right) and the sensual (which exists only as the correlate of some real entity that encounters it). . . . [Real things] only make contact indirectly, through a *sensual* form that is the mediator between them" (DeLanda and Harman 24): forms of two objects and the architectonic form in the indirect architectonic perspectivist form that orders their relationship. As we have seen, Harman's conceptions of real and sensual objects transform the conventional idea of perspective, with which Harman started in *Tool-Being*, into a distinctive Harmanesque variant of perspectivist form. The distinctiveness of Harman's variant becomes even more elaborate in *The Quadruple Object*, which diagrams varying ways real and sensual objects do and do not relate to one another. *Quadruple Object* adds the additional element we saw earlier in its use of Husserl to distinguish in the sensual object the sense in which it is always one, a tower, and a sense in which it has multiple changing qualities, Husserl's changing perceptions of the tower as he circles it. A similar distinction between one object and multiple qualities appears in the real object, which appears to be conceived by analogy with Husserl's object, since strictly speaking the real object is supposedly accessible only partially, in a perspective, not as a whole. Hence, the aforementioned shorthand: RO, RQ, SO, SQ.

That form is Harman's fundamental existent means that it is on the level of form that one finds his ultimate priority in his metaphysical turn to thing. It is important to keep this in mind insofar as his analyses do not always foreground this level. His ultimate priority is often implicit. One conveniently concise example appears in a 2020 text, the previously referenced "Realism with a Straight Face," which as its subtitle explains, is "A Response to Leonard Lawler." For Lawlor, realism is limited to "the ontological conditions of consciousness." Such a realism would be equivalent to Kant's account, analyzed at the end of chapter four, of the noumenal thing-in-itself of the human subject, as distinct from the noumenon beyond experience that the *Critique of Pure Reason* declares is inaccessible. Lawlor affirms, "I do not see how one can return back beyond Kant's Copernican Revolution. As Kant showed, if there is a reality beyond the forms in which things are given to us, the noumenal, then we can say nothing about it." Harman denies that there is anything realist in the normal sense of the term about "the ontological conditions of consciousness." That does not mean, however, that Kant is antirealist for Harman, who goes on, in a passage quoted earlier, "If we are nevertheless inclined to call Kant a 'realist'—as I am so inclined—then this clearly has nothing to do with his pursuit of the transcendental categories of experience, but only with what escapes such categories: namely the infamous *Ding an sich,* or thing-in-itself." In other words, Harman explains, Kant is realist not because he "think[s] there is a reality to which we have direct access," but rather, because he is "committed to the notion that reality means that which escape any such access." Reality escapes not because of Kant's divide between phenomena and noumena, but because "[t]he thing-in-itself is something we *deduce* from the fact that . . . no number of views of a house suffice to add up to a house" (99, 99, 102, 102–03, 105). Because it is deduced from perspectivist "views," importantly, it is posterior to Harman's ultimate priority, perspectivist form. Fundamental for Harman is the statement in *Guerilla Metaphysics,* quoted earlier, "The important thing is that any object, at any level of the world, has a reality that can be endlessly explored and viewed from numberless perspectives without ever being exhausted by the sum of these perspectives."

In this debate with Lawlor, Harman debates Merleau-Ponty too, albeit briefly in an endnote. He references a passage in *Phenomenology of Perception* in which Merleau-Ponty outlines a view of an object that combines both what he sees and what he does not see: "When I look at the lamp on my table, I attribute to it not only the qualities visible from where I am, but also those which the chimney, the walls, the table can 'see'"; Merleau-Ponty then changes examples, shifting from lamp to house, to conclude, "the house itself is not the house seen from nowhere, but the house seen from everywhere" (79). Unlike Harman, Merleau-Ponty attributes perspectives to the chimney, walls, and table that surround his lamp simply because they are there even though they are totally passive. So conceived, perspectives would be necessary insofar as anything anywhere is always surrounded by equivalents to chimneys, walls, and tables. Harman, by contrast, envisions perspectives as enactments, typically giving examples of interactions, including even the collision of rocks in which the rocks produce caricatures of one another. As we have seen, Harman views sensual objects as involving intentionality, the idea central in phenomenology that a mental act intends an object (*Quadruple Object* 21), while broadening this agency beyond phenomenology's human-centeredness. Perspectives are thus happenings, dependent on the agency of intentionality that may or may not be enacted. Hence, in the absence of any enactments, a house may be ignored, whereas for Merleau-Ponty a house is always under surveillance.

In dialoguing with Lawlor, then, Harman depicts a house (1) that he knows is "out there" because there are perspectivist views of it and (2) that is inaccessible because it eludes perspectivist views, no matter how many. This inaccessibility is understood because it is deduced from an ultimate priority, perspectivist form. Contrastingly, the claim that the house withdraws prompts the "why?" question because such withdrawal does not appear to be deducible from anything; the term "withheld" does no better. Over time, "withdrawal" may be seen to characterize the early Harman more than the later one.

Furthermore, Harman claims that even if we cannot say what the noumenon is, we can still say something about it, presumably from the standpoint of the multiple perspectives that capture something about the object even if the whole object is inaccessible. Harman justifies this view with the example of Socrates: "There is no passage in the Platonic dialogues where Socrates successfully defines anything, but this hardly means that Socrates does not succeed in saying anything of value" ("Realism" 105; see also DeLanda and Harman 139). For Harman, Socrates becomes the embodiment of the essence of philosophy, conceived not as knowledge but as *philosophia*, the love of knowledge (*Art 2*, 30–31). This depiction of Socrates becomes fundamental.

What appears in this dialogue with Lawlor is the inferential chain following from Harman's ultimate priority, not the priority itself. That priority appears in the passage quoted earlier in which Harman insists that it is "something in the world" that requires him to make his perspectivist distinction in the indirect contact between real objects that withdraw and sensual objects that do not. It is this "something," this form, a real thing for Harman, that requires Harman's distinction, his thought, thus marking Harman's metaphysical turn to thing.

Importantly, when Harman says "something in the world" requires his fundamental distinction, he is not intuiting this "something" through perspectivist eyes. This "something" is not like a house that would look different viewed from different perspectives. This "something," rather, explains why things look different from different perspectives. This "something" is a form that is ultimate reality for Harman and he accesses it directly, independently of his normal, day-to-day perspectivist view of things, like the perspectivist views of his bridge by human and non-human agents. This nonperspectivist view of perspective is defined with clarity by Babette E. Babich's definition of the term "perspectivalism" that this chapter uses in its title. In Babich's words,

> I employ the *adjectival* noun form of *perspectivalism* in an attempt to avoid the relativistic confusion inherent in the word *perspectivism*. As I construe the term, perspectivalism (a perspectival philosophy) is not an instance of perspectivism (perspectivist philosophy) but rather a reflective collection of perspectivisms, that is, a philosophy built up on the idea that the world is replete with different viewpoints and different from every perspective. . . . Thus perspectivalism does not, as perspectivism seems to, connote the view that all knowledge is no more than interpretation, the representation of a particular perspective. . . . In the critical spirit of Kant, a perspectivist philosophy reflects the epistemic fact of perspective and traces its origins and seeks to outline its critical consequences. (46; Babich's italics)

A perspective on a house, Russell's perspectivist view of a penny, Morton's Husserlian perspectives on a coin—all such perspectives are partial, "no more than interpretation, the representation of a particular perspective." Babich's point is to distinguish such interpretation from the "perspectival" that grasps the perspectivist form that explains why perspectives are always limited. Perspectival is to perspectives on house, penny, and coin as ultimate priority is to posterior consequences of this priority. The perspectival is the "something" in Harman's "requiring me" passage. As Harman in the course of an ordinary day produces all the sensual objects that constitute his experience that day, Harman is perspectivist. But when he philosophizes about how entities ranging from humans to rocks are similarly perspectivist in their production of sensual objects in their encounters with one another, he transcends perspective to speak as a perspectivalist.

Particularly revealing is a passage in which Harman recognizes with special clarity that the quasi-Kantian realism he defends in debating Lawlor is not the fundamental realism in his philosophy. Given the importance and infrequency of such clarity, the passage merits full quotation:

> Now, many philosophers claim to be realists despite upholding the Kantian duopoly of human and world. They think that to posit some unarticulated reality beyond experience is enough to escape idealism. Perhaps they are right; perhaps they do deserve the name of realists. But if that is the case, then there is little reason to be excited about realism. Against such claims, we should always observe the following litmus test: no philosophy does justice to the world unless it treats all relations as equally relations, which means as equally translations or distortions. (*Quadruple Object* 46)

From the standpoint of this passage there is "little reason to be excited about [the] realism" Harman defends in debating Lawlor. For the realism exemplified by the example of the house in that debate is posterior to Harman's ultimate priority, his perspectivalism. It is from the standpoint of this perspectivalism that one deduces that this house eludes the "translations and distortions" of perspectivist views of it, no matter how many.

Similarly, Harman states that no object "can be modeled by any form of knowledge. . . . No reconstruction of that object can step in for it in the cosmos" (*Quadruple Object* 73). This statement is true in Harman's philosophy because it is a consequence of his knowledge of perspectivalism, whereby any object is inscribed within perspectivist form, so that the only access to it is through the "translations and distortions" of perspectives. By definition, perspective is partial and thus a distortion, a caricature. That no knowledge is possible on the level of objects is an inference from knowledge on the level of form, the ultimate priority of perspectivalism, full recognition of which by Harman may be inhibited by his reservations about onto-theology.[54]

While Harman makes his commitment to form clear, he remarks, almost as an aside, "I have no objection to formalization, as long as it does not claim to exhaust the reality of things themselves and makes no pretensions to the absolute" ("Response" 150). Harman's ultimate priority is not an absolute in this sense because it is a form, not "the reality of things themselves." Consider the hypothetical of a God who creates a world in which things, ranging from humans to inanimate objects, have perspectivist relations to one another. In this hypothetical, the ultimate priority of perspectivalism in Harman would not be ultimate because it would be derived from something prior, namely, God. There is no such God or anything comparable in Harman's philosophy. His ultimate priority resides in his perspectivalism, his beginning, posterior to nothing.

McKeon defines a metaphysical turn, as in the passage in this chapter's epigraph, as one in which "knowledge is treated as a relation of consequences established in thought to consequences encountered in things" ("Principles" 388). In Harman's case, perspectivalism on the level of thought, established on the basis of his intuition in the "requiring me" passage, explains the capacities and functionings of particular

---

54. Harman frequently expresses agreement with Heidegger's notion of onto-theology: "I agree . . . that we should avoid onto-theology: the notion that one particular being could serve as the explanation for being as a whole" (DeLanda and Harman 86). Harman's perspectivalism is a realism of form, of formal causation, a form of being that explains why the world is replete with perspectives, one form of being thus explaining being as a whole replete with perspectives. It is not clear whether this form is Platonic, apart from matter, or hylomorphic, always informing matter. In either case, this form would appear to qualify as onto-theology. A variant of this issue of onto-theology is posed by Latour's *Irreductions*. In commenting on this text, Harman observes that "[t]hough the specific claim of *Irreductions* is that nothing can be reduced to anything else," Latour nonetheless "does perform one master reduction," the reduction to "actors"; Harman adds, "Presumably it is impossible to do theoretical work without some sort of reduction, in the sense of taking certain aspects of reality to be more important than others" (*Bruno* 40–41). Is not such reduction onto-theology?

perspectives on the level of things, ranging from perspectivist caricatures of one another that occur when rocks collide with one another to human perspectives on such objects as houses, pennies, and coins. Intuiting how perspective is "organized to function," perspectivalism explains the functioning of particular perspectives. The full explanatory power of Harman's perspectivalism appears in his analysis of how RO, RQ, SO, and SQ are "organized to function" in multiple relations.

RO, RQ, SO, SQ

Harman reminds us, "Recall that the sensual is what exists only in relation to the perceiver, and that the real is whatever withdraws from that relation" (*Quadruple Object* 110). But the perceiver is also a real object, the source of the sensual object, as when Husserl sees the tower. There would be no sensual objects without the real objects that produce them. Conversely, a real object can stand alone, producing no sensual objects, at least for a time, while in a "dormant" state ("Time" 15). This term "dormant" is well chosen, for when one is awake it is hard to imagine not producing sensual objects continuously. Rocks are different. Presumably, a rock produces a sensual object only when some disruption results in something like Harman's example of a rock colliding with another rock and producing a perspectivist "caricature or objectification" of it.

The objecthood of real and sensual objects accounts for their resistance to absorption into holistic totality. *Tool-Being* laid down as fundamental that objects resist such totalization without retreating to traditional notions of substance. Notably, though, Harman concedes that he retreats to some degree insofar as he deploys "an Aristotelian-sounding distinction between the unity of a substance and its plurality of traits" (*Quadruple Object* 95; see also Delanda and Harman 51). Even more, he suggests that his "metaphysics of objects" offers "a weirder version of Aristotle's theory of substance" (*Quadruple Object* 93). Objects continue to be what they were in *Tool-Being* insofar as they consist of relations internally and are capable of entering into relations externally without absorption into holistic totalization (*Quadruple Object* 112). But the conceptualization of objects undergoes developments, as we have seen, as Harman transforms the conventional idea of perspective with which he began by taking ownership of a distinctive perspectivist form consisting of the relation between sensual and real objects, each of which is itself a form similar to the form of Aristotelian substance.

In sensual objects, the relation of object to its qualities is clear. Importantly, qualities can change during the experience of such an object. The qualities in the sensual object of the tower that Husserl produces change as Husserl circles the tower, seeing it from different perspectives, in sunlight in one, in shadows in another, and so on, but the tower is always there, independent of these qualities, rather than reduced to them as in Hume.

In real objects, the relation of object to its qualities is far from clear because Harman characterizes it differently in different places. Most commonly, especially in his early work, a real object is said to withdraw, thus identified by one quality, its agential capacity to withdraw. But in later work, as suggested by his analogies of objects to Aristotle's substances, he says more and more about objects, nowhere more so than in the real objects of the American Civil War and the Dutch East India Company to be considered later in the context of Harman's views of causality. In between these extremes, there is Harman's claim that *Moby Dick*, cited as a representative example of an object, "differs from its own exact length and its own modifiable plot details, and is a certain *je ne sais quoi* or substance able to survive certain modifications and not others" ("Well-Wrought Broken Hammer" 202). One can thus identify an object by distinguishing the modifications it can survive from those it cannot. For this procedure, there is an analogous classical precedent. Consider a human being named "A" who is a white musician. One could peel away the properties of whiteness and musical skills, and "A" would still be a human being. One could do this knowing the essence of a human being that would allow one to distinguish essential from accidental properties. In Harman's analogy, essence becomes *je ne sais quoi*. In place of Aristotle, Harman installs Socrates, who says things of value without ever coming to a clear definition of an essence.

As noted earlier, Harman's Socratic skepticism is metaphysical rather than epistemological, based not on limitations of human faculties à la Kant but on formal causes in the real world that limit access of one object to another. Aristotle's metaphysics has four causes; Harman subtracts final, material, and even efficient insofar as colliding rocks only make indirect contact. Formal causes are all that remain but they are existents, existents that are the one thing that is known, the thing that explains the skepticism.

Harman uses for formalistic modeling the fourfold shorthand of RO, RQ, SO, and SQ. These four can be related in varying ways. "For any group that contains four elements," Harman observes, "ten permutations should be possible in principle." The ten permutations are ten forms that for Harman exhaust the "different kinds of relations [that] are possible in the cosmos" (*Quadruple Object* 124, 108). These permutations do not totalize the cosmos, totalizing being impossible for Harman's cluttered objects, but instead explain the untotalizable relations among objects in the cosmos. One can never penetrate a real object exhaustively Harman tells us over and over, but one can penetrate exhaustively the formal relations among objects in the cosmos.

Formal possibilities, in short, exhaust the possible relations in the cosmos. Here, more than anywhere, one sees the equation of the real to the formal in Harman's ultimate priority, the real being an essential component of any ultimate priority because it is the real that authorizes the inferences from the ultimate priority. In Harman's case, four elements yield ten permutations with a certainty akin to mathematics. The permutations flesh out the skepticism in Harman's perspectivalism.

Harman supplies terms for each of these ten permutations. Listed here are the ten in alphabetical order, each of which will be italicized when it is illustrated below: confrontation, contiguity, duplicity, eidos, emanation, essence, sincerity, space, time, withdrawal. Time, space, essence, and eidos are the "quadruple," the "bedrock for further constructions" (*Quadruple Object* 99). The architectonic perspectivist form manifests itself whenever an element from the RO/RQ side is related to an element from the SO/SQ side.

Time (SO/SQ) is on the sensual side. Sensual qualities "are always already linked with a sensual object, and hence do not need to contract into the object, since they *emanate* from it." When Husserl circles the tower, he sees the tower as an unchanging object and its qualities as changing with every step. Time is the "name for this tension between sensual objects and their sensual qualities" (*Quadruple Object* 132, 100). The sensual object registers the time experienced by a real object such as Husserl. "The experience of time is an experience of change within continuity," Harman propounds, adding, "In Husserlian terms, it is the relative endurance of sensual objects amidst a constant shift of adumbrations" (DeLanda and Harman 122).

Essence (RO/RQ) is on the real side. It is the name for the "tension between the real object and its real qualities." Harman comes perhaps closest to Aristotle when he links *essence* with "causation": "We have seen that this [linking real qualities in a single real object] requires a kind of fusion that we have called essence, and linked with the phenomenon of causation" (*Quadruple Object* 101, 132). Harman does not elaborate, but causation here would appear to be limited to formal causation, a watered-down Aristotle.

Space (RO/SQ) is the perspectivist gap between the real object and the indirect relation to it through sensual qualities. Harman illustrates by depicting himself as related to Osaka, Japan, whether he is in Cairo or Osaka, but "[w]hatever sensual profile the city displays to [him]," it "will differ from the real Osaka that forever withdraws into the shadows of being. This interplay of relation and nonrelation is precisely what we mean by *space*" (*Quadruple Object* 100). Additionally, Harman sees clock-time as spatial, distinct from the experiential time in sensual objects, because it has to do with changes in real objects rather than sensual experience" (DeLanda and Harman 122). Presumably, then, clock-time would measure the time it would take Harman, a real object, to change location from Cairo to Osaka.

Eidos (SO/RQ): one grasps *eidos* "through a process of eidetic variation: we imagine a house from many different viewpoints, stripping away its shifting properties that arise and then vanish" in order to identify "an inner nucleus of the house, an eidos that makes it what it is for those who perceive it." Even though the house is withdrawn from the totality of perspectives, evidently a multitude of perspectives can identify a core nucleus of essential, real qualities. Here the difference between the sensory and the intellectual is important, not unimportant as we saw earlier: these real qualities "can only be known through categorial intuition: the work of the intellect and not of the senses" (*Quadruple Object* 101).

Sensual qualities coexist with real qualities. Sensual qualities are accidental, can come and go without any impact on the real object and its qualities, whereas the real qualities are essential for the object to be what it is. The name for this relation between real and sensual qualities is "*duplicity*." The sensual object may be an idealist illusion that mistakenly sees gallows as a tree. When the mistake is corrected the qualities take on a new character, the relation between the new and the old being not recognition, which is too human-centered, but "*confrontation*." When not an illusion, the relation between the real object and the sensual object is "*sincerity*" (*Quadruple Object* 128, 103, 128).

The sensual object, as quoted earlier, "exists only in relation to the perceiver" in the perspectival architectonic. This "exists" should be underlined. For Harman, perception is a reality. "While it is true that perceptions are transient, not purely physical," Harman concedes, "these points disqualify them as objects only for those who accept needless traditional views of what an object is," adding, "For in fact my perception of a tree does meet the criteria for an object" because it is "unified" and "irreducible to its pieces in isolation." What is perhaps most notable in Harman's sensual object is that the perceiver, normally seen as independent of the perspectivist view, becomes part of the object, interior to it. "If I perceive a tree," Harman explains "this sensual object and I do not meet up inside my mind, and for a simple reason: my mind and its object are two equal partners in the intention, and the unifying term must contain both" (*Quadruple Object* 117, 115–16). For Harman, we recall, "any given intentional act *is itself a new reality*" (*Dante's Hammer* 12), and this reality takes the form of a sensual object. Regarding intentionality, Harman says that it took him seventeen years to understand fully Husserl's assertion "that intentionality is both one and two," "two" in the sense that the "I" who intends and the "tree" intended are distinct, "one" in the sense that in the intention, the two become one ("Time" 9).

But while the observer of a tree becomes part of the sensual object, the observer may also observe a nearby house, an additional sensual object. Multiple sensual objects are linked in the relation of "*contiguity*," this linkage occurring in the "same field of experience for a single observer: I encounter not just one sensual object at a time, but many," whereas "two real objects coexist in the manner of "*withdrawal*" (*Quadruple Object* 128). Is contiguity possible, given Harman's insistence that sensual objects "do not meet up inside [his] mind"? A sensual object is a distinctive reality that contains Harman and an object such as a tree. Harman and a house adjoining the tree constitute another sensual object, that is, another distinctive reality. Harman's contiguity, then, presupposes that Harman can be in two distinctive objects at the same time. One can imagine phenomenal images of the tree and the house in his mind at the same time, but he insists that sensual objects are not in his mind but are instead distinctive objects that are real. It is also obvious that Harman, a real object, produces countless sensual objects in the course of a day. While discussions of Harman typically focus on withdrawn real objects, such objects are dwarfed by the far larger number of sensual objects. Sensual objects are also present, available for careful analysis, whereas one logically can say nothing about withdrawn real objects, although Harman says a lot about them in the name of Socrates, beginning with the attribution of the agency in the term "withdrawal."

Harman analogizes his fourfold of time, space, essence, and eidos to the fourfold of earth, air, fire, and water that Empedocles found, but contrasts the two by noting that earth, air, fire, and water are "physical elements," whereas his four appear in innumerable entities (*Quadruple Object* 142). To be more precise, he should say that his four are forms that may be realized in an indefinite number of matters. It is because they are forms that they are not limited by characteristics of any physical particulars such as earth, air, fire, and water.

Additionally, *The Quadruple Object* is notably marked by a large number of graphs that represent the forms that for Harman are what is real. Form is what Harman accesses directly and about which he offers knowledge. His ultimate priority of form, his explainer, explains why there are two kinds of objects, each with its distinctive qualities, these objects and qualities related in ten ways that exhaust the possibilities in the cosmos. The reality of form is primary. The realities of real and sensual objects are derivative. Their relation to form, a noted earlier, is not altogether clear insofar as the relation of form to matter is left blurry. This relation is one relation Harman ignores. Is it the same everywhere in a flat ontology? Or are there differences in matter that make a difference? But for differences in matter to matter Harman would presumably have to grant matter an existential status that he has resisted to date.

CAUSALITY AND AESTHETICS

The topics of causality and aesthetics are not commonly seen as close. Causality is typically associated with science, which is commonly opposed to art. Harman paradoxically is and is not an exception. He is an exception insofar as one can find causality and aesthetics closely associated in his work early in his career. He is not an exception insofar as in the course of his development, there is a shift in emphasis from causality to aesthetics that appears to widen the difference between them, more in line with the conventional opposition. Furthermore, in theorizing aesthetics, Harman draws on the shorthand from *Quadruple Object*, featuring a variant of RO-SQ, to theorize what he calls "formalism" in *Art and Objects*, published in 2020. Among the arts, architecture in particular appears to be most deeply influenced by Harman's work (*Object-Oriented Ontology* 246–52). Harman now teaches at SCI-Arc (Southern California Institute of Architecture).

The early close association between causality and aesthetics appears in *Guerilla Metaphysics*. Harman announces in its opening pages that while the focus in *Tool-Being* was on "objects exist[ing] in utter isolation," the focus in this new book is on how, despite this isolation, "carpentry" occurs: "The subject matter of a carpentry of things in object-oriented philosophy is the shifting communication and collision between distinct entities" (1, 2). Two sides of this carpentry may be distinguished. On one side there is a concern with causality that occasions *Guerilla*'s consideration of the notion of vicarious causation, a precursor of his aspirational essay "On Vicarious Causation." On the other side there is a concern with aesthetics, one sign of which is a lengthy consideration of "An Essay in Esthetics by Way of a Preface" by José Ortega y Gasset in *Guerilla*'s chapter on metaphor, chapter eight. Harman returns to Ortega's theory of metaphor in "Aesthetics Is the Root of All Philosophy," chapter two in his 2018 *Object-oriented Ontology*, rewriting the earlier consideration with an analysis informed by RO-SQ.

In his presentation at the 2007 Speculative Realism Workshop, and later in his review of this presentation in *Speculative Realism*. Harman positions vicarious causation as central in the initial stages of the development of his philosophy. At the Workshop, he proclaims, "The *Collapse* article ["On Vicarious Causation," published in *Collapse* in 2007] is about as far as I've gotten. I've gotten only a little bit further than that" ("Presentation" 375). Recapitulating his development, he recounts that in his reading of Heidegger he concluded, as discussed earlier, that theory and practice equally distort the withdrawn real object; second, considering that in their withdrawal, objects withdraw from one another as well, he asked how they can impact one another causally ("Presentation" 370–71, 373; *Speculative Realism* 93, 95). This prompted his coinage "vicarious causation" ("Presentation" 375) and his finding the vehicle for such causation in Husserl, specifically in Husserl's "sensual or intentional object" ("Presentation" 375, 377; "On Vicarious Causation" 197; *Speculative Realism* 96–97). Harman proclaims, "There's not really any discussion in physics of what happens when one thing influences another," adding that the neglect of formal causation in physics is a particular shortcoming, countering, "Forms do all the work in Aristotle and elsewhere, and that's what I want to retain" ("Presentation" 406).

"On Vicarious Causation" is remarkably aspirational. "The supposed great debate over causation between skeptics [presumably Hume] and transcendental philosophers [presumably Kant]," Harman complains, "is at best a yes-or-no dispute as to whether causal necessity exists, and in practice is just an argument over whether it can be known," leaving little room for "active discussion of the very nature of causality." "In classical terms," Harman proclaims, "we must speculate once more on causation while forbidding its reduction to efficient causation. Vicarious causation, of which science so far knows nothing, is closer to what is called formal cause" (188, 190). Efficient causation is probably the first thing the topic of causality brings to mind. Red billiard ball hits blue ball, blue ball moves; red ball is efficient cause of blue ball's movement. Harman rules out such causation, claiming real objects never make direct contact. Their contact is always indirect, perspectivist or "vicarious" in form. Rocks colliding form perspectivist caricatures of one another; billiard balls do the same. This formal causation, "of which science so far knows nothing," is what Harman ambitiously promises to reveal.

Subsequent work has failed to live up to these early ambitions. Vicarious causation appears in the 2018 comprehensive *Object-Oriented Ontology: A New Theory of Everything*, but only briefly, taking a decidedly backseat to other topics treated far more extensively, especially aesthetics. Vicarious causation even appears to give way to compositional causation, discussed below.

The discussion of the real objects of "I" and "pine tree" in "On Vicarious Causation" is one that Harman later corrects, "I would no longer say that the intentional relation between me and the sensual tree is what contains the two parts, and it is strange that I ever said so in the first place," explaining, "[I]t is not my *intentional* relationship with the tree that contains the two pieces of the relation (which is contact, not relation). Instead, this honor goes to the relation between the real me and the real tree, however this may occur. Due to Asymmetry such relation can never be direct, but only by means of some sensual mediator" (*Prince of Networks* 210–11). It is the perspectivist form of indirect contact in the "sensual mediator" that vicariously substitutes for direct contact. This sensual object is the effect of intentionality, a cause whose source is the "real me." This cause is asymmetrical, coming solely from the "real me" to add the new reality of the sensual object that mediates the relation between the "real me" and the "real tree." The sensual object, as discussed earlier, is Harman's synonym for Husserl's intentionality, preferable insofar as it conveys more clearly "that we do not speak here of the real world beyond human access where only real objects belong" (*Quadruple Object* 26).

But Harman's autocritique does not extend to asking why he used the example of the "real me" and the "pine tree" in the first place. It is true that one can imagine vicarious causal relations between "real me" and "pine tree." Looking at "pine tree," "real me" creates a "sensual object" of it (vicarious cause), one that convinces "real me" that it needs pruning and to begin cutting branches accordingly. But this causality is contingent, an effect of a contingent decision by "real me," which is not the kind of causality that underwrites Harman's prediction in his plutonium example, discussed earlier. This prediction presupposes that plutonium's lethal causality is unleashed by physical necessity. That is why its lethality is predictable, unlike the unpredictability of what "real me" may or may not do in interacting with the "pine tree." The intentionality informing the creation of the sensual object that mediates the relation between "real me" and "pine tree" is inherently a mode of contingent causality, like the causality in Husserl circling the tower, far different from the causality in plutonium's lethality and thus not likely to revolutionize the theorizing of causality in any way that would measure up to the aspirations of "On Vicarious Causation."

Intentionality also implies the presence of human consciousness, so that for Harman one must conceive intentionality broadly to go beyond its normal scope to include such matters as one rock's "caricature" of the rock with which it collides. Such "caricature" is a contingent, new reality, like an effect of intentionality. Better terminology is needed to encompass the modes of indirect contact extending from humans to rocks. One commentator suggests "connection" might do the job because it does not "necessarily imply any form of awareness" (Ferro 574).

Harman's plutonium example reflects his early interest in causality; his failure to return to it may reflect limitations in his effort to conceive causality as indirect contact. To overcome these limitations, Harman suggests that vicarious causation "owes much" to occasionalism (*Object-Oriented Ontology* 150; see also "On Vicarious Causation" 218–20). Like vicarious causation, occasionalism is an alternative to efficient causality. In this doctrine, which flourished in Europe as late as the seventeenth century, most notably in Malebranche, "the impact of one billiard ball upon another is an *occasion* for God to move the second ball" (*Cambridge Dictionary* 543; my italics); the first ball is thus not the efficient cause of movement in the second ball, as one might think in a commonsensical understanding of efficient causality. Vicarious causation, introduced as we saw as an alternative to Humean skepticism and Kantian transcendentalism, looks for an analogue to occasionalism's God in the sense that it looks to something independent of two objects to explain a causal process that occurs between them even though they cannot come into direct contact with one another, so that one cannot be the efficient cause of what happens to the other.

Occasionalism's reliance on God dates it, of course, but Harman contends that vicarious causation shows that one can keep occasionalist structure while dispensing with God. Furthermore, "Hume and Kant certainly do not agree with the occasionalist view that causation must always have God as a mediator," Harman observes, "But what they do share in common with occasionalism is the view that *one special entity in particular* is the site of causation: namely, the human mind" (*Object-Oriented Ontology* 165). Oddly, then, Harman aspires to find in vicarious causation an alternative to the debate between Humeans and Kantians, but ends up putting Hume and Kant, occasionalism, and vicarious causation in the same basket.

This "owes much" is eventually combined with radical revisions of occasionalism. Harman pronounces that "OOO cannot accept the findings of occasionalism," as well as the variants in Hume and Kant, "because *no entity at all*—whether God, the human mind or anything else—should be permitted to make direct contact with other objects when this is forbidden in principle to everything else" (*Object-Oriented Ontology* 150). Furthermore, reliance on God, the human mind, or any other single thing falls short when compared to Latour's "doctrine of local occasionalism," which Harman celebrates as "probably Latour's greatest achievement in philosophy" and as introducing possibly "an unprecedented theme in the long history of metaphysics." The key is "local," which means that the vicarious mediator is not any single thing but varies from situation to situation. Presumably one example would be the sensual object that prompts "real me" to prune "pine tree" in my hypothetical. Harman underlines that it also means that the local mediator might fail, something "always denied, for obvious reasons, to God" (*Prince Networks* 112, 115).

By contrast to vicarious causation, compositional causation "holds that any relation between separate things produces a new composite object" (*Object-Oriented Ontology* 167). Harman takes this causation to the extreme in claiming that a midair collision between two airplanes is such a new object even if it exists for only a few seconds. Harman also subscribes to another mode of causation closely related to if not identical with compositional causation, one that comes from "the late Lynn Margolis, who distinguishes between moments of gradual change and moments of *symbiosis* between separate organisms in which change leads to an organism different in kind from its predecessors" (*Object-Oriented Ontology* 111; see also "On Landscape Ontology"). Harman does not limit "symbiosis" to biology (*Object-Oriented* 112), so that a midair collision would also appear to instantiate symbiosis as much as compositional causation.

Harman applies symbiosis extensively in "The American Civil War," one of the main sections in *Object-Oriented Ontology*. One well-known event in the Civil War is the Emancipation Proclamation, which Harman identifies "as a symbiosis because it transformed the nature of the war by broadening its goals and further uncovering its ultimate outcome" (133). In his analysis of the Civil War, Harman identifies a number of such symbiotic transformations that link the Civil War's beginning to its end. Here, symbiosis appears to identify significant modifications in one object, the Civil War, rather than a succession of new objects. *Immaterialism* adds, "*The key to understanding social objects is to hunt for their symbioses*" (*Immaterialism* 117).

Treatment of the Civil War as a social object, like the treatment of the Dutch East India Company in *Immaterialism: Objects and Social Theory*, evidences Harman's interest in broadening his philosophizing to encompass social objects formed historically. These objects appear to be real rather than sensual, but even though that means that they presumably withdraw, Harman analyzes them in considerable detail, adding that even more could obviously be said; Harman even suggests that an "OOO interpretation of the Civil War could easily run to hundreds of pages" and that one day he may even "attempt it" (*Object-Oriented Ontology* 134). Harman goes even closer to classical metaphysical realism in his extensive analysis in *Immaterialism* of the Dutch East India Company. He concludes with a set of fifteen "provisional rules" for the formation of such social objects (114–26), a set that is on the slope toward what Aristotle called "commensurately universal" attributes, both universal and essential (*Posterior Analytics* 1.4.73b–26–31, *Basic Works* 117), thus deepening the analogies to Aristotle that he sees on the level of the form of objects. The term "provisional" applies to the analysis rather than the object. In other words, one's understanding of the process by which social objects are formed may improve but the process itself will not change. Harman even appears to proceed in Aristotelian fashion from what is better known to us in the historical record to what is better known in the being of historical objects. He says explicitly that *Immaterialism* "is an *ontology* rather than a history" (40).

There is a polemical side to the analyses of these historical objects. Both target Latour's ANT. Harman has for years combined his indebtedness to and admiration for Latour with faulting him for "overmining." Harman captures the core of his critique in one sentence: "To treat objects solely as actors forgets that a thing acts because it exists rather than existing because it acts" (*Immaterialism* 7). To make his case for this priority of existence, Harman penetrates the depths of these supposedly withdrawn existent objects. Such penetration is not new, but it is deeper here than in other places. This greater penetration cannot be justified on the ground that these are historical objects; given Harman's dismissal of matter, there is no basis in his philosophy for treating historical objects differently on the ground that their matter differs from non-historical objects. Such penetration seems to in the direction of metaphysical realism, away from skepticism. But Socrates seems now to occupy a permanent place in Harman's philosophy as the proper model for philosophy. Socrates justifies extensive movement in the direction of metaphysical realism while ensuring that this movement always stops short of such realism, consistent with the "translations or distortions" discussed earlier in the relations between the real and the sensual.

Turning from causality to aesthetics, one can begin with the aesthetic counterpart to vicarious causality in *Guerilla Metaphysics*, namely, "allure," a mode of allusion. In 2007, the year "On Vicarious Causation" appeared, Harman also published "Aesthetics as First Philosophy: Levinas and the Non-Human," which finds in Levinas evidence for concluding, "Allure is not just a theory of art, but a theory of causal relations in general" (30). Harman's example of the "real me" and the "pine tree" is arguably more readily suitable for consideration of aesthetics than vicarious causality. It is notable that a relation analogous to that between "real me" and "pine tree," namely, that between the reader or viewer of art and the art work itself, becomes central in the "formalism" that Harman develops in his later aesthetics. (*Art* 32–33, 45).

Harman's view of Socrates as exemplar of philosophy conceived as the love of knowledge rather than the acquirement of knowledge might be viewed as transforming the negativity of loving knowledge that can never be acquired into the positivity of aesthetic experience. In any case, it is definitely in the direction of this positivity that Harman's philosophizing has been heading in recent years and perhaps for good. Science has, Harman argues, "browbeaten us into the assumption that the only options are knowledge on one side and ignorant gesticulation on the other," adding, "This crude vision of human cognition has never made any sense in the arts" ("Realism" 105).

Even though Harman's influence appears to be greatest in the realm of architecture and his *Art and Objects* is largely about the visual arts, Harman draws mainly on literary arts in philosophizing about aesthetics. The title of his 2012 essay in *New Literary History*, "The Well-Wrought Broken Hammer: Object-Oriented Literary Criticism," alludes to Cleanth Brooks's *The Well-Wrought Urn: Studies in the Structure of Poetry*, published in 1947, a major contribution to the ascendency that the formalism known as the New Criticism enjoyed during the middle decades of the twentieth century (Brooks does not hyphenate "well wrought").

The New Critics prioritized the intrinsic form of the literary work over author, reader, and content. They stigmatized analysis of a work in terms of the author's intention or the reader's response in classic essays coauthored by W. K. Wimsatt and Monroe C. Beardsley, "The Intentional Fallacy" (1946) and "The Affective Fallacy" (1949), both reprinted in Wimsatt's *The Verbal Icon: Studies in the Meaning of Poetry*, published in 1967. In *The Well Wrought Urn*, Brooks stigmatizes reducing a work to its content in "The Heresy of Paraphrase," which Harman sums up approvingly as claiming, "A poem cannot be translated into literal prose statement" ("Well-Wrought Broken Hammer" 189). This is the component of New Critical formalism that Harman incorporates into the formalism he espouses eight years later in *Art and Objects*, where he stigmatizes it as "*literalism*" (x).

While Harman applauds Brooks's stigmatizing of literalism, he rejects Brooks's argument justifying it. For Brooks, the words in a literary work derive their meaning from their relations to other words in the work. The dictionary meaning of the words in the work might be metaphorized as the clay with which the writer begins before giving it its distinctive shape in the literary work. Consequently, the closer one comes to stating the meaning of the work, the closer one comes to simply repeating the words in the work. Paraphrasing the words instead of repeating them is heretical. This argument Harman rejects: "In one sense it is obviously true that he [Brooks] views the poem as existing in pristine isolation from the rest of the cosmos. Yet once we have entered the gates of the poem, nothing is autonomous at all according to Brooks: instead, we inhabit a holistic wonderland in which everything is defined solely by its interrelations with everything else" ("Well-Wrought Broken Hammer" 190). In other words, for Harman, seeing a word defined by its relation to other words is equivalent to reducing a hammer to its relations to other objects in the process in which it functions. That the hammer breaks evidences that it cannot be so reduced, that it has an existence independent of the relations in which it participates. Hence, Harman rejects Brooks's analysis by looking in the literary work for an analogue to the breaking of the hammer. In other words, what could show that while on one level everything in the literary work may be related to everything else, there is another level that is independent of reduction to such holistic interrelations?

Harman's answer, "[W]e cannot identify the literary work with the exact current form it happens to have." Translating this principle into a method of criticism, Harman offers the method of interpreting *Moby Dick* discussed earlier. The object-oriented critic "might try to show how each text resists internal holism by attempting various *modifications* of these texts," such as shortening *Moby Dick* "to discover the point at which it ceases to sound like *Moby Dick*" ("Well-Wrought Broken Hammer" 201, 201–02). Theoretically, then, in each text there is internal holism on one level and a core independent of this holism on another level.

That Harman made this argument in 2012 suggests that at that time he envisioned a "Well-Wrought Broken Hammer" that would be like New Critical formalism in prioritizing the form of the individual work (the "well-wrought" aspect) but depart from that formalism by envisioning variants of the work as equal instances of this form (the "broken hammer" aspect). His formalism in *Art and Objects* departs from this centering on the individual work, substituting for it the combination of the work and the reader or viewer, which aligns with the reader response criticism that rebelled against new criticism's formalism.

This departure evolves out of many years of reflection on metaphor largely inspired by the Ortega essay mentioned above. Harman credits this essay with "open[ing] the doors" for him at an early age to what eventually became "object-oriented philosophy" (*Guerilla Metaphysics* 98), an age when he had yet to read Heidegger (*Object-Oriented Ontology* 72). While Heidegger's influence evidently later surpassed Ortega's, Harman here gives Ortega a degree of precedence. Returning to this essay repeatedly, Harman testifies to taking eighteen years to understand it (*Object-Oriented Ontology* 72). The capstone of this evolution is recorded in *Object-Oriented Ontology*, where he theorizes metaphor in terms of *Quadruple Object*'s shorthand, identifying it as RO-SQ. In *Quadruple Object*'s fourfold, RO-SQ is space (114). Perhaps metaphor is to be seen as in some sense a variant of space; not sure. Harman's theory of metaphor does authorize a spatial relationship between the work of art and the agent who experiences the work of art.

Harman himself uses the word "bizarre" to describe his use of RO-SQ to define metaphor, in effect the formal cause of metaphor. He takes his example from Ortega's essay, quoting from it: "we are to see the image of a cypress through the image of a flame; we *see it as* a flame, and vice versa." Harman corrects the "vice versa" on the ground that seeing a flame as a cypress is a different metaphor; metaphor is asymmetrical. Then, he proposes that because Ortega's essay "led us to the formulation that art is an object-quality tension of the type RO-SQ, we have the problem of knowing exactly what plays the role of RO in the metaphor 'the cypress is a flame'" (*Object-Oriented Ontology* 74, 74–75, 82).

One thing Harman values in Ortega is his distinction between the observable image of a thing, such as a cypress, "and the *executant* reality of things in their own right, quite apart from how they are seen or used." Harman readily translates this distinction into his between sensual and real objects. As a real object, the actual cypress withdraws, so that, Harman insists, "Not even the vastest army of beautiful metaphors could exhaustively allude to the cypress in its inwardness." One must thus look elsewhere for the RO in "the cypress is a flame." Here is Harman's discovery of the needed RO:

> Nonetheless, since objects and qualities always come together for OOO, the metaphor only works because the flame-qualities somehow become fused with an *object*, not just an inscrutable void where the cypress used to be. This leaves us with only one option, which we must embrace even if the consequences seem initially bizarre. For if the real cypress is just as absent from the metaphor as it is from thought and perception, there is nonetheless one real object that is never absent from our experience of art: namely, *we ourselves*. Yes, it is we ourselves who stand in for the absent cypress and support its freshly anointed flame-qualities. (*Object-Oriented* 78, 82, 83)

Implications of this theorizing appear in *Art and Objects*, where metaphor is deemed a "performance art" in which the spectator is the performer. Metaphor is thus the core model for what Harman calls "Theatrical Aesthetics." The fusion of spectator and art work constitutes the object in Harman's formalism, now aligned not with new critical formalism but with "reader response criticism" (68–69, 64, 70).

On its last two pages, *Art and Objects* contrasts different roles for the spectator in his formalism by drawing on McLuhan's distinction between hot and cold mediums. A cold medium is one "in which insufficient information is given, so that some detail must be provided by the beholder, yielding an effect that is often hypnotic" (178). A hot medium does the opposite, constraining spectators by leaving them little or no room to perform. Harman concludes that "the many hot forms that dominated modernity" may give way in the coming years to cold forms (179). In this move to cold mediums, Harman forecasts, the art form that may dominate is "architecture, which is inherently cold insofar as we wander it freely and never grasp it at once, meaning that it cannot be equated with any specific series of profiles in the manner of illusionistic painting, the novel or film" (179).

Harman's formalism thus allows him to define the vanguard direction in the world of art. Whether the metaphysical turn will follow him in this aesthetic direction remains to be seen.

Ultimate Priority, Again

Gratton begins the final section of his chapter on Harman, mentioned earlier, with the point that "each philosopher has a depiction of the absolute, or a method that begins with a given starting point." This passage is of interest here in this chapter's conclusion because it considers Harman in the context of the problem that this book addresses with the notion of an ultimate priority. Gratton sees absolute and method as distinct because he says, "Harman's claim is not methodological, but is a depiction of the real or absolute" (100, 101). In the absence of further elaboration, Gratton's meaning is not altogether clear. Suffice it to say, an ultimate priority would appear to combine what Gratton separates with "absolute" on one side and "method" on the other side. His "absolute" would appear to be equivalent to the ultimate priority, defined as that existent in a philosophy that is prior to the inferential chain that follows from it; his "method" would appear to be equivalent to the inferential chain following from the ultimate priority that is informed by the nature of this existent.

Gratton has difficulties understanding Harman's "real or absolute," however, because he looks for it in the wrong place. This is understandable insofar as Harman's talk of objects withdrawing encourages it. Because withdrawal puts Harman's absolute "out of view as *other*," Gratton cannot find the answers he is looking for: "The question is how to account for an interiority that is closed off: is it one thing behind all objects? All different objects in themselves? Processes of becoming that throw up appearances of objects? Are they but *monads* unrelated to one another through time and space?" In Gratton's view, because Harman does not answer such questions, his "absolute" could be almost anything: "The problem is, once it is put out of view as *other*, then it is difficult to see why it shouldn't be pure indeterminacy as in Schelling, or number as in the Pythagoreans, or firstness or *prius* as in Peirce, and so on, given all the absolutes that metaphysicians have made their starting point" (101).

Harman responds to this critique briefly, but rather than address the problem of ultimate priority, he reiterates his analysis, discussed early in this chapter in contrasting Heidegger's turn against thought to Harman's turn to thing by turning against Heidegger. Harman contends that this analysis demonstrates that there must be "a submerged entity that is never fully expressed in any of its practical *or* theoretical appearances and is ultimately unexpressed even in its brute causal relations with non-human things" (*Skirmishes* 138). It is unlikely that Harman's response would satisfy Gratton insofar as it simply indicates that his "submerged entity" is "put out of view," which is precisely the problem for Gratton.

While Harman's ultimate priority evidences itself in his reasoning, it is not altogether clear that Harman himself recognizes this priority for what it is. He comes close in the handful of places where he affirms strongly the primacy and existential status of formal causes. He comes closest when he says in the passage quoted earlier that "something in the world" requires him to distinguish between "real objects that withdraw and sensual ones that don't." That "something" is a form, specifically the perspectival form that informs relations everywhere in the combination of contact and no contact in indirect contact.

The priority of this form appears in a passage that Gratton himself quotes in his analysis of Harman, a passage quoted earlier in this chapter. This passage should have alerted Gratton to look in a different place for

Harman's absolute. This is the passage in which Harman says that there is "little reason to be excited" about a realism based on "posit[ing] some unarticulated reality beyond experience," then counters, "Against such claims we should always observe the following litmus test: no philosophy does justice to the world unless it treats all relations as equally relations, which means as equally translations or distortions" (93, quoting *Quadruple Object* 46), that is, as equally perspectivist indirect contacts. Harman, of course, often depicts himself as a realist precisely because he claims there is an "unarticulated reality beyond experience," as in his debate with Lawlor, but his self-depiction in this passage is more accurate than his usual self-depiction. Perspectivalism, a formal cause, is his fundamental reality.

The priority of this fundamental reality appears in another passage that Gratton quotes a few pages later, one that echoes the bridge example in *Tool-Being*: "The geological survey of a mountain and the climbing of that mountain have a very different structure, but what both have in common is their failure to exhaust the mountain in its very being. The geologist must always leave many of its features unnoticed, while the climber also fails to grasp aspects of the mountain that are relevant for birds, ants, snow leopards, or yeti" (95, quoting *Quentin* 184; writing before the second edition of *Quentin*, Gratton quotes from the first edition, where the passage appears on 135). In the sentence that follows this passage, Harman echoes the turn from Heidegger discussed early in this chapter: "In short, human theory and human praxis are both translations or distortions of the subterranean reality of mountain-being, which is no more exhausted by sentient action than by sentient thought" (*Quentin* 184). Here, perspectivalism is clearly the ultimate priority from which it follows, in Harman's inferential chain, that mountain "being" eludes the multiple agents that Harman imagines because they are limited to the slivers of the mountain that appear in their varying perspectives, that is, their "translations or distortions."

This mountain example exhibits Harman's best argument for an object's inaccessibility because it establishes this inaccessibility in an inferential chain beginning with perspectivalism that shows why multiple agents, either individually or collectively, fail to "exhaust" the mountain's "being." There is no need here to attribute to the mountain the mysterious agency of withdrawal or withholding. "At the heart of OOO," Harman states clearly in a passage quoted earlier, "is the idea that the real object undergoes *translation* into a sensual one, so there is no isomorphy between the two; the form itself changes between one place and another." Geologist, mountain climber, birds, ants, snow leopards, and yeti—all exhibit the conventional idea of perspective in the sense that each, by having contact with one part of the mountain, is kept during this contact from having contact with other parts. Harman takes ownership of an original variant of perspective by theorizing the contact as a translation of one form (RO, RQ) into another form (SO, SQ).

This example also illustrates the metaphysical structure of Harman's skepticism. Harman is not a realist but a skeptic, one who sees in Socrates a model for his skepticism. The structure is the perspectival structure in which sensual objects mediate everyone's distinctive relation to the mountain. Insofar as sensual objects can be illusory, they do not even guarantee the existence of the mountain.

Contrastingly, an Aristotelian approach would use the distinction between better known to us and better known in being to privilege the geologist. Geologist, mountain climber, birds, ants, snow leopards, and yeti all have sensual objects of the mountain that are on the side of better known to us. The geologist can go from this level to the level of better known in being insofar as the geologist can explain how the mountain got there, how it could disappear, and so on. Aristotle is a realist, Harman is a skeptic. In the name of flat ontology, Harman puts geologist, mountain climber, birds, ants, snow leopards, and yeti all on the same skeptical level.

The missing chapter in Harman's work is one on the relation of form to matter. If form is joined to matter, differences in matter would matter in some way. If form is separate from matter then his metaphysical turn as perspectivalism is a paradoxical Platonic skepticism. A form separable from matter may or may not be an eternal form. Presumably for Harman form is contingent rather than eternal, so that if he sees form as separable from matter his skepticism would be quasi-Platonic. Whether Harman's aesthetic formalism will one day lead him to address the problem of form and matter remains to be seen. At this point, his metaphysical turn gets no farther than a form that informs a Socratic skepticism.

6 Turn against Turn

> ... it is no less true that the nature of things, in so far as it is known, is determined by philosophic principles than that philosophic principles are determined, in so far as they are verified, by the nature of things.
>
> —McKeon, "Philosophic Bases of Art and Criticism," p. 464.

Chapter one asks, "Can one find in philosophical turns themselves a reason to favor one turn over the others?" A specific turn offers reasons for preferring it to its predecessor, but this question is broader. Is there a basis for preferring one turn to the others on the basis of the evidence of the turns themselves.

Such a general criterion is arguably implicit in Kant's arguments for his turn. Put simply, this criterion is that a turn that produces consensus is preferable to any turn that produces controversy. In *Prolegomena to Any Future Metaphysics*, he complains, "in all ages one metaphysics has contradicted another," when there actually should be a "single book to which you can point as you do to Euclid, and say: This is metaphysics" (21, 20). Euclid no longer serves to make Kant's point, but his point is nonetheless clear. This complaint reiterates the passage in the Preface to the first edition of *Critique of Pure Reason*, where Kant proclaims, "The battlefield of these endless controversies is called metaphysics." He returns to this theme in his Preface to the second edition, where he again depicts metaphysics as "a battleground quite peculiarly suited for those who desire to exercise themselves in mock combats, and in which no participant has ever yet succeeded in gaining even so much as an inch of territory, not at least in such manner as to secure him in its permanent possession." By contrast, Kant speaks admiringly of modern science for its success in getting past such endless controversy to produce genuine knowledge. To duplicate this success, he proposes "by way of experiment" his turn from thing to thought (7, Aviii; 21, Bxv; 22, Bxvi).

Kant, then, saw his turn as an "experiment" promising consensus to replace the inconclusive controversies of metaphysics. That, of course, did not happen. Instead, to this day, we live with the "*Kant wars*," Robert

Hanna's term for the seemingly endless controversies not just between Kantians and antiKantians but even among Kantians themselves (75). If metaphysical controversy is a reason for rejecting a metaphysical turn to thing, Kantian controversy is a reason for rejecting a Kantian turn to thought.

But what needs to be rejected, of course, is Kant's criterion for preferring one turn to another. The turns charted in McKeon's historical semantics indicate that philosophers cannot even agree for more than a century or so about the subject matter of philosophy. The subject matter of the linguistic turn now appears more dated with each passing day. Furthermore, agreement about subject matter is combined, as we saw particularly in chapter three, with debate about what it is exactly that makes the subject matter ultimately prior, a debate that involves subtle differences in views of the subject matter itself. If there is a basis for a preferential order among turns, Kant's criterion is not it. One must look elsewhere.

A different criterion appears in Rorty's observation, repeating a quotation from chapter four, that "the Cartesian claim that we can have certainty only about our ideas" fostered "the notion that we can only know about objects a priori if we 'constitute' them," adding that "Kant was never troubled by the question of how we could have apodictic knowledge of these 'constituting activities,' for Cartesian privileged access was supposed to take care of that" (*Philosophy Mirror* 137–38). Privileged access to the "constituting activities" of thought, the location of the ultimate priority in a turn to the subject matter of thought, remained the basis for preferring Kant's turn as his dream of consensus failed to materialize. This privileging also proved easy to extend to the subject matter of words and acts because the ultimate priority in this subject matter also consists of "constituting activities" in human beings. In recent centuries, then, this privileging was consistent with turns first to thought, then to language and action. Because "constituting activities" are directly accessible, turns to thought or language and action came to be preferred to a turn to thing, which is independent of such "activities." This preference appeared in the favoring of antirealism over realism. Meillassoux's term "correlation" encapsulates the structure of this antirealism.

This argument from "constituting activities" is a confession of what this book terms "exemptionalism," explicitly justifying direct, intuitive access to ultimate priorities in "constituting activities" in the subject matters of thought and language, while denying such access to the subject matter of thing, allowing instead only indirect mediated access. Notably, Harman denies this distinction between direct and mediated accessibility claiming that "it is not true that I have any more intimate access to language or consciousness or the conditions of speech-acts than I do to a pile of rocks" (*Towards* 86).

Turns in McKeon's cycle are all turns to subject matters that are distinctive realities. This consideration undermines the opposition between antirealism and realism because the antirealisms based on thought and language are actually two distinctive realities. Undermining this opposition may have been the meaning, or a meaning, of the term "subversive" that McKeon used, as we saw near the end of chapter one, in making his prediction of a metaphysical turn. Philosophy is always based on the reality of a subject matter, a reality considered prior to the other possibilities. As we saw in chapter three, the trajectory of the narrative of the linguistic turn was informed by the recognition that the prioritizing of language over thought early in the turn was insufficient. To complete the turn, it would be necessary to prioritize language over thing as well. Translating this narrative of inquiry into this chapter's epigraph, one could say that the turn in the twentieth century to the subject matter of language determined the "nature of things, in so far as it is known" in the sense that it was only through the mediation of language that anything was deemed knowable. This is the pragmatic side of McKeon's historical semantics in the sense that a turn, such as the turn to language and action, is a human process. The realist side is the distinctiveness of the subject matter of language and action that functions as arbiter in the debates among philosophers that enacted the linguistic turn. Philosophies are or are not "verified" by this arbiter. Variants of this process occur in each turn.

The argument from "constituting activities" pridefully distinguishes itself from the metaphysical realism based on the subject matter of thing. But this distinction is unfounded. This argument's blindness resides in its failure to see that these "activities," be they thought or language, are as directly accessible to metaphysical realism as to proponents of thought or language. As we saw in chapter one, Johnston and Gabriel show that an ontology underwrites Kant's epistemology. As Gabriel summed the point up concisely, "The subject with its conceptual capacities actually exists; it is part of the world." This reality would correspond to the reality Aristotle considers in *De Anima*. Similarly, we saw McKeon, near the end of chapter two, contrasting two rhetorics based on contrasting assumptions about language, one of which is Aristotle's *Rhetoric*. McKeon's point that rhetoric establishes "object[s] of attention" has been referenced repeatedly. The rhetorical establishment of such "object[s]" presupposes, as we saw McKeon explain in chapter three, that "[w]hat is, is established by the convictions and agreements of men." Aristotle's *Rhetoric* explains this variant of "what is" by showing how the artful use of persuasion can produce such "convictions and agreements" among humans in the limited areas of deliberative, judicial and epideictic rhetoric, which together comprise a part of reality.

Metaphysical realism thus accesses the realities of the subject matters of thought and language. This realism contains these subject matters, which are parts of reality. Visualizing it, one could imagine the subject matter of metaphysical realism as a big circle and the subject matters of thought and language as smaller circles inside, each separate from the other. Metaphysical realism is broader than the others, to recall Harman's use in chapter five of the opposition between broadening and narrowing in insisting that philosophy is about "everything."

Ultimate priority in metaphysical realism is thus located in an encompassing subject matter that includes the real "constituting activities" of thought and language, as well as a reality in which human "constituting activities" have no part. Ultimate priority in thought is located in a narrower subject matter, a reality that does not extend beyond conceptualization, an issue Brassier addresses in "Concepts and Objects," to be considered in the next section. In the subject matter of language and action, ultimate priority, as we saw at the end of chapter three, is located in the still narrower subject matter, the reality of the arbitrariness of the word by virtue of which each word is an act of invention that makes it prior to any use of the invented word.

The sequence in McKeon's cycle indicates that in the course of history philosophy narrows first to the subject matter of thought, then to the subject matter of language and action. Narrowing to language and action ends the narrowing process, as suggested by Meillassoux's call for a return to the "*great outdoors*," a *Cri de Coeur* to turn from centuries of stifling narrowing to the full reality of metaphysical realism.

The evidence of the turns themselves thus tells us that the metaphysical turn to thing is the turn to be preferred to the others. It includes the others, but they do not include it. Instead, they needlessly narrow the subject matter of philosophy, needlessly because these narrower subject matters are contained in metaphysical realism.

A meaning of McKeon's use of the term "subversive" may be that his cycle subverts other views of the history of philosophy by revealing that it is instead a process in which turns from metaphysical realism narrow philosophy before turning back to metaphysical realism. Could that revelation motivate staying with metaphysical realism?
Brassier among the Turns

The Cambridge Dictionary of Philosophy's defines "metaphysical realism" as the view that there are "real objects" that "exist independently of our experience or our knowledge of them." It adds that the chief objection to it is "that we can form no conception of real objects, as understood by it, since any such conception must rest on concepts we already have and on our language and experience" (488). This objection, when it takes hold, begins the narrowing of the subject matter of philosophy.

Brassier appears to see a way past this objection by envisioning the possibility of solving "the fundamental problem of philosophy," which he defines as combining the assumption that there is "no cognitive ingress to the real save through the concept" with the assumption that "the real itself is not to be confused with the concepts through which we know it" ("Concepts" 47). We thus need the concept to find the real, yet when we find the real, we need somehow to recognize it as real independently of the concept. This method appears in "Concepts and Objects," which Harman credits with being "no doubt [Brassier's] most significant piece of work since *Nihil Unbound*" (*Speculative Realism* 40). Brassier's method improves upon his earlier magical thinking, discussed in chapter four. It is his approach to the problem, as we saw in chapters four and five, that Meillassoux and Harman attempt to solve in their different ways, Harman with his "requiring me" passage and Meillassoux with his version of intellectual intuition. In both cases there is intuitive direct access to a reality that qualifies as a metaphysical thing that is prior to the subject matters of thought and language.

While Brassier is presumably concerned with demonstrating that the solution to his "fundamental problem" is to be found in the metaphysical turn to thing, he rejects intellectual intuition vociferously, not only in a turn to thing but also in a turn to thought.

> Thus it is not clear why our access to the structure of concepts should be considered any less in need of critical legitimation than our access to the structure of objects. To assume privileged access to the structure of conception is to assume *intellectual intuition*. But this is to make a metaphysical claim about the

> essential nature of conception; an assumption every bit as dogmatic as any allegedly metaphysical assertion about the essential nature of objects. ("Concepts" 56; my italics)

A turn to the subject matter of thought is the first stage in the narrowing of philosophy. To call this turn metaphysical does not lessen this narrowing, but calling it metaphysical does indicate that thought is a subject matter where one can locate an ultimate that is in a sense prior to thing and language. As we saw in considering Kant at the end of chapter four, despite Kant's prohibition of accessing the noumenon, the thing-in-itself, Kant does access the noumenon of the human subject, where this "structure of conception" is housed. That ultimate priorities can be found in the subject matters of thought and language is the basis of McKeon's reference, near the end of chapter two, to these subject matters as variant metaphysical subject matters.

What is thus notable from the standpoint of McKeon's cycle is Brassier's recognition of an important parallel between two of the turns in McKeon's cycle. Turns to thought and thing are turns to the realities of distinctive subject matters, turns that to complete themselves require intuitive direct access to the ultimate priorities in these subject matters.

While Brassier surprises us by eliminating the use of intellectual intuition to solve his "fundamental problem of philosophy," he surprises us a second time when he laments doing so in the sense that he concedes that by virtue of this elimination, he does not have answers to questions that would seem to need answering to solve this "problem." For in his penultimate paragraph, looking longingly through a window in a metaphysical department store of things, he asks and answers, "How can we acknowledge that scientific conception tracks the in-itself without resorting to the problematic metaphysical assumption that to [do] so is to conceptually circumscribe the 'essence' (or formal reality) of the latter? For we want to be able to claim that science knows reality without resorting to the Aristotelian equation of reality with substantial form. This is to say that the structure of reality includes but is not exhausted by the structure of discretely individuated objects" ("Concepts" 64–65). The twofold implication is that whatever help Aristotle might provide to solve this "problem" is limited not only by his intellectual intuition of "essence" but also by his equation of substance to individuals.

It is true that for Aristotle primary substance is an individual. *Categories*, chapter five, gives as examples of substance a particular man or horse. But individual objects do not exhaust Aristotle's reality. As we saw in chapter two, *Posterior Analytics* features the example of the eclipse of the moon. Unlike a man or a horse, an eclipse is constituted by relations, specifically relations of the kind that Newton mapped in helping to launch modern science. This eclipse of the moon helped Aristotle illustrate the contrast, also discussed in chapter two, between what is better known to us through empirical experience and what is better known in being. On the basis of empirical experience one could say that an eclipse occurs when "the moon fails to produce shadows though she is full and though no visible body intervenes between us and her" (93a38–39, *Basic Works* 168). This is empirical experience that is better known to us. But this empirical experience does not reveal the cause of an eclipse. For that you need the supersensible intellect to go beyond the empirical to figure out how sun, earth, and moon are "organized to function" in an eclipse. But that brings one back to the intellectual intuition that Brassier rejects.

Brassier considers Meillassoux again, having considered him earlier in *Nihil Unbound*, but ignores his variant of intellectual intuition. Instead, he questions why Meillassoux even thinks, as we saw in chapter four, that the correlationist argument is a strong argument. Because of this supposed strength, Brassier recognizes, Meillassoux thinks "correlationism can only be overcome from within" by exposing "the contingency of the correlation" ("Concepts" 60). But Brassier does not consider how Meillassoux does this. Instead, he presents his solution to the "fundamental problem" as an overcoming of correlationism superior to Meillassoux's overcoming of it from within.

This solution, the biggest surprise of all, takes place in the subject matter of language and action, which turns out to be Brassier's subject matter. Here, there is no mention of intellectual intuition. Instead, in the manner characteristic of exemptionalism, the reality of this subject matter is accessed directly in an intuition of how it is "organized to function" in a fashion that solves the "fundamental problem," explaining how concept leads to the object, which nonetheless is independent of the concept, not to be confused with it. In other words, Brassier performs an intellectual intuition, presumably without realizing it, in any case without acknowledging it. Given his strong rejection of intellectual intuition, one would expect him to explain why what he does differs from intellectual intuition, but that does not appear to occur to him. What may explain this omission is the shift in subject matter. Unlike the subject matter of thing or thought, the subject matter of language and action in the age of the linguistic turn becomes a "constituting activity" that seems to be an immediate reality at one's fingertips.

In the subject matter of language and action, Brassier's own solution takes the form of an analysis of semantic reference, one that makes distinctions by using different font styles: "We will use 'Saturn' when mentioning the word and **Saturn** when designating the concept for which the word stands." Furthermore, "the word 'Saturn' must be understood to mean the *referent* of the concept **Saturn**," so that the word stands for the concept by meaning the referent of the concept ("Concepts" 61). Saturn, the existent planet, is different from both word and concept. On the basis of these distinctions, Brassier draws two conclusion.

> First, when I say that Saturn does not need to be posited in order to exist, I am not saying that the meaning of the concept **Saturn** does not need to be posited by us in order to exist—quite obviously, the concept **Saturn** means what it does because of us, and in this sense it is perfectly acceptable to say that it has been "posited" through human activity.

The "meaning" of the word, importantly, is the referent of the concept, so that "meaning" is pointing at what the concept conceptualizes. The conceptualization is relative to "us," while the word points at what is independent of us. Second,

> But when I say that Saturn exists un-posited, I am not making a claim about a word or a concept; my claim is rather that the planet which is the referent of the word "Saturn" existed before we named it and will probably still exist after the beings who named it have ceased to exist, since it is something quite distinct both from the word 'Saturn' and the concept **Saturn** for which the word stands. ("Concepts" 61, 61-62)

Saturn, the existent planet, is thus seen through the concept by means of the word pointing at the referent of the concept, but this existent planet is independent of the concept.

This solution is anticipated by Frege's famous analysis of sense and reference. "Evening star" and "morning star" are two terms. Each means the referent of a concept. This referent is the existent planet Venus. But in one case, "morning star" is the conceptualization, whereas in the other "evening star" is the conceptualization. In both Frege and Brassier, the linguistic points, but the object pointed at is accessible only through this linguistic lens. The linguistic turn insists only that one cannot step outside language and, having direct access to both extra-linguistic reality and a linguistic statement, judge whether they correspond. Because such judgment is impossible, reality is always mediated through language, and mediations can differ, the way "morning star" differs from "evening star." Brassier's concept, which he stresses is relative to "us," is his mediation.

Brassier's concept points at Saturn without explaining anything about Saturn. In Aristotelian terms, Brassier answers only one of the four questions of inquiry distinguished at the beginning of the second book of *Posterior Analytics*, the question of "is it?" One can easily imagine an observer of an eclipse affirming that it occurred without knowing "what it is?" in the sense of "'essence' (or formal reality)" that explains how moon, earth, and sun are "organized to function" in the production of an eclipse.

In sum, Brassier's intuits how language is "organized to function." He simply does this without any reflection on how he does it. He denounces intellectual intuition, but makes no attempt to explain how what he does differs from intellectual intuition. He simply does what he does, like others examined in this book, beginning with Williams in chapter two. Intellectual intuition seems to be occurring often but without recognition.

Intellectual intuition of thing as prior to thought and language is the intuition needed for the metaphysical turn. Harman and Meillassoux both have moments of such intuition. Harman's is left undeveloped and Meillassoux's seems applicable only to the correlationist in the dialogue about death. These shortcomings notwithstanding, in their moments of intellectual intuition Harman and Meillassoux advance the metaphysical turn, something Brassier sets out to do but does not accomplish. The obstacle he appears unable to overcome, as we saw in chapter four, is his view, following Kant, that intellectual intuition creates its object, something only God can do. To the contrary, intellectual intuition appears in the role of language in his argument. Brassier does not create language but he does offer an intuition of how it is "organized to function." Others may differ, but in their debates, as we saw in chapter three, the arbiter will be the way language is actually "organized to function."

PUTNAM AND ARISTOTLE

Putnam's paraphrase of Aristotle's intellectual intuition of form, encapsulated in "organized to function," appears as we saw earlier in "Aristotle after Wittgenstein." In an endnote to this essay, Putnam indicates that he wrote it to consider "the viability of neo-Aristotelian metaphysics," an idea, he adds, "inspired by conversations with John Haldane during [his] stay in St. Andrews in the fall of 1990." He tests it, moreover, "after Wittgenstein," that is, by twentieth-century standards.

The extent of the viability he finds peaks in his insightful paraphrase of Aristotelian intellectual intuition. This peak appears in this essay in a brief narrative context that amounts to a literary interlude in an otherwise philosophical discourse. It is as if Putnam wants the reader to see the peaking of his embrace of Aristotle as something that occurs outside of his normal self, working in his study, something he seems to think is needed even though the essay as a whole indicates clearly that this embrace is limited. In any case, he describes this peak as a thought experiment, explaining that he finds "such thought experiments are best conducted while taking [his] dog, Shlomit, on a walk in the woods and marshes of Arlington and Lexington" (79, 71).

Putnam then returns to his study to conclude with his reservations about Aristotle, one relatively brief, the other significantly longer and more to the point it turns out. The brief reservation is summed up in one passage:

> The difficulty is that very often we have the structure of the things we refer to just dead wrong. For Aristotle, living before the successive scientific revolutions, this does not seem to have been a problem because he could assume that at a certain point we would just get the structure right. But in fact even the structure of something as familiar as water is something that we did not succeed in getting right for over two thousand years, and even today we have only a very approximate account of the structure of water. (73)

Leaving aside the speculation that attributes remarkable prescience to Aristotle, one puzzles over the "very often" that would appear to concede that sometimes we do get it right. Maybe that happens infrequently, but even so, it happens.

This water example, however, turns out to be a red herring. Putnam's substantial reservation begins, "The greatest difficulty facing someone who wishes to hold an Aristotelian view is that the central intuition behind that view, that is, the intuition that a natural kind *has* a single determinate form (or 'nature' or 'essence') has become problematical." The problem, in other words, is not that we don't get the structure of a "natural kind" right, but that the idea of a "natural kind" is "problematical."

At this point, Putnam's dog returns, not on a leash for a walk in the woods, but as an example of a dog owner's dog to consider alongside an evolutionary biologist's dog and a molecular biologist's dog. Putnam emphasizes that he is "not saying that just *anything* can be regarded as the nature of a kind from some point of view or other." Rather, he is saying that consideration of something like dogs from these three points of view "presupposes language users who are already in contact with a world, not minds in the abstract or languages in the abstract which have to somehow be related to a world. . . . Certainly, the Aristotelian insight that objects have structure is right, provided we remember that what counts as the structure of something is relative to the ways in which we interact with it" (74, 78).

Here is Putnam's departure from Aristotle. For Aristotle, there is the empirical object relative to us, to our senses, which would differ from person to person depending on their sensory interaction with it. By contrast, what is better known in being is furthest from sense, from the perspectives of different individuals or the same individual at different times. Grasping what is better known in being would appear to be equivalent to the "minds in the abstract or languages in the abstract" that Putnam dismisses. Putnam departs from Aristotle because his object stays on the level of what is better known to us. This object is the interaction on this level, so that there are as many objects as there are perspectivist interactions. (Just to avoid confusion, Putnam should not be confused with Harman. Putnam's perspectives are limited to humans, arising from human language and action interacting with things. Harman's perspectives include humans, but extend to non-humans and inanimate things.)

Putnam's subject matter thus consists of perspectivist interactions. Dog owner, evolutionary biologist, and molecular biologist have three distinct perspectives on dogs deriving from their distinctive intentions. Putnam underlines this point, "Talk of interests and points of view is, of course, intentional talk" ("Aristotle" 78). Putnam elaborates in considerable detail on the differences in the way dog owners, evolutionary biologists, and molecular biologists see dogs through their distinctive perspectives.

But one needs to ask what enables Putnam to elaborate on these differences. He is able to do so because he speaks as a "perspectivalist," Babich's term that was discussed at length in chapter five. As a perspectivalist, Putnam intuits the structure common to all perspectives to see how perspective is "organized to function." Having intuited this structure, he can attribute to differences in perspective the differences in what dog owners, evolutionary biologists, and molecular biologists see in dogs.

In speaking as a perspectivalist, Putnam rises from the level of what is better known to us to the level of what is better known in the being of perspectives. In doing so, he is more like Aristotle than he realizes. But he does so in practice rather than in philosophical comprehension. What he does in practice, he denies ultimately philosophically.

This denial appears strikingly in his essay's last sentence. In a coda-like final word following a semicolon, he says, "it seems that the hope of reducing the notion of intentionality to a metaphysical notion of structure (or 'form') which itself has no intentional presuppositions is illusory" ("Aristotle" 79). In other words, the perspectival is impossible because one can never escape the intentions informing one's perspective to comprehend perspectives in general, the way Russell, as we saw in chapter three, escapes his perspective on a penny to comprehend perspectives in general on the same penny. Putnam puts himself rigorously on the level of what is better known to him, denying the existence of Aristotle's level of better known in being, in this case the being of perspectives.

In doing so, Putnam denies philosophically what he does in practice. For this coda denies the perspectivalism that enables his analyses of dog owners, evolutionary biologists and molecular biologists. In the absence of perspectivalism, anything Putnam can say not only about his dog but also about the points of view of others toward dogs is mediated by his intentional presuppositions as a dog owner. Whatever he says about the perspectives of evolutionary or molecular biologists is dog-ownerish, not accurate analyses of those perspectives, of what and why they see what they see.

Continuing the Metaphysical Turn

Chapter one indicated that philosophical turns often inspire renewed interest in figures from earlier periods. Meillassoux finds in Aristotle a form of argument that he uses to develop the "anhypothetical principle" in his variant of intellectual intuition. Harman, in a passage quoted in chapter one, observes that Aristotle is not among "the most fashionable classic philosophers in present-day continental thought," but that "once we start to look at individual things as the central topic of philosophy, Aristotle's dominant position is hard to overlook." Looking through an Aristotelian lens at Husserl's model of objects, on which he relies heavily, Harman sees it is "basically the same thing as substance vs. accident in Aristotle" (quoted in chapter five). This model becomes crucial for Harman in his discrimination in *The Quadruple Object* of multiple interrelations between RO, RQ, SO, SQ.

Both Harman and Meillassoux, however, largely ignore what is most distinctive and most relevant in Aristotle's realism in the context of climate change, namely, its tripartite structure, consisting of natural, artifactual, and practical realities. For Meillassoux, all realities are the same insofar as they all arise ultimately from the contingency of *"may-being."* An existent "World" has "constancies" chartable by science, but it may be displaced by a different "World" with different "constancies" at any time. Coexisting "Worlds" would parallel Aristotle's coexisting realities, but Meillassoux's coexisting "Worlds" all arise through a similar contingent process, whereas the different realities in Aristotle arise in different ways, these differences making his tripartite structure of realities distinctively suitable for mapping the reality of climate change. Harman's real objects arise from contingency, specifically contingent formal integrations of relations, yet retain a degree of independence of these relations, evidenced in their capacity to disintegrate, to break. As we saw in chapter five, Harman insists that *"all* beings are broken equipment."

Harman misleads in claiming that "Aristotle and his heirs grant the title of 'substance' only to certain privileged things in the world, usually those that exist by nature" (*Prince Networks* 17). Leaving "heirs" aside, in addition to things that exist by nature, that is, an internal cause independent of humans, Aristotle's substances include things, ranging from technologies to tragedies, which require a human producer, an external cause, to take materials such as wood and stone that would not become a house on their own and turn them into a house. Similarly, the materiality of words would not become a tragedy on their own but require a tragedian. When Aristotle defines the substance of tragedy in *Poetics*, chapter six, he uses the same word for substance, *ousía*, which he uses in the chapter on substance in *Categories*, chapter five.[55] A definition is a secondary substance because it references a species rather than an individual, primary substance, but "those things are called substances within which, as species [e.g., tragedy], the primary substances [e.g., individual tragedies] are included" (2a14–15, *Basic Works* 9). Houses and tragedies are productive realities, by contrast to the practical realities of ethics and politics, which result from actions, natural in the way a habit becomes a second nature and humanly produced in the way a habit can be changed. Produced and practical realities arise from nature in a process in which the human is "an entity acting among, and conditioned by, other entities" (McKeon, "Experience and Metaphysics" 223). But nature is a necessary rather than a sufficient condition of their reality. Nature is the source of the capacities that enable humans to add nonnatural realities to natural realities, but these nonnatural realities cannot be reduced to nature.

Aristotle's tripartite structure of realities, because it includes two realities that consist of what humans add to reality, comprehends the reality of climate change, where humans create their own reality to an unprecedented extent. Latour references this development in 2014, remarking that early in his career he studied human agency in the construction of scientific facts about phenomena, but that now one must in some cases consider the human agency in the "very existence of the phenomena those facts are trying to document" ("Agency" 2).

It is, of course, accurate to say that humans have long lived in a reality partly of their own creation. In doing so, moreover, they have not been alone. Beavers build dams, birds build nests, and so on. But there is a point at which changes in quantity become changes in quality. What is now happening may have long been a theoretical possibility, but only today is this possibility being realized in reality. Michel Serres defines this newness thus: "Global history enters nature; global nature enters history: this is something utterly new in philosophy" (4).

Latour's *We Have Never Been Modern*, perhaps his best book, contends that while the modern world that emerged in the seventeenth cen-

---

55. Kenneth Telford's exemplary translation of the *Poetics* (Gateway Editions, 1961) is exceptional in using "substance" in chapter six to translate *ousía*. Telford includes an invaluable index correlating the Greek words in the *Poetics* to the English words he uses to translate them.

tury took as its premise the Cartesian dualism that divided mind and physical nature absolutely, it turned out never to be modern insofar as it actually produced hybrids of mind and nature. Hydroelectric power, for example, combines nature and human technology to produce electric power for millions. Instead of dividing mind and nature, modernism filled the world with hybrids of the two, making it harder and harder to separate them. Furthermore, unintended consequences produced another level of hybrids, none more momentous than climate change.

Climate change is Bill McKibben's concern in *The End of Nature*, appearing in 1989. Humans are a causal factor in climate change and climate affects everything on planet earth, so that there is no longer a nature independent of humans. Here, Cartesian "constituting activities" appear greater than ever, broadening beyond thought and language to human actions that impact the climate. In subsequent decades, these "constituting activities" attracted more attention, including philosophical attention. Notable and influential examples are Timothy Morton's *Ecology without Nature* and *Dark Ecology*. In this philosophical view, a level beyond these "constituting activities" would be the "*Nature*" that no longer is there. Here, global history absorbs global nature, leaving it no way to enter history.

These "constituting activities" are Aristotle's productive and practical realities. But metaphysical realism, the realism that is prior to the stages of narrowing in McKeon's cycle of turns, includes a "nature" beyond such human "constituting activities," a level that is their necessary but not sufficient cause. Aristotle's tripartite structure of realities calls upon us to find this "nature" even though we live in an age when it is not obviously "out there" in the way it used to be.

This "nature" appears obliquely in climate summits, unimaginable not too long ago, in which government leaders around the world meet periodically agree to measures designed to shape the planet's climate. These leaders largely agree on what they would like the climate to be, so that if "constituting activities" were all that was involved, agreement would be easy. Assume, for example, that human "constituting activities" extend to control of what a given amount of greenhouse gases will do to the climate. If amount X is producing a climate humans do not want, then they could flip a switch to change what X produces, so that henceforth it will produce not what it produced in the past but the climate humans want going forward. No change in human practices would be needed. But, of course, human action cannot change what a given amount will do. There is a nature, a level of cause and effect in what greenhouse gases do that is independent of human action. Humans can only impact this cause by increasing or reducing the amount of greenhouse gases that they emit into the atmosphere. Here, global nature enters history. Agreement on reduction, of course, is far from easy. Not surprisingly, the results of these climate summits have been mixed.

This level of cause and effect independent of human action is independent nature, the third reality in Aristotle's tripartite structure. Human impact on reality is considerable but it is limited to the other two parts in the tripartite structure of realities, the practical and the productive. Practical and productive realities are what increase or decrease the greenhouse gases human emit. These are the realities where humans can have an impact. The third reality in Aristotle's structure is what climate science investigates. This reality exemplifies Meillassoux's *"great outdoors,"* for it is "not relative to us . . . existing in itself regardless of whether we are thinking of it or not" (*After Finitude* 7).

What needs to be figured out is how the three parts in Aristotle's tripartite structure are best "organized to function." In this case, "organized to function" is not a fixed structure because there is nothing fixed about what the human parts do in the structure. But it is a structure that can come to be and perpetuate itself to produce a climate in which humans can flourish as well as they have in the past. For this to happen, history entering into nature has to limit itself in compliance to the dictates of nature entering history.

Changes in human thinking needed for this structure to come to be may be prefigured today in the overcoming in some academic fields of the long-standing division between science and the humanities. Modern science, when it emerged in the seventeenth century, came into conflict with the way humans generally viewed themselves. These views initially were mainly religious. Later, they took various forms that C. P. Snow put under the umbrella of the humanities in claiming in the 1950s that there were "two cultures," one scientific, the other humanistic. But in the context of climate change in particular and the Anthropocene in general, scientific findings have inspired academic interdisciplinary programs in the environmental humanities. These new programs teach humans to see themselves in new ways by focusing their attention, as in the idea of "eco footprint," on their place in the ecological order of life on earth. Ethics now includes environmental ethics. Ecocriticism studies literature for its insights into the relation between humans and nature. Philosophy includes environmental philosophy. And so on.

While the tripartite structure of reality is unchanged since Aristotle's time insofar as its three realities remain the same, the result of this structure is changing in our time insofar as the productive and the practical, particularly the productive reality of technologies, now play a larger role in how the three together are "organized to function." This transformed structure is the realism in the new metaphysical realism that should come to fruition in the coming decades of the twenty-first-century.

Works Cited

Adler, Mortimer J. *Philosopher at Large: An Intellectual Autobiography.* Macmillan, 1977.
Anscombe, G. E. M. *An Introduction to Wittgenstein's Tractatus.* 2nd ed., Harper, 1959.
Aristotle. *The Basic Works of Aristotle,* edited by Richard McKeon, Random, 1941.
Ayer, Alfred Jules. *Language, Truth and Logic.* 2nd ed., Dover, 1952.
—. *Logical Positivism.* Free Press, 1959.
Babich, Babette E. *Nietzsche's Philosophy of Science: Reflecting Science on the Ground of Art and Life.* SUNY P, 1994.
Backman, Jussi. "Transcendental Idealism and Strong Correlationism: Meillassoux and the End of Heideggerian Finitude." *Phenomenology and the Transcendental,* edited by Sara Heinämaa, Mirja Hartimo, and Timo Miettinen, Routledge, 2014, pp. 276–94.
Badiou, Alain. *Logics of Worlds: Being and Event, 2.* Translated by Alberto Toscano, London, Continuum, 2009.
—. *Manifesto for Philosophy: Followed by "The (Re)turn of Philosophy" and "Definition of Philosophy."* Translated by Norman Madarasz, SUNY P, 1999.
Baldwin, Thomas. "Presence, Truth, and Authenticity." *Derrida's Legacies: Literature and Philosophy,* edited by Simon Glendinning and Robert Eaglestone, Routledge, 2008, pp. 107–17.
Bender, John, and David B. Wellbery. *The Ends of Rhetoric: History, Theory, Practice.* Stanford UP, 1990.
Bergmann, Gustav. *Logic and Reality.* U of Wisconsin P, 1964.
—. *The Metaphysics of Logical Positivism.* U of Wisconsin P, 1967.
—. "Some Remarks on the Ontology of Ockham." *Meaning and Existence.* U of Wisconsin P, 1960, pp. 144–54.
Beyond the Tractatus *Wars: The New Wittgenstein Debate,* edited by Rupert Read and Matthew A. Lavery, Routledge, 2011.
Biesecker, Barbara A. "Rethinking the Rhetorical Situation from within the Thematic of Différance." *Philosophy and Rhetoric,* vol. 22, no. 2, 1989, pp. 110–30.
Booth, Wayne C. "The Revival of Rhetoric." *PMLA,* vol. 80, no. 2, 1965, pp. 8–12.
—. "Richard McKeon's Pluralism: The Path between Dogmatism and Relativism." *Pluralism,* pp. 213–30, 265–70.
Bouveresse, Jacques. "Reading Rorty: Pragmatism and Its Consequences." *Rorty and His Critics,* pp. 129–46.

Brassier, Ray. "Concepts and Objects." *Speculative Turn*, pp. 47–65.
—. *Nihil Unbound: Enlightenment and Extinction*. Palgrave Macmillan, 2007.
—. "Postscript: Speculative Autopsy." Wolfendale, *Object-Oriented*, pp. 409–21.
—. "Presentation by Ray Brassier." *Speculative Realism*, pp. 308–33.
Bronzo, Silver. "The Resolute Reading and Its Critics: An Introduction to the Literature." *WittgensteinStudien*, vol. 3, no. 1, 2012, pp. 45–80.
Bryant, Levi. "BREAKING: Alexander Galloway Heroically Pleads for New Realists to Stop Eating Kittens," *Larval Subjects, Wordpress.com*, 10 December 2012. Accessed 11 December 2012.
—. *The Democracy of Objects*. Open Humanities, 2011. http://hdl.handle.net/2027/spo.9750134.0001.001.
—. Foreword. Adam S. Miller. *Speculative Grace: Bruno Latour and Object-Oriented Theology*. Fordham UP, 2013, pp. xiii–xix.
Burke, Kenneth. *Attitudes toward History*. 1937. 3rd ed., U of California P, 1984.
—. *A Grammar of Motives*. 1945. U of California P, 1969.
—. *Language as Symbolic Action: Essays on Life, Literature, and Method*. U of California P, 1966.
—. *Permanence and Change: An Anatomy of Purpose*. 1935. 3rd ed., U of California P, 1984.
—. *The Philosophy of Literary Form: Studies in Symbolic Action*. 1941. 3rd ed., U of California P, 1973.
The Cambridge Dictionary of Philosophy, edited by Robert Audi. Cambridge UP, 1995.
Carnap, Rudolf. "Autobiography." *The Philosophy of Rudolf Carnap*, edited by Paul Arthur Schilpp, Open Court, 1963, pp. 1–84. Library of Living Philosophers 11.
—. *Introduction to Semantics*. Harvard UP, 1942.
—. *The Logical Syntax of Language*. Translated by Amethe Smeaton, Littlefield, 1959.
Chomsky, Noam. *Syntactic Structures*. London, Mouton, 1965.
Colebrook, Claire. "The Linguistic Turn in Continental Philosophy." *History of Continental Philosophy*, edited by Alan D. Schrift, vol. 6, London: Ashgate, 2011, pp. 279–309.
Conant, James. "The Method of the *Tractatus*." *From Frege to Wittgenstein: Perspectives on Early Analytic Philosophy*, edited by Erich H. Reck, Oxford UP, 2002, pp. 374–462.
Conley, Thomas M. *Rhetoric in the European Tradition*. U of Chicago P, 1994.
Creath, Richard. "Logical Empiricism." *Stanford Encyclopedia of Philosophy*, https://plato.stanford.edu. Accessed 3 Oct. 2014.
Critics and Criticism: Ancient and Modern, edited by R. S. Crane, U of Chicago P, 1952.

Danisch, Robert. "The Absence of Rhetorical Theory in Richard Rorty's Linguistic Pragmatism." *Philosophy and Rhetoric*, vol. 46, no. 2, 2013, pp. 156–81.

—. *Building a Social Democracy: The Promise of Rhetorical Pragmatism*. Lexington Books, 2015.

Davidson, Donald. "Coherence Theory of Truth and Knowledge." *Subjective, Intersubjective, Objective*, Oxford, Clarendon Press, 2001, pp. 137–53.

—. "A Nice Derangement of Epitaphs." *Truth, Language, and History*, Oxford, Clarendon Press, 2005, pp. 89–107.

—. "On the Very Idea of a Conceptual Scheme." *Inquiries into Truth and Interpretation*. Oxford, Clarendon Press, 1984, pp. 183–98.

DeLanda, Manuel and Graham Harman. *The Rise of Realism*. Cambridge, Polity Press, 2017.

De Man, Paul. *Allegories of Reading: Figural Language in Rousseau, Nietzsche, Rilke, and Proust*. Yale UP, 1979.

Depew, David J. "Between Pragmatism and Realism: Richard McKeon's Philosophical Semantics." *Pluralism*, pp. 29–53.

Derrida, Jacques. "And Say the Animal Responded," interview by JeanLuc Nancy. *The Animal That Therefore I Am*. Translated by David Wills, edited by MarieLouis Mallet, Fordham UP, 2008, pp. 119–40.

—. "Declarations of Independence." *New Political Science*, no. 15, 1986, pp. 715.

—. "Differance." Derrida, *Speech*, pp. 129–60.

—. *Limited Inc*. Edited by Gerald Graff, Northwestern UP, 1988.

—. *Of Grammatology*. Translated by Gayatri Chakravorty Spivak, Johns Hopkins UP, 1976.

—. *Positions*. Translated by Alan Bass, U Chicago P, 1981.

—. "Psyche: Inventions of the Other." Translated by Catherine Porter, *Reading De Man Reading*, edited by Lindsay Waters and Wlad Gozich, U of Minnesota P, 1989, pp. 25–65. Theory and History of Literature 59.

—. "Remarks on Deconstruction and Pragmatism." Mouffe, pp. 77–88.

—. *Rogues: Two Essays on Reason*. Translated by PascaleAnne Brault and Michael Nass, Stanford UP, 2005.

—. *Speech and Phenomena and Other Essays on Husserl's Theory of Signs*. Translated by David B. Allison, Northwestern UP, 1973.

—. *Writing and Difference*. Translated by Alan Bass, U of Chicago P, 1978.

Diamond, Cora. "Realism and Resolution: Reply to Warren Goldfarb and Sabina Lovibond." *Journal of Philosophical Research*, vol. 22, 1997, pp. 75–86.

—. *The Realistic Spirit: Wittgenstein, Philosophy, and the Mind*. MIT P, 1991.

Doxtader, Erik. "The Rhetorical Question of Human Rights—A Preface." *Quarterly Journal of Speech*, vol. 96, no. 4, 2010, pp. 353–79.

Dummett, Michael. *Origins of Analytical Philosophy*. Harvard UP, 1994.

Edmonds, David. *The Murder of Professor Schlick: The Rise and Fall of the Vienna Circle*. Princeton UP, 2020.

Ennis, Paul J. *Continental Realism*. Winchester, UK: Zero, 2011.
Farrell, Thomas. "From Semantics to Praxis: Some Old Tricks for the New Pluralism." *Pluralism* 189–212, 263–65.
Ferguson, Kennan. *William James: Politics in the Pluriverse*. Rowman and Littlefield, 2007.
Ferro, Floriana. "Object-Oriented Ontology's View of Relations: A Phenomenological Critique." *Open Philosophy*, vol. 2, 2019, pp. 566–81. doi.org/10.1515/opphil20190040.
Finkelstein, Louis, ed. *Thirteen Americans: Their Spiritual Autobiographies*. 1953. Kennikat Press, 1969.
Frege, Gottlob. *The Foundations of Arithmetic: A Logico-Mathematical Enquiry into the Concept of Number*. Translated by J. L. Austin, Blackwell, 1953.
Gabriel, Markus. *Transcendental Ontology: Essays in German Idealism*. London: Bloomsbury, 2013.
Galloway, Alexander R. "The Poverty of Philosophy: Realism and Post-Fordism." *Critical Inquiry*, vol. 39, no. 2, 2013, pp. 347–66.
Garver, Newton. "Preface." *Speech and Phenomena and Other Essays on Husserl's Theory of Signs*. Northwestern UP, 1973, pp. ix–xlii.
Gasché, Rodolphe. *The Tain of the Mirror: Derrida and the Philosophy of Reflection*. Harvard UP, 1986.
Gilson, Etienne. *The Unity of Philosophical Experience*. Charles Scribner's Sons, 1937.
Goldfarb, Warren. "Metaphysics and Nonsense: On Cora Diamond's *The Realistic Spirit*." *Journal of Philosophical Research*, vol. 22, 1997, pp. 57–73.
—. "I want You to Bring Me a Slab: Remarks on the Opening Sections of the *Philosophical Investigations*." *Synthese*, vol. 56, no. 3, 1983, pp. 265–82.
Grant, Iain Hamilton. "Mining Conditions: A Response to Harman." *Speculative Turn*, pp. 41–46.
Gratton, Peter. "After the Subject: Meillassoux's Ontology of 'What May Be.'" *Pli: Warwick Journal of Philosophy*, vol. 20, 2009, pp. 55–79.
—. *Speculative Realism: Problems and Prospects*. London: Bloomsbury, 2014.
Gross, Neil. *Richard Rorty: The Making of an American Philosopher*. U of Chicago P, 2008.
Gross, Paul R. and Norman Levitt. *Higher Superstition: The Academic Left and Its Quarrels with Science*. Johns Hopkins, 1994.
Habermas, Jürgen. *The Political Discourse of Modernity*. Translated by Frederick Lawrence, MIT, 1995.
Hacker, P. M. S. *Wittgenstein's Place in TwentiethCentury Analytic Philosophy*. Blackwell, 1996.
Hacking, Ian. *The Social Construction of What?* Harvard UP, 1999.
Hallward, Peter. "Anything Is Possible: A Reading of Quentin Meillassoux's *After Finitude*." *Speculative Turn*, pp. 130–41.

Hanna, Robert. "The Kant Wars and the Three Faces of Kant." *Contemporary Studies in Kantian Philosophy*, no. 5, 2020, pp. 73–94.

Harman, Graham. "Aesthetics and the Tension in Objects." *[met]afourisms: Art Practice and Documentation*. Malta: Midsea Books, no date, pp. 11–19.

—. "Aesthetics as First Philosophy: Levinas and the Nonhuman." *Naked Punch*, no. 9, 2007, pp. 21–30.

—. "Answering a Question about 'Why Has Critique Run out of Steam?'" *Object-Oriented Philosophy*, Wordpress.com, 2 April 2012. Accessed 18 July 2012.

—. "Aristotle with a Twist." *Speculative Medievalisms: Discography*, edited by The Petropunk Collective, Brooklyn, Punctum Books, 2013, pp. 227–53.

—. *Art and Objects*. Cambridge, UK: Polity P, 2020.

—. *Bells and Whistles: More Speculative Realism*. Winchester, UK: Zero Books, 2013.

—. *Bruno Latour: Reassembling the Political*. London: Pluto Press, 2014.

—. "The Current State of Speculative Realism." *Speculations: A Journal of Speculative Realism*, vol. 4, 2013, pp. 22–28.

—. *Dante's Broken Hammer: The Ethics, Aesthetics, and Metaphysics of Love*. London: Repeater Books, 2016.

—. "Fear of Reality: On Realism and InfraRealism." *The Monist*, vol. 98, no. 2, pp. 126–44.

—. *Guerilla Metaphysics: Phenomenology and the Carpentry of Things*. Open Court, 2005.

—. *Heidegger Explained: From Phenomenon to Thing*. Open Court, 2007. Ideas Explained Series 4.

—. "I Am Also of the Opinion That Materialism Must Be Destroyed." *Environment and Planning D: Society and Space*, vol. 28, 2010, pp. 772–90.

—. *Immaterialism: Objects and Social Theory*. Cambridge, UK: Polity, 2016.

—. "Interview with Graham Harman." ASK/TELL, 23 July 2011. Accessed 18 July 2020.

—. "Johnston's Materialist Critique of Meillassoux." *Umbr(A)*, vol. 1, 2013, pp. 29–48.

—. "Marginalia on Radical Thinking: An Interview with Graham Harman." skepoet, *Wordpress.com.*, 1 June 2012. Accessed 3 October 2014.

—. "Materialism and Speculative Realism: A Response to Critics." *Modern Painters*, March 2014, pp. 50–51. Accessed 25 March 2014.

—. "Meillassoux's Virtual Future." *continent*, vol. 1, no. 2, 2011, pp. 78–91.

—. "New Post on Object-Oriented Philosophy: Reference in Documenta Review." *Object-Oriented Philosophy*, *Wordpress.com.*, 5 July 2012. Accessed 11 July 2012.

—. *Object-Oriented Ontology: A New Theory of Everything*. UK: Pelican, 2018.

—. "On Landscape Ontology: An Interview with Graham Harman," by Brian Davis. *faslanyc* 1 July 2012. Accessed 1 August 2012.

—. "On the Undermining of Objects: Grant, Bruno, and Radical Philosophy." *Speculative Turn*, pp. 21–40.
—. "On Vicarious Causation." *Collapse*, no. 2, 2007, pp. 187–221.
—. "Presentation by Graham Harman." *Speculative Realism*, pp. 367–407.
—. *The Prince and the Wolf: Latour and Harman at the LSE*. Winchester, UK: Zero Books, 2011.
—. *The Prince of Networks: Bruno Latour and Metaphysics*. Melbourne: re.press, 2009. www.repress.org
—. "Propositions, Objects, Questions," interview by Jon Roffe. *Parrhesia: A Journal of Critical Philosophy*, no. 21, 2014, pp. 23–52.
—. *The Quadruple Object*. Winchester, UK: Zero Books, 2011.
—. "Quentin Meillassoux: A New French Philosopher." *Philosophy Today*, vol. 51, no.1, 2007, pp. 104–17.
—. *Quentin Meillassoux: Philosophy in the Making*. 2nd ed., Edinburgh UP, 2015.
—. "Realism with a Straight Face: A Response to Leonard Lawlor." *New Realism and Contemporary Philosophy*, edited by Gregor Kroupa and Jure Simoniti, Bloomsbury Collections, pp. 99–112. Accessed 3 July 2020.
—. "Response to Nathan Coombs." *Speculations: A Journal of Speculative Realism*, vol. 1, 2010, pp. 145–52.
—. *Skirmishes: With Friends, Enemies, and Neutrals*. Punctum Books, 2020. https://punctumbooks.com
—. *Speculative Realism: An Introduction*. Cambridge, UK: Polity Press, 2018.
—. "Time, Space, Essence, and Eidos: A New Theory of Causation." *Cosmos and History: The Journal of Natural and Social Philosophy*, vol. 6, no. 1, 2010, pp. 1–17.
—. *Tool-Being: Heidegger and the Metaphysics of Objects*. Open Court, 2002.
—. *Towards Speculative Realism: Essays and Lectures*. Winchester, UK: Zero Books, 2010.
—. "Undermining, Overmining, and Duomining: A Critique." ADD Metaphysics, edited by Jenna Sutela, Aalto, Finland, Aalto University Digital Design Laboratory, 2013, pp. 40–51.
—. *Weird Realism: Lovecraft and Philosophy*. Winchester, UK: Zero Books, 2012.
—. "The Well-Wrought Broken Hammer: Object-Oriented Literary Criticism." *New Literary History*, vol. 43, no. 2, 2012, pp. 183–203.
Hartle, Ann. *Montaigne and the Origins of Modern Philosophy*. Northwestern UP, 2013.
Head, Dominic. "The (Im)possibility of Ecocriticism." *Writing the Environment*, edited by Richard Kerridge and Neil Sammells, London, Zed, 1998.
Heidegger, Martin. *Being and Time*. 1927. Translated by John Macquarrie and Edward Robinson, Harper, 1962.
Human Rights: Comments and Interpretations, A Symposium edited by UNESCO. Columbia UP, 1949.

Hutto, Daniel D. *Wittgenstein and the End of Philosophy*. Palgrave Macmillan, 2003.

Ijsseling, Samuel. *Rhetoric and Philosophy in Conflict: An Historical Survey*. The Hague: Martinus Nijhoff, 1976.

James, Henry. *The Art of the Novel: Critical Prefaces*. Charles Scribner's Sons, 1962.

James, William. *Essays in Radical Empiricism* and *A Pluralistic Universe*, edited by Ralph Baron Perry, Dutton, 1971.

Jeler, Ciprian. "Why Meillassoux's Speculative Materialism Struggles with Ancestrality." *Annals of Philosophy, Social and Human Disciplines*, vol. 2, 2014, pp. 11–32.

Johnston, Adrian. "Hume's Revenge: À Dieu, Meillassoux?" *Speculative Turn*, pp. 92–113.

Joy, Eileen. "Weird Reading." *Speculations: A Journal of Speculative Realism*, vol. 4, 2013, pp. 28–34.

Kahn, Charles H. "Aristotle on Thinking." *Essays on Aristotle's* De Anima," edited by Martha C. Nussbaum and Amélie Oksenberg Rorty, Clarendon Press, 1992, pp. 359–79.

Kant, Immanuel. *Critique of Judgment*. Translated by J. H. Bernard, Hafner, 1951.

—. *Critique of Pure Reason*. Translated by Norman Kemp Smith, St. Martin's Press, 1965.

—. *Foundations of the Metaphysics of Morals*. Translated by Lewis White Beck, BobbsMerrill, 1959.

—. *Prolegomena to Any Future Metaphysics*. Translated and edited by Lewis White Beck, BobbsMerrill, 1950.

Kates, Joshua. *Essential History: Jacques Derrida and the Development of Deconstruction*. Northwestern UP, 2005.

Koopman, Colin. "Rorty's Linguistic Turn: Why (More Than) Language Matters to Philosophy." *Contemporary Pragmatism*, vol. 8, 2011, pp. 61–84.

Kuhn, Thomas K. *The Structure of Scientific Revolutions*. 2nd ed., U of Chicago P, 1970.

Lanham, Richard A. *The Electronic Word: Democracy, Technology, and the Arts*. U of Chicago P, 1993.

Latour, Bruno. "Agency at the Time of the Anthropocene." *New Literary History*, vol. 45, no. 1, 2014, pp. 1–18.

—. *We Have Never Been Modern*. Translated by Catherine Porter, Harvard UP, 1993.

—. "Why Has Critique Run Out of Steam? From Matters of Fact to Matters of Concern." *Critical Inquiry*, vol. 30, no. 2, 2004, pp. 225–48.

Lawlor, Leonard. "Jacques Derrida." *Stanford Encyclopedia of Philosophy*, https://plato.stanford.edu. Accessed 16 April 2018.

The Linguistic Turn: Essays in Philosophical Method, edited by Richard M. Rorty, 2nd ed., U of Chicago P, 1992.

MacIver, R. M., editor. *Moments of Personal Discovery*. 1952. Kennikat Press, 1969.

Marx, Karl. *Capital: A Critique of Political Economy*. Vol. 1, translated by Ben Fowkes, Penguin, 1976.

McKeon, Richard. "Aristotle's Conception of Language." *Critics and Criticism*, pp. 176–231.

—. "Being, Existence, and That Which Is." McKeon, *Selected Writings*, vol. 1, pp. 244–55.

—. "The Circumstances and Functions of Philosophy." *Philosophers on Their Own Work*, pp. 99–112.

—. "Criticism and the Liberal Arts: The Chicago School of Criticism." McKeon, *Selected Writings*, vol. 2, pp. 11–41.

—. "De Anima: Psychology and Science." *Journal of Philosophy*, vol. 27, 1930, pp. 673–90.

—, editor. *Democracy in a World of Tensions, A Symposium prepared by UNESCO*. U of Chicago P, 1951.

—. "Dialectical and Political Thought and Action." *Ethics: An International Journal of Social, Political, and Legal Philosophy*, vol. 65, no. 1, 1954, pp. 1–33.

—. "Dialogue and Controversy in Philosophy." *Philosophy and Phenomenological Research*, vol. 17, no. 2, 1956, pp. 143–63.

—. "Discourse, Demonstration, Verification, and Judgment." McKeon, *Selected Writings*, vol. 2, pp. 157–96.

—. "Experience and Metaphysics." McKeon, *Selected Writings*, vol. 1, pp. 222–28.

—. "Experience and Reality: Problems and Categories." Course lecture, Philosophy of Communications and the Arts: Rhetoric and Poetic, Department of Philosophy, University of Chicago, 26 July 1967.

—. "The Flight from Certainty and the Quest for Precision." McKeon, *Selected Writings*, vol. 1, pp. 229–43.

—. *Freedom and History and Other Essays: An Introduction to the Thought of Richard McKeon*, edited by Zahava K. McKeon, U of Chicago P, 1990.

—. "The Future of Metaphysics." *The Future of Metaphysics*, edited by Robert E. Wood, Quadrangle Books, 1970, pp. 288–308.

—. "Knowledge and World Organization." *Foundations of World Organization: A Political and Cultural Appraisal, Eleventh Symposium of the Conference on Science, Philosophy and Religion in Their Relation to the Democratic Way of Life, New York, 5–8 September 1950*, edited by Lyman Bryson et al., Harper, 1952, pp. 289–329.

—. "Literary Criticism and the Concept of Imitation in Antiquity." *Critics and Criticism*, pp. 147–75.

—. "The Methods of Rhetoric and Philosophy: Invention and Judgment." McKeon, *Selected Writings*, vol. 2, pp. 97–103.
—. *On Knowing—The Natural Sciences*, edited by David B. Owen and Zahava K. McKeon, U of Chicago P, 1994.
—. *On Knowing—The Social Sciences*, edited by David B. Owen and Joanne K. Olson, U of Chicago P, 2016.
—. "A Philosopher Meditates on Discovery." McKeon, *Selected Writings*, vol. 1, pp. 41–60.
—. "The Philosophic Bases of Art and Criticism." *Critics and Criticism*, pp. 463–545.
—. "The Philosophic Bases and Material Circumstances of the Rights of Man." *Ethics: An International Journal of Social, Political, and Legal Philosophy*, vol. 58, no. 3, 1948, pp. 180–87.
—. "Philosophic Semantics and Philosophic Inquiry." McKeon, *Selected Writings*, vol. 1, pp. 209–21.
—. "Philosophy and Method." *Selected Writings*, vol. 1, pp. 183–208.
—. "Philosophy of Communications and the Arts." McKeon, *Selected Writings*, vol. 2, pp. 307–25.
—. *The Philosophy of Spinoza: The Unity of His Thought*. 1928. Ox Bow P, 1987.
—. "A Philosophy for UNESCO." *Philosophy and Phenomenological Research*, vol. 8, no. 4, 1948, pp. 573–86.
—. "Pluralism of Interpretations and Pluralism of Objects, Actions, and Statements Interpreted." McKeon, *Selected Writings*, vol. 2, pp. 51–69.
—. "Power and the Language of Power." *Ethics: An International Journal of Social, Political, and Legal Philosophy*, vol. 68, no. 2, 1958, pp. 98–115.
—. "Principles and Consequences." *Journal of Philosophy*, vol. 56, 1959, pp. 385–401.
—. "Propositions and Perceptions in the World of G. E. Moore." *Philosophy of G. E. Moore*, pp. 453–80.
—. "Rhetoric in the Middle Ages." *Critics and Criticism*, pp. 260–96.
—. *Selected Writings of Richard McKeon*, edited by Zahava K. McKeon and William G. Swenson, vol. 1, Philosophy, Science, and Culture; vol. 2, Culture, Education, and the Arts, U of Chicago P, 1998–2005.
—. "Thomas Aquinas' Doctrine of Knowledge and Its Historical Setting." *Speculum*, vol. 3, no. 4, 1928, pp. 425–44.
—. "The Uses of Rhetoric in a Technological Age: Architectonic Productive Arts." *The Prospect of Rhetoric*, edited by Lloyd F. Bitzer and Edwin Black, PrenticeHall, 1971, pp. 44–63.
—. *Thought, Action, and Passion*. U of Chicago P, 1954.
McLuhan, Marshall. *The Classical Trivium: The Place of Thomas Nashe in the Learning of His Time*, edited by W. Terrence Gordon, Gingko P, 2006.
Meillassoux, Quentin. *After Finitude: An Essay on the Necessity of Contingency*. Translated by Ray Brassier, London, Continuum, 2008.

—. "Badiou and Mallarmé: The Event and the Perhaps." Translated by Alley Edlebi, *Parrhesia: A Journal of Critical Philosophy*, no. 16, 2013, pp. 35–47.

—. "The Contingency of the Laws of Nature." Translated by Robin Mackay, *Environment and Planning D: Society and Space*, vol. 30, 2012, pp. 322–34.

—. "Decision and Undecidability of the Event in *Being and Event I* and *II*." Translated by Alyosha Edlebi, *Parrhesia: A Journal of Critical Philosophy*, no. 19, 2014, pp. 22–35.

—. From *Divine Inexistence: An Essay on the Virtual God*. Translated by Nathan Brown, *Parrhesia: A Journal of Critical Philosophy*, no. 25, 2016, pp. 20–40.

—. From *Divine Inexistence: An Essay on the Virtual God*. Translated by Graham Harman, Harman, *Quentin* 224–87.

—. "History and Event in Alain Badiou." Translated by Thomas Nail, *Parrhesia: A Journal of Critical Philosophy*, no. 12, 2011, pp. 1–11.

—. "The Immanence of the World Beyond." Translated by Peter Candler et al. *The Grandeur of Reason: Religion, Tradition and Universalism*, edited by Peter M. Chandler, Jr. and Conor Cunningham, London: SCM P, 2010. 444–78.

—. Interview by Rick Dolphijn and Iris van der Tuin. Translated by MariePier Boucher, *New Materialism: Interviews and Cartographies*, edited by Rick Dolphijn and Iris van der Tuin, Open Humanities P, 2012, pp. 1–9. Accessed 19 Nov. 2012.

—. Interview by Graham Harman. Translated by Graham Harman. Harman, *Quentin* 208–23.

—. "Iteration, Reiteration, Repetition: A Speculative Analysis of the Meaningless Sign." Translated by Robin Mackay. Freie Universität, Berlin, 20 April 2012. Lecture. Accessed 22 Aug. 2016.

—. "Metaphysics, Speculation, Correlation." Translated by Taylor Adkins, *Pli: The Warwick Journal of Philosophy*, vol. 22, 2011, pp. 1–25.

—. *The Number and the Siren: A Decipherment of Mallarmé's Coup de Dés*. Translated by Robin Mackay. Sequence Press, 2012.

—. "Potentiality and Virtuality." Translated by Robin Mackay, *Speculative Turn*, pp. 224–36.

—. "Presentation by Quentin Meillassoux." *Speculative Realism*, pp. 408–49.

—. *Science Fiction and Extro-Science Fiction*. Translated by Alyosha Edlebi, Univocal, 2015.

—. "The Spectral Dilemma." *Collapse*, no. 4, 2008, pp. 261–75.

—. "Time without Becoming." Middlesex University, London, 8 May 2008. Address. Accessed 3 July 2016.

Merleau-Ponty, Maurice. *Phenomenology of Perception*. Translated by Colin Smith, Routledge, 2002.

Moody, Ernest A. *The Logic of William of Ockham*. 1935. Russell and Russell, 1965.

Morsink, Johannes. "World War Two and the Universal Declaration." *Human Rights Quarterly*, vol. 15, no. 2, 1993, pp. 357–405.

Morton, Timothy. "Here Comes Everything: The Promise of Object-Oriented Ontology." *Qui Parle*, vol. 19, no. 2, 2011, pp. 163–90.

—. *Hyperobjects: Philosophy and Ecology after the End of the World*. U of Minnesota P, 2013. posthumanities 27.

Mouffe, Chantal, editor. *Deconstruction and Pragmatism: Simon Critchley, Jacques Derrida, Ernesto Laclau and Richard Rorty*. Routledge, 2006.

Nietzsche, Friedrich. "On Truth and Lies in a Nonmoral Sense." *Philosophy and Truth: Selections from Nietzsche's Notebooks of the Early 1870s*. Translated and edited by Daniel Breazeale, Humanities P, 1979, pp. 79–91.

—. *The Will to Power*. Trans. Walter Kaufmann and R. J. Hollingdale. RandomVintage, 1968.

O'Brien, Dennis. "One Mind in the Truth: Richard McKeon, a Philosopher of Education." *Pluralism*, pp. 77–91, 244–46.

Olson, Elder. "Richard McKeon: 19001985." *Remembering the University of Chicago: Teachers, Scientists, and Scholars*, edited by Edward Shils, U of Chicago P, 1991, pp. 300–06.

Peramatzis, Michail. *Priority in Aristotle's Metaphysics*. Oxford UP, 2011.

Philosophers on Their Own Work. Vol. 1, edited by André Mercier and Maja Svilar, Bern und Frankfurt, Verlag Herbert Lang, 1975.

The Philosophy of G. E. Moore, edited by Paul Arthur Schilpp, 2nd ed., Tudor Publishing, 1952.

Plochmann, George Kimball. *Richard McKeon: A Study*. U of Chicago P, 1990.

Pluralism in Theory and Practice: Richard McKeon and American Philosophy. Edited by Eugene Garver and Richard Buchanan, Vanderbilt UP, 2000.

Putnam, Hilary. "Aristotle after Wittgenstein." *Words and Life*, edited by James Conant, Harvard UP, 1994, pp. 62–81.

—. "How Old Is Mind?" *Exploring the Concept of Mind*, edited by Richard M. Caplan, U of Iowa P, 1986, pp. 31–49.

Quine, Willard Van Orman. "Epistemology Naturalized." Quine, *Ontological*, pp. 69–90.

—. "Existence and Quantification." Quine, *Ontological*, pp. 91–113.

—. *From a Logical Point of View*. 2nd ed., Harper, 1961.

—. "Identity, Ostension, and Hypostasis." Quine, *From a Logical*, pp. 65–79.

—. "Linguistics and Philosophy." Quine, *Ways*, pp. 56–58.

—. "Meaning and Translation." *The Structure of Language: Readings in the Philosophy of Language*, edited by Jerry A. Fodor and Jerrold J. Katz, Prentice-Hall, 1964, pp. 460–78.

—. "On What There Is." Quine, *From a Logical*, pp. 1–19.

—. *Ontological Relativity and Other Essays*. Columbia UP, 1969.

—. "Ontological Relativity." Quine, *Ontological*, pp. 26–68.

—. "Speaking of Objects." Quine, *Ontological*, pp. 1–25.

—. "Two Dogmas of Empiricism." Quine, *From a Logical*, pp. 20–46.
—. *The Ways of Paradox*. Rev. ed. Harvard UP, 1976.
—. *Word and Object*. MIT P, 1960.
Read, Rupert. "Throwing Away 'The Bedrock.'" *Proceeding of the Aristotelian Society*, vol. 105, 2005, pp. 81–98.
Ricketts, Thomas. "Pictures, Logic, and the Limits of Sense in Wittgenstein's *Tractatus*." *The Cambridge Companion to Wittgenstein*, edited by Hans Sluga and David G. Stern, Cambridge UP, 1996, pp. 59–99.
Roffe, Jon. "Time and Ground: A Critique of Meillassoux's Speculative Realism." *Angelaki: Journal of the Theoretical Humanities*, vol. 17, no. 1, 2012, pp. 57–67.
Rorty, Richard. *Consequences of Pragmatism (Essays: 1972–1980)*. U of Minnesota P, 1982.
—. *Contingency, Irony, and Solidarity*. Cambridge UP, 1989.
—. "Deconstruction and Circumvention." *Critical Inquiry*, vol. 11, no. 1, September 1984, pp. 1–23.
—. "Derrida and the Philosophical Tradition." Rorty, *Truth*, pp. 327–50.
—. "Derrida on Language, Being, and Abnormal Philosophy." *Journal of Philosophy*, vol. 74, 1977, pp. 673–81.
—. *Essays on Heidegger and Others: Philosophical Papers*. Vol. 2, Cambridge UP, 1991.
—. "Feminism and Pragmatism." Rorty, *Truth*, pp. 202–27.
—. "Introduction." *Empiricism and the Philosophy of Mind*, by Wilfrid Sellars, Harvard UP, 1997, pp. 1–12.
—, ed. *The Linguistic Turn: Essays in Philosophical Method, with Two Retrospective Essays*. U of Chicago P, 1992.
—. *Objectivity, Relativism, and Truth: Philosophical Papers*. Vol 1, Cambridge UP, 1991.
—. *Philosophy and the Mirror of Nature*. Princeton UP, 1979.
—. *Philosophy and Social Hope*. London, Penguin, 1999.
—. *Philosophy as Cultural Politics: Philosophical Papers*. Vol. 4, Cambridge UP, 2007.
—. "Realism, Categories, and the 'Linguistic Turn.'" *International Philosophical Quarterly*, vol. 2, 1962, pp. 307–22.
—. "Remarks on Deconstruction and Pragmatism." Mouffe 13–18.
—. "Response to John McDowell." *Rorty and His Critics*, pp. 123–28.
—. "Response to Simon Critchley." Mouffe, pp. 41–46.
—. *Truth and Progress: Philosophical Papers*. Vol. 3, Cambridge UP, 1998.
—. "Untruth and Consequences." Review of *Killing Time: The Autobiography of Paul Feyerabend*, by Paul Feyerabend, *The New Republic*, 31 July 1995, pp. 32–36.
—. "Wittgenstein and the Linguistic Turn." Rorty, *Philosophy as Cultural*, pp. 160–75.

—. "Wittgenstein, Heidegger, and the Reification of Language." Rorty, *Essays on Heidegger*, pp. 50–65.

Rorty and His Critics, edited by Robert B. Brandom, Blackwell, 2000.

Ross, Sir David. *Aristotle*. 5th ed., London, Methuen, 1949.

Russell, Bertrand. "Introduction." Wittgenstein, *Tractatus*, pp. ix–xxii.

—. *Our Knowledge of the External World*. 1914. London: George Allen & Unwin, 1922.

Saussure, Ferdinand de. *Course in General Linguistics*. Translated by Wade Baskin, edited by Charles Bally, et al., McGraw-Hill, 1966.

Schlick, Moritz. "The Future of Philosophy." *Linguistic Turn*, pp. 43–53.

—. "The Turning Point in Philosophy." *Logical Positivism*, pp. 53–59.

Selinger, William. "The Forgotten Philosopher: A Review Essay on Richard McKeon." *Review of Politics*, vol. 80, 2018, pp. 137–50. Accessed 8 April 2018.

Selzer, Jack. *Kenneth Burke in Greenwich Village: Conversing with the Moderns, 1915–1931*. U of Wisconsin P, 1996.

Serres, Michel. *The Natural Contract*. Translated by Elizabeth MacArthur and William Paulson, U of Michigan P, 1995.

Shaviro, Steven. *The Universe of Things: On Speculative Realism*. U of Minnesota P, 2014. Posthumanities 30.

Simonson, Peter. "Richard McKeon in the Pragmatist Tradition." *Recovering Overlooked Pragmatists in Communication: Extending the Living Conversation about Pragmatism and Rhetoric*, edited by Robert Danisch, Cham, Switzerland, Palgrave Macmillan, 2019.

Slaughter, Joseph. *Human Rights, Inc.: The World Novel, Narrative Form, and International Law*. Fordham UP, 2007.

Speculative Realism: Ray Brassier, Iain Hamilton Grant, Graham Harman, Quentin Meillassoux. Collapse, no. 3, 2007, pp. 306–449.

The Speculative Turn: Continental Materialism and Realism, edited by Levi Byrant, Nick Srnicek, and Graham Harman. Melbourne: re.press, 2011. www.repress.org

Spivak, Gayatri Chakravorty. Translator's Preface. *On Grammatology*, by Jacques Derrida, Johns Hopkins UP, 1976, pp. ix–lxxxvii.

Toulmin, Stephen E. "From Logical Analysis to Conceptual History." *The Legacy of Logical Positivism: Studies in the Philosophy of Science*, edited by Peter Achinstein and Stephen F. Barker, Johns Hopkins P, 1969, pp. 25–53.

Uebel, Thomas. "Vienna Circle." *Stanford Encyclopedia of Philosophy*, https://plato.stanford.edu. Accessed 3 Oct. 2014.

Watkins, Christopher. *Difficult Atheism: PostTheological Thinking in Alain Badiou, JeanLuc Nancy, and Quentin Meillassoux*. Edinburgh UP, 2011.

Watson, Walter. *The Architectonics of Meaning: Foundations of the New Pluralism*. SUNY P, 1985.

—. "McKeon: The Unity of His Thought." *Pluralism*, pp. 10–28, 231–39.

—. "McKeon's Semantic Schema." *Philosophy and Rhetoric*, vol. 27, no. 2, 1994, pp. 85–103.
—. "Types of Pluralism." *Monist*, vol. 73, no. 3, 1990, pp. 350–66.
Wegener, Charles W. "Memoirs of a Pluralist." *Pluralism*, pp. 92–109, 246.
Wess, Robert. "Burke's Dialectic of Constitutions." *Pre/Text*, vol. 12, no. 1–2, 1991, pp. 10–30.
—. Burke's McKeon Side: Burke's Pentad and McKeon's Quartet." *Kenneth Burke and His Circles*, edited by Jack Selzer and Robert Wess, Parlor Press, 2008, 49–67.
—. *Kenneth Burke: Rhetoric, Subjectivity, Postmodernism*. Cambridge UP, 1996.
—. "A McKeonist Understanding of Kenneth Burke's Rhetorical Realism in Particular and Constructionism." KB Journal, 11.1, Summer 2015, kbjournal.org.
West, Cornel. "Nietzsche's Prefiguration of Postmodern American Philosophy." *boundary 2*, vol. 9, no. 3 and vol. 10, no. 1, 1981, pp. 241–69.
White, Morton, editor. *The Age of Analysis: 20th Century Philosophers*. Mentor, 1955.
—. *Toward Reunion in Philosophy*. Cambridge: Harvard UP, 1956. Print.
Williams, Bernard Arthur Owen. "Metaphysical Arguments." *The Nature of Metaphysics*, edited by D. F. Pears, Macmillan, 1957, pp. 39–60.
Wittgenstein, Ludwig. *Philosophical Investigations*. Translated by G. E. M. Anscombe, Blackwell, 1968.
—. *Tractatus LogicoPhilosophicus*. Translated by D. F. Pears and B. F. McGuinness, Routledge, 1921.
Wolfendale, Peter. *Object-Oriented Philosophy: The Noumenon's New Clothes*. UK, Urbanomic, 2014.

About the Author

Robert Wess is emeritus professor of English at Oregon State University. He received a BA, MA, and PhD at the University of Chicago. While at Chicago, time in Richard McKeon's classroom inspired Wess to become a lifelong student of McKeon's work, publishing a few articles on him and Kenneth Burke along the way and now publishing this book on him that is the product of years of work. Wess attended the 1984 conference at which the Kenneth Burke Society was formed and later received the Society's Distinguished Service Award (1999) and Lifetime Achievement Award (2017). He served as the Society's president from 2005 to 2008.

Wess is the author of *Kenneth Burke: Rhetoric, Subjectivity, Postmodernism* (1996) and coeditor (with Jack Selzer) of *Kenneth Burke and His Circles* (2008). His articles have been published in such journals as *KB: The Journal of the Kenneth Burke Society*, *Modern Philology*, *Pre/Text*, *The Minnesota Review*, *ISLE: Interdisciplinary Studies in Literature* and *Environment*, and *Restoration*.

Photograph of the author by Sandra Wess. Used by permission.

Index

activism, 57, 150–151
Adler, Mortimer J.: *The Idea of Freedom*, 42
aesthetics, 44, 226, 230, 233
agnosticism, 167–171
alchemy, 4
anglophone, 10
Anscombe, G. E. M., 65–66, 68, 71–72
Anselm, St., 13
anthropocentrism, 3
Aquinas, St., Thomas, 32–33, 39
arche-fossil, 152–153, 156–158, 169, 186
architecture, 4, 155, 220, 227, 230
Aristotelianism, ix
Aristotle, 8, 20–22, 27–31, 50, 64, 79, 81, 100, 106, 109–113, 121, 160–162, 164–165, 190, 202, 208–209, 215–218, 221, 225, 233, 236–237, 239–240, 242–250; *De Anima*, 28, 63, 236; *Posterior Analytics*, 29, 30, 64, 79, 225, 240, 242; *The Categories*, 52, 239, 247
assimilation, 140
Auger, Pierre, 41
Augustine, St., 84–85
Austin, J. L., 33, 54, 123, 128
axiom, 123, 162–163
Ayer, A. J., 35, 56, 62, 65, 67–72, 90, 94; *The Revolution in Philosophy*, 56

Babich, Babette E., 212–213, 245
Backman, Jussi, 48, 172
Badiou, Alain, 51, 131–132
Baldwin, James, 120

Balzac, Honoré de, 107
Barjavel, Rene, 143
Beardsley, Monroe C., 227
Beasley, James, 38
Bender, John, 51
Bergmann, Gustav, 59, 60, 62–64, 73–74, 98
Bergson, Henri, 12, 72
biology, 58, 61, 225
Bitzer, Lloyd F., 45
Black, Edwin, 45, 106, 110
Blakesley, David, xi
Booth, Wayne C., 13, 38–39, 50; *The Rhetoric of Fiction*, 13, 39
Bouveresse, Jacques, 104
brand, 4
Brassier, Ray, 3, 27, 29, 134, 144, 146, 152, 160–161, 172, 198, 199, 237–242; *Nihil Unbound*, 144, 146, 152, 161, 238, 240
Brooks, Cleanth, 227–228
Burke, Kenneth, 33, 37–39, 54, 72, 79, 83–86, 91, 98, 102, 107, 108, 113, 116, 128, 138–140; *A Grammar of Motives*, 128
Byrant, Levi, 201

Cantor, Georg, 147
capitalism, 5
caricature, 185, 203, 214–215, 223
Carnap, Rudolf, 36, 57, 60, 81–82, 98
Carr, Edward Hallett, 41
causality, 55, 105, 174–175, 189, 216, 220–223, 226
chemical theory, 89, 93
Chomsky, Noam, 80, 92
Christianity, 57, 62, 170–171

267

Cicero, 13, 45
Civil War, 216, 225
Clark, Andy, xi
class, 34–35, 40, 124
codification, 15
Coetzee, J. M., 124
Colebrook, Claire, 72, 79, 94
colonialism, 124
Columbia University, 14, 20–21, 38
Conant, James, 77, 78, 80–81
confrontation, 105, 124, 169, 217–218
constancy, 140–141, 144, 146, 154–155
constructivism, 1, 101
contiguity, 217, 219
contingency, 112, 131, 135, 138–141, 143–147, 150–151, 153–154, 155, 160–161, 164, 173, 240, 246
convention, 78–79, 81, 96, 116, 129, 150
Copernicus, Nicolaus, 8, 49, 210
correlationism, 7, 8, 130–133, 136–137, 139, 142, 149, 152–156, 159, 160–174, 207, 240, 242
countercompositional, 209
Crane, R. S.: *Critics and Criticism; Ancient and Modern*, 21, 44
Creath, Richard, 58, 61, 65, 67
criterion of verifiability, 67, 69
criticism, ix, 20, 21, 65, 74, 83, 142–144, 162, 228, 230

Danisch, Robert, 15, 106
Davidson, Donald, 86, 97–99, 102, 105, 107, 111–112, 128–129
de Man, Paul, 129
deconstruction, 32, 79, 104, 114, 121, 127, 200
Democritus, 13, 21–22

Depew, David J., xi, 14, 16
Derrida, Jacques, 8, 10, 32, 50, 52, 54, 56–57, 61, 103–104, 107–108, 110, 113–128, 133, 137, 141, 176, 195, 200–205; *Limited In*, 125–126, 202; *Of Grammatology*, 52, 54, 61, 202; *Speech and Phenomena*, 52, 113, 120, 200; *Writing and Difference*, 52
Descartes, Rene, 28, 105, 123, 135–136
Desilet, Gregory, xi
Dewey, John, 13–15, 19, 181
Diamond, Cora, 75–79, 85, 129; *The Realistic Spirit; Wittgenstein, Philosophy, and the Mind*, 75, 77–78
discourse, 47–48, 63, 79, 96, 98, 105, 108, 113, 116, 118, 139, 141, 144, 158, 201, 243
displacement, 65–66, 98, 107, 116, 124, 126, 128, 144, 155, 181
dissertation, ix, 14, 35, 113, 197, 199
distinctions: basic, 1, 10–11, 47–48, 135, 140
dogma, 90, 98, 106
Doxtader, Erik, 41
drama, 83, 86–87, 162–163, 191
dualism, 98, 102, 199, 248
Dummett, Michael, 59–60, 73–74, 78, 94
duomining, 194
duplicity, 217–218
Dutch East India Company, 193, 216, 225

ecocriticism, 124
eidos, 120, 217–218, 220
Einstein, Albert, 62, 142–143
emanation, 217

empiricism, 25–26, 28–29, 35–36, 48, 58–59, 62, 65, 67–69, 71, 72–73, 82–87, 90–95, 97–98, 100, 102, 105, 107, 113, 116, 175, 203, 240, 244
Ennis, Paul J., 159
Enos, Theresa, 45
epistemology, 4, 11–12, 16, 62, 63, 66–67, 125, 165, 175, 201, 207, 236
epoch, 52, 64, 109, 119
equal footing, 37, 198–199
essence, 38, 79, 85, 111, 120, 125, 145, 155, 173, 193, 195, 198, 212, 216–218, 220, 239, 242, 244
Ethics (journal), 41, 249
ex nihlio, 126, 140–141, 146–147, 162
exceptionalism, 10, 23–24
exemptionalism, 10, 27, 86, 101, 111, 174, 235, 240
existent, 10, 16, 23–24, 26, 36, 47, 53, 58–59, 64, 83, 102, 108, 117, 125–126, 140, 149, 153, 157–158, 175, 193, 205, 210, 226, 230–231, 241, 246
extraterrestrial, 157–158

fallacy, 194, 197
Farrell, Thomas, 13
fiction, 83, 123, 143
Flew, Antony, 56
formalism, 21, 62, 220, 226–228, 230, 233
Foucault, Michael, 50
foundationalism, 105, 112
Frege, Gottlob, 54, 58, 60, 73, 74, 78, 80, 241
Freud, Sigmund, 119
Friedmann, Georges, 41

Galileo, 109–112
Galloway, Alexander R., 5, 6

Garver, Eugene, xi, 113
gender, 124
geography, 4
Gilbert, Margaret, 56
Gilson, Etienne, 19, 20, 37
God, 132, 134, 149, 151, 161, 170, 171, 214, 223–224, 242
Goldfarb, Warren, 76, 85
Goldsmiths University, 3, 7
Gottlieb, Johann, xi
grammar, 113
Grant, Iain Hamilton, 3, 134, 194
Gratton, Peter, 8, 142, 151, 154, 159, 166–167, 172, 178, 230–232; *Speculative Realism; Problems and Prospects*, 178
Gross, Paul R., 45, 54–57, 67, 72, 74, 86, 102, 137, 202
grounding, 9, 23, 84, 104

Häaglund, Marin, 134
Hacker, P. M. S., 35, 57, 58–59, 60, 62
Hacking, Ian, 87, 88
Haldane, John, 243
Hallward, Peter, 142
Hanna, Robert, 235
Harman, Graham, *Immaterialism; Objects and Social Theory*, 225; *Object-Oriented Ontology; A New Theory of Everything*, 6, 179, 190, 203–204, 206, 220, 222–225, 228–229; *Prince of Networks*, 152, 186, 191, 196, 197, 198, 222; *Quentin Meillassoux; Philosophy in the Making*, 3, 5, 132, 142; *The Quadruple Object*, 3, 178, 183–184, 188, 190, 195, 206, 209, 220, 246; *Tool-Being; Heidegger and the Metaphysics of Objects*, 5, 178; *Weird Realism; Lovecraft and Philosophy*, 202
Hartle, Ann, 135
Head, Dominic, 124

270   Index

Hegel, Georg Wilhelm Friedrich, 107, 150, 167, 168
Heidegger, Martin, 4, 8, 16, 50, 59, 61, 107, 114, 119, 138, 172, 179–184, 187, 191–192, 196, 198, 200, 205–206, 214, 221, 228, 231–232; *Being and Time*, 5, 181
Henderson, David, xi
heterogeneity, 14
holism, 6, 89, 90–91, 96–97, 100–101, 110, 215, 228
holism, holistic, 104, 228
Hollanda, Sergio Barque de, 41
holoscopic, 22–23, 31
Homer, 90, 91, 94, 98, 101, 144, 148
Hoy, David Couzens, 110
humanism, 40
Hume, David, 12, 13, 25, 142–143, 147, 169, 190, 216, 221, 223–224
Husserl, Edmund, 63, 120, 123, 184, 188, 189–191, 206, 209, 210, 215–217, 219, 221–223, 246
Hutto, Daniel D., 74–76, 98
Huxley, Julian, 40
hypothesis, hypotheses, 67, 69, 149, 162, 195

idealism, 36, 55, 102, 137, 153, 159–161, 168–172, 186, 190, 213, 218
Ijsseling, Samuel, 50
inferential chain, 102–103, 110, 212, 230, 232
insolubilia, 63
intellectual self-concept, 57
intentionality, 189–190, 211, 219, 222–223, 245
intersubjectivity, 94, 96, 120, 153
intuition, 9, 26–31, 90, 100, 101, 104, 107, 117, 138, 160, 161, 164, 168, 170, 172–173, 176, 207–208, 214, 218, 238–240, 242–243, 244, 246
irony, 5, 103, 157

James, William, 12
Jeler, Ciprian, 153, 154
Johnston, Adrian, 12, 16, 142–143, 147, 169, 175, 236
Joy, Eileen, xi, 10, 11

Kahn, Charles H., 31
Kant, Immanuel, ix, 2, 7–14, 27, 31, 46–49, 51, 58–59, 67, 69, 101, 105, 130, 136, 151, 160–161, 166–168, 172, 174–176, 178–180, 187, 188, 203, 205, 210, 212, 216, 221, 224, 234–236, 239, 242; *Critique of Pure Reason*, ix, 8–9, 168, 174–175, 210, 234
Kimball, George, 14
Koopman, Colin, 103, 104
Kuhn, Thomas, 32, 88, 108

Lanham, Richard, 37–38
Laruelle, François, 161–164
Laski, Harold J., 41
Latour, Bruno, 1, 2, 55, 101, 102, 196–199, 214, 224, 226, 247; *We Have Never Been Modern*, 247
Lawlor, Leonard, 52, 210–213, 232
Leibniz, Gottfried Wilhelm, 193–194, 198, 208
Levenstein, Benjamin, xi
Levinas, Emmanuel, 119, 226
Levitt, Norman, 54–55, 67, 72, 74, 86, 102, 137, 202
lexicon, 8
linearity, 32–34, 61
linguistic turn, ix, 1, 2, 10–11, 17, 28, 30, 33, 35, 40, 46, 50, 51–55, 57–60, 62–64, 66–75,

77, 79–80, 83–84, 88–90, 97–98, 101, 103–104, 107–110, 113, 116, 120, 127–128, 130, 135–137, 139, 149, 153–155, 165, 201–204, 235–236, 241–242
literal, 21, 67–69, 227
Lo, Chung-Shu, 41
Locke, John, 105
logocentrism, 32, 61, 79, 104, 114, 120–123
Lovecraft, H. P., 202

Mailloux, Steven, xi, 45
Mallarmé, Stéphane, 131
Marx, Karl, 5, 148, 150, 167
materialism, 3, 135, 152, 194
matrix, 13
may-being, 148–151, 159–160, 170–171, 173, 179, 246
McKeon, Richard, *Freedom and History; The Semantics of Philosophical Controversies and Ideological Conflicts*, 44; *Freedom and History and Other Essays*, 15, 22, 44; *Making and Unmaking the Prospects for Rhetoric*, 45; *Rhetoric; Essays in Invention and Discovery*, 48; *Selected Writings of Richard McKeon*, 15, 22, 48; *The Philosophy of Spinoza; The Unity of His Thought*, 14, 36; *Thought, Action, and Passion*, 19, 21, 130
McKibben, Bill, 248; *The End of Nature*, 248
McLuhan, Marshall, 113, 230
McNabb, Richard, 45
mediation, 55–56, 64, 67, 99–102, 111, 121, 131, 175, 187, 202, 236, 242
medieval, 35, 113
Meillassoux, Quentin, *After Finitude; The Necessity of Contingency*, 7; *Divine Inexistence; An Essay on the Virtual God*, 131; *Divine Inexistence and After Finitude*, 178; *Science Fiction and Extro-Science Fiction*, 143
Melville, Herman: *Moby Dick*, 216, 228
Merleau-Ponty, Maurice, 211
meroscopic, 22, 23, 31
Metaphysical Society of America, 47
metaphysics, ix, 1–8, 11, 12, 17, 19, 20, 25–27, 33–34, 37–38, 46–50, 60–61, 65, 68, 82–83, 101–102, 104, 109, 123–125, 130, 133–136, 138–139, 141, 144, 146, 148, 150, 158, 164, 169, 173–174, 178–180, 182–183, 188, 196, 199–201, 203, 207, 210, 212, 214, 215–216, 224–226, 230, 233–239, 242–245, 248, 250
Mitchell, William, xi
mode of production, 5
modes of interpretation, 23
modus operandi, 126
Montaigne, Michel de, 135–136
Moody, Ernest, 63
Moore, G. E., 35–36, 44, 63
Morton, Timothy, 58, 82, 184, 200, 212, 248; *Dark Ecology*, 248

Nashe, Thomas, 113
naturalism, 112, 139
Nelböck, John, 62
New Literary History (journal), 110, 227
Newton, Isaac, 106, 112–113, 142–143, 240
nihilism, 5, 151
Nikam, N. A., 19
nominalism, 63
nonlinguistic, 53, 56, 69, 71, 74–75, 88, 96, 98–99, 102, 105–106, 110–111, 115, 119

272 Index

noumenon, 27, 174–175, 188, 210–211, 239
novelty, 78–79, 81, 96, 112, 128–129, 147, 192

object-oriented ontology, 2, 4–6, 12, 48, 84, 93–94, 118, 147–148, 154–155, 171, 173, 179–180, 184, 195, 200–201, 203, 205–206, 220, 224–226, 2229, 232, 233, 236
object-oriented philosophy (OOP), 2, 3, 4, 6, 182, 198, 221, 228
occasionalism, 223–224
Ockham, William, 63
Olson, Elder, 13
ontology, 2, 4–6, 12, 48, 84, 93–94, 118, 147–148, 154, 155, 171, 173, 179–180, 201, 220, 226, 233, 236
Open Humanities Press, 1
organized to function, 28–29, 31, 90, 100–102, 111, 119, 121, 164, 172, 174–176, 208, 215, 240, 242–243, 245, 249, 250
Ortega y Gasset, José, 221
overmining, 194, 196, 197, 226
Oxford English, 79

paradigm, 32, 88
paradox, 41, 54, 62, 121, 139, 177
Penn State University, 38
Peramatzis, Michail, 29
perception, 25, 30, 48, 66, 184, 190, 218, 219, 229
Perelman, Chaim, 41
perennis philospohia, 20
perspectivism, 31, 44, 79, 92, 99–100, 183–189, 191, 194–195, 199, 200, 203, 206–207, 209–215, 217–219, 222, 232–233, 244, 245

phenomena, 10, 35, 72, 78, 98, 120, 140, 174–175, 188, 203, 210, 218, 247
Plato, 13, 20–22, 123; *Republic*, 13, 44
Plochmann, George Kimball, 14, 20–22, 31, 33–35, 37–41, 44, 48; *Richard McKeon; A Study*, 20
pluralism, ix, 10, 12–13, 17–18, 20–22, 39, 43–44, 176
poetry, 83
politics, 126, 148, 151, 247
Porrovecchio, Mark J., 45
positivism, 16, 28, 34–35, 37, 57, 58, 60, 62, 64–71, 73, 76–77, 79, 82–90, 98, 100, 105, 107–110, 181
postulate, 162
pragmatism, 14–16, 46, 65, 87, 91, 101, 104, 148–149, 174, 178
predestination, 151
presence-at-hand, 181–182
presupposition, 69
Princeton University, 56
principles, 9, 13, 22–24, 31, 38, 40, 57, 67, 71–72, 82, 100, 126, 139–141, 145, 153, 155, 161–163, 168, 170, 194, 203, 217, 224, 228, 246
Protagoras, 164
Proust, Marcel, 107, 116
Puritan, 151
Putnam, Hilary, 28–29, 31, 90, 97, 100–101, 164, 243–245
Pythagoras, 154

Quine, W. V. O., 84–102, 104–106, 111, 144, 148, 196; *Ontological Relativity and Other Essays*, 88; *Word and Object*, 87–88, 94, 98

race, 124
radical translation, 85–87

Read, Rupert, 75, 77, 78, 79
ready-to-hand, 181–182
realism, 2–6, 8, 15, 26, 36, 46, 77–79, 131, 136, 159, 163, 166, 169, 178–179, 200, 202, 207, 210, 213–214, 225–226, 232, 235–238, 246, 248, 250
reality/appearance distinction, 109
reciprocal priority, 46
redescription, 109–112
reductionism, 90, 106
relativism, 20
religion, 149, 150
Renaissance, 45, 63, 136
rhetoric, 14, 17, 22, 33–34, 37–40, 44–45, 48–52, 58, 63, 68, 78, 103–104, 106–108, 113, 115, 117, 126, 201, 237
Ricketts, Thomas, 74–75, 98
Ricoeur, Paul, 41
Roffe, Jon, 145
Rorty, Richard, 44, 52–54, 56–60, 62, 64–65, 69–71, 79, 89, 93, 96, 98, 103–119, 136–139, 144, 175, 201, 235; *Contingency, Irony, and Solidarity*, 103, 105, 109; *Philosophy and the Mirror of Nature*, 53, 104, 106, 108; *Philosophy as Cultural Politics*, 115; *The Linguistic Turn; Recent Essays in Philosophical Method*, 44, 46, 52, 56, 57, 59, 60, 65, 111
Ross, Alf, 41
Rousseau, Jean-Jacques, 123, 150
Russell, Bertrand, 35, 63–64, 68, 74, 99–100, 184, 212, 245
Ryle, Gilbert, 56

Sacks, Jonathan, ix
Saint Paul, 112
Saint-Simon, Henri de, 107
satire, 54–55, 67, 120, 202
Saussure, Ferdinand de, 86, 116–118, 155

scheme, 34, 37, 57, 88–90, 92–93, 96, 98, 100, 102, 108
Schlick, Moritz, 57, 59–64, 68; *Space and Time in Contemporary Physics*, 62
Schlipp, Paul Arthur: *The Library of Living Philosophers*, 35
selection, 13, 22, 31, 35, 41, 60
Selinger, Evan, xi, 50
Sellars, Wilfred, 104–106
Selzer, Jack, 38
semantic, 22, 31, 241
sensory perception, 83–84
sexual orientation, 124
Shaviro, Steven, 136
Shlick, Mortiz, 62
significance, 23, 58, 66–69
signified, 54, 117, 127, 155, 203
signifier, 127, 155
sign-language, 66, 72
Simonson, Peter, 14
Socrates, 80–81, 211–212, 216, 219, 226, 233
Somerhausen, Luc, 41
sophistry, 51, 149, 150
sophists, 150, 164
Southern Illinois University, 20, 22
Soviet Union, 148
space, 9, 14, 105, 131, 155–158, 168, 182, 187, 217–218, 220, 229, 231
speech-act theory, 33, 54
Spinoza, Baruch, 14, 35–36
stimulus, 86–89, 93, 95, 185
Strawson, P. F., 60
subjectalism, 134, 154, 186
subjectivism, 169
Swift, Jonathan, 119–120
syllogism, 23
symbiosis, 225

taxonomy, 179, 187, 199
term d'art, 4
terminology, 30–31, 58, 189, 223

Thales of Miletus, 19
theme, 48, 107, 201, 224, 234
theology, 83, 214
theory of language, 33
theory of symbolic action, 54
thesis, 57, 65, 79, 109, 118, 132, 154, 162, 172, 206
transcendentalism, 3, 31, 105, 113, 115–117, 137, 158–159, 166, 168, 178, 210, 221

Uebel, Thomas, 67
ultimate priority, 9–10, 12, 23–27, 31, 46–48, 52–54, 56, 59, 69, 70, 75, 79, 84, 88–91, 98–104, 106, 108, 110–112, 116–117, 119, 127–128, 130, 133, 135, 148–149, 159–160, 173–174, 187, 207, 208, 210–214, 217, 220, 230– 232, 235, 237
undermining, 194, 197
UNESCO, 39–41
Universal Declaration of Human Rights (UN), 41
universals, 23, 29–31, 63, 100, 137–140, 147–149, 225
University of Chicago, ix, 14, 20, 36–38
University of Rochester, 13
USSR, 151

verbalism, 45

verificationism, 66–67, 82
Vienna Circle, 35–36, 57–59, 65, 81
visual arts, 4, 227

Watkin, Christopher, 132
Wegener, Charles, 38–39, 50
Wellbery, David E., 51
White, Morton, 58, 82–83, 96
Williams, Bernard, 25–29, 47–48, 94, 100, 242
Wimsatt, W. K., 227
Wittgenstein, Ludwig, 28, 35, 57–60, 62–63, 65, 66, 68, 71–78, 80, 81, 84–85, 90, 103–104, 243; *Philosophical Investigations*, 65, 84, 85; *Remarks on the Foundations of Mathematics*, 77; *Tractatus Logico-Philosphicus*, 57
Wolfendale, Peter, 3, 182–183; *Object-Oriented Philosophy*; *The Noumenon's New*, 3, 6, 192, 196
Woodbridge, Frederick J. E., 14–15, 19
Woolgar, Steve, 1
Wordsworth, William, 97, 105
writing, xi, 12, 62, 65, 68, 98–99, 110, 115, 117, 119, 123–124, 127, 137, 177–178, 191, 196, 198, 232

Zubiri, Xavier, 193